The Best Casserole Cookbook Ever

THE
Best
Casserole
COOKBOOK EVER

With More Than 500 Recipes!

○ ○ ○ ○ ○

by Beatrice Ojakangas
photographs by Susie Cushner

CHRONICLE BOOKS
SAN FRANCISCO

Library of Congress Cataloging-in-Publication
Data available.

ISBN: 978-0-8118-5624-9

Manufactured in the United States of America

Designed by Katie Heit
Food Styling by Jee Levin
Prop Styling by Lynn Butler

10 9 8 7 6 5 4 3 2 1

Chronicle Books LLC
680 Second Street
San Francisco, California 94107

www.chroniclebooks.com

Dedicated to all lovers of casseroles and hot dishes.

ACKNOWLEDGMENTS

While writing this book, I likened the process to shoveling a six-foot snow bank with a teaspoon. Anyone who lives in Minnesota can identify with this. We have overdosed on casseroles, and more than one got buried in my walk-in cooler a bit too long. I started freezing them, and when the freezer filled up, I was grateful for friends who offered to help me retrieve the space.

I want to thank especially my husband, Dick, who was my ready tester, taster, and sometimes dishwasher, and who calls himself not just a "clean plate clubber," but also a "clean casserole clubber." Thanks also go to many friends and family members who contributed recipes and helped test and eat these recipes. I am, because of them, most blessed.

Thanks to Jane Dystel, my patient agent, who encouraged me to write this book, and Bill LeBlond, senior editor at Chronicle Books, who not only gave me the opportunity to write this book but believed that I could actually do it in a year.

Many thanks to Amy Treadwell, project editor at Chronicle Books, who gave me the choice of sending the book in either hard copy or electronically. When I chose the electronic option, Amy aptly answered, "The trees will thank you." And so it was that all six hundred–some pages amazingly flew across the country through the Internet. Thanks, too, to Deborah Kops for her excellent work in editing this monumental manuscript.

TABLE OF CONTENTS

INTRODUCTION

THE CASSEROLE IS BACK

○ ○ ○ ○ ○

Casseroles are making a comeback. They are all about home, food, family, and friends, whether you are cooking alone or together, no matter what season. Not only are casseroles fast and easy to make, but they can be healthy as well, with the addition of whole grains, legumes, and vegetables.

The word "casserole" can refer either to the dish that the food is cooked in or to the food itself. In Minnesota, however, the food is called a "hot dish." In other parts of the country, it might be called a "covered dish."

Casseroles became popular in the 1950s, mainly because they got the cook in and out of the kitchen fast. This was about the time that canned soups became vastly popular, and cooks were convinced that they, too, saved enormous amounts of time.

Today's casseroles have a greater variety of flavors, and they're fresher, too. We have embraced many dishes and ingredients from abroad, and we're also using more fresh vegetables, many of which are now available in convenient, ready-to-use packages. Ingredients like sun-dried tomatoes, brined olives, dried exotic mushrooms, flavored oils, and fresh herbs, which were not readily available in the past, are at our fingertips now.

In this book, there may be an occasional recipe here and there that uses a canned soup. However, my personal preference is to avoid ingredients that we've recently found to be unhealthy, such as monosodium glutamate (MSG), partially hydrogenated fats, and high-fructose corn syrup (a sweetener widely used in beverages and fruits). Read the labels.

It is my hope that you will find more than a few useful recipes in this book, as well as suggestions for those times when what to fix for a meal presents obstacles like (1) "I don't have time for fancy preparations," or (2) the opposite, "I really want to serve something special," or (3) "I want to serve something wonderful but I don't have the time," or (4) "I need to make it ahead and leave the baking for the final hour." Throughout this book there will be information to help you overcome these obstacles.

I love to entertain and usually have dreams of elegance and formality. But when it comes down to it, hospitality and conviviality are more important. As a result, we've had a lot of fun with our testing parties. When our guests took a recipe, made it, and offered suggestions, they invested themselves in the process, and proudly presented the results. This happened time and time again as we tested the recipes in this book.

CASSEROLE COOKWARE

○ ○ ○ ○ ○

A casserole dish itself can be made of ovenproof glass, porcelain, earthenware, or enameled cast iron. Glass, porcelain, and earthenware do not conduct heat quickly, but they do retain heat, so they are good choices for casseroles. Dishes made from one of these three materials can go from freezer to oven without problems, but they cannot be used for stove-top cooking like cast-iron or enameled cast-iron casseroles can. Most casseroles are attractive enough to go from oven to table.

In some of the recipes, we specify the size of a casserole dish in quarts, rather than giving its dimensions. This is because if you know the volume, you can use a casserole or baking dish with a different shape and dimensions. I have casserole dishes that are round, oval, square, rectangular, and even star-shaped. Any of them would work for most casseroles that call for a shallow casserole dish of a certain volume. To determine the volume of an odd-shaped dish, you can simply measure it using quarts of water. If there is no size indicated on the bottom of a dish, I mark it with a permanent marker. Ovenproof dishes that have the size on the bottom, like a 9-by-13-inch baking dish, often include the volume. Dish dimensions do make a difference in baking time. If the depth of the dish, and therefore the food, is greater, it will need to bake longer than it would in a shallow dish. Some casseroles fare best when they are baked in a deep casserole dish with a cover. The recipes indicate when this type of dish is needed.

FREEZING & THAWING BAKED CASSEROLES

○ ○ ○ ○ ○

To successfully freeze foods, there are some simple rules you need to follow. The two most important bits of advice are to make sure you wrap the foods very well and to keep track of what is in your freezer. Freezer burn happens when food becomes dehydrated as a result of improper packing and being held too long.

To freeze casseroles:
Cool completely after baking and cover with plastic wrap or waxed paper, and then with foil. Label the dish with its name, date of preparation, number of servings, and hints on how to reheat the food.

To thaw frozen casseroles:
Remove from the freezer at least 8 hours ahead or defrost overnight in the refrigerator, then reheat in the oven to serving temperature. In a pinch, you can thaw a casserole in the microwave, but be sure it is in a microwave-safe container. Microwaves tend to thaw foods from the outside in. The center may still be frozen while the outside is burning. To avoid this, use a low setting and turn the food often.

ASSEMBLING & REFRIGERATING CASSEROLES BEFORE BAKING

○ ○ ○ ○ ○

Many of the recipes that follow can be assembled, covered, and refrigerated for several hours, or even a day. If you have chilled a casserole for more than a few hours, remove it from the refrigerator when you preheat the oven. That will give the ingredients and the dish a chance to warm up a bit.

HOSTING A POTLUCK

○ ○ ○ ○ ○

Casseroles can be shared with pride. "Can I bring something?" These are words we often hear when we invite friends or family to a party. The idea seems so American, but it is actually done the world over.

Although the term "potluck" suggests a random assortment of dishes, it's likely to turn out better if the host does a little bit of organizing. The term itself has an old-fashioned ring to it. We might visualize ladies in their Sunday bonnets, teetering on high heels, carrying large dishes covered with checkered cloths. But potluck parties are an ideal form of entertaining for the contemporary host or hostess who would like to gather friends together, but who is too busy to do all of the cooking.

If you are organizing a potluck, you can make a point of asking each person to bring a favorite dish. If you can, be more specific—for example, "Your special turkey-and-stuffing casserole would be perfect," or "Can you bring your wonderful vegetable casserole?" The more than 500 recipes in this book are all great choices for a potluck, and most of them are very portable, requiring no elaborate last-minute preparation.

A potluck with a theme can be a lot of fun for a group of

friends. Themes like Italian, French, Scandinavian, German, or South American can pique everyone's imagination. I know of families who, for their annual holiday gatherings, ask people to bring foods that start with the letter "C" or "H" or that are a certain color.

If you choose to organize your potluck, here are some more ideas. (1) ask guests to bring a family favorite dish; or (2) assign each guest to bring either an appetizer, main dish, or dessert; or (3) as the host, you can provide the main dish and ask the guests to bring appetizers and side dishes.

When assigning dishes, be considerate of guests who are traveling a long distance, and recommend they bring non-perishables, such as cookies, bread, or pickles. If you have oven space, suggest a ready-to-bake casserole that can be kept cold until they arrive. At the party, it is always helpful to label dishes. I use 3-inch white ceramic tiles, purchased on sale from a hardware store, and write with a felt-tip pen the names of various dishes.

The tiles are easily washed clean for use another time.

It is the host's responsibility to provide serving utensils, pot holders, dishes, and silverware. It's also nice to have small disposable containers for leftovers and cards for sharing recipes (ask guests to bring recipes). Be sure to have plenty of spatulas and big spoons for serving.

Put beverages into a large container, such as a barrel, tub, or planter, with ice to keep them cold. Be sure to have nonalcoholic beverages available.

KEEPING FOOD SAFE

○ ○ ○ ○ ○

Keep hot foods hot (above 145°F) and cold foods cold (below 45°F) to avoid bacterial growth. Never leave foods at room temperature for more than 2 hours. It is not a good idea to let food sit out all afternoon. Instead, designate the time of serving and keep it to less than 2 hours before; refrigerate leftovers immediately.

If you have a large number of guests, set out small platters of food and replenish them as needed. When replenishing perishable food, replace or wash the platter first to prevent contamination.

To prevent guests from "double dipping" with their eating utensils, put a spoon in each dip or spread so they can drop a small amount on their plates.

Provide adequate places for people to dispose of garbage and deposit used dishes. Keep garbage away from food that will be served. Don't mix dirty and clean dishes.

TOOLS FOR YOUR KITCHEN

○ ○ ○ ○ ○

You don't need a lot of tools, but there are some that make life much easier for the cook.

———

KNIVES AND HAND TOOLS
○ 8- to 10-inch chef's knife for cutting and chopping
○ Serrated knife for slicing breads, tomatoes, and soft fruit

- Paring knife
- Potato peeler
- Can opener
- Box grater
- Zester or Microplane for removing zest from citrus fruits
- Wooden spoons for cooking
- Large metal spoons, some of them slotted, for serving
- Whisk
- Tongs
- Rubber spatulas

CUTTING BOARDS
- Two boards, one designated for raw meat and fish, to prevent cross-contamination. The new thin, plastic cutting sheets are handy, and they come two or three in a pack. (Never cut cooked meat on the same board on which it was cut before cooking.)

MEASURING TOOLS
- Set of measuring spoons. It usually includes table-spoon, teaspoon, ½ teaspoon, and ¼ teaspoon measures; some sets include ½ table-spoon and ⅛ teaspoon measures, too.

- Set of dry cup measures. It usually includes 1 cup, ½ cup, ⅓ cup, and ¼ cup measures. (Dry measures are always used to measure the dry ingredients by leveling with the top of the cup.)
- Liquid measuring cups. These have markings for fractions of a cup. It is handy to have both 1-cup and a 2-cup measures.

BOWLS
- Set of nested glass bowls. These are great because glass can be used in the microwave.

- Set of metal bowls, usually three or four bowls that nest together.

POTS AND PANS
- Medium saucepan with a lid
- Small nonstick skillet
- Medium or large skillet with a lid
- Medium or large Dutch oven
- Large pot for pasta
- Roasting pan with a rack, which can double as a lasagna pan

CASSEROLES
(glass, porcelain, or enameled cast iron)
- 2- to 4-cup for appetizers
- 1-quart for small dishes, 6- or 8-quart for larger dishes, and one or two sizes in between
- Shallow casseroles in oval, rectangular, square, and novelty shapes
- Deep, heavy casseroles (or a Dutch oven) with lids
- 9-by-13-inch baking dish

- And, of course, good hot pads!

Chapter 1
CASSEROLE BASICS

○ ○ ○ ○ ○

The whole idea of this chapter—in fact, the idea behind this whole book—is to offer healthier, tastier casserole choices. One simple way to accomplish this is to make your own sauces to replace the "cream of" soups. Of course, if you don't really care, you can go ahead and use canned soups.

Here's my rationale for making your own sauce: While "cream of" soups offer convenience, they are high in sodium. Just read the labels. You'll also notice MSG (monosodium glutamate), partially hydrogenated fat or oil (a source of trans fats), and various chemical flavor enhancers.

Each of the basic sauce recipes here replaces one can (10¾ ounces) of concentrated soup. You can use them in your favorite casserole recipes. If the casserole recipe calls for 2 cans, just double the sauce recipe. You will have less sodium and fewer unknowns in your food, which ultimately gives you more control over what you are feeding yourself and your family.

If you use purchased broths, select the low-sodium varieties. I look for organic broths that are low in salt. If you would like to make your own, you will find simple recipes for making three kinds of broth: chicken (page 25), beef (page 26), and vegetable (page 27). Again, making your own gives you more control over what you are eating.

BASIC MIX 'N' MATCH
MEAL-IN-ONE-CASSEROLE RECIPE

Casseroles are basically a combination of meat, pasta, rice, beans, or veggies with a sauce and perhaps a topping, baked in the oven until bubbly. A friend once described a casserole as a blend of inspiration and what's on hand. Certain elements are important for a one-dish meal or, as we say in Minnesota, a "hot dish." To inspire you to be creative (or help you clean out the refrigerator), here is a basic plan.

○———————————————— SERVES 6 ————————————————○

FOR THE PROTEIN
(SELECT 1 OR COMBINE A FEW TO EQUAL 2 CUPS):

Chopped hard-cooked egg

Diced cooked chicken or turkey

Diced cooked ham

Cooked ground beef

Cooked beef or pork, shredded or cubed

Cooked fish, flaked

Cooked shelled shrimp

Cooked dry beans, peas, or other legumes

FOR THE STARCH
(SELECT 1 OR MORE TO EQUAL 3 CUPS COOKED):

Pasta in fancy shapes, shells, or tubes, such as penne or elbow macaroni

Wide or narrow egg noodles, or strands of pasta, such as spaghetti or linguine

Long- or short-grain brown or white rice or wild rice

———————

FOR THE VEGETABLE
(SELECT 1 OR MORE TO EQUAL 2 CUPS COOKED):

Broccoli florets

Green beans, trimmed and cut into ½-inch pieces

Peas

Zucchini, sliced, diced, or chopped

Sautéed chopped or sliced onion and/or sliced mushrooms

———————

FOR THE SAUCE
(SELECT 1 TO MEASURE 1¼ TO 2 CUPS):

Basic White Sauce (page 18), or 1 can (10¾ ounces) condensed cream of mushroom, celery, or a similar soup

Basic Egg Sauce (page 19), or 1 can condensed cream of mushroom, celery, or a similar soup

Basic Cheese Sauce (page 20), or 1 can condensed cream of mushroom, celery, or a similar soup

Basic Mushroom Sauce (page 22), or 1 can condensed cream of mushroom, celery, or a similar soup

Sour cream or mayonnaise

Whole, stewed, or diced tomatoes, with juice

———

FOR THE FLAVOR INGREDIENTS
(SELECT 1 OR MORE TO EQUAL
¼ TO ½ CUP):

Chopped celery

Chopped onion

Sliced black olives

———

FOR THE HERBS
(SELECT 1 OR MORE, 1 TEASPOON
DRIED TO 3 TABLESPOONS FRESH):

Mixed dried or chopped fresh herbs, such as basil, thyme, marjoram, and rosemary

FOR THE TOPPING
(SELECT 1 OR MORE TO EQUAL
¼ TO ½ CUP):

Grated or shredded cheese, such as Swiss, Cheddar, Monterey Jack, or Parmesan

Buttered breadcrumbs

1. Preheat the oven to 350°F. Lightly butter a 2½- to 3-quart casserole.

2. Select and prepare the ingredients of your choice from each of the categories listed above.

3. Mix the protein, starch, and vegetables in a large bowl. In a smaller bowl, mix the sauce, flavor ingredients, and herbs. Spread the starch mixture in the bottom of the casserole and pour the sauce over the top. Sprinkle with the topping.

4. Bake, covered, for 30 minutes. Uncover and bake for another 15 minutes, or until heated through.

BASIC WHITE SAUCE

This thick white sauce is a basic replacement for a can of "cream of" soup, and you can use it in your favorite casserole recipe. To make a sauce to replace cream of chicken soup, substitute chicken broth for the milk. To replace cream of mushroom soup, sauté ½ pound sliced mushrooms in the butter before adding the flour and substitute beef broth for the hot milk. Add any seasonings according to your taste.

MAKES 1¼ CUPS;
REPLACES 1 CAN (10¾ OUNCES) CONDENSED SOUP

4 tablespoons butter

¼ cup all-purpose flour

½ teaspoon salt

¼ teaspoon pepper

1 cup hot milk

1. In a medium saucepan, melt the butter. Stir in the flour, salt, and pepper and cook over medium heat, stirring constantly, for 3 minutes, or until the mixture is smooth and bubbly.

2. Whisk in the hot milk, keeping the mixture smooth and free of lumps. Bring to a boil, whisking constantly, reduce the heat, and cook until thickened and smooth. Use the sauce hot, or cover and refrigerate until ready to use.

BASIC EGG SAUCE

Use this mixture, which does not require any stove-top cooking, when you don't want to make Basic White Sauce (facing page). Use it to replace 1 can of "cream of" soup. The proportions are easy to remember: Just add 2 eggs to 1 cup milk and season to your taste. To use as a replacement for cream of chicken soup, substitute chicken broth for the milk.

MAKES 1¼ CUPS;
REPLACES 1 CAN (10¾ OUNCES) CONDENSED SOUP

1 cup milk

2 large eggs

½ teaspoon salt

¼ teaspoon pepper

Mix together the milk, eggs, salt, and pepper in a medium bowl. Pour over any unbaked casserole that requires 1 can (10¾ ounces) of condensed soup.

BASIC CHEESE SAUCE

This easy-to-make sauce is a great binder for casseroles, and it can also be spooned over cooked cauliflower or broccoli, poached eggs, chicken breasts, or even fish.

MAKES 2½ CUPS;
REPLACES 2 CANS (10¾ OUNCES EACH) CONDENSED SOUP

4 tablespoons butter

¼ cup all-purpose flour

½ teaspoon salt

1 pinch cayenne pepper

⅛ teaspoon dry mustard

2 cups hot milk

1 cup shredded Cheddar cheese

1. In a medium saucepan, melt the butter. Stir in the flour, salt, cayenne, and dry mustard until blended.

2. Whisk in the hot milk, bring to a boil, lower the heat, and cook, whisking constantly, until thickened and smooth. Add the cheese and stir until smooth. Use the sauce hot, or cover and refrigerate until ready to use.

BÉCHAMEL SAUCE

Béchamel sauce, or French white sauce, is often used in creamed dishes and casseroles. In the '50s, the sauce began to be replaced in everyday cooking by a cream soup of one sort or another. Made from scratch, this sauce will provide a fresher flavor for your dishes.

MAKES ABOUT 2¼ CUPS SAUCE;
REPLACES 2 CANS (10¾ OUNCES EACH) CONDENSED SOUP

4 tablespoons (½ stick) butter

¼ cup all-purpose flour

1 cup homemade (page 25) or prepared chicken broth, heated

½ cup cream or undiluted evaporated milk, heated

Salt

Dash of nutmeg

1. In a saucepan over medium heat, melt the butter, add the flour, and cook together for 2 to 3 minutes to remove the flour's raw taste.

2. Whisk in the heated broth and cream, stirring constantly, and cook until smooth and thick. Season with salt to taste and nutmeg. Use the sauce hot, or cover and refrigerate until ready to use.

BASIC MUSHROOM SAUCE

Mushroom sauce made with fresh mushrooms and beef broth makes a flavorful alternative to cream of mushroom soup. Use it in your favorite casserole recipe. For a richer and deeper flavor, instead of common white button mushrooms, use wild mushrooms such as morels or chanterelles, or shiitake or cremini mushrooms.

MAKES 1¾ CUPS;
REPLACES 1 CAN (10¾ OUNCES) CONDENSED SOUP

4 tablespoons butter

½ pound mushrooms, finely chopped

¼ cup onions, finely diced

¼ cup all-purpose flour

½ teaspoon salt

⅛ teaspoon pepper

1 cup homemade (page 26) or prepared beef broth, heated

1. In a medium saucepan, melt the butter over medium heat. Add the mushrooms and onions and sauté until aromatic. Add the flour, salt, and pepper, stirring until the mushrooms and onions are thoroughly coated.

2. Gradually add the beef broth and stir until the sauce is thickened, about 3 to 5 minutes. Use the sauce hot, or cover and refrigerate until ready to use.

SAVORY TOMATO SAUCE

When tomatoes are not in season, canned tomatoes are best. Use this sauce with cooked pasta or whenever a recipe calls for tomato sauce.

MAKES 3 CUPS

2½ cups peeled vine-ripened tomatoes or canned tomatoes, chopped (see Note)

3 tablespoons butter

1 medium onion, minced

3 tablespoons all-purpose flour

½ teaspoon dried thyme

Salt

Pepper

1. Whirl the tomatoes in a food processor or blender to puree.

2. In a 2-quart heavy saucepan, melt the butter over medium heat. Add the onion and cook for 3 to 5 minutes, until the onion is soft. Blend in the flour and stir over medium heat for 2 minutes, stirring until the onion is coated with flour.

3. Gradually add the pureed tomatoes to the onion mixture, stirring constantly. Cook, stirring, until thickened and smooth. Add the thyme and salt and pepper to taste. Use the sauce hot, or cover and refrigerate until ready to use.

○ ○ ○ ○ ○

NOTE: Fresh, vine-ripened tomatoes in season have great flavor. The rest of the year, however, the tomatoes from the supermarket are relatively tasteless. In most cases, canned tomatoes can be substituted in casseroles. Since they are usually picked at the height of the season, they actually have more flavor than those pale, out-of-season fresh tomatoes.

QUICK ALFREDO SAUCE

Alfredo sauce is credited to Chef Alfredo di Lello, who combined it with cooked fettuccine in the early 1900s. Since then, we've found many ways to use this sauce and even make changes in its preparation. In this simple-to-make version, cream cheese replaces the cream in the original sauce.

MAKES ABOUT 2¾ CUPS

1 package (8 ounces) cream cheese

1 cup milk

4 tablespoons butter

1 cup grated Parmesan cheese

1. Combine all of the ingredients in a medium saucepan and place over low heat.

2. Heat until the ingredients are melted and well combined, stirring frequently, approximately 15 minutes. Use in a casserole or simply pour over the pasta of your choice. Use the sauce hot, or cover and refrigerate until ready to use.

BASIC CHICKEN BROTH

The best thing about making your own chicken broth is that you decide what goes in it, and you can vary the flavors, too. For instance, you can add fresh herbs, more or less onion, and even garlic, if you prefer. A concentrated chicken broth is easy to make by simply boiling down the final product until it is thick or syrupy. Store it in the freezer in measured amounts, such as 1 or 2 cups, and use as needed.

MAKES 2 QUARTS

3 pounds chicken bones, or 1 whole stewing hen, rinsed and cut up

1 large onion, quartered

1 carrot (leave skin on), cut into 1-inch chunks

1 rib celery, cut into 1-inch chunks

2 sprigs fresh parsley

1 bay leaf

1 sprig fresh thyme, or ½ teaspoon dried thyme

3 quarts cold water

1 teaspoon salt, plus more to taste

1 teaspoon pepper, plus more to taste

1. Put all of the ingredients in a large stockpot and bring to a boil over high heat. Reduce the heat to low and simmer, partially covered, for 2 to 3 hours, or until the chicken is falling off the bones (if you have used a stewing hen). Check the stock every 30 minutes and skim off and discard any foam that rises to the surface.

2. Strain the broth. If you have used a hen, pick large pieces of meat off the bones and reserve for making soup. Discard the bones and vegetables.

3. Season the broth with more salt and pepper to taste. Cool and refrigerate until the fat has congealed. Remove the solid fat from the top of the broth and discard.

4. To store, measure the broth into heavy-duty resealable plastic bags, label, and freeze.

BASIC BEEF BROTH

For a deep, rich broth, roast the bones and vegetables before proceeding to step 2. A long, slow simmer of at least 3 hours is essential for a flavorful broth. For a clearer one, avoid boiling.

MAKES 3½ QUARTS

3 to 4 pounds meaty beef bones, such as short ribs or shank, tail, and/or neck bones

1 large onion (leave skin on), roughly chopped (see Note)

3 large carrots (leave skin on), roughly chopped

3 stalks celery, including leaves, roughly chopped

1 large tomato, chopped

8 whole black peppercorns

4 sprigs fresh parsley

1 bay leaf

1 tablespoon salt

2 teaspoons dried thyme

2 cloves garlic (optional)

4 quarts water

1. Preheat the oven to 450°F, and roast the bones and vegetables for about 30 minutes, if desired.

2. Combine all of the ingredients in a large stockpot. Bring the mixture to a boil and immediately reduce the heat. Simmer, partially covered, for 3 hours, or until the meat is falling off the bones. Check the stock every 30 minutes and skim and discard any foam that rises to the top of the pot.

3. Strain the broth well, pressing down on the meat and vegetables to extract their juices. Discard the meat, bones, and vegetables.

4. Cool and refrigerate until the fat has congealed. Remove the solid fat from top of the broth and discard. Taste and add seasonings as desired.

5. To store, measure the broth into heavy-duty resealable plastic bags, label, and freeze.

○ ○ ○ ○ ○

NOTE: The onion skin will add color to the broth.

BASIC VEGETABLE BROTH

Vegetable broth is perfect for vegetarian dishes. If you wish, collect the ingredients in resealable plastic bags and freeze until you have time to make this flavorful broth. To further concentrate the flavor, simmer the finished broth until it is reduced to 4 cups. Add water, cream, or milk to thin it when you use it in a sauce.

— MAKES 2½ QUARTS —

1 tablespoon olive oil

2 cups potato peels from scrubbed potatoes

1 large onion (leave skin on), coarsely chopped (see Note, facing page)

1 cup coarsely chopped mushrooms

2 stalks celery, including leaves, coarsely chopped

2 large carrots (leave skin on), coarsely chopped

1 bunch green onions (white and green parts), coarsely chopped

6 to 8 large cloves garlic, chopped

1 bunch fresh parsley

6 sprigs fresh thyme

2 bay leaves

1 teaspoon salt

3 quarts water

1. In a large stockpot, heat the olive oil over medium-high heat. Add the potato peels, onion, mushrooms, celery, carrots, green onions, and garlic cloves. Cook, stirring frequently, for 10 minutes.

2. Add the parsley, thyme, bay leaves, salt, and water and bring to a boil. Lower the heat and simmer, uncovered, for 1 hour and 30 minutes.

3. Strain the broth and discard the vegetables. Cool the broth. Refrigerate or measure into resealable freezer bags and freeze until ready to use.

BASIC COOKED RICE

Many recipes suggest that you "serve over hot fluffy rice." Here is a basic recipe that will provide four ½-cup servings.

MAKES 2 CUPS COOKED RICE

1¾ cups water

¾ teaspoon salt

1 tablespoon butter or olive oil (optional)

1 cup white or brown rice

1. In a medium saucepan, bring the water, salt, and butter or oil (if using) to a boil over high heat.

2. Stir in the rice slowly, so as not to disturb the boiling.

3. Cover, reduce the heat, and simmer for 20 to 30 minutes for white rice, or 35 to 45 minutes for brown rice.

4. Fluff the rice with a fork.

COOKED WILD RICE

Perfectly cooked wild rice is tender, but not entirely opened up. When wild rice is overcooked, it almost explodes into curly, white grains and gets mushy. Wild rice is the seed of a wild grass. It complements all sorts of main courses, from beef to fish. I seldom mix it with another type of rice because the cooking times will vary. In fact, the cooking time may vary from one package of wild rice to the next, depending on how the rice was processed, meaning how much the grain has been dried.

MAKES 2 CUPS

⅔ cup wild rice

2½ cups water

½ to 1 teaspoon salt

1. Put the rice into a strainer and run hot tap water over it until the water runs clear. This will remove any dust and foreign particles.

2. Bring the water and salt to a boil in a medium, heavy saucepan and add the wild rice. Stir, cover, and lower the heat. Simmer the rice for 30 to 40 minutes, without stirring, until tender.

3. Drain the excess water from the rice. It should be tender but not curled or mushy. Some kernels will be open, but others will be just tender.

COOKED DRIED BEANS

You can use this recipe to cook any variety of beans. If time is short, use the "quick soak" method, but if possible, soak the beans overnight. Extra cooked beans can be frozen for later use.

○──────────── MAKES 6 TO 8 CUPS COOKED BEANS ────────────○

1 pound dried beans (about 2 cups)

Quick method: Rinse and sort the beans in a large pot and add 6 to 8 cups hot water, covering the beans by at least 2 inches. Bring to a rapid boil for 2 minutes. Remove from the heat. Cover and let stand for 1 hour. Drain and rinse the beans and put them back in the pot. Add hot water to cover the beans by 2 inches, bring to a simmer, and simmer gently, with the lid tilted slightly, until the beans are tender, about 1½ to 2 hours.

Overnight method: Rinse and sort the beans in a large pot. Add 6 to 8 cups cold water or enough to cover the beans by 2 inches. Let stand overnight for at least 6 to 8 hours. Drain and rinse the beans. Put them back in the pot and add 6 cups hot water or enough to cover the beans by 2 inches. Simmer gently, with the lid tilted slightly, until the beans are tender, about 1½ to 2 hours.

To make it easy to use the beans, cool them completely, separate into 2-cup batches, and freeze in plastic bags for later use.

CARAMELIZED ONIONS

Caramelized onions are delicious baked over chicken breasts (see Chicken Breasts with Caramelized Onions on page 501). They are also delicious on grilled hamburgers and open-faced sandwiches. This is one of my favorite ways to prepare them. A bit of brown sugar gives the onions a start on sweetness. Some cooks like to make a heaping skillet full of onions. They cook down as they brown. If you make these ahead of time so they're ready to use, pack them in freezer bags or containers, marked with the date and amount.

MAKES ABOUT 2 CUPS

2 tablespoons butter

2 large sweet onions (about 2 pounds), thinly sliced

2 teaspoons packed light brown sugar

1. Melt the butter in a large skillet; add the onions and cook over medium-high heat for 10 minutes, or until well browned. Reduce the heat to medium and cook for another 30 minutes, or until soft, stirring frequently.

2. Add the brown sugar and stir until dissolved. Keep warm until ready to use. Or transfer to a covered container and refrigerate for up to 2 days or freeze up to 4 weeks.

FLAKY PASTRY

Including lemon juice and egg in the dough is an old-fashioned trick for making a flaky pastry. Use this recipe for pies with savory or sweet fillings. For a double-crust pie, double all of the ingredients except the egg; replace the egg yolk with 1 whole large egg.

MAKES ONE 8- OR 9-INCH PIECRUST

¾ cup all-purpose flour

¼ teaspoon salt

5 tablespoons chilled butter or lard

1 large egg yolk

1 teaspoon fresh lemon juice

2 to 4 tablespoons ice water

1. In a large bowl, combine the flour and salt. Using a pastry blender, two knives, or a pastry fork, cut in the butter or lard until the fat is the size of dried peas. Alternatively, combine the ingredients in a food processor with the steel blade in place, and pulse.

2. In a small bowl, whisk together the egg yolk, lemon juice, and 2 to 3 tablespoons of the ice water. Drizzle the egg mixture over the flour mixture. With a fork or spatula, mix until the pastry holds together in a ball, adding more ice water if necessary.

3. Turn out onto a work surface and knead lightly once or twice to shape the dough into a ball. Wrap in aluminum foil or plastic wrap and refrigerate until firm, about 30 minutes, before rolling out the dough. Proceed as directed in the recipe you are using.

Variation
Whole-Wheat Pastry: Substitute ¾ cup whole-wheat flour for ¾ cup of the all-purpose flour in the recipe.

FOOLPROOF HARD-COOKED EGGS

Here's how to cook eggs and avoid the green ring around the yolk.

Large eggs

1. Put the eggs into a pot, and cover with cold water by 1 to 2 inches. Place over high heat and bring to a boil, then remove from the heat. Cover, and let the eggs sit in the hot water for exactly 15 minutes.

2. Place the eggs, still in the pan, under cold running water and continue running the water over the eggs until the water in the pan is cold. These eggs will be easy to shell if you do it immediately.

NOTES: To make chilled eggs easier to shell, bring some water to a boil in a saucepan. Plunge the eggs in the boiling water for 10 seconds, remove, and put them in ice water.

To shell the eggs, tap them on the countertop to crack the shells all over. Remove the shells, beginning at the flatter end of the egg.

TACO SEASONING MIX

One good reason to make your own taco seasoning mix is that you can control what is in it. If you wish, you can make it less spicy by reducing the cayenne pepper or more spicy by adding more.

2 tablespoons onion powder

2 tablespoons chili powder

2 teaspoons paprika

1 teaspoon cayenne pepper

1½ teaspoons dried oregano leaves

½ teaspoon dried marjoram leaves

1 tablespoon salt

¼ teaspoon black pepper

2 tablespoons cornstarch

1 tablespoon minced garlic

1 teaspoon ground cumin

Combine all of the ingredients in a small bowl and blend well. Store at room temperature in a tightly closed container, such as a canning jar or plastic container. Use within 6 months.

ROASTED PEPPERS

Several recipes call for roasted peppers. You can roast any type of bell pepper as well as large chile peppers, such as anchos or poblanos. Roast the peppers in the oven or over a gas range or grill.

Bell peppers or large chile peppers

Olive oil or vegetable oil

1. Preheat the oven to 500 to 550°F and cover a baking sheet with aluminum foil. Or prepare a very hot fire in a charcoal grill. Or turn the gas burner and hood fan on high.

2. Coat the peppers lightly with oil (if roasting on a gas burner, do not oil the peppers). Roast on the baking sheet in the oven or on the grill or burner. As the peppers develop charred spots, turn them over using a pair of long tongs. Continue roasting until the peppers are charred all over, about 15 minutes in the oven or 10 to 15 minutes on the grill.

3. Put the peppers in a paper bag or wrap in the foil used to cover the baking sheet. Allow to steam and cool for 10 to 15 minutes. Remove the stems and seeds and pull off the thin skins.

Chapter 2

CASSEROLE APPETIZERS & FIRST COURSES

Many of the recipes in this chapter serve a large number of people. When we serve appetizers, it's often for a party or a potluck, where we want to serve a bigger crowd. The advantage of casserole appetizers is that most of them can be assembled ahead, covered, and refrigerated, to be baked just before serving. This makes them easy to bring to a party—providing you let the host or hostess know your dish will need a few minutes in the oven. If you bake just before you leave your kitchen, be sure to keep the dish hot in an insulated tote bag.

○ ○ ○ ○ ○

*The recipes are organized here by numbers
of servings, starting with smaller yields.*

○ ○ ○ ○ ○

BUTTERY PORTOBELLO MUSHROOMS WITH FRIED SAGE LEAVES

The flavors of butter-fried sage, lemon, and portobello mushrooms make this an outstanding first course. It's easiest to serve the mushrooms whole for a sit-down meal. For a "walk around" party, I like to cut the mushrooms into squares and serve with toothpicks.

SERVES 4

4 large portobello mushrooms (see Note)

4 tablespoons butter

¼ cup olive oil

5 bunches fresh sage leaves (about 40 leaves)

Salt

Pepper

1 lemon, halved

1. Preheat the oven to 400°F.

2. Trim the stems off the mushrooms and save for another use or discard. Arrange the mushrooms, gill sides up, in a shallow casserole.

3. In a small skillet, heat the butter and olive oil until bubbly. Add the sage leaves and cook over medium heat until the leaves are crispy.

4. Arrange the sage leaves on the mushrooms and drizzle the caps with the butter and olive oil mixture. Sprinkle with salt and pepper to taste.

5. Bake, uncovered, for 10 minutes, or until the mushrooms are tender. Squeeze the lemon over the mushrooms and serve.

○ ○ ○ ○ ○

NOTE: For serving buffet-style, cut the mushrooms into 1-inch squares before you put them in the casserole. Serve with sliced bread, or offer toothpicks for spearing.

SPICY CHEESE AND GREEN CHILE DIP

Serve this dip with raw veggies, crisp tortilla chips, or sliced crusty bread.

1 can (14½ ounces) stewed tomatoes, drained

1 medium red onion, cut into 1-inch chunks

¼ cup packed chopped fresh parsley

1 can (4 ounces) diced green chiles with their juice

1 medium clove garlic

1 tablespoon white wine vinegar

1 teaspoon dried oregano

½ teaspoon salt

2 cups shredded Monterey Jack cheese, divided

1. Preheat the oven to 375°F. Coat a 1-quart ovenproof crock or casserole with cooking spray.

2. Put the drained tomatoes, onion, parsley, chiles, garlic, vinegar, oregano, and salt in a food processor with the steel blade in place. (Alternatively, you might use a blender, but be careful not to overprocess the mixture.) Process the mixture until the tomatoes and onions are coarsely chopped. Transfer to the casserole, stir in ½ cup of the shredded cheese, then top with the remaining 1½ cups cheese. (At this point you can cover and refrigerate the dish and heat it just before serving.)

3. Bake, uncovered, for 20 minutes or until the dip is hot and the cheese is melted. Serve hot.

CREAMY CRAB SPREAD WITH ALMONDS

Assemble this appetizer ahead of time and store it in the refrigerator. It's a perfect one to take to a potluck and heat when you arrive.

SERVES 6

Butter for the dish

1 package (8 ounces) cream cheese, softened (see Note)

2 cans or packages (6 ounces each) crabmeat, picked through

1 small onion, chopped

Pinch of cayenne pepper

⅓ cup sliced almonds

Crackers or melba toast for serving

1. Preheat the oven to 350°F. Butter a small 3-cup casserole.

2. In a small bowl, mix the cream cheese, crabmeat, onion, and cayenne pepper. Spoon into the casserole and sprinkle with the almonds. Bake, uncovered, for 10 to 15 minutes, until bubbly. Serve with crackers or melba toast.

NOTE: To soften cream cheese, remove from the foil wrapper and place on a microwave-safe dish. Microwave for 10 seconds at high power.

SWISS MUSHROOMS AU GRATIN

Offer these juicy baked mushrooms with slices of crusty French bread. Instead of white button mushrooms, you can use baby bellas, morels, oyster mushrooms, or other flavorful mushrooms.

SERVES 6

3 tablespoons butter, plus extra for the dish

2 tablespoons minced shallots or green onions (white and green parts)

1½ pounds mushrooms, sliced

1 teaspoon salt

1 teaspoon fresh lemon juice

2 tablespoons sherry

1½ cups heavy cream, divided

3 large eggs

Pinch of ground nutmeg

⅛ teaspoon pepper

¼ cup shredded Swiss cheese

1. Preheat the oven to 375°F. Butter a 1½-quart shallow casserole or gratin dish.

2. In a large skillet, melt the 3 tablespoons butter, add the shallots, and sauté for 2 minutes, stirring. Stir in the mushrooms, salt, lemon juice, and sherry. Cook for 10 minutes, or until the liquid has been absorbed. Add 1 cup cream. Bring to a boil and continue boiling for about 5 minutes, or until the cream is reduced to a thick sauce.

3. In a medium bowl, beat the eggs and the remaining ½ cup cream. Stir the mushroom mixture into the egg mixture and transfer to the buttered dish. Sprinkle with the nutmeg, pepper, and Swiss cheese.

4. Bake, uncovered, for 15 to 20 minutes, or until bubbly.

SHIITAKE MUSHROOMS WITH GRUYÈRE

These mushrooms are just a little slurpy and sloppy, but so delicious!
They are actually easier to serve as a first course at a sit-down meal.

SERVES 6 TO 8

7 tablespoons butter

1 pound shiitake or baby bella mushrooms, sliced

¼ teaspoon ground nutmeg

Salt

Pepper

¼ cup heavy cream

6 to 8 slices French bread, about 1 inch thick

½ cup shredded Gruyère or Swiss cheese

Chopped fresh parsley for garnish

1. Preheat the oven to 400°F. In a large skillet, melt the butter over medium heat. Add the mushrooms and sauté for 10 minutes, or until the liquid has evaporated. Reduce the heat to medium-low and stir in the nutmeg, salt and pepper to taste, and cream. Cook until thickened.

2. Arrange the bread slices in a shallow 1½-quart casserole or an 8-inch square baking dish. Make a slight indentation in the center of each slice. Spoon the mushroom mixture over the slices and sprinkle with the cheese.

3. Bake, uncovered, for 10 minutes, or until the cheese is melted. Garnish with the parsley.

CRAB AND SWEET CURRY QUICHE

Curry powder is a blend of twenty or more spices and herbs, including cardamom, cloves, cinnamon, coriander, mace, and nutmeg. These are all "sweet" spices, as opposed to hot spices like chiles and black pepper. Select a mild curry powder for this recipe to bring out the flavor of the crab. Serve the quiche cut into small triangles for an appetizer or in larger wedges for a first course. It also makes a delicious main course for a light lunch or supper.

SERVES 8

1 recipe Flaky Pastry (page 32)

2 tablespoons minced shallots

1 tablespoon butter

1 teaspoon sweet curry powder

1 cup shredded cooked crabmeat, well drained

2 tablespoons minced fresh chives

1 tablespoon all-purpose flour

1½ cups shredded Swiss cheese, divided

3 large eggs

1 cup light cream or half-and-half

½ teaspoon salt

Dash of Tabasco sauce

1. Prepare the pastry and chill in the refrigerator. Preheat the oven to 350°F.

2. *While the pastry is chilling, prepare the filling:* Sauté the shallots in the butter for about 2 minutes and add the curry powder. Transfer to a medium bowl and add the crabmeat, chives, and flour.

3. Roll out the chilled pastry into a 12-inch circle and transfer to a 9-inch tart or pie pan. Trim and crimp the edges.

4. Spread half the cheese in the bottom of the pastry shell. Top with the crab mixture and sprinkle with the remaining cheese.

5. In a small bowl, whisk together the eggs, cream, salt, and Tabasco sauce, and pour over the filling in the pastry shell.

6. Bake for 35 to 40 minutes, or until the filling is lightly browned and a knife inserted near the center comes out clean. Serve warm or at room temperature.

BEEF AND ANCHO CHILE CHEESE DIP

An ancho chile is a broad dried chile, 3 to 4 inches long, which ranges in flavor from mild to hot. In its fresh, green state, the ancho is called a "poblano" chile. You can either pulverize the dried, deep-red pod (seeds removed) into a powder yourself, or you can buy it in powder form. One good source is Penzeys, a nationally known purveyor of spices. This appetizer will remind your guests of nachos, a favorite appetizer of kids and teens alike.

SERVES 8

1 pound lean ground beef

1 tablespoon ancho chile powder

Salt

½ teaspoon dried marjoram

1 can (15½ ounces) seasoned chili beans

1 can (10 ounces) diced tomatoes and green chiles with their juice

2 cups crumbled queso fresco (Mexican farmers' cheese) or feta cheese, divided

1. Preheat the oven to 350°F. Coat a 1½-quart shallow casserole with cooking spray.

2. In a large nonstick skillet, cook the beef over medium heat, stirring to separate the clumps of meat, until no pink remains, about 10 minutes.

3. In a large bowl, combine the cooked beef with the chile powder, salt to taste, the marjoram, chili beans, tomatoes and chiles with their juice, and 1 cup of the cheese. Spread out in the prepared casserole and sprinkle the remaining cup of cheese evenly over the top. (At this point you can cover and refrigerate the dip for up to 1 day. Add an extra 5 minutes to the baking time.)

4. Before serving, bake, uncovered, until the cheese is melted, 20 to 25 minutes. Serve hot with tortilla chips, crackers, bread, or freshly cut vegetables.

EGGPLANT AND GARLIC SLATHER

A slather is something you spread generously on crisp croutons or toasted slices of French bread. Try this as a sauce for pasta, as well. To allow the flavors to develop, make this slather ahead and refrigerate for an hour or two, or even a day in advance.

——————————————— SERVES 8 ———————————————

1 large eggplant, or 5 to 7 small Japanese eggplants (1½ pounds total)

2 teaspoons olive oil, divided

2 whole heads garlic

2 tablespoons balsamic vinegar

¼ cup chopped fresh basil

2 to 3 tablespoons nonfat plain yogurt

½ teaspoon salt

¼ teaspoon pepper

⅔ cup grated Parmesan cheese, divided

French bread slices, toasted, for serving

1. Preheat the oven to 350°F. Coat a shallow 4-cup casserole with cooking spray.

2. Cut a few slits in the eggplant(s). Rub all over with 1 teaspoon olive oil and place in a shallow roasting pan or on a rimmed baking sheet. Drizzle the garlic heads with the remaining 1 teaspoon olive oil. Wrap them in foil and place on the same tray as the eggplants.

3. Bake the garlic and eggplant until the eggplant wrinkles and starts to collapse, about 1 hour. Remove from the oven. Cool enough to be able to handle.

4. Cut the eggplant in half and scrape the pulp into the bowl of a food processor. Squeeze the

garlic cloves out of their skins and into the food processor. Add the vinegar, basil, yogurt, salt, and pepper. Process until almost smooth.

5. Spread half the puree in the casserole dish. Top with half the Parmesan cheese, and spread the remaining puree over the cheese. Sprinkle with the remaining Parmesan cheese. (The slather can be made up to this point 12 hours in advance. Cover and refrigerate until ready to bake.)

6. Before serving, preheat the oven to 400°F. Bake the slather, uncovered, for 10 to 15 minutes, until bubbly. Serve hot with slices of French bread.

ROASTED GARLIC AND ONION BEAN SPREAD

The length of this recipe makes it look difficult. It is actually simple, especially if you roast the garlic and onion the day before you make the dip. They infuse this delicious hot dip with subtle flavors.

SERVES 10

2 cans (16 ounces each) pinto beans, rinsed and drained

3 tablespoons olive oil

4 teaspoons chili powder

1 teaspoon ground cumin

1 large roasted yellow onion, chopped (see Note, facing page)

4 large cloves roasted garlic, chopped (see Note, facing page)

1 teaspoon Tabasco sauce

2 cups shredded Monterey Jack cheese, divided

Salt

Chopped fresh cilantro for garnish

Tortilla chips for serving

1. Preheat the oven to 400°F.

2. Puree the beans in a food processor.

3. Heat the olive oil in a heavy saucepan. Add the chili powder and cumin and stir over medium heat until aromatic. Add the pureed beans to the saucepan. Stir in the chopped roasted onion and garlic and cook, stirring, for 5 minutes.

4. Stir in the Tabasco and 1 cup of the cheese and season with salt to taste. Pour into a shallow 1½-quart casserole and sprinkle the remaining cup of cheese over the top. (The spread can be covered and refrigerated at this point for up to 6 to 8 hours.)

5. Before serving, place the casserole in the oven until heated through and the cheese

is melted. Sprinkle with chopped cilantro and serve with tortilla chips.

∘ ∘ ∘ ∘ ∘

NOTES: To roast the onion, rub a large yellow-skinned onion with oil (do not peel the onion). Wrap in heavy-duty aluminum foil, crimping it at the top to close tightly. Place in a pre-heated 400°F oven for 1 to 1½ hours, or until the onion is soft. Allow to cool in the foil before peeling and chopping.

To roast the garlic, cut the top off of a large, firm head of garlic, exposing the tips of the garlic cloves. Place on a square of heavy-duty aluminum foil. Drizzle with some olive oil and sprinkle with a little salt. Wrap the garlic in the foil, and tightly crimp the top to close. Place in a preheated 400°F oven for 30 to 40 minutes, or until soft. Cool, then press gently on the bottom to push the soft roasted cloves from their skins.

DILLED CHIPPED BEEF DIP

Chipped beef, the wafer-thin slices of salted and smoked dried beef, is also referred to as "dried beef," and usually comes packed in small jars. Here, rather than mixing it with the usual cream sauce, we've made it into an appetizer, which is tasty on crackers or lavash.

SERVES 10

2 tablespoons butter

1 small onion, chopped

1 tablespoon fresh lemon juice

¾ cup sour cream

1 package (8 ounces) cream cheese, softened (see Note)

1 teaspoon dried dill weed

1 jar (3 ounces) dried beef, chopped

½ cup chopped pecans

1. Preheat the oven to 350°F.

2. In a large skillet, melt the butter and sauté the onion over medium-low heat until tender, about 5 minutes. Add the lemon juice and cook for 2 minutes.

3. Add the sour cream, cream cheese, dill weed, and dried beef to the skillet and stir until all of the ingredients are well combined. Pour the mixture into an 8-inch square baking dish and top with the pecans.

4. Bake, uncovered, for 15 to 20 minutes until bubbly.

○ ○ ○ ○ ○

NOTE: To soften cream cheese, remove from the foil wrapper and place on a microwave-safe dish. Microwave for 10 seconds at high power.

QUICK AND EASY CHILE CON QUESO DIP

You can assemble the ingredients for this party dip, cover it, and refrigerate until an hour or so before your party. Slip it into the oven, and it will be ready when your first guests arrive.

SERVES 10

2 cups shredded Monterey Jack cheese

1 package (8 ounces) cream cheese, softened (see Note, facing page)

1 can (10 ounces) diced tomatoes and green chiles

½ cup picante sauce or salsa (mild, medium, or hot)

Tortilla chips for serving

1. Preheat the oven to 350°F.

2. Combine all of the ingredients except the tortilla chips in a 1-quart casserole. Cover and bake for 20 to 25 minutes, until the cheese is melted and the dip is bubbly.

3. Serve with crisp tortilla chips.

JALAPEÑO CHILE CON QUESO

Jalapeño pepper can make this version of chile con queso spicy hot. Remember, though, when handling hot peppers, to wear rubber gloves and keep your hands away from your face, especially your eyes!

SERVES 10

2 tablespoons butter

2 green onions, minced (white and green parts)

1 poblano pepper, seeded and diced

1 teaspoon ground cumin

1 large tomato, diced

1 can (4 ounces) diced green chiles

1 jalapeño pepper, seeded and diced (optional)

1 package (8 ounces) cream cheese, cubed

½ cup heavy cream or sour cream

1 cup shredded Monterey Jack cheese

Chopped fresh cilantro for garnish

Tortilla chips or raw vegetables for serving

1. Preheat the oven to 350°F.

2. Melt the butter in a small skillet and add the green onions and poblano pepper. Sauté for about 5 minutes, until tender.

3. In a 1-quart casserole, combine the green onion mixture, cumin, tomato, diced chiles, jalapeño pepper (if using), cream cheese, and heavy or sour cream. (At this point the casserole can be covered and refrigerated for up to 1 day. Add 5 minutes to the baking time.)

4. Bake, uncovered, for 30 minutes, or until bubbly. Sprinkle with the Monterey Jack cheese and cilantro. Serve hot with tortilla chips or raw vegetables for dipping.

BEAN AND BURGER SPREAD

Think of this spread when you are planning a large party or picnic, or if you need to bring something to a potluck affair. This is an appetizer that appeals to meat-loving teens. To reduce the saltiness, substitute low-sodium cheese for the Cheddar and diced canned tomatoes for the taco sauce.

— SERVES 12 TO 16 —

1 can (16 ounces) refried beans

1 pound lean ground beef

1 medium sweet onion, diced, divided

1 can (4 ounces) diced green chiles

½ cup sliced black olives, plus more for garnish

2½ cups shredded Cheddar or Jack cheese

1 cup taco or chile sauce (mild, medium, or hot)

Tortilla chips for serving

1. Preheat the oven to 350°F.

2. Spread the bottom of a 9-by-13-inch baking dish with the refried beans.

3. In a large nonstick skillet, brown the beef and half of the onion over medium-high heat.

4. Spread the beef and onion mixture over the refried beans. Sprinkle with the green chiles, ½ cup olives, the cheese, and the remaining half of the onion. Drizzle with taco sauce. (The casserole can be covered and refrigerated at this point for up to 12 hours. Add 5 to 10 minutes to the baking time.)

5. Bake, uncovered, for 20 to 30 minutes, until bubbly. Garnish with more black olives and serve with tortilla chips.

BROCCOLI AND PARMESAN SLATHER

This hot, savory spread is perfect to serve buffet-style with rounds of toast, crackers, or raw vegetables.

SERVES 12

1 package (10 ounces) frozen chopped broccoli, or 1 medium head fresh broccoli

1 cup light or regular mayonnaise

1 tablespoon fresh lemon juice

1 tablespoon dried basil leaves

1 teaspoon chili powder

½ cup chopped fresh chives

½ cup chopped fresh parsley

1 cup grated Parmesan cheese

1. Preheat the oven to 350°F.

2. If using frozen broccoli, cook according to package directions and drain. If using fresh broccoli, cut off and discard tough ends from stalks. Peel the remaining stems if the skin is tough. Cook in boiling water for 10 minutes, or until tender; drain and chop.

3. In a food processor with the steel blade in place, combine the broccoli, mayonnaise, lemon juice, basil, chili powder, chives, parsley, and Parmesan cheese. Transfer to a shallow 1-quart casserole.

4. Bake, uncovered, for 20 minutes, or until heated through and browned on top. Serve hot.

———

Variation: Try this with cauliflower, and substitute shredded Cheddar for the Parmesan.

CHILE-CHEESE OMELET SQUARES

These are satisfying little bites of omelet spiked with chiles and hot pepper cheese. You can make these squares ahead of time, wrap them well, and refrigerate. Reheat just until warm before serving.

SERVES 12

8 large eggs, beaten

½ pound mushrooms, sliced

1 can (4 ounces) chopped green chiles

4 slices bacon, cooked and diced, or ½ cup diced cooked ham

1 cup shredded spicy pepper cheese

1. Preheat the oven to 350°F. Coat a shallow 1-quart casserole with cooking spray.

2. In a large bowl, whisk together the eggs, mushrooms, chiles, bacon, and cheese and pour the mixture into the casserole dish. Bake, uncovered, for 20 minutes, or until set. Cool and cut into 1-inch squares. Serve with toothpicks.

CURRIED MUSHROOMS

Here is a slightly different take on a curry. You can serve these mushrooms as a vegetarian main dish as well as a first course.

SERVES 12

4 tablespoons butter

2 cups chopped onions

2 cloves garlic, minced

1 cup chopped celery

1½ pounds mushrooms

1½ teaspoons salt

1 teaspoon ground cumin

1 teaspoon ground cinnamon

1 teaspoon ground turmeric

1 teaspoon grated fresh ginger

½ teaspoon dry mustard

½ teaspoon ground cloves

2 large cooking apples, such as Fuji, Gala, or Granny Smith, peeled and chopped

3 large tomatoes, peeled, seeded, and chopped

3 tablespoons shredded coconut

1 tablespoon honey

2 tablespoons fresh lemon juice

Crisp toast rounds or toasted pita triangles for serving

Sliced or slivered almonds, toasted, for garnish (see Note)

1. Preheat the oven to 350°F.

2. In a large skillet, melt the butter and add the onions and garlic. Sauté for 5 minutes, or until tender. Transfer to a 2-quart casserole and add the celery. Remove the stems from the mushrooms and chop the stems. Stir the stems, mushroom caps, and salt into the casserole.

3. Bake, covered, for 30 minutes or until the mushrooms have released their juices.

4. Meanwhile, in a small bowl, mix together the cumin, cinnamon, turmeric, ginger, mustard, and cloves. Stir into the mushroom mixture and add the apples, tomatoes, coconut, honey, and lemon juice. Return the casserole to the oven and bake, uncovered, for 25 minutes, or until all the ingredients are just tender; do not overcook. Cover and let stand 10 minutes before serving. Spoon onto crisp toast rounds or pita triangles and garnish with toasted almonds.

ooooo

NOTE: To toast the almonds, spread them out on a cookie sheet and toast in a 350°F oven for about 10 minutes, stirring occasionally, until the nuts are fragrant and lightly browned.

JARLSBERG CHEESE SPREAD

The nutty flavor of Jarlsberg cheese, melted into a baked spread, goes equally well with bread, crackers, or sliced fresh apple. The last time I made this, I thought I had Jarlsberg in the fridge, but it was actually a Swedish fontina. I used it anyway, with excellent results.

SERVES 12

2 cups shredded or diced Jarlsberg cheese

2 tablespoons minced red onion

½ cup mayonnaise

1. Preheat the oven to 400°F. Coat a shallow 1-quart casserole with cooking spray.

2. In a medium bowl, mix the cheese, onion, and mayonnaise and spread in the bottom of the casserole. Bake, uncovered, for 15 minutes, or until hot and bubbly.

BAKED MUSHROOMS WITH GARLIC AND CHEESE

Provide a small container of toothpicks and some crusty French bread for serving these delicious, cheesy mushroom tidbits. If the mushrooms are large, cut the slices into quarters; if they're medium-size, just halve them. Tiny button mushrooms can be left whole.

SERVES 12

1 pound mushrooms, sliced

4 large cloves garlic, sliced

7 tablespoons butter, plus more for the dish

1 teaspoon kosher salt

½ teaspoon pepper

½ cup grated Parmesan cheese

Slices of French bread for serving

1. Preheat the oven to 400°F. Butter a shallow 1½-quart casserole.

2. Arrange the mushrooms in the casserole in an even layer and top with the sliced garlic. Dot with the butter and sprinkle with salt and pepper. Bake, uncovered, for 20 minutes, or until bubbly. Sprinkle with the cheese.

3. Serve the mushrooms with slices of French bread.

PARMESAN AND SUN-DRIED TOMATO QUICHE

For a tasty filling that is relatively low in fat, use evaporated milk.
Don't use skim, though—a little fat carries flavor!

FOR THE PASTRY:

1 cup all-purpose flour

½ teaspoon salt

¼ cup vegetable or canola oil

2 to 3 tablespoons milk

FOR THE FILLING:

2 tablespoons unsalted butter

½ cup chopped onions

½ cup sun-dried tomatoes, chopped
(not oil-packed)

½ cup grated Parmesan cheese

4 large eggs

2 cups light cream or
evaporated milk

½ teaspoon salt (optional)

⅛ teaspoon ground nutmeg

1. Preheat the oven to 425°F.

2. *To make the pastry:* With a fork, stir together the flour, salt, and oil in a medium bowl until the mixture is crumbly. Stir in enough milk to moisten the flour and form moist crumbs. Flatten into a disk and place between sheets of waxed paper. Chill for 10 to 15 minutes. Roll out the pastry into a 9- or 10-inch square to fit an 8- or 9-inch square baking pan, preferably with removable sides. Transfer to the pan and crimp the edges. With a fork, pierce several holes in the crust and bake for 10 minutes. Remove from the oven. If the dough has puffed up, gently press down.

3. *To make the filling:* Melt the butter in a heavy nonstick skillet over medium heat. Add the onions and sauté for 5 minutes, or until softened.

4. Spread the onions in the bottom of the partially baked crust. Sprinkle with the sun-dried tomatoes and Parmesan cheese.

5. Whisk the eggs, cream, salt (if using), and nutmeg in a medium bowl and pour over the onion mixture. Bake the quiche for 15 minutes at 425°F. Lower the temperature to 350°F and bake for another 25 to 30 minutes, or until set and the tip of a knife comes out clean when inserted in the center.

BAKED RICOTTA WITH GARLIC AND HERBS

In this easy and delicious casserole, the ricotta bakes down into a creamy cheese sauce. It makes a perfect appetizer for a buffet-style meal.

SERVES 12

1 tablespoon olive oil

2 cups ricotta cheese

1 teaspoon salt

½ teaspoon pepper

4 cloves garlic, minced

¼ cup chopped fresh herbs, such as basil, rosemary, and thyme

¼ cup heavy cream

12 slices French bread, toasted or grilled, for serving

1. Preheat the oven to 300°F.

2. Coat a 1-quart casserole with the olive oil.

3. In a large bowl, stir the ricotta together with the salt, pepper, garlic, herbs, and cream.

Transfer to the casserole. Bake, uncovered, for about 15 minutes, until the cheese is creamy and hot. Serve with the French bread slices.

SPINACH AND PARMESAN SLATHER

Put these ingredients together in a pretty little casserole dish so that it will be ready to pop into the oven 15 minutes before your guests arrive.

SERVES ABOUT 12

1 bag (9 ounces) fresh spinach leaves

1 cup grated Parmesan cheese

½ cup regular or low-fat mayonnaise

½ cup regular or low-fat sour cream

1 clove garlic, minced

1 tablespoon fresh lemon juice

1 tablespoon Dijon mustard

1 teaspoon dried basil

½ teaspoon salt

⅛ teaspoon cayenne pepper

½ cup pine nuts

Slices of crusty French bread or freshly cut vegetables for serving

1. Preheat the oven to 400°F. Butter a shallow 1- to 1½-quart casserole.

2. Put the spinach in a large bowl and cover with boiling water. Press the leaves down into the water until they wilt. Drain the spinach well and squeeze out all the liquid.

3. Combine the spinach, Parmesan, mayonnaise, sour cream, garlic, lemon juice, mustard, basil, salt, and cayenne in a food processor fitted with the steel blade. Process until the spinach is finely chopped, but not pureed. Alternatively, chop the spinach by hand and combine with the remaining ingredients except the pine nuts and bread slices. Spoon into the buttered casserole and sprinkle with the pine nuts. (At this point the casserole can be covered and refrigerated overnight. Add 5 minutes to the baking time.)

4. Bake, uncovered, for 15 minutes, or until lightly browned. Serve hot with the bread or vegetables.

HERBED CHICKEN TERRINE WITH EXOTIC FRUIT SALSA

Each slice of this beautiful meat loaf reveals a round of white chicken breast, surrounded by a puree of spinach and herbs. It is absolutely perfect for a summertime dinner party and ideal because you can make this terrine up to 3 days ahead of time. It needs to be chilled so that it can be cut into slices for serving. To save time, you can skip steps 1 and 2 and buy a rotisserie chicken breast from the supermarket. The recipe is a little fussy, but really worth the effort!

○———————————— SERVES 12 ————————————○

1 whole chicken (3½ to 4 pounds)

1 lime, halved

1 medium onion

2 tablespoons butter, cut into pieces

3 cups baby spinach leaves, divided

Leaves of 8 sprigs fresh tarragon

⅔ cup heavy cream

3 large eggs

1½ to 2 teaspoons salt

1 teaspoon freshly ground black pepper

1 pound sliced bacon

FOR THE EXOTIC FRUIT SALSA:

½ cup fresh orange juice

1 cup finely diced mango

1 cup finely diced papaya

1 cup finely diced pineapple

1 Scotch bonnet chile, stem and seeds discarded, minced

½ cup finely diced red onion

3 tablespoons olive oil

Salt

Pepper

1. To roast the chicken, preheat the oven to 400°F. Or preheat a charcoal grill and bank the coals for indirect heat.

2. Wash the chicken and pat dry with paper towels. Squeeze lime juice over the chicken and in the cavity. Put the lime halves into the cavity along with the onion. Dot the chicken with butter. Place the chicken on a rack in a roasting pan and roast in the oven for 1½ hours, or until a leg jiggles easily and an instant-read thermometer inserted in the thigh reads 185°F. Or grill for 1½ hours, covered. Melt the butter and brush the chicken 2 or 3 times while grilling. Remove from the oven or grill and cool. Reduce the oven temperature to 325°F (or preheat the oven if you were grilling the chicken).

3. Remove the breast meat in 2 big chunks and set aside. Remove the skin and bones from the chicken carcass and put the meat into a food processor fitted with the steel blade.

Add the roasted onion, 1 cup of the spinach leaves, the tarragon leaves, cream, eggs, salt, and pepper. Puree until smooth.

4. If you have one, line a narrow, loaf-shaped terrine with a tight-fitting lid with bacon slices. Otherwise, line a regular loaf pan. Spread 1 cup of the remaining baby spinach leaves evenly over the bottom of the terrine, covering the bacon.

5. Spread half of the pureed mixture over the spinach layer and top with the breast meat (tear into smaller pieces if necessary), so that there is a continual strip of the breast meat from one end of the terrine to the other. Top with the remaining pureed mixture. Spread the remaining 1 cup spinach leaves over the top.

6. Lap the ends of the bacon pieces over the top (they will not entirely cover it). Cover the top of the terrine with a strip of parchment or waxed paper. Place the cover on top to seal the terrine, or cover tightly with foil.

7. Set into a large roasting pan and add enough hot water to come halfway up the sides of the terrine or loaf pan. Bake for 2 hours.

8. *Meanwhile, make the Exotic Fruit Salsa:* In a small saucepan, bring the orange juice to a boil over medium-high heat and cook, stirring, until reduced to about 2 tablespoons. Remove from the heat and allow to cool slightly. Combine the mango, papaya, pineapple, chile, onion, and olive oil in a large bowl and stir in the juice. Season with salt and pepper.

9. Cool the terrine completely, unmold, and cut into thin slices. Serve with spoonfuls of the salsa.

TERRINE OF HERBS AND PORK

Many years ago, I attended a weeklong series of cooking classes with Simone Beck (coauthor, with Julia Child, of the famed *Mastering the Art of French Cooking,* volumes I and II). I think this is the only recipe that has remained in my repertoire, and even these many years later it is still a favorite summertime "meat loaf." I've adjusted and changed the recipe over the years. I like to bake this in a narrow enameled cast-iron terrine with a lid. After it has cooked and cooled, you can cut as many slices as you like and refrigerate the remainder. Because of all the herbs and spices, it keeps well and is wonderful for an impromptu lunch, served with a salad.

— SERVES 16 —

1 pound reduced-sodium sliced bacon, divided

1 pound lean ground pork

1 cup minced onion

2 cloves garlic, minced

1 package (10 ounces) frozen chopped spinach, cooked and drained

1 tablespoon chopped fresh tarragon leaves, or 2 teaspoons dried

1 teaspoon fresh rosemary leaves, or ½ teaspoon dried

1 teaspoon fresh oregano leaves, or ½ teaspoon dried

1 teaspoon fresh thyme leaves, or ½ teaspoon dried

1 teaspoon fresh or dried marjoram leaves

2 teaspoons salt

½ teaspoon pepper

¼ teaspoon ground nutmeg

½ cup dry sherry

2 tablespoons unflavored gelatin

1 cup heavy cream

4 large eggs, lightly beaten

½ pound boiled ham, cut into ½-inch dice

1. Preheat the oven to 350°F. Line a 1½-quart loaf pan or terrine with the bacon slices, overlapping them slightly. You'll have about 4 slices left over. Cut them into ½-inch pieces and cook in a skillet over medium heat until crisp. Remove the bacon from the skillet and reserve; pour out all but 2 tablespoons of the bacon fat.

2. Put the pork into a large bowl. Add the onion and garlic to the bacon fat and sauté over medium heat for 3 minutes, stirring. Add to the pork along with the spinach, all of the herbs, the salt, pepper, nutmeg, sherry, and gelatin. (The gelatin does not need to be softened first.) Mix well and add the cream and eggs.

3. Turn half of the mixture into the loaf pan and pat down evenly. Top with the cooked bacon and boiled ham and press down slightly into the meat mixture. Spread the remaining meat mixture on top and lap the ends of the bacon over the top of the meat.

4. Cover with a strip of parchment or waxed paper. If your pan has no lid, cover tightly with foil. Otherwise, place the lid on top of the parchment paper.

5. Place the loaf pan or terrine inside a large roasting pan and add 1 inch of boiling water to the larger pan. Bake the terrine for 1 hour and 45 minutes, or until an instant-read thermometer inserted near the center registers 165 to 170°F. Remove from the oven and cool on a rack. Place a weight on top

of the terrine, ideally something rectangular that will press the loaf evenly. I often place a narrow cutting board on top and then weight it down with a couple of cans of vegetables. Chill for at least 4 hours, or overnight.

6. To serve, turn the terrine out onto a serving plate or cutting board and slice. Refrigerate any leftover terrine for up to 4 days or freeze for up to 1 month.

SWEET ONION, ROSEMARY, AND CHEESE SLATHER

Hot spreads such as this one are so appealing and yet easy to put together. The sweet onions are juicy and mild, so even though they are plentiful, they don't overpower the spread.

SERVES 16

2 tablespoons butter

2 large sweet onions (about 2½ pounds total), coarsely chopped

1 clove garlic, minced

2 cups shredded Swiss cheese

1 cup mayonnaise

1 teaspoon dried rosemary, crushed

½ teaspoon Tabasco sauce

½ cup shredded Parmesan cheese

Crackers for serving

1. Preheat the oven to 350°F. Coat a shallow 1½-quart casserole with cooking spray.

2. In a large nonstick skillet over medium-high heat, melt the butter and sauté the onions and garlic until tender, 20 to 25 minutes. Remove from the heat. Add the Swiss cheese, mayonnaise, rosemary, and Tabasco sauce.

3. Transfer to the casserole dish. Bake, uncovered, for 20 minutes until lightly browned. Sprinkle with the Parmesan cheese and serve with crackers.

SUN-DRIED TOMATO AND ARTICHOKE SLATHER

Slather toasted slices of French bread with this creamy, hot spread. It makes a lot, so when I prepare it, I freeze half and am happy to have an appetizer in reserve for another party. Thaw the frozen portion for an hour or two at room temperature before baking.

SERVES ABOUT 24

1 can (14 ounces) artichoke hearts, drained

½ cup julienned oil-packed sun-dried tomatoes, drained

1 cup grated Parmesan cheese

1 cup low-fat sour cream

1 clove garlic, minced

1 tablespoon fresh lemon juice

1 teaspoon Dijon mustard

2 cups shredded Jarlsberg, Gruyère, or Swiss cheese

⅛ teaspoon cayenne pepper

¼ cup pine nuts

French bread slices, toasted, or freshly cut vegetables for serving

1. Preheat the oven to 400°F. Butter a 4-cup shallow casserole.

2. Combine the artichokes, sun-dried tomatoes, Parmesan cheese, sour cream, garlic, lemon juice, and mustard in a food processor fitted with the steel blade. Process until all ingredients are coarsely chopped. Mix in the cheese and cayenne.

3. Turn the mixture into the casserole and spread out evenly. Sprinkle with the pine nuts and bake, uncovered, for 15 minutes, or until lightly browned. Serve hot with the bread or vegetables.

Chapter 3
NO-KNEAD CASSEROLE BREADS

The casserole breads in this chapter are for cooks who are not only short of time, but also have had inhibitions about bread baking. The upside of baking your own breads is that you know exactly what is in them. You can avoid fat, especially trans fats, which have proven to be unhealthy.

These are old-fashioned breads that require no kneading. Some, like the spoon breads, are pudding-like. Most, however, can be sliced. What separates them from most yeast breads is that they have a high ratio of liquid to flour and therefore are beaten, rather than kneaded.

Because a casserole bread is almost a batter, the bread often has a rather rough surface, and may have a moist, open texture when sliced. All are irresistible, smell wonderful when they're baking, and are healthy breads to serve your family and guests.

CORNMEAL SPOON BREAD

Spoon breads are traditionally served as a side dish. They are scooped out of the casserole dish with a spoon, but are often eaten with a fork. Spoon bread goes especially well with roasted chicken, or it can be served with a cheese sauce as a luncheon main course. If you serve it with fruit salad on the side, you will have an old-fashioned "ladies' luncheon menu."

SERVES 4 TO 6

2 tablespoons butter, plus extra for the dish

2 cups milk

1 teaspoon sugar

1 teaspoon salt

⅔ cup yellow cornmeal

4 large eggs, separated

1. Preheat the oven to 375°F. Butter a 2-quart casserole.

2. Combine the milk, the 2 tablespoons butter, the sugar, and salt in a saucepan. Bring to a boil and slowly add the cornmeal, stirring constantly. Cook for 3 to 5 minutes, or until thickened. Remove from the heat and let cool slightly.

3. With a fork, beat the egg yolks in a small bowl. Add a small portion of the hot mixture to the eggs, and stir well. Return the egg yolk mixture to the pan and mix well.

4. Beat the egg whites in a medium bowl until soft peaks form, then fold into the cornmeal mixture. Transfer to the buttered casserole and bake for 35 minutes, or until firm.

IRISH WHEAT AND OATMEAL BREAD

Consider serving this grainy bread with a hot bowl of vegetable soup. The Irish often leaven whole-grain breads like this one with baking powder or baking soda. This is a slightly heavy bread, which is delicious cut into thin slices and slathered with butter.

SERVES 10

1 tablespoon butter, melted, plus extra for the pan

2 cups all-purpose flour, plus extra for dusting

1 cup whole-wheat flour

1¼ cups quick-cooking or old-fashioned rolled oats

1½ tablespoons baking powder

1 tablespoon salt

1 large egg

¼ cup honey

1½ cups milk

1. Preheat the oven to 350°F. Butter a 5-by-9-inch bread pan and dust with the all-purpose flour.

2. In a large bowl, mix the 2 cups all-purpose flour, the whole-wheat flour, rolled oats, baking powder, and salt. In a medium bowl, mix the egg, honey, and milk.

3. Pour the liquid ingredients into the dry ingredients and stir together until the dry ingredients are moistened. The mixture will not be smooth.

4. Transfer to the prepared bread pan and bake for 1 hour and 15 minutes, or until crusty and a skewer inserted near the center comes out clean. Drizzle the 1 tablespoon melted butter over the hot loaf and turn out onto a wire rack to cool.

POLENTA SPOON BREAD

More like a soufflé than a bread, polenta spoon bread is delicious with a simple meal of roast chicken and steamed vegetables. Serve it with melted butter, gravy, or a white sauce flavored with lemon juice (see page 18).

SERVES 6

1 tablespoon butter, plus extra for the dish

1½ cups water

1½ cups polenta or cornmeal

1 teaspoon salt

1½ cups milk, divided

2 large eggs, separated

2 teaspoons baking powder

Extra butter, white sauce, or gravy for serving

1. Preheat the oven to 400°F. Butter a 1½-quart casserole or soufflé dish.

2. Bring the water to a boil in a medium saucepan. Combine the polenta and salt and stir into the boiling water. Cook, stirring, until thickened, about 15 minutes. Add 1 cup of the milk and cook, stirring, until smooth, about 5 minutes.

3. Beat the remaining ½ cup milk and the egg yolks together. Add a small amount of the polenta mixture to temper the egg yolks, and stir well. Stir into the hot polenta mixture in the saucepan. Mix in the 1 tablespoon butter and the baking powder and stir until smooth.

4. Beat the egg whites with an electric mixer in a medium bowl until stiff and fold into the mixture. Pour the batter into the prepared dish and bake until puffed and golden, 35 to 40 minutes. Serve hot with butter, white sauce, or gravy.

CINNAMON BUBBLE BREAD

The "bubbles" in this loaf of bread are little rounds of dough, which are rolled in cinnamon and sugar, and then piled into a baking pan. The bread tastes a lot like cinnamon rolls, and is fun to serve for breakfast or brunch, or with coffee. Use two forks or a pair of tongs to pull apart the bubbles.

SERVES 8 TO 10

6 tablespoons butter, melted, divided, plus extra for the dish

1 cup warm water (105 to 115°F)

2 packages (¼ ounce each) active dry yeast

2 tablespoons plus 1 cup sugar, divided

1 cup milk, scalded and cooled to lukewarm

2 teaspoons salt

4½ cups all-purpose flour, divided

2 tablespoons ground cinnamon

1. Generously butter a deep 2-quart casserole. Pour the warm water into a large bowl and stir in the yeast and the 2 tablespoons sugar. Let stand until foamy, about 5 minutes.

2. Add the milk, salt, 4 tablespoons of the melted butter, 1 cup of the flour, and ½ cup sugar; beat until smooth. Gradually beat in the remaining flour to make a stiff, satiny, smooth dough.

3. Cover with a kitchen towel and let rise until doubled in size, about 45 minutes. Turn out the dough onto a lightly oiled work surface. Divide the dough into quarters. Divide each quarter into quarters again, to make 16 pieces. Cut each of the pieces in half to make 32 pieces total.

4. Pour the remaining 2 tablespoons melted butter into a small dish. In another small dish mix the remaining ½ cup of sugar and the cinnamon. Roll each piece of dough first in the butter and then in the cinnamon sugar. Place the dough pieces in the buttered casserole in even layers. Cover with a kitchen towel and let rise in a warm place until doubled in size, about 45 minutes.

5. Meanwhile, preheat the oven to 375°F. Bake the bread for 35 to 45 minutes, or until browned and a skewer inserted in the center of the loaf comes out clean. Cool in the casserole for 5 minutes. Invert onto a serving dish and serve warm, pulling apart the pieces.

WHOLE-WHEAT BUBBLE BREAD

Here's another version of a healthy bubble bread, which is fabulous served hot from the oven. In the unlikely event that you have bread left over, you can freeze it in plastic bags. Or cut it into cubes and use it in a breakfast strata.

SERVES 8 TO 10

2 tablespoons butter at room temperature, plus extra for the dish

1 ¼ cups warm water (105 to 115°F)

1 package (¼ ounce) active dry yeast

2 tablespoons light or dark brown sugar

1½ teaspoons salt

2 large eggs

1½ cups whole-wheat flour

2 to 2½ cups all-purpose flour

½ cup (1 stick) butter, melted

1 cup wheat germ

1. Generously butter a 2-quart casserole or a 10-inch tube pan.

2. Pour the warm water into a large bowl; stir in the yeast and brown sugar. Let stand until foamy, about 5 minutes. Stir in the salt, 2 tablespoons of the softened butter, the eggs, and whole-wheat flour, and beat well. Let rest for 15 minutes, or until the mixture begins to look puffy.

3. Add 2 cups of the all-purpose flour gradually, beating to keep the mixture smooth, and adding enough flour to make a stiff dough. Let rest for another 15 minutes.

4. Turn out the dough onto a lightly floured surface. Clean and butter the bowl. Knead the dough for 10 minutes, or until smooth and satiny, adding all-purpose flour as necessary to keep the dough from sticking.

Put the dough into the buttered bowl, turning to coat the dough lightly with butter.

5. Cover with a kitchen towel, and let rise in a warm place until doubled in size, about 1 hour. Turn out onto a lightly oiled work surface. Divide the dough into quarters. Divide each quarter into quarters again, to make 16 pieces. Cut each of the pieces in half to make 32 pieces total.

6. Pour the melted butter into a small bowl. Pour the wheat germ into another small bowl. Shape each piece of dough into a round ball and roll in the melted butter and then in the wheat germ. Place the dough pieces in the buttered casserole in even layers. Cover and let rise in a warm place until doubled in size, 45 minutes to 1 hour.

7. Meanwhile, preheat the oven to 375°F. Bake the bread for 35 to 45 minutes, or until a skewer inserted in the center of the loaf comes out clean. Cool in the casserole for 5 minutes, then invert onto a serving dish. To serve, pull apart with forks.

HONEY MUSTARD BUBBLE BREAD

This bread is perfect with a soup or salad. There are many variations on bubble bread, which is also known as "monkey bread." Here, little balls of yeast dough are rolled in honey and mustard and piled into a baking pan to rise and bake.

SERVES 8 TO 10

4 tablespoons butter, melted, plus extra for the dish

1 cup warm water (105 to 115°F)

2 packages (¼ ounce each) active dry yeast

2 tablespoons sugar

1 cup milk, scalded and cooled to lukewarm

2 teaspoons salt

2 tablespoons olive oil

4½ cups all-purpose flour, divided

¼ cup honey

¼ cup Dijon mustard

1. Generously butter a deep 2-quart casserole. Pour the warm water into a large bowl and stir in the yeast and sugar. Let stand until foamy, about 5 minutes.

2. Add the milk, salt, olive oil, and 1 cup of the flour; beat until smooth. Gradually beat in the remaining flour to make a stiff, satiny, smooth dough.

3. Cover with a kitchen towel and let rise until doubled in size, about 45 minutes. Turn out the dough onto a lightly oiled work surface. Divide the dough into quarters. Divide each quarter into quarters again, to make 16 pieces. Cut each of the pieces in half to make 32 pieces total.

4. Mix the honey and mustard in a small dish. Roll each piece of dough in the honey and mustard mixture. Place the dough pieces in the buttered casserole in even layers. Drizzle with the 4 tablespoons of melted butter. Cover with a kitchen towel and let rise in a warm place until doubled in size, about 45 minutes.

5. Meanwhile, preheat the oven to 375°F. Bake the bread for 35 to 45 minutes, or until browned and a skewer inserted in the center of the loaf comes out clean. Cool in the casserole for 5 minutes. Invert onto a serving dish and serve warm, pulling apart the pieces.

CARAWAY AND CHEDDAR CASSEROLE BREAD

The caraway gives a distinctive flavor and texture to this cheesy batter bread, which is a no-knead, yeast-raised bread. Baked in a straight-sided 3-quart soufflé dish, it is very attractive.

SERVES 10

1½ cups warm water (105 to 115°F)

2 packages (¼ ounce each) active dry yeast

3 tablespoons dark brown sugar

1½ teaspoons salt

2 large eggs, at room temperature

1 cup rolled oats, quick-cooking or old-fashioned

3½ cups all-purpose flour, divided

2 cups shredded Cheddar cheese

3 tablespoons caraway seeds

Melted butter for brushing the loaf

1. In a large bowl, dissolve the yeast in the warm water. Stir in the sugar, salt, eggs, and oats.

2. Add 1¾ cups of the flour and beat with an electric mixer for 2 to 3 minutes until the dough is very smooth. Cover with a kitchen towel and let rest for 5 minutes.

3. Add the cheese, caraway seeds, and 1 more cup flour and beat until well blended. Work in the remaining ¾ cup flour until it is no longer visible in the dough.

4. Cover and let rise in a warm place until doubled, about 30 minutes.

5. Stir down the dough and turn out into a greased 3-quart deep casserole or soufflé dish or two 8½-by-4½-inch loaf pans. Cover and let rise for 45 minutes to 1 hour, or until the batter reaches the top of the pan.

6. Meanwhile, preheat the oven to 350°F. Bake the bread for 45 minutes to 1 hour for the large round bread, or 35 to 40 minutes for the 2 loaves. Remove from the dish or pans and cool on a rack. Brush with melted butter.

CHEESE, OLIVE, AND PINE NUT CASSEROLE BREAD

Loaded with lots of flavors and textures, this no-knead bread can enhance almost any meal. It's perfect with a Mediterranean-style dinner. For the main course, choose a lasagna, pasta, or a Moroccan beef tagine.

SERVES 8 TO 10

½ cup warm water (105 to 115°F)

2 packages (¼ ounce each) active dry yeast

1 tablespoon sugar

1 teaspoon salt

2 tablespoons butter

1½ cups milk, scalded and cooled to lukewarm

1 large egg, beaten

4 cups all-purpose flour

¼ pound sharp Cheddar cheese, cut into ½-inch cubes (about 1 cup)

20 pitted mixed green and black olives (preferably kalamata for the black), halved

½ cup pine nuts

1. In a large bowl, combine the warm water, dry yeast, sugar, salt, butter, milk, and egg. Let stand for 5 minutes, or until the mixture begins to bubble.

2. Stir in the flour a little at a time until a very stiff batter forms. Beat with an electric mixer for 2 minutes. Cover with a kitchen towel and let stand for 15 minutes.

3. Stir in the Cheddar cheese, olives, and pine nuts. Butter a 3-quart round casserole or two 9-by-5-inch loaf pans. Turn the batter into the casserole or pans. Let rise for 45 minutes, or until the batter reaches the top of the dish or pans.

4. Meanwhile, preheat the oven to 375°F. Slash the top of the bread diagonally a few times with a sharp knife. Bake the 9-by-5-inch loaves for 35 to 40 minutes or the large loaf for 55 to 60 minutes, or until a wooden skewer inserted in the center of the loaf comes out clean and dry. Remove from the dish or pans and cool on a rack.

CINNAMON SALLY LUNN

Dating back to eighteenth-century England, a classic Sally Lunn is a slightly sweet, cakelike bread that is great for breakfast or brunch. Originally it was baked as a large bun, split horizontally, and slathered with thick clotted cream.

SERVES 8 TO 10

1 cup warm water (105 to 115°F)

2 packages (¼ ounce each) active dry yeast

¼ cup sugar

1 cup milk, scalded and cooled to room temperature

5 cups all-purpose flour, divided

2 large eggs, lightly beaten

⅓ cup butter, melted

1½ teaspoons salt

Ground cinnamon for sprinkling

1. In a large bowl, combine the water, yeast, and sugar. Mix well and let stand for 5 minutes, or until foamy. Stir in the milk and 2 cups of the flour and beat until smooth.

2. Beat in the eggs, butter, and salt and add enough flour to make a stiff, smooth dough (you may not need to add all of the flour).

3. Cover with a kitchen towel and let rise in a warm place until doubled in size, about 1 hour.

4. Generously butter a deep 2½-quart casserole or a 10-inch tube pan. Sprinkle the inside generously with cinnamon so the entire surface is dusted.

5. Stir down the batter and transfer to the casserole. Let rise in a warm place until the batter is within 1 inch of the top of the pan, about 45 minutes.

6. Meanwhile, preheat the oven to 350°F. Bake the bread for 45 minutes, or until a skewer inserted in the center of the loaf comes out clean and dry. Turn out of the casserole and serve hot.

MILK AND HONEY CASSEROLE BREAD

Honey brings out the nutty flavor of whole wheat in this bread. You will need 1 large or 2 smaller casseroles for this bread. A dish with straight sides, such as a soufflé dish, works best.

SERVES 12

1 cup milk

½ cup (1 stick) butter

½ cup honey

2 teaspoons salt

1 cup warm water (105 to 115°F)

2 packages (¼ ounce each) active dry yeast

1½ cups whole-wheat flour

4 cups bread flour or all-purpose flour

1. Pour the milk into a small saucepan and place over medium-high heat until scalded (about 200°F). Remove from the heat and add the butter, honey, and salt. Let stand until cooled to lukewarm and the butter is melted.

2. Meanwhile, in a large bowl, mix the warm water and dry yeast. Stir and let stand for 5 minutes, or until the yeast foams.

3. Stir the cooled milk mixture, whole-wheat flour, and 1 cup of the bread flour into the yeast mixture. With an electric mixer, beat at high speed for 2 minutes.

4. With a wooden spoon, beat in the remaining bread flour, a cupful at a time, and continue beating to make a sticky, soft dough. Cover with plastic wrap and let rise for 1 hour.

5. Coat one 3-quart casserole or two 1½-quart casseroles with cooking spray. Transfer the dough to the casserole(s) and let rise again for 1 hour.

6. Meanwhile, preheat the oven to 375°F. Bake the bread for 1 hour for the larger casserole or for 45 minutes for the smaller ones. Remove from the oven, turn out the loaves onto racks, and cool.

NO-KNEAD ARTISAN-STYLE CASSEROLE BREAD

The great flavor of this rather effortless bread comes from the long and slow rising period. When baked in a preheated casserole, it develops a nice crustiness. You will need a cast-iron Dutch oven or an enameled cast-iron pot (such as Le Creuset's) for baking the bread. This method was developed by Jim Lahey, the owner of the Sullivan Street Bakery in New York City, and reproduced by the food writer Mark Bittman in the *New York Times*. I found this method works well, but I have adapted it to my own favorite bread recipe.

SERVES 8 TO 10

2 cups tepid water (about 100°F)

1 teaspoon active dry yeast

2 teaspoons salt

4 to 4½ cups all-purpose flour

1. In a large bowl, stir the water and yeast together. Let stand for about 5 minutes, until the yeast is dissolved. Stir in the salt and 2 cups of the flour. Beat with a large spoon until smooth, then slowly add the remaining flour to make a rough, shaggy dough. It should look quite moist, but still hold together in a ball. Cover with plastic wrap and let rise at room temperature for at least 6 hours, or until the dough is dotted with bubbles.

2. Lightly flour a work surface and turn out the dough. Sprinkle with a little more flour and, using a dough scraper, lift the dough over onto itself to form a ball. Cover with a kitchen towel and let stand for 15 minutes.

3. Coat the kitchen towel generously with flour and place the ball of dough on top. Dust with more flour, cover with another kitchen towel, and allow to rise for about 2 hours, or until more than doubled in size.

4. Preheat the oven to 450°F. While the oven preheats, place a 4- to 5-quart heavy pot or Dutch oven into the oven, along with its lid, to preheat as well. This will take 20 to 30 minutes. When the dough is doubled and the pot is hot, place the pot on a board or trivet. Remove the towel covering the dough. Carefully slide your hand under the towel beneath the dough, pick up the towel and dough, and invert the loaf into the hot pot. Cover with the lid and bake for 30 minutes. Remove the lid and bake for another 15 to 30 minutes, until crusty. Turn out onto a rack to cool.

GOLDEN RAISIN AND WALNUT CASSEROLE BREAD

Cut thick slices of this bread and toast them for breakfast or coffee break. To make cinnamon toast, sprinkle the toasted and buttered bread with sugar and cinnamon.

SERVES 10

¼ cup warm water (105 to 115°F)

1 package (¼ ounce) active dry yeast

1 cup milk, scalded and cooled

¼ cup sugar

4 tablespoons butter, softened

1 teaspoon salt

2 large eggs, lightly beaten

1 cup golden raisins

2¾ to 3 cups all-purpose flour

1. In a large bowl, dissolve the yeast in the warm water. Let stand until foamy, about 5 minutes. Stir in the milk, sugar, butter, salt, eggs, and raisins.

2. Add the flour a little at a time, beating with an electric mixer until the dough is about the same consistency as cookie dough.

3. Cover with a kitchen towel and let stand in a warm place until doubled in bulk, about 1½ hours.

4. Butter a 2½- to 3-quart casserole. Stir the dough down and turn into the casserole. Cover and let rise until puffy, about 1 hour.

5. Meanwhile, preheat the oven to 350°F. Bake the bread for 25 to 30 minutes, or until a skewer inserted in the center of the loaf comes out clean and dry.

WHOLE-WHEAT RAISIN CASSEROLE BREAD

The combined flavors of honey, raisins, and whole wheat make this an all-time favorite for kids as well as adults.

SERVES 12

1 cup milk

½ cup (1 stick) butter

½ cup honey

2 teaspoons salt

1 cup warm water (105 to 115°F)

2 packages (¼ ounce each) active dry yeast

1½ cups whole-wheat flour

1 cup light or dark raisins

1 cup chopped walnuts

4 cups bread flour or all-purpose flour

1. Pour the milk into a small saucepan and place over medium-high heat until scalded (about 200°F). Remove from the heat and add the butter, honey, and salt. Let stand until the butter is melted and the mixture is cooled to lukewarm.

2. Meanwhile, in a large bowl, mix the warm water and dry yeast; stir and let stand for 5 minutes until the yeast foams.

3. Stir the cooled milk mixture, whole-wheat flour, raisins, walnuts, and 1 cup of the flour into the yeast mixture. With an electric mixer, beat at high speed for 2 minutes.

4. With a wooden spoon, beat in the remaining 3 cups flour, a cupful at a time, moistening all of the flour to make a sticky, soft dough. Cover with plastic wrap and let rise for 1 hour.

5. With cooking spray, coat one 3-quart casserole or two 1½-quart casseroles, preferably with straight sides. Put the dough in the casserole(s), cover with a kitchen towel, and let rise again for 1 hour until almost doubled.

6. Meanwhile, preheat the oven to 375°F. Bake the bread for 1 hour for the large casserole or 45 minutes for the smaller ones. Remove from the oven, turn the loaves out of baking pans, and cool on racks.

ROSEMARY AND PARMESAN CASSEROLE BREAD

Bake this in a shallow casserole, and you will end up with something that looks and tastes like classic focaccia!

2 packages (¼ ounce each) active dry yeast

½ cup warm water (105 to 115°F)

1 cup creamed cottage cheese, warmed (see Note)

2 tablespoons sugar

2 tablespoons extra-virgin olive oil, divided, plus extra for the dish

2 teaspoons dried rosemary leaves, crushed

1 teaspoon salt

1 large egg

2 cups all-purpose flour

2 tablespoons grated Parmesan cheese

1. In a large bowl, dissolve the yeast in the warm water and set aside until foamy, about 5 minutes.

2. Add the warmed cottage cheese, sugar, 1 tablespoon of the olive oil, the rosemary, salt, and egg. Add the flour and beat well to make a stiff dough.

3. Cover with plastic wrap and let rise in a warm place for about 1 hour, or until doubled in bulk.

4. Brush a 9-by-13-inch shallow baking dish or pan with olive oil. Press the dough into the dish so it covers the bottom completely, including the corners. Cover with a kitchen towel and let rise in a warm place for about 1 hour, or until doubled in bulk.

5. Meanwhile, preheat the oven to 350°F. Drizzle the top of the dough with remaining 1 tablespoon olive oil and sprinkle with the grated Parmesan cheese. Bake for 30 to 35 minutes, until golden. Serve warm, cut into squares.

○ ○ ○ ○ ○

NOTE: To warm the cottage cheese, spoon into a glass 1-cup measure and microwave on high power for 30 seconds.

THREE-GRAIN CASSEROLE BREAD

You just stir up this dough, let it rise, and turn it into a casserole for baking. So simple! And it's so healthy, too, with all those grains.

SERVES 10

2 cups warm water (105 to 115°F)

2 packages (¼ ounce each) active dry yeast

3 tablespoons honey

1 cup nonfat dry milk

2 tablespoons butter, softened or melted

2 teaspoons salt

½ cup old-fashioned or quick-cooking rolled oats, plus extra for sprinkling

½ cup dark rye flour

1¼ cups whole-wheat flour

2½ cups unbleached all-purpose flour

1. Pour the warm water into a large bowl and stir in the yeast and honey until dissolved. Let stand until foamy, about 5 minutes.

2. Stir in the dry milk, butter, salt, the ½ cup oats, the rye flour, and whole-wheat flour and beat until smooth (you may do this with an electric mixer).

3. Slowly add the all-purpose flour, beating by hand or with the electric mixer (switching to a wooden spoon when the dough becomes too thick), until the dough resembles a thick cookie dough. Cover with a kitchen towel and let rise for 1 hour, or until doubled.

4. Generously butter a 2½- to 3-quart casserole and sprinkle the bottom and sides with rolled oats. Turn the batter into the casserole and sprinkle with more rolled oats. Let rise in a warm place until doubled in bulk, about 45 minutes.

5. Preheat the oven to 350°F. Bake the loaf for 45 minutes or until a skewer inserted in the center of the loaf comes out clean and dry. Remove from the oven and cool in the casserole on a rack for 10 minutes. Turn the bread out of the dish and finish cooling on the rack.

Chapter 4

BREAKFAST & BRUNCH CASSEROLES

Breakfast casseroles are perfect for entertaining early-morning guests. What's more, most of the recipes in this chapter can be assembled in the evening and baked in the morning, leaving time for other last-minute preparations if you are hosting a brunch.

Here are more than forty recipes. Most of them center on eggs and all that you can do with them, but there is one no-egg breakfast included, too. These recipes run the gamut from baked omelets, breakfast pies, ever-popular stratas, and hash-brown breakfasts to baked French toast, puffy baked pancakes, grits, polenta, and individual breakfast casseroles.

○ ○ ○ ○ ○

CONTINUED ON NEXT PAGE...

ARTICHOKE AND SALSA BREAKFAST CASSEROLE

For breakfast or brunch, a side of sliced fresh oranges, drizzled with a little balsamic vinegar, complements this egg-based casserole beautifully. Serve it with Cinnamon Bubble Bread (page 71).

SERVES 6

6 tablespoons tomato salsa (mild or medium)

1 can (14 ounces) artichokes, drained, rinsed, and chopped

¾ cup shredded sharp Cheddar cheese

¾ cup shredded Monterey Jack cheese

10 large eggs

1 cup light sour cream

6 tablespoons grated Parmesan cheese

1. Preheat the oven to 350°F. Coat 6 individual ovenproof dishes (6 to 8 ounces each) or one shallow 2-quart casserole with cooking spray.

2. Spread 1 tablespoon salsa in the bottom of each dish or all 6 tablespoons over the bottom of the large casserole dish. Spread the artichokes evenly over the salsa. Top with the shredded Cheddar and Monterey Jack cheeses (2 tablespoons each for the individual dishes).

3. Whisk the eggs and sour cream together, pour over the cheese in the dish(es), and top with the Parmesan. (At this point the dish(es) can be covered and refrigerated for up to 12 hours. Add 5 to 10 minutes to the baking time.)

4. Bake, uncovered, for 30 to 35 minutes or until set. Serve warm.

CHILE-WRAPPED CHEESE IN A BAKED PUFFY OMELET

The chile-wrapped Monterey Jack cheese gives this omelet a Southwestern flavor. Serve it as a simple main dish for lunch or brunch.

SERVES 6

½ pound Monterey Jack cheese

1 can (4 ounces) whole peeled green chiles

6 large eggs, separated

⅓ cup all-purpose flour

¾ teaspoon salt

1. Preheat the oven to 400°F. Butter a shallow 2-quart casserole or an 8-inch square baking dish.

2. Cut the cheese into strips ½ inch thick and 3 inches long. Remove and discard the seeds from the chiles. Cut each chile lengthwise into 3 strips. Wrap a chile strip around each piece of cheese; set aside.

3. In a large bowl, beat the egg whites with an electric beater until soft peaks form. Without washing the beaters, in a small bowl, beat the egg yolks until creamy. Beat in the flour and salt.

4. Fold the egg whites into the yolk mixture. Spread half of the egg mixture in the bottom of the buttered casserole. Top with the chile-wrapped cheese. Add the remaining egg mixture.

5. Bake, uncovered, for 15 to 20 minutes, or until set.

EGG AND MUSHROOM BAKED OMELET

This is so quick to put together, it could become a favorite breakfast when you have overnight guests.

8 large eggs, beaten

½ pound mushrooms, sliced

½ cup chopped green onions (green and white parts)

4 slices bacon, cooked and diced, or ½ cup diced cooked ham

¼ pound shredded cheese, such as Cheddar, Swiss, or Jarlsberg

1. Preheat the oven to 350°F. Coat a shallow 1-quart shallow casserole with cooking spray.

2. In a large bowl, whisk together the eggs, mushrooms, green onions, bacon, and cheese. Pour the mixture into the dish and bake, uncovered, for 20 minutes, or until set. Cut into squares to serve.

SPANISH POTATO OMELET

In Spain this is called a potato tortilla, and it is often served in little squares on the tapas table. We think it is also a tasty breakfast dish. It's a great way to use leftover cooked potatoes.

SERVES 6

6 large eggs

2 cups peeled and cooked potatoes, cut into ½-inch dice

1 small onion, finely chopped

1 green pepper, minced

12 green stuffed Spanish olives, sliced

1 teaspoon salt

¼ pound cooked ham, cut into ½-inch cubes

1. Preheat the oven to 350°F. Coat a 9-inch round pie pan with cooking spray.

2. In a large bowl, beat the eggs until fluffy. Stir in the remaining ingredients and turn into the prepared pan.

3. Bake, uncovered, for 40 to 45 minutes, until the center is set. Cut into wedges to serve.

EGG CASSEROLE WITH CHILES AND COTTAGE CHEESE

This comes together in a flash! The butter melts in the baking pan in the oven while the oven preheats. Meanwhile, you quickly stir up the egg mixture. The green chiles and chili powder give this a Southwestern twist.

SERVES 8

4 tablespoons butter

10 large eggs

2 cups cottage cheese

1 pound Monterey Jack cheese, shredded

2 cans (4 ounces each) chopped green chiles

1 tablespoon chili powder

½ cup all-purpose flour

1 teaspoon baking powder

½ teaspoon salt

Sour cream for serving

Tomato salsa for serving

1. Preheat the oven to 350°F. Melt the butter in a 9-by-13 inch baking dish in the oven as it preheats. Remove the pan from the oven before the butter browns.

2. Beat the eggs until foamy. Mix in the cottage cheese, Monterey Jack cheese, chiles, chili powder, flour, baking powder, and salt.

3. Turn the mixture out into the dish with the melted butter and bake, uncovered, for 45 to 50 minutes, until the center is set. Let stand for 10 minutes before cutting. Serve with sour cream and salsa to spoon over individual servings.

EGGS FLORENTINE IN A CASSEROLE

This is reminiscent of an egg dish we enjoyed in New Orleans years ago at Brennan's Restaurant. It can be assembled ahead of time and refrigerated overnight.

SERVES 4

3 tablespoons butter at room temperature

1 package (10 ounces) chopped frozen spinach

3 tablespoons all-purpose flour

1½ cups milk, heated

4 large eggs, poached (see Note)

1 teaspoon salt

½ teaspoon pepper

½ cup grated Parmesan cheese or shredded mild Cheddar cheese

1. Preheat the oven to 400°F. Butter a shallow 1½-quart casserole with 1 tablespoon of the butter.

2. Cook the spinach according to package instructions and drain well.

3. In a small saucepan, over medium-high heat, melt the remaining 2 tablespoons butter. Blend in the flour and gradually whisk in the milk, stirring constantly, until thickened and bubbly.

4. Spread out the spinach in the prepared dish. Arrange the poached eggs over the spinach and pour the white sauce on top. Sprinkle with the salt, pepper, and cheese. (At this point the casserole can be covered and refrigerated. Add 10 minutes to the baking time.)

5. Bake, uncovered, for 3 to 5 minutes, or until the cheese is melted.

○ ○ ○ ○ ○

NOTE: To poach eggs, bring 2 inches of water to a simmer in a large skillet. Crack the eggs, one at a time, into a saucer. Slide the eggs, one at a time, into the simmering water. Baste the eggs with the boiling water and cook until done to your liking, about 3 minutes. With a spatula, lift the eggs from the water.

EGG, BACON, MUSHROOM, AND CHEESE CASSEROLE

This savory custard could be served for brunch or supper. Add a green or fresh fruit salad, freshly baked muffins, and hot coffee for a winning menu!

SERVES 6

1 tablespoon butter, plus extra for the dish

4 slices bacon

8 green onions, thinly sliced (white and green parts)

1 pound mushrooms, sliced

8 large eggs

1 cup milk

1 teaspoon salt

⅛ teaspoon pepper

2½ cups shredded Cheddar cheese

1. Preheat the oven to 350°F. Butter a shallow 2-quart casserole.

2. In a large skillet, cook the bacon until crisp; drain well and crumble. Add the green onions and the 1 tablespoon butter to the pan and cook for 2 minutes, stirring. Add the mushrooms and cook for 2 to 3 minutes more, then remove from the heat.

3. In a medium bowl, beat the eggs, milk, salt, and pepper together. Stir in the cheese and the mushroom mixture. Pour into the prepared dish and bake, uncovered, for 30 to 35 minutes, or until puffed and set.

BROCCOLI AND MUSHROOM FRITTATA

A frittata is a perfect way to use vegetables left over from last night's supper. Add them to the vegetables already in this colorful frittata. Make this tasty egg dish in just minutes for breakfast or for a brunch main dish.

SERVES 6

3 tablespoons butter

1 cup mushrooms, sliced

1 medium onion, chopped

½ medium red bell pepper, cut into 1-by-¼-inch strips

4 cups broccoli florets, blanched (see Note)

1 cup leftover cooked vegetables, such as peas, beans, or carrots (optional)

9 large eggs

1 teaspoon salt

1 cup shredded Cheddar cheese

1. Preheat the broiler. Melt the butter in an ovenproof, nonstick 10-inch skillet until sizzling. Add the mushrooms, onion, bell pepper strips, broccoli, and leftover vegetables, if using. Cook over medium heat until the mushrooms and onion are tender and the vegetables are hot, 3 to 4 minutes.

2. Beat the eggs and salt in a large bowl until frothy and pour into the skillet with the vegetables. Cook over medium heat, lifting slightly with a spatula to allow the uncooked portion to flow underneath, until the eggs are almost set, 3 to 4 minutes.

3. Sprinkle with cheese.

4. Broil about 8 inches from the heat until the cheese is melted and the eggs are set, 3 to 4 minutes.

○ ○ ○ ○ ○

NOTE: To blanch broccoli florets, bring a pot of water to a boil. Drop the florets into the water and cook for 1 to 2 minutes, until bright green.

NORWEGIAN BAKED CHEESE OMELET

Cheese is the backbone of the Scandinavian breakfast and brunch, and this omelet is made with nutty Norwegian Jarlsberg. It's really quick to make!

4 large eggs

¼ cup water

½ teaspoon salt

2 tablespoons butter

¾ cup sliced green onions (white and green parts)

1 cup diced cooked ham

1 red bell pepper, seeded and cut into rings

¾ pound Jarlsberg cheese, cut into 1-inch cubes

Chopped parsley for garnish

1. Preheat the oven to 400°F.

2. In a medium bowl, whisk together the eggs, water, and salt. Melt the butter in a heavy flameproof shallow casserole or gratin dish over medium heat. Sauté the green onions, ham, and bell pepper for 3 to 4 minutes, until the green onions are bright green and the pepper is hot. Pour the egg mixture over them and sprinkle with the cheese cubes.

3. Bake, uncovered, for 15 to 20 minutes, until the egg mixture is set and the cheese is melted. Garnish with chopped parsley.

SAUSAGE, CHEESE, AND EGG CASSEROLE

This easy casserole is so quick to assemble, you can probably put it together while the oven preheats!

SERVES 8

12 large eggs, lightly beaten

⅓ cup all-purpose flour

½ teaspoon baking powder

10 ounces lean pork or turkey breakfast sausage, cooked and crumbled

2 cups shredded Monterey Jack cheese

1½ cups low-fat cottage cheese

½ pound mushrooms, sliced

1. Preheat the oven to 375°F. Butter a 9-by-13-inch glass baking dish.

2. In a large bowl, mix the eggs, flour, and baking powder. Stir in the sausage, shredded cheese, cottage cheese, and mushrooms.

3. Pour the mixture into the prepared baking dish and bake, uncovered, for 30 to 35 minutes, until set.

SOUTHWESTERN BREAKFAST CASSEROLE

I first had this spicy egg, cheese, and sausage casserole for breakfast in a wonderful inn in Santa Fe, New Mexico.

6 ounces bulk-style chorizo sausage

½ onion, finely chopped

4 cans (4 ounces each) whole mild green chiles, drained

½ pound queso fresco (Mexican farmers' cheese), finely crumbled

8 large eggs, beaten

¼ teaspoon pepper

Tomato salsa for serving

1. Preheat the oven to 350°F. Butter an 8-inch square baking dish.

2. Place a medium skillet over medium-high heat. Add the chorizo and cook, breaking up with a fork, until browned, about 4 minutes. Add the onion and sauté for 3 to 4 minutes longer, stirring, until the onion is tender. Remove from the heat.

3. Cut each chile lengthwise in half and remove the membranes and seeds. Line the bottom of the dish with half the chiles, arranging them cut-sides up.

4. Sprinkle half of the chorizo mixture over the chiles and cover with half of the cheese.

5. Beat the eggs in a medium bowl and add the ground pepper. Cover the cheese layer with half of the beaten eggs. Top with the remaining chiles in one layer, and layer the remaining chorizo and then the cheese on top. Pour the remaining egg mixture over the cheese.

6. Bake, uncovered, for 30 to 40 minutes, until the casserole is set. Let stand for about 5 minutes before cutting into squares. Serve the squares topped with salsa.

SPINACH AND FETA BAKE

For a change in your evening routine, make this breakfast dish for supper.

SERVES 6

2 tablespoons butter, plus extra for the dish

1 medium red bell pepper, chopped

1 medium onion, chopped

3 cups baby spinach leaves

½ cup milk

8 large eggs

½ teaspoon salt

¼ teaspoon pepper

½ cup crumbled feta cheese

1 medium tomato, chopped, for garnish

1 tablespoon chopped fresh basil for garnish

1. Preheat the oven to 350°F. Butter a 9-inch pie pan.

2. In a medium skillet, melt the 2 tablespoons butter and add the bell pepper and onion. Cook over medium heat, stirring occasionally, until the vegetables are crisp-tender, 3 to 4 minutes. Add the spinach and continue cooking, stirring occasionally, until the spinach is wilted.

3. In a medium bowl, whisk together the milk, eggs, salt, and pepper. Stir in the cheese and the vegetable mixture. Pour into the pie pan.

4. Bake, uncovered, for 30 to 35 minutes, or until the eggs are set in the center and the edges are lightly browned. Let stand for 5 minutes. Garnish with the tomato and basil, cut into wedges, and serve.

SPINACH, HAM, AND EGG CASSEROLE

Serve this for brunch or as a side dish for dinner. Assemble it ahead of time and refrigerate it for up to 1 day, if you wish.

SERVES 6

2 tablespoons butter at room temperature

1 bag (1 pound) fresh baby spinach leaves

1 cup milk

3 tablespoons all-purpose flour

1 tablespoon dry mustard

1 teaspoon salt

½ cup shredded Cheddar cheese

½ pound deli ham, cut into ½-inch cubes

4 hard-cooked eggs, peeled and diced

1. Preheat the oven to 350°F. Grease a 1½-quart shallow casserole with a small amount of the butter.

2. Heat the remaining butter in a large skillet or wok over medium heat and add the spinach. Cook, stirring, until the spinach leaves are wilted. Add the spinach to the casserole.

3. In a saucepan, combine the milk, flour, mustard, and salt. Heat to boiling, whisking constantly. Cook for 3 minutes, stirring, until the mixture is thickened.

4. Sprinkle the spinach with the cheese and ham and pour the sauce over all. (At this point the casserole can be covered and refrigerated. Add 5 minutes to the baking time.)

5. Bake, uncovered, for 15 to 20 minutes, or until heated through. Remove from the oven and top with the hard-cooked eggs.

BREAKFAST EGG AND SUN-DRIED TOMATO PUFF

This dish puffs with the help of self-rising flour, which is popular in the South, but is not as readily available in the North. If you can't find it, you can make your own (see Note) or use Bisquick. Serve this with Cinnamon Sally Lunn (page 77) or toasted slices of Whole-Wheat Raisin Casserole Bread (page 81).

— SERVES 8 —

2 tablespoons butter at room temperature

6 large eggs, beaten

2 cups milk

1 cup self-rising flour (see Note)

1 medium onion, chopped

½ cup finely chopped sun-dried tomatoes

½ cup chopped mushrooms

2 cups shredded Colby Jack or Cheddar cheese

1. Preheat the oven to 350°F. Coat a 9-by-13-inch baking dish with 1 tablespoon of the butter.

2. In a large bowl, whisk together the eggs, milk, and flour until smooth.

3. In a large nonstick skillet, melt the remaining 1 tablespoon butter over medium heat. Add the onion, sun-dried tomatoes, and mushrooms and sauté, stirring, until the onions are soft.

Stir the vegetables into the egg mixture and mix in the cheese.

4. Pour into the prepared casserole. Bake, uncovered, for 35 to 40 minutes, until set. Serve hot.

○ ○ ○ ○ ○

NOTE: If you don't have self-rising flour on hand, add 1 teaspoon baking powder and ½ teaspoon salt to 1 cup all-purpose flour.

BREAKFAST POTATO PIE

This rather unusual dish is heaven for potato lovers! To keep the potatoes from turning brown after shredding, rinse in cold water and drain well.

SERVES 6 TO 8

2 tablespoons butter at room temperature

½ pound bacon, diced

¼ cup finely diced green bell pepper

¼ cup finely diced red bell pepper

1 small onion, chopped

8 large eggs

1 pound russet potatoes, peeled and shredded

2¾ cups shredded sharp Cheddar cheese

1 teaspoon salt

½ teaspoon pepper

1. Preheat the oven to 350°F. Coat a 10-inch pie or quiche dish with 1 tablespoon of the butter.

2. In a medium nonstick skillet, cook the bacon until crisp; remove the bacon and set aside. Drain all but 1 tablespoon of the bacon drippings. Add the peppers and onion and sauté over medium heat for 3 to 5 minutes, until soft.

3. Whisk the eggs in a large bowl. Stir the potatoes into the eggs. Add the bacon and the vegetable mixture. Pour into the prepared pan and spread out the mixture evenly. Top with the cheese and sprinkle with salt and pepper.

4. Bake for 45 minutes, or until set.

CRUSTLESS VEGGIE QUICHE

There is lots of flavor here from the garlic, vegetables, and herbs.
The low-fat cheese makes it healthy, too.

SERVES 4

2 teaspoons butter, softened

1 large clove garlic, chopped

1 cup chopped broccoli

½ cup shredded carrot

2 green onions, sliced (white and green parts)

4 large eggs, beaten, or an equivalent amount of Egg Beaters

2 tablespoons water

½ teaspoon salt

1 tablespoon chopped fresh basil, or 1 teaspoon dried basil

½ cup shredded part-skim or regular Monterey Jack cheese

Sliced, seeded, and deribbed red bell pepper rings for garnish

1. Preheat the oven to 400°F. Grease a 9-inch pie pan with 1 teaspoon of the butter.

2. In a 10-inch nonstick skillet, melt the remaining 1 teaspoon butter and add the garlic, broccoli, carrot, and green onions. Cook over medium heat, stirring occasionally, until the vegetables are crisp-tender, 4 to 5 minutes. Spread over the bottom of the pie pan.

3. In a medium bowl, whisk the eggs, water, and salt together. Pour over the vegetable mixture and sprinkle with the basil.

4. Bake for 25 minutes or until set. Sprinkle the cheese over the top and garnish with the red pepper rings. Let stand until the cheese melts before serving.

CHEESE AND SAUSAGE BREAKFAST PIE

Here is a quichelike breakfast dish that's absolutely satisfying!

1 recipe Flaky Pastry (page 32)

2 cups shredded mozzarella cheese

1 pound breakfast sausage, chopped, cooked, and drained

6 large eggs

½ cup milk

2 tablespoons snipped fresh chives

1. Prepare the pastry and chill in the refrigerator. Preheat the oven to 325°F.

2. Roll out the chilled pastry into a 12-inch circle and transfer to a 9-inch pie pan. Trim and crimp the edges.

3. Line the unbaked pie shell with 1 cup of the shredded cheese. Top with the sausage and the remaining cheese.

4. In a small bowl, beat the eggs and milk. Pour over the cheese layer evenly. Sprinkle with the chives.

5. Bake for 35 to 40 minutes, or until set.

CHICKEN AND ASPARAGUS BREAKFAST PIE

Similar to a quiche, this breakfast pie is perfect for a special brunch with friends or family. Start out with mimosas and add a freshly baked bread such as Whole-Wheat Bubble Bread (page 72).

SERVES 6 TO 8

FOR THE PASTRY:

1 cup all-purpose flour

¼ teaspoon salt

6 tablespoons chilled butter, cut into pieces

2 tablespoons chopped fresh chives

2 tablespoons cold water

FOR THE FILLING:

2 cups shredded Cheddar cheese

1 cup shredded cooked chicken

6 slices bacon, cooked until crisp and cut into 1-inch pieces

¼ pound asparagus

1½ cups half-and-half or milk

4 large eggs, lightly beaten

¼ teaspoon salt

⅛ teaspoon pepper

1. Preheat the oven to 400°F.

2. *To make the pastry:* In a food processor with the steel blade in place, combine the flour and salt; add the butter pieces. Process using on/off pulses about 8 times, until the mixture resembles coarse crumbs. Or, use a fork or pastry blender to cut the butter into the flour. Stir in the chives and then the water to make a crumbly dough. Shape into a ball.

3. On a lightly floured work surface, roll out the dough to make a 12-inch circle. Ease into a 10-inch pie pan, pressing the dough firmly against the bottom and sides. Crimp or flute the edges.

4. *To make the filling:* Spread the cheese over the bottom of the crust and top with the chicken. Sprinkle bacon over the chicken. Arrange the asparagus spears like the spokes of a wheel on top of the bacon.

5. Stir together the half-and-half, eggs, salt, and pepper in a medium bowl, and pour over the mixture in the pan. Bake for 40 to 45 minutes, or until golden and the center is set. Let stand for 10 minutes before serving.

HASH BROWN–CRUSTED POTATO PIE

Equally suitable for brunch or supper, this hearty breakfast pie only requires a side of fresh fruit or a salad for a satisfying meal.

SERVES 6

3 large eggs

½ cup milk

½ teaspoon salt

3 cups frozen shredded hash brown potatoes, thawed

5 tablespoons butter, melted

1 cup finely chopped cooked ham

1 cup shredded Cheddar or Swiss cheese

½ cup finely chopped onions

½ cup chopped green bell peppers

¼ cup diced red bell peppers

1. Preheat the oven to 425°F.

2. Mix the eggs, milk, and salt together in a medium bowl. Blot the potatoes between sheets of paper towels to remove excess moisture. Press the potatoes into the bottom and up the sides of an ungreased 9-inch pie pan. Drizzle with the melted butter.

3. Bake the crust for 25 minutes, or until lightly browned. Cool in the pan on a wire rack. Lower the oven heat to 375°F.

4. Spread the ham over the bottom of the crust. Top with the cheese, onions, and green and red bell peppers. Pour the egg and milk mixture over all.

5. Bake the pie for 35 to 40 minutes, or until set. Remove from the oven and let rest for 10 minutes before cutting and serving.

POTATO CRUST BREAKFAST PIE

We made 50 of these pies to feed 300 people for a brunch at church. When we compared the taste of a pie made with fresh tomatoes with one made with canned, the canned won out.

— SERVES 6 —

FOR THE CRUST:

⅓ cup butter at room temperature, plus extra for the pan

¾ cup instant mashed potato flakes

¾ cup all-purpose flour

¼ cup grated Parmesan cheese

¼ teaspoon salt

¼ cup water

FOR THE FILLING:

1½ cups shredded Cheddar cheese

¼ cup instant mashed potato flakes

1 can (14½ ounce) diced tomatoes, drained

1 cup sliced mushrooms

FOR THE EGG MIXTURE:

5 large eggs

¼ cup sour cream

¾ teaspoon salt

1. Preheat the oven to 350°F. Butter a 9-inch pie pan.

2. *To prepare the crust:* In a medium bowl, stir the ⅓ cup butter, ¾ cup mashed potato flakes, the flour, Parmesan cheese, and ¼ teaspoon salt together until well mixed and crumbly. Drizzle the water over the dry ingredients and stir with a fork until the dough holds together.

3. Press the dough into the pie pan with your fingers and flute the edges. Bake for 10 minutes, or until the crust feels dry.

4. *To make the filling:* Spread ½ cup of the shredded cheese, the ¼ cup mashed potato flakes, tomatoes, and mushrooms evenly over the top. Top with the remaining 1 cup cheese.

5. *To make the egg mixture:* Beat together the eggs, sour cream, and ¾ teaspoon salt. Carefully pour over the ingredients in the pie shell, poking a hole here and there to allow the mixture to permeate the filling.

6. Bake for 25 to 30 minutes, until a knife inserted in the center comes out clean and the filling is set. Cool for about 10 minutes before cutting and serving.

BAKED CINNAMON-MAPLE FRENCH TOAST

Remember this simple dish when you have houseguests. Put it together the night before and refrigerate it, covered. It's perfect for a leisurely winter morning. Your guests will wake up to the great smells of cinnamon and maple as the French toast bakes.

—————————————— SERVES 8 ——————————————

1 loaf 2-day-old French bread, cut into 1-inch-thick slices

12 large eggs

2 tablespoons pure maple syrup

1 quart heavy cream

1½ tablespoons vanilla extract

Cinnamon for garnish

Butter at room temperature, for serving

Warmed maple syrup for serving

1. Put the bread slices in a 9-by-13-inch baking dish.

2. In a large bowl, whisk together the eggs, maple syrup, heavy cream, and vanilla. Pour over the bread and let set for 1 hour. Turn the slices, cover, and refrigerate overnight.

3. In the morning, turn the bread once again and sprinkle with cinnamon. Let stand for 15 minutes before baking.

4. Preheat the oven to 350°F. Bake the French toast, uncovered, for 40 to 45 minutes, until the toast feels firm to the touch and no egg mixture appears around the edges. Serve with butter and warmed maple syrup.

BAKED COCONUT FRENCH TOAST WITH TROPICAL FRUIT COMPOTE

This is definitely a summery brunch dish. When strawberries are in season, add them to the compote as well.

○———————————————— SERVES 8 ————————————————○

FOR THE COMPOTE:

1½ cups chopped pineapple

1 cup chopped mango

1 cup chopped papaya

1 cup chopped kiwifruit

3 tablespoons sugar

3 tablespoons fresh lime juice

FOR THE FRENCH TOAST:

16 slices French bread (1 inch thick), cut on the diagonal

1¼ cups light coconut milk

6 large eggs, lightly beaten

½ cup sugar

1 tablespoon vanilla extract

½ cup sweetened flaked coconut

1. *To prepare the compote:* Combine the pineapple, mango, papaya, kiwifruit, sugar, and lime juice in a serving bowl. Cover and chill for 8 hours or overnight.

2. *To make the French toast:* Coat a 9-by-13-inch baking dish with cooking spray. Arrange the bread in a single layer in the bottom. Combine the coconut milk, eggs, sugar, and vanilla, stirring with a whisk. Pour evenly over the bread, and turn the bread over to coat. Cover and refrigerate for 8 hours or overnight.

3. Preheat the oven to 350°F.

4. Remove the bread mixture from the refrigerator and uncover. Turn the bread slices over, and sprinkle evenly with the flaked coconut. Let stand at room temperature for 15 minutes. Bake, uncovered, for 30 minutes, or until the coconut is golden. Serve warm with the fruit compote.

BAKED FRENCH TOAST WITH PRALINE AND MAPLE SYRUP

You might serve this with sliced fresh strawberries when they are in season. In winter, serve with sliced bananas and oranges on the side.

SERVES 6 TO 8

1 cup (2 sticks) butter, plus extra for the dish

One loaf (1 pound) French bread

8 large eggs

2 cups half-and-half

1 cup milk

2 tablespoons granulated sugar

½ teaspoon salt, or more to taste

1 teaspoon vanilla extract

1 teaspoon ground cinnamon, divided

½ teaspoon ground nutmeg, divided

1 cup packed light brown sugar

1 cup chopped pecans

2 tablespoons light corn syrup

Maple syrup for serving

1. Butter a 9-by-13-inch baking dish. Cut the bread into 20 slices, about 1 inch thick. Arrange the slices in the baking dish in 2 rows, overlapping the slices.

2. In a large bowl, combine the eggs, half-and-half, milk, sugar, salt, vanilla, ½ teaspoon of the cinnamon, and ¼ teaspoon of the nutmeg. Beat with a rotary beater or whisk until blended but not bubbly.

3. Pour the mixture over the bread slices, making sure all are covered evenly with the milk and egg mixture. Spoon some of the mixture in between the slices. Cover with foil and refrigerate overnight. Remove from the refrigerator 15 minutes before baking.

4. Preheat the oven to 350°F.

5. For the praline topping, in a medium bowl, combine the 1 cup butter, the brown sugar, pecans, corn syrup, the remaining ½ teaspoon cinnamon, and the remaining ¼ teaspoon nutmeg. Spread the praline mixture evenly over the bread. Bake for 35 to 40 minutes, until puffed and lightly browned and the center of the casserole is set. Serve with maple syrup.

BAKED PECAN-STUFFED FRENCH TOAST

Pumpkin pie spice—a combination of cinnamon, ginger, allspice, and cloves—has a special affinity for egg and milk mixtures. This is a perfect choice for a holiday breakfast or brunch.

SERVES 8

1 cup firmly packed light or dark brown sugar

½ cup (1 stick) butter

2 tablespoons honey

1 cup chopped pecans, toasted (see Note)

1 large loaf (1 pound) French bread, cut into ½-inch-thick slices

½ pound cooked ham, finely chopped (2 cups)

6 large eggs, beaten

1⅔ cups milk

1 teaspoon vanilla extract

1 tablespoon sugar

1 teaspoon pumpkin pie spice (see Note)

Maple syrup for serving

1. Combine the brown sugar, butter, and honey in a small saucepan. Cook over medium heat, stirring frequently, until the butter melts and the sugar dissolves, 2 to 3 minutes. Pour into an ungreased 9-by-13-inch baking dish. Sprinkle with the pecans. Top with half of the bread slices, and scatter the ham on top.

2. Combine the eggs, milk, and vanilla in a large bowl and beat until well mixed. Dip the remaining bread slices in the egg mixture on one side only. Place over the ham, dipped side down. Pour the remaining egg mixture over the bread slices. Combine the sugar and pumpkin pie spice in a small bowl and sprinkle over the top. Cover the baking dish and refrigerate for 4 hours or overnight. Remove from the refrigerator 15 minutes before baking.

3. Preheat the oven to 350°F.

4. Uncover the French toast and bake for 50 to 55 minutes, or until golden brown and a knife inserted in the center comes out clean. Let stand for 10 minutes. Cut into 8 servings. Serve with maple syrup.

○ ○ ○ ○ ○

NOTES: If you don't have pumpkin pie spice, substitute ½ teaspoon ground cinnamon, ¼ teaspoon ground ginger, ⅛ teaspoon ground nutmeg, and ⅛ teaspoon ground cloves.

To toast the pecans, preheat the oven to 350°F. Spread out the nuts on a cookie sheet and bake, stirring occasionally, for 5 to 10 minutes, until aromatic and lightly browned.

BLUEBERRY-MAPLE FRENCH TOAST WITH BLUEBERRY SAUCE

You definitely want to use fresh blueberries with this one. When I made it with frozen blueberries, the blueberry juice turned the French bread and custard a sickly shade of purple while baking. The flavor was still delicious, however, and our granddaughter just about devoured the whole thing!

SERVES 8

1 large loaf (1 pound) French bread, crust removed

1 package (8 ounces) cream cheese

1 cup fresh blueberries

12 large eggs, beaten

2 cups milk

⅓ cup maple syrup

FOR THE BLUEBERRY SAUCE:

1 cup sugar

1 cup water

2 tablespoons cornstarch

1 tablespoon butter

1 cup blueberries

1. Cut the bread into 1-inch cubes and spread half in a 9-by-13-inch baking dish. Cut the cream cheese into cubes and scatter over the bread. Scatter the blueberries evenly on top and cover with the remaining half of the bread cubes.

2. Mix the eggs, milk, and maple syrup in a large bowl and pour over the bread mixture. Cover and refrigerate overnight. Remove from the refrigerator 30 minutes before baking.

3. Preheat the oven to 350°F. Cover the dish with aluminum foil and bake the French toast for 30 minutes. Uncover and bake for 30 minutes longer, until set.

4. *While the French toast bakes, make the blueberry sauce:* Combine the sugar, water, cornstarch, and butter in a medium saucepan. Place over medium heat and boil for 3 minutes, stirring constantly. Stir in the blueberries, reduce the heat, and simmer for 8 to 10 minutes, until the blueberries burst.

5. Slice the French toast and serve warm with the warm blueberry sauce.

CINNAMON AND APPLE–STUFFED FRENCH TOAST CASSEROLE

Here's another idea for breakfast or brunch. It's a very flexible recipe. Assemble the casserole a day ahead if you like, or just before baking. For other fruit flavors, check the variations below.

SERVES 4

4 large slices sourdough bread, crust removed, and cubed

1 package (8 ounces) cream cheese, cubed

1 large Golden Delicious or Granny Smith apple, peeled and chopped

6 large eggs

1 cup milk

1½ teaspoons ground cinnamon

3 tablespoons powdered sugar for garnish

1. Preheat the oven to 375°F. Arrange half the bread cubes in an 8-inch square baking dish. Distribute the cream cheese cubes evenly over the bread. Distribute the chopped apple over the top, and cover with the remaining bread cubes.

2. Beat the eggs, milk, and cinnamon together in a medium bowl and pour over all. Bake for 35 minutes, uncovered. Sprinkle with powdered sugar before serving.

Variations

Fresh Blueberry–Stuffed French Toast Casserole: Substitute 2 cups blueberries for the apple and proceed with the recipe.

Fresh Strawberry–Stuffed French Toast Casserole: Substitute 2 cups sliced strawberries for the apple and proceed with the recipe.

Toasted Almond and Peach–Stuffed French Toast: Replace the apples with 2 large peaches, peeled and sliced. Scatter the peaches over the cream cheese cubes, sprinkle with ½ cup toasted slivered almonds, and proceed with the recipe.

HAM AND CHEESE–STUFFED FRENCH TOAST

I served this to a group of my husband's friends who get together once a year. It was a real favorite. For a lunch or supper dish, serve it with sauerkraut on the side.

SERVES 8

½ cup (1 stick) butter at room temperature, divided, plus extra for the dish

12 to 14 slices rye bread with caraway seeds

3 tablespoons Dijon-style mustard

1 sweet onion, thinly sliced

¾ pound Asiago, Swiss, or Cheddar cheese, thinly sliced or shredded

¾ pound thinly sliced cooked ham

6 large eggs

2½ cups milk

1 tablespoon chopped fresh basil, or 1 teaspoon dried basil

1 teaspoon salt

1½ cups fine dry breadcrumbs or panko (see Note)

¼ cup grated Parmesan cheese

1. Butter a 9-by-13-inch baking dish. Using 3 tablespoons of butter, lightly butter all of the bread slices on one side. Spread the mustard on top. Arrange half of the bread slices, mustard side up, in the baking pan in one layer; cut to fit if necessary.

2. Heat 1 tablespoon of the remaining butter in a skillet over medium-low heat and add the onion. Sauté for 25 to 35 minutes, stirring often, until the onion is softened. Spread the onion evenly over the bread slices. Top with half the sliced cheese and all of the ham. Cover with the remaining cheese and then the remaining bread slices. Press the layers together.

3. Beat the eggs, milk, basil, and salt together in a medium bowl. Pour evenly over the layers, pressing them down slightly so they absorb the mixture. Cover and refrigerate for several hours or overnight. Remove from the refrigerator 1 hour before baking.

4. Preheat the oven to 375°F. Mix the breadcrumbs with the remaining 4 tablespoons butter and the Parmesan cheese in a medium bowl. Sprinkle over the casserole. Bake, uncovered, for 35 to 40 minutes, until the top is golden brown and the egg mixture is set. Remove from the oven and allow to rest for 10 minutes before serving. To serve, cut into squares.

○ ○ ○ ○ ○

NOTE: Panko are Japanese–style coarse breadcrumbs, which stay crisp longer than regular dried breadcrumbs.

HOT PEPPER STRATA

The "hot" comes easily with a sprinkle of red pepper flakes, but be sure to add them according to your taste!

SERVES 8

10 slices whole-wheat bread

2 cups sliced mushrooms

1 cup sliced green onions (white and green parts)

1 can (4 ounces) diced green chiles

3 cups shredded sharp Cheddar cheese

6 large eggs

2 cups milk

1 tablespoon Dijon mustard

1 to 3 teaspoons red pepper flakes

1 cup crushed tortilla chips

1. Butter a 9-by-13-inch baking dish.

2. Remove the crusts from the bread and put the crusts (not the bread) into a food processor fitted with the steel blade. Process to make crumbs and set aside until you're ready to bake the strata.

3. Line the baking dish with half the bread slices in one layer, cutting them to fit if necessary. Top with half the mushrooms, half the green onions, half the green chiles, and half the cheese. Cover with the remaining bread slices, mushrooms, green onions, chiles, and cheese.

4. Whisk together the eggs, milk, mustard, and red pepper flakes in a medium bowl. Pour over the ingredients in the dish. Cover and refrigerate for 4 hours or overnight. Remove from the refrigerator 30 minutes before baking.

5. Preheat the oven to 350°F. Mix the reserved breadcrumbs with the tortilla chips and sprinkle over the top of the casserole. Bake, uncovered, or 55 minutes, or until set. Let stand for 10 minutes before serving.

MUSHROOM-STUFFED CROISSANT CASSEROLE

Make this with day-old croissants. This is another savory dish that is assembled the night before.

SERVES 4

1 tablespoon butter, plus extra for the dish

4 plain croissants, split horizontally

2 cups sliced mushrooms

¼ cup sliced green onions (white and green parts)

4 large eggs

1 cup milk

1 cup shredded Swiss cheese

1 cup shredded mozzarella cheese

¼ cup grated Parmesan cheese

1. Butter a 9-inch square casserole. Arrange the croissant bottoms, cut sides up, in the bottom of the dish.

2. Melt the 1 tablespoon butter in a skillet and add the mushrooms and green onions. Sauté over medium heat, stirring, for 2 to 3 minutes, until the liquid is evaporated. Remove from the heat.

3. Whisk the eggs and milk together in a small bowl and pour half of the mixture over the croissants. Top with the mushroom mixture. Top with the cheeses, then pour the remaining liquid over the top.

4. Position the croissant tops, cut side down, over the bottoms, with the filling mixture in between. Cover and refrigerate overnight. Remove from the refrigerator 30 minutes before baking.

5. Preheat the oven to 350°F.

6. Bake the casserole for 35 to 40 minutes, or until set. Let stand 10 minutes before serving.

ONION AND GOAT CHEESE BREAD PUDDING

Have it for breakfast, brunch, or supper—this meatless main dish is delicious any time. Serve it with a refreshing salad of some kind, one with fresh fruit or marinated vegetables.

5 tablespoons butter at room temperature, plus extra for the dish

1 loaf (1 pound) sourdough bread, sliced, crusts removed, and cut into ¾-inch cubes

3 bunches green onions, cut into ½-inch lengths (white and green parts)

1 large clove garlic, finely chopped

½ teaspoon salt

Dash of cayenne pepper

4 large eggs

1½ cups heavy cream

¾ cup sour cream

1 tablespoon chopped fresh basil, plus extra for garnish

1 log (10½ ounces) goat cheese, crumbled

1. Preheat the oven to 400°F. Butter a 9-by-13-inch baking dish.

2. Spread out the bread cubes on an ungreased baking sheet and toast for 10 minutes, turning them often, and making sure they don't burn.

3. In a large skillet, melt the 5 tablespoons butter and add the green onions and garlic. Sauté over medium-high heat for 3 minutes, or until the green onions are aromatic. Add the salt and cayenne pepper.

4. Whisk the eggs, cream, and sour cream together in a large bowl. Add the sautéed green onions, the 1 tablespoon basil, and the crumbled cheese. Fold in the toasted bread cubes and turn into the prepared baking dish. Cover and refrigerate overnight. Remove from the refrigerator at least 30 minutes before baking.

5. Preheat the oven to 350°F. Bake, covered with aluminum foil, for 25 minutes. Uncover and bake for another 20 minutes, or until the top is browned, the edges are bubbly, and the center is cooked. Sprinkle with additional chopped basil.

SAUSAGE AND CHEDDAR EGG DISH

Make-ahead breakfast casseroles are really convenient, and this is one of our favorites.

6 large eggs

1 cup half-and-half

2 tablespoons green onions, chopped (white and green parts)

1 teaspoon salt

½ teaspoon pepper

1 tablespoon butter at room temperature

6 slices Texas toast or another thick-cut, crusty white bread

1 pound spicy pork sausage, cooked and drained

1 cup grated Cheddar cheese

1. In a medium bowl, beat the eggs. Add the half-and-half and green onions. Mix well, season with the salt and pepper, and set aside.

2. Spread the butter over the bottom and sides of a 9-by-13-inch baking dish. Line the dish with the bread, cutting and rearranging, if needed. Sprinkle the bread with the cooked sausage and the cheese. Pour the egg mixture over all. Cover and refrigerate overnight. Remove from the refrigerator 30 minutes before baking.

3. Preheat the oven to 350°F. Uncover the dish and bake for 35 to 40 minutes, or until the casserole is set in the center. Let stand 5 to 10 minutes before cutting into serving pieces.

BELL PEPPER AND SAUSAGE STRATA

I bake a lot of French bread, and often some of the loaf goes uneaten.
I cut these hunks into cubes, crusts and all, and freeze them.
Here's how I use them!

SERVES 6

1 package (12 ounces) frozen pork breakfast sausage, thawed and crumbled

⅓ cup chopped green bell pepper

⅓ cup chopped red bell pepper

6 cups day-old French bread cubes (¾-inch cubes)

1½ cups half-and-half or undiluted evaporated milk

4 tablespoons butter, melted

3 large eggs

1 teaspoon onion salt

1½ cups shredded Cheddar cheese

1. In a heavy skillet over medium heat, cook the sausage and green and red peppers for about 4 minutes, until the sausage is browned and the peppers are crisp-tender. Drain off the fat if necessary.

2. In a large bowl, combine the cooked mixture with the bread cubes and turn into an ungreased 8-inch square baking dish or a shallow 2-quart casserole.

3. Combine the half-and-half, butter, eggs, and onion salt. Pour evenly over the bread mixture in the pan. Sprinkle the cheese evenly on top. Cover tightly and refrigerate overnight. Remove from the refrigerator 30 minutes before baking.

4. Preheat the oven to 350°F. Uncover the strata and bake for 55 to 60 minutes, or until a knife inserted in the center comes out clean and the cheese is melted. Let stand for 5 minutes before serving.

TURKEY SAUSAGE, EGG, AND CHEDDAR BAKE

Low-fat turkey breakfast sausage comes in frozen logs, available in the freezer section of your market, and sometimes in bulk packages, sold at the meat counter. A variety of breads, from rye to wheat, are perfect in this breakfast dish. I like to save ends of bread, cut them into cubes, and store in zip-top bags in the freezer. When I have about 5 cups, I put this casserole together.

SERVES 6

1 pound bulk turkey breakfast sausage

6 slices assorted day-old bread, cubed

1 cup shredded Cheddar cheese

6 large eggs

2 cups milk

1 teaspoon salt

1 teaspoon dry mustard

⅛ teaspoon cayenne pepper

1. Butter a 9-by-13-inch baking dish. In a skillet, crumble and cook the sausage over moderate heat until browned. Drain well.

2. Spread half of the bread cubes in the baking dish. Top with half of the cheese and all of the sausage. Cover the sausage with the remaining bread cubes and the remaining cheese.

3. Mix the eggs, milk, salt, dry mustard, and cayenne pepper in a large bowl. Pour this mixture over the ingredients in the dish. Cover and refrigerate for at least 12 hours. Remove from the refrigerator 30 minutes before baking.

4. Preheat the oven to 350°F. Uncover the dish and bake for 1 to 1½ hours, or until set (baking time will vary, depending on how cold the ingredients are).

THREE-CHEESE BREAKFAST CASSEROLE

Manchego is Spain's most famous cheese. It was made originally from the milk of Manchego sheep, which grazed on the famous plain of La Mancha. Sometimes, when I have just a dried heel of the cheese left, I combine it with other cheeses I have on hand and transform its marvelous flavor into a breakfast casserole.

SERVES 6

6 tablespoons butter at room temperature

6 slices thick-cut bread, crusts trimmed

½ teaspoon pepper

½ cup shredded Swiss cheese

½ cup shredded sharp Cheddar cheese

½ cup shredded Manchego cheese

1½ cups whole milk

6 large eggs

2 teaspoons fresh oregano leaves, or ½ teaspoon dried oregano

1. Butter 6 individual 8-ounce ramekins or one 9-inch square baking dish using 1 tablespoon of the butter.

2. With the remaining 5 tablespoons butter, spread one side of each slice of bread with butter. Place a single slice, buttered side up, in each ramekin, or lay the buttered slices in the baking dish. Grind some pepper over each slice of bread.

3. Mix the three types of cheese together. Sprinkle each bread slice in a ramekin with ¼ cup of the cheese mixture, or sprinkle all of the cheese over the bread in the baking dish. Beat the milk with the eggs in a medium bowl and add the oregano. Pour over the cheese and bread in the ramekins or baking dish. Cover and refrigerate overnight.

4. The next morning, preheat the oven to 350°F. Remove the casserole(s) from the refrigerator 30 minutes before baking and uncover.

5. Bake the ramekins for 20 to 25 minutes or the larger dish for 35 to 40 minutes, until puffed and golden brown. Serve immediately.

EGGS BENEDICT CASSEROLE

With this safe method of cooking eggs for hollandaise sauce, we can once again enjoy this classic dish without worry. The casserole method allows you to do most of the preparation ahead of time and serve with ease.

SERVES 6

12 slices toasted white or wheat bread, crusts removed

12 slices Canadian bacon

12 cold large eggs

FOR THE HOLLANDAISE SAUCE:
6 large egg yolks

½ cup water

¼ cup fresh lemon juice

1 cup (2 sticks) cold butter, each stick cut into eighths

¼ teaspoon salt

¼ teaspoon paprika

Chopped fresh parsley for garnish

1. Preheat the oven to 250°F. Butter a 9-by-13-inch baking dish. Place the toast pieces side by side in the baking dish and top each with Canadian bacon.

2. Poach the eggs in 3 batches: In a deep skillet, bring 2 to 3 inches of water to a boil. Reduce the heat and maintain the water at a gentle simmer. Break 4 cold eggs into a bowl. Holding the bowl close to the water's surface, slip the eggs into the water. Cook until the whites are completely set and the yolks begin to thicken but are not hard, about 3 to 5 minutes. With a slotted spoon, lift out the eggs and place them, one at a time, onto the bacon-topped toasts. Repeat with the remaining eggs. (At this point the casserole can be covered and refrigerated overnight. Take out of the refrigerator 15 minutes before baking.)

3. *To make the hollandaise sauce:* In a small saucepan, beat together the egg yolks, water, and lemon juice. Cook over very low heat, stirring constantly, until the mixture bubbles at the edges.

4. Whisk in the butter, 1 piece at a time, and continue whisking until all the butter is melted and the sauce is thickened. Stir in the salt and paprika. Remove from the heat and cover and chill if not using immediately. (To reheat, transfer to the top of a double boiler or a bowl suspended over a saucepan of simmering water and whisk briskly until the sauce is smooth and pourable.)

5. To finish the casserole, drizzle hollandaise sauce over the poached eggs. Bake for 15 minutes, or until heated through. Garnish with the chopped fresh parsley.

BAKED GRITS WITH CHEESE

Easy and filling, this falls into the "comfort foods" category—
perfect for breakfast, brunch, or a light supper.

2 tablespoons butter, plus extra for the dish

4 cups water

1 teaspoon salt

1 cup cornmeal grits or polenta

1 large egg

⅓ cup heavy cream

1 teaspoon pepper

1 cup grated Gruyère cheese

⅓ cup grated Parmesan cheese

1. Preheat the oven to 350°F. Butter a 2-quart casserole.

2. In a medium saucepan, heat the water and salt to boiling. Gradually whisk in the grits and cook, whisking constantly, until thickened, about 15 minutes.

3. Whisk the egg, cream, the 2 tablespoons butter, and pepper together in a small bowl. Stir into the cooked grits along with the Gruyère and Parmesan cheese. Transfer to the casserole.

4. Bake, uncovered, for about 45 minutes, until set. Remove from the oven and let sit for about 5 minutes before serving.

GRITS, CHEESE, AND EGG BREAKFAST CASSEROLE WITH TOMATO SALSA

Put this hearty casserole on the menu for a Tex-Mex brunch or lunch. Serve with a simple bean dish, along with the fresh salsa.

SERVES 6

4 tablespoons butter, melted, plus extra for the dish

4 cups water

2 teaspoons salt

1 cup cornmeal grits

6 large eggs, beaten

1 tablespoon onion, finely chopped

1 cup milk

½ cup yellow cornmeal

2 tablespoons all-purpose flour

1 teaspoon baking powder

1 pound bulk pork sausage, cooked and drained

2 cups shredded Monterey Jack cheese

½ teaspoon paprika

Roasted Tomato Salsa (recipe follows) for serving

1. Preheat the oven to 350°F. Butter a 9-by-13-inch baking dish or baking pan.

2. Bring the water and 1 teaspoon salt to a boil in a large deep saucepan over high heat. Gradually add the grits, reduce the heat to medium, and cook, stirring often, until thick, about 30 minutes. Set aside to cool slightly.

3. In a large bowl, mix the eggs, onion, remaining 1 teaspoon salt, the milk, cornmeal, flour, baking powder, and the 4 tablespoons butter. Stir in the cooked grits.

4. Spread the cooked pork sausage evenly over the bottom of the casserole and spread the cornmeal mixture on top. Spread the cheese over the top and sprinkle evenly with paprika. (The casserole can be assembled ahead of time up to this point, covered, and refrigerated overnight. Remove from the refrigerator 30 minutes before baking.)

5. Bake, uncovered, for 45 to 50 minutes, or until firm in the center. Let stand for 5 minutes before serving. Accompany with Roasted Tomato Salsa.

ROASTED TOMATO SALSA
MAKES ABOUT 2 CUPS

6 Roma (plum) tomatoes, quartered lengthwise, then halved crosswise

1 red onion, cut into 1-inch dice

1 jalapeño pepper, seeded and cut into eighths

2 tablespoons olive oil

Juice from ½ lime

Salt and pepper

½ cup chopped fresh cilantro

1. Preheat the oven to 450°F. Line the inside of a shallow baking pan with foil and coat with cooking spray.

2. In a large bowl, toss the tomatoes, onion, and pepper with the olive oil and spread out in the pan. Roast for 10 minutes and let cool in the pan.

3. Transfer the mixture to a medium serving bowl and season with the lime juice, salt and pepper to taste, and cilantro.

GRITS AND EGGS

These grits are baked with eggs and cheese to make one of the most basic of grits casseroles, and a very satisfying one at that.

SERVES 6

4 cups water

1 teaspoon salt

1 cup cornmeal grits

3 large eggs, separated

2 teaspoons baking powder

½ cup shredded sharp Cheddar cheese

1. Preheat the oven to 325°F. Butter a shallow 2-quart casserole.

2. In a large deep saucepan over high heat, bring the water and salt to boiling and stir in the grits. Lower the heat to medium and cook, stirring often, for 30 minutes, or until thick. Set aside for a few minutes to cool slightly.

3. Beat the egg yolks in a small bowl. Stir in a small amount of the grits to temper them, then stir the yolks into the pan full of grits.

4. Beat the egg whites until stiff with an electric mixer, and fold into the grits mixture. Fold in the baking powder and cheese. Transfer to the casserole and bake, uncovered, for 35 to 40 minutes, until slightly browned and puffy. Serve immediately.

POLENTA, CHEESE, AND EGG CASSEROLE

You can make this casserole ahead of time, cover, and refrigerate, and do the baking just before serving.

6 cups water

1½ cups polenta or coarse yellow cornmeal

1 pound Cheddar cheese, shredded

3 large eggs, beaten

3 teaspoons seasoning salt

2 pounds bulk sausage, crumbled, cooked and drained

1 teaspoon paprika

1. Preheat the oven to 350°F. Butter a deep 3-quart casserole.

2. In a large saucepan, bring the water to a boil and slowly whisk in the polenta. Cook, stirring, over high heat until thickened. Lower the heat and stir in the cheese.

3. Stir a small amount of the cooked polenta into the beaten eggs to temper them, then stir the egg mixture into the polenta in the saucepan along with the salt, cooked sausage, and paprika. Pour into the casserole and bake, uncovered, for 1½ hours, or until set.

MUSHROOM AND POTATO BREAKFAST CASSEROLE

The low-fat dairy products bring the total fat content down (despite the bacon) to make a healthier breakfast casserole. If you serve this for brunch, add a baby spinach salad with sliced fresh strawberries when in season, and dress with a simple vinaigrette with a bit of honey added.

SERVES 4

4 slices white or whole-wheat bread, crusts removed

6 large eggs

1½ cups skim or low-fat milk

4 slices bacon, cooked and crumbled

¼ cup shredded reduced-fat Cheddar cheese, divided

¼ cup shredded reduced-fat Swiss cheese, divided

⅓ cup sliced mushrooms

½ cup frozen shredded hash brown potatoes, thawed

1. Coat an 8- or 9-inch square baking dish with cooking spray and arrange the bread slices across the bottom, overlapping them slightly.

2. In a large bowl, beat the eggs, milk, bacon, 2 table-spoons of the Cheddar cheese, 2 tablespoons of the Swiss cheese, and the mushrooms. Pour the mixture over the bread slices and sprinkle with the potatoes, then sprinkle with the remaining cheese. Cover and refrigerate over-night. Remove 30 minutes before baking.

3. Preheat the oven to 350°F. Bake, uncovered, for 40 to 45 minutes, or until lightly browned and the eggs are set.

HASH BROWN BREAKFAST CASSEROLE

This is one of those casseroles that you can make ahead or not—whatever best suits your schedule. Frozen hash brown potatoes save time here without compromising taste.

SERVES 6

1 pound bacon

2 tablespoons butter

2 onions, chopped

2 cups sliced mushrooms

4 cups frozen shredded hash brown potatoes, thawed

1 teaspoon salt

½ teaspoon pepper

6 large eggs

1½ cups milk

2 tablespoons chopped fresh parsley

1 cup shredded mild to sharp Cheddar cheese

1. Preheat the oven to 400°F. Separate the bacon slices and arrange on a large rimmed baking sheet. Place in the oven as it preheats and bake until the bacon is crisp, 10 to 12 minutes. Drain off the fat.

2. Using 1 tablespoon of butter, coat a shallow 3-quart casserole.

3. Melt the remaining tablespoon of butter in a nonstick skillet. Add the onions and mushrooms and sauté over medium heat, stirring, for 5 to 10 minutes, until the onions are tender.

4. Arrange the potatoes in the bottom of the dish, and sprinkle with the salt and pepper. Top with the cooked bacon slices, then the onions and mushrooms.

5. In a large bowl, beat the eggs with the milk and parsley. Pour over the casserole and top with the cheese. (The casserole can be assembled up to this point, covered, and refrigerated. Add 15 minutes to the baking time.)

6. Bake the casserole, uncovered, for 45 minutes, or until set and the cheese is melted. Serve immediately.

LUMBERJACK HASH BROWNS, EGG, AND CHEESE CASSEROLE

As its name suggests, this casserole is perfect for a day of skiing, snowshoeing, or just snow shoveling, thanks to its substantial stick-to-the-ribs quality.

SERVES 6

4 tablespoons butter, plus extra for the dish

12 large eggs

1 cup plain regular or nonfat yogurt

1 teaspoon salt

¼ cup chopped sweet onions

2 cups shredded fresh potatoes, preferably russets

1 cup shredded sharp Cheddar cheese

1. Preheat the oven to 350°F. Butter a 9-by-13-inch glass baking dish.

2. In a large bowl, beat the eggs, yogurt, and salt together.

3. In a medium skillet over medium-high heat, melt the 4 tablespoons butter and add the onions and potatoes. Sauté for 3 to 4 minutes, until the vegetables are beginning to soften.

4. Add the onion-potato mixture to the egg mixture and transfer to the prepared casserole. Bake, uncovered, for 30 to 35 minutes, or until a knife inserted in the center of the mixture comes out clean. Top with the cheese, cut into 6 generous portions, and serve.

NO-EGG BREAKFAST POTATO HOT DISH

Add this dish to a brunch menu just for variety. It is also a great way to use leftover cooked potatoes.

SERVES 6

2 teaspoons butter

1 small onion, minced

4 cups diced cooked potatoes

8 slices bacon, cooked and crumbled

1 cup shredded Cheddar or Swiss cheese

¼ cup sliced pimiento-stuffed green olives

½ cup light mayonnaise

1. Preheat the oven to 350°F. Coat an 8-inch square baking dish with cooking spray.

2. Melt the butter in a nonstick skillet, and cook the onion over medium-high heat until tender, about 5 minutes.

3. Transfer the onion to a large bowl and add the potatoes, cooked bacon, cheese, olives, and mayonnaise, stirring until well mixed. Transfer to the prepared baking dish. Bake, uncovered, for 30 to 35 minutes, until lightly browned and bubbly around the edges. Serve immediately.

POTATO-CRUSTED HAM AND CHEESE BAKE

Hash browns form a hearty crust for this easy brunch or lunch dish. This is lovely with a fresh fruit salad and hot muffins.

SERVES 6

2 cups frozen shredded hash brown potatoes, thawed

1 cup light cream or half-and-half

4 large eggs

¼ teaspoon pepper

1 cup cubed cooked ham (½-inch cubes)

¼ cup finely sliced green onions (white and green parts), divided

¼ cup finely chopped red bell pepper, divided

1 cup shredded medium or sharp Cheddar cheese, divided

1. Preheat the oven to 375°F. Coat a 9-inch pie pan with cooking spray and press the potatoes onto the bottom and up the sides of the pan. Bake for 10 minutes.

2. Combine the cream, eggs, and pepper in a medium bowl and beat until well mixed. Stir in the ham, 2 tablespoons of the green onions, and 2 tablespoons of the red pepper. Sprinkle half of the cheese over the potatoes. Pour the egg mixture over the cheese.

3. Bake, uncovered, for 35 to 40 minutes, or until a knife inserted in the center comes out clean. Top with the remaining cheese, 2 tablespoons green onions, and 2 tablespoons red pepper. Let stand for 10 minutes before serving.

SAGE, POTATO, BACON, AND CHEESE CASSEROLE

When sage is growing in my garden, I often make this breakfast casserole. It's a also a good recipe to make when you have some leftover potatoes.

— SERVES 8 —

1 pound sliced bacon, diced

1 medium sweet onion, chopped

8 large eggs, lightly beaten

4 cups diced cooked potatoes

2 cups shredded mild Cheddar cheese

1½ cups small-curd cottage cheese

1¼ cups shredded Swiss cheese

2 tablespoons chopped fresh sage leaves, or 1 tablespoon dried

1. Preheat the oven to 350°F. Butter a 9-by-13-inch glass baking dish.

2. Spread out the bacon and onion on a rimmed baking sheet and bake until the bacon is browned and crisp, about 10 minutes. Drain.

3. Transfer the bacon and onion to a large bowl and stir in the eggs, potatoes, cheeses, and sage. Transfer to the prepared baking dish. Bake, uncovered, for 25 to 30 minutes, or until the eggs are set. Let stand for 10 minutes before serving.

HERB-BAKED CHEESE AND EGG CASSEROLE

You can multiply the quantities in the ingredients list to accommodate any number of guests. This is really a per-serving recipe. Bake it in individual custard cups or 4- to 6-ounce ramekins.

SERVES 1

1 tablespoon butter, melted

1 large egg

1 tablespoon half-and-half

1 tablespoon shredded mild Cheddar cheese

Pinch of dried basil

Pinch of dried oregano

Pinch of dried thyme

Pinch of dried parsley

Pinch of pepper

2 teaspoons grated Parmesan cheese

Dash of paprika

1. Preheat the oven to 350°F. Pour the butter into an individual ovenproof casserole or ramekin. Top with the egg. Spoon the half-and-half over the top and sprinkle with the Cheddar cheese, the herbs, pepper, Parmesan, and paprika.

2. Place in a larger baking dish and add 1 inch of boiling water to the larger dish. Bake for 20 minutes, or until the egg is set. When done, run a knife around the edge and drain off any extra liquid.

PUFFY OVEN APPLE PANCAKE

Large and puffy baked pancakes are popular throughout Europe;
I was first introduced to this recipe in Finland. The proportion of eggs,
milk, and flour varies from one recipe to another, but this is my favorite.
It puffs up to make a golden, crusty cradle. I like to fill it with fruit
or berries at the table. Cook the sautéed apple slices while the pancake
bakes and bring them to the table in a serving bowl. A 17-inch slope-
sided paella pan is perfect for baking the pancake.

— SERVES 4 —

FOR THE PANCAKE:

1½ cups all-purpose flour

1½ cups milk

6 large eggs

1 tablespoon sugar

1 teaspoon salt

½ cup (1 stick) butter

FOR THE APPLE FILLING:

2 large Golden Delicious or Granny Smith Apples, peeled and sliced

2 tablespoons butter

¼ cup light or dark brown sugar

Whipped cream for serving (optional)

1. *To make the pancake:* In a bowl, whisk together the flour, milk, eggs, sugar, and salt until no lumps remain. Let stand for 30 minutes. (You can mix the batter the night before, cover, and refrigerate. Remove from the refrigerator when you begin preheating the oven.)

2. Preheat the oven to 450°F. While the oven preheats, place a large slope-sided baking pan or ovenproof skillet into the oven and add the butter. When the butter is melted, remove from the oven.

3. Pour the pancake mixture into the heated pan and return to the oven. Bake the pancake for 15 to 20 minutes, until the edges are puffed high and golden.

4. *To make the apple filling:* While the pancake bakes, in a medium skillet, sauté the apples in the butter until tender, 5 to 10 minutes. Add the brown sugar and stir until dissolved. Transfer to a serving bowl.

5. To serve the pancake, be sure guests are at the table when you bring it in, as it will slump quickly. Cut the pancake into quarters, and fill each serving with sautéed apples. Pass whipped cream on the side, if desired.

SWEDISH LINGONBERRY PANCAKE CASSEROLE

Many people enjoy their Swedish pancakes, which are as thin as crêpes, with lingonberry preserves. Here's a way to make the pancakes ahead of time and reheat them in casserole form so that you, the cook, will be able to enjoy the fruits of your labor. This makes a pretty presentation when you unmold the casserole onto a serving plate. Cut into wedges to serve.

SERVES 6

3 tablespoons butter, melted, plus extra for the dish

½ cup sugar

1 tablespoon cinnamon

3 large eggs

2 ½ cups milk

1 ¼ cups flour

½ teaspoon salt

Vegetable oil for cooking the pancakes

1 jar (14 ounces) lingonberry preserves, plus extra for serving (optional)

Whipped cream for serving

1. Preheat the oven to 325°F. Butter an 8-inch round casserole or soufflé dish. Stir the sugar and cinnamon together in a small bowl.

2. In a large bowl, beat the eggs with half the milk. Add the flour and salt and stir until smooth. Stir in the 3 tablespoons melted butter and the remaining milk; the batter will be thin.

3. Heat a griddle or large nonstick skillet with about 1 tablespoon of vegetable oil. For each pancake, pour about ¼ cup batter onto the griddle and cook over medium heat for about 1 minute, until the pancake develops golden brown spots on the bottom side. With a spatula, turn the pancake and cook until golden brown, about 30 seconds. Continue cooking the pancakes, adding more oil to the pan as needed. You will end up with about 15 or 16 thin pancakes, about 8 inches in diameter.

4. Place each pancake into the prepared casserole as it is cooked. Sprinkle each with cinnamon sugar and spread with lingonberry preserves and layer them in the casserole dish. (At this point the casserole can be covered and refrigerated for serving later.)

5. Before serving, bake, uncovered, for 15 minutes or until heated through. Cut into wedges and serve with whipped cream and additional lingonberry preserves, if desired.

THREE CHEESES AND CHILE CUSTARD

This baked custard makes a tasty breakfast, but it can also be cut into small squares and served with crisp tortilla chips as a snack or appetizer. To make this casserole even quicker and easier, purchase already shredded cheeses.

SERVES 6

4 large eggs

½ teaspoon baking powder

¼ cup whole-wheat flour

½ teaspoon dry mustard

1 cup cottage cheese

1 cup shredded Cheddar cheese

1 cup shredded Monterey Jack cheese

2 cans (4 ounces each) chopped green chiles

Sliced avocado for garnish

Tomato salsa (mild, medium, or hot) for garnish

1. Preheat the oven to 350°F. Coat a 2-quart shallow casserole with cooking spray.

2. In a large bowl, beat the eggs. Add the baking powder, flour, and mustard and stir until smooth. Stir in the cheeses and chiles. Pour into the casserole and bake, uncovered, for 25 to 30 minutes, until set.

3. To serve, cut into squares and garnish with slices of avocado and dollops of salsa.

Chapter 5
POULTRY CASSEROLES

○ ○ ○ ○ ○

Chicken offers such a variety of choices, it can be mind-boggling: cook it whole, cut it into pieces, leave the bone in and skin on or not. No wonder it is a favorite with adults and children alike.

The bland flavor of chicken makes it easily adaptable to many cuisines. Flavored with curry and coconut milk, it becomes a Vietnamese dish (page 158). Made with ginger, garlic, and chiles and served over basmati rice, it is transformed into an Indian-inspired biryani (page 157).

What's more, chicken is high in protein but relatively low in fat, particularly the breast. Chicken breast becomes dry if overcooked, however, so it is a perfect candidate for casseroles. Enjoy classics such as Country Captain Casserole (page 152), French coq au vin in a casserole (page 184), King Ranch Chicken (page 170), and Chicken Marengo (page 178), Napoleon's favorite.

The casseroles in this chapter use various types of chicken meat: boneless breasts; bone-in breasts; whole chicken, cut up; just legs or thighs; and cooked chicken meat. There are also some recipes made with turkey and duck.

○ ○ ○ ○ ○

CONTINUED ON NEXT PAGE...

ASIAGO CHICKEN

Asiago is a semifirm Italian cheese with a rich, nutty flavor. If you can't get it, Norwegian Jarlsberg is a great substitute. Add a salad and bread to the menu, and you've got a really easy meal that is perfect for family or entertaining.

SERVES 8

4 tablespoons butter, melted, plus extra for the dish

8 boneless, skinless chicken breast halves (about 2 pounds total; see Note)

½ pound mushrooms, sliced

1 green bell pepper, seeded and diced

8 slices Asiago or Jarlsberg cheese

1½ cups milk

¼ cup all-purpose flour

½ cup sour cream

1½ cups dried herb stuffing mix

1. Preheat the oven to 350°F. Butter a 9-by-13-inch baking dish.

2. Rinse the chicken breast halves and pat dry with paper towels. Place in the baking dish and top with the mushrooms, bell pepper, and sliced cheese.

3. Mix the milk, flour, and sour cream in a small bowl and pour over the chicken breasts. Sprinkle the stuffing mix over evenly and drizzle with the 4 tablespoons melted butter.

4. Bake, uncovered, for 30 to 35 minutes, or until the chicken breasts are cooked through.

○ ○ ○ ○ ○

NOTE: If the chicken breast halves are very large, cut them in half, either lengthwise or crosswise, to make the servings uniform.

CHICKEN AND BROWN RICE CASSEROLE

Canned soups are high in sodium, but many love them for their convenience. Canned cream of chicken soup is an alternate ingredient here. For a healthier choice, make the Béchamel Sauce (page 21) before you begin to put this together.

SERVES 4

4 boneless, skinless chicken breast halves (about 1¼ to 1½ pounds total)

Kosher salt

Pepper

1 recipe Béchamel Sauce (page 21), or 1 can (10¾ ounces) cream of chicken soup

1 cup low-sodium chicken broth or water

¾ cup quick-cooking, long-grain brown rice

2 cups fresh or frozen vegetables, thawed if frozen, such as beans, peas, corn, or any of the many combinations available in your market's frozen food section

½ cup shredded Cheddar cheese

1. Preheat the oven to 375°F. Rinse the chicken breasts and pat dry with paper towels. Sprinkle with salt and pepper.

2. Combine the sauce or soup, chicken broth or water, rice, and vegetables in a shallow 8-by-12-inch baking dish. Top the rice layer with the chicken breasts. Spray a sheet of aluminum foil with cooking spray and cover the baking dish with the foil.

3. Bake for 45 minutes, or until the chicken is cooked through. Remove the foil and top the casserole with the cheese. Return to the oven for 5 minutes, or until the cheese melts.

CREAMY BAKED CHICKEN BREASTS

Put this one on your list of comfort foods. The chicken breasts, which are coated with a creamy, rich-tasting sauce spiked with dry white wine, bake over a bed of rice. Water chestnuts add a nice crunch. The sauce is made quickly in the same skillet you use to brown the chicken.

SERVES 6

2 cups cooked long-grain rice

6 boneless, skinless, chicken breast halves (1¾ to 2 pounds total; see Note)

1 teaspoon salt

¼ teaspoon pepper

4 tablespoons butter

2 tablespoons all-purpose flour

1 cup undiluted evaporated milk or light cream

¾ cup dry white wine or water

½ pound mushrooms, sliced

1 can (8 ounces) sliced water chestnuts, drained and rinsed

1 red or green bell pepper, seeded and diced

1 cup frozen or fresh green peas

¼ teaspoon dried thyme

1. Preheat the oven to 350°F. Coat a 9-by-13-inch baking dish with cooking spray. Spread the rice evenly over the bottom.

2. Rinse the chicken breasts and pat dry with paper towels. Sprinkle with the salt and pepper. Heat 2 tablespoons of the butter in a large non-stick skillet and brown the chicken pieces quickly on both sides over medium-high heat. Arrange the chicken on top of the rice in the baking dish.

3. Reduce heat to medium. Add the remaining 2 tablespoons butter to the pan and stir in the flour; whisk in the milk or cream, wine, mushrooms, water chestnuts, bell pepper, peas, and thyme. Heat to boiling, remove from the heat, and pour the sauce over the chicken.

4. Coat a sheet of aluminum foil with cooking spray, cover the baking dish, and bake for 25 minutes. Uncover and continue baking for another 10 to 15 minutes, or until the chicken is cooked through.

○ ○ ○ ○ ○

NOTE: For convenience, buy already boned and skinned breast halves. If yours are large, weigh out a total of 1¾ to 2 pounds, and split the breasts in half lengthwise. (Freeze any extra to use later.)

CHICKEN BAKED IN BEER

Beer adds a flavor boost to this dish, enhancing the taste of the chicken and the mushrooms. What can you do with the other half of the can of beer? Make Beer Biscuits, of course! (The recipe is on the facing page.) To reduce the fat in this dish, remove the skin from the chicken breasts.

SERVES 6

3 whole bone-in chicken breasts, split in half and skinned

¼ cup all-purpose flour

1 teaspoon salt

½ teaspoon pepper

2 tablespoons vegetable oil

1 recipe Béchamel Sauce (page 21)

½ pound mushrooms, sliced

½ can (¾ cup) beer, preferably dark, alcoholic or nonalcoholic

Toasted slivered almonds (see Note) for garnish

Beer Biscuits (facing page) for serving

1. Preheat the oven to 350°F. Coat a shallow 9-by-13-inch baking dish with cooking spray.

2. Rinse the chicken breasts and pat dry with paper towels. Mix the flour, salt, and pepper in a shallow bowl and toss the chicken in the mixture to coat.

3. Heat the oil in a large non-stick skillet. Add the chicken breasts and brown over medium-high heat on both sides. Remove to the baking dish.

4. Make the Béchamel Sauce (you can use the skillet you browned the chicken in to make the sauce).

5. Top the chicken with the mushrooms and pour the sauce over all evenly, followed by the beer. Bake, uncovered, for 1 hour, or until chicken is cooked. When ready to serve, sprinkle with the almonds. Serve with Beer Biscuits.

○ ○ ○ ○ ○

NOTE: To toast the almonds, spread on a baking sheet and place into a 350°F oven. Toast for 5 to 10 minutes, stirring often, until lightly browned.

BEER BISCUITS

MAKES 6 LARGE BISCUITS

2 cups all-purpose flour

3 teaspoons baking powder

1 teaspoon salt

4 tablespoons butter or shortening

½ can (¾ cup) beer

1. Preheat the oven to 450°F.

2. In a large bowl, stir together the flour, baking powder, and salt. Cut in the butter or shortening with a pastry blender until the mixture resembles coarse meal. With a fork, stir in the beer and continue stirring until the dry ingredients are moistened.

3. Roll out the dough to a 1-inch thickness and, with a 3-inch round cookie cutter, cut into 6 rounds.

4. Place the rounds on an ungreased baking sheet and bake for 10 to 12 minutes, until golden brown. Serve hot.

CHICKEN BREASTS IN MUSHROOM SAUCE

Here's another easy, easy casserole that is great for company, but also when time is running short. You can easily double or triple the recipe for more people. To make this casserole healthier, I prefer to make my own mushroom sauce.

SERVES 4

4 boneless, skinless chicken breast halves (about 1¼ pounds total)

3 tablespoons all-purpose flour

1 cup sour cream

1 recipe Basic Mushroom Sauce (page 22), or 1 can (10¾ ounces) cream of mushroom soup

½ cup dry white wine

1. Preheat the oven to 325°F. Wash the chicken breasts and pat dry with paper towels. Place them in a shallow 9-by-13-inch baking dish.

2. Mix the flour, sour cream, sauce or soup, and wine in a medium bowl and pour over the chicken. Bake, uncovered, for 45 minutes to 1 hour, until the chicken is cooked through.

HAVARTI-STUFFED CHICKEN BREASTS

The creamy Havarti and herb butter create a luscious, saucy filling for the rolled chicken. For a perfect springtime menu, serve steamed asparagus and offer a crusty French bread to sop up the tasty sauce.

SERVES 8

½ cup (1 stick) butter at room temperture, plus extra for the dish

8 boneless, skinless chicken breast halves (about 2 pounds total)

½ teaspoon seasoned salt

½ teaspoon dried oregano

½ teaspoon chopped fresh parsley

¼ pound Havarti cheese, plain or herbed, cut into 8 strips

½ cup seasoned breadcrumbs

½ cup dry white wine

Avocado slices for garnish

Tomato wedges for garnish

1. Preheat the oven to 375°F. Butter a shallow 9-by-13-inch baking dish. Rinse the chicken breasts and pat dry with paper towels.

2. Place the chicken breasts between sheets of plastic wrap. Pound with the flat side of a meat mallet until thin and about doubled in size. Sprinkle with salt.

3. Combine the ½ cup butter, oregano, and parsley in a small bowl and spread about ½ tablespoon of the butter mixture over each chicken breast. Top each with a strip of cheese at one end.

4. Roll the chicken breasts, starting with the end that has the cheese, and tucking in the edges so that the rolls are the same length. (At this point you can freeze the stuffed chicken. Thaw in the microwave or defrost for 8 hours in the refrigerator. If cold, add a few minutes to the baking time.)

5. Melt the remaining butter mixture and brush over the chicken rolls. Then roll in the seasoned breadcrumbs. Place the rolls in the baking dish in a single layer.

6. Pour the wine over the casserole. Bake, uncovered, for 30 to 40 minutes, or until the chicken is cooked through and browned on top. (Be careful not to overcook the chicken breasts.) Garnish with the avocado slices and tomato wedges.

CHICKEN CACCIATORE ON POLENTA

The word *cacciatore* is Italian for "hunter," and it also describes chicken simmered in a well-seasoned tomato sauce. This hunter-style chicken is served over a bed of precooked polenta, which is available at many supermarkets.

3 tablespoons olive oil

2 packages (1 pound each) prepared polenta with basil and garlic

2 cloves garlic, minced

1 small red bell pepper, seeded and chopped

1 small green bell pepper, seeded and chopped

½ cup chopped sweet onion

1½ pounds boneless, skinless chicken breast, cut into bite-size pieces

1 can (14½ ounces) diced tomatoes with their juice

1 can (8 ounces) tomato sauce

2 teaspoons dried oregano or basil, crushed

½ teaspoon dried rosemary, crushed

¼ cup dry white wine

1. Preheat the oven to 375°F. Brush a 9-by-13-inch baking dish with 1 tablespoon of the olive oil. Slice the polenta into rounds and arrange on the bottom in one layer.

2. In a skillet, heat the remaining 2 tablespoons oil, add the garlic, and sauté over medium heat until aromatic. Brush the polenta lightly with some of the oil. Add the peppers and onion to the skillet and sauté in the remaining oil for 5 minutes.

3. Spread the chicken pieces over the polenta and top with the bell pepper and onion mixture.

4. Mix the diced tomatoes with their juice, tomato sauce, oregano or basil, rosemary, and wine and pour evenly over the ingredients in the casserole. Bake, uncovered, for 30 minutes, or until the chicken is cooked through.

CHICKEN, SHIITAKE, AND SNOW PEA CASSEROLE

It's easy to put together this dish with authentic Asian flavors if you keep a few basic ingredients on hand, like soy sauce, sherry, oyster sauce, water chestnuts, and cashews.

SERVES 4

3 tablespoons peanut or vegetable oil

1 large onion, halved, and thinly sliced

2 cups cooked rice

4 boneless, skinless chicken breasts halves (about 1 pound)

1 tablespoon soy sauce

3 tablespoons sweet sherry

3 tablespoons oyster sauce

2 whole cloves garlic, lightly crushed and peeled

1 slice fresh ginger, ⅛ inch thick

2 teaspoons cornstarch

¼ pound shiitake mushrooms, trimmed and sliced

¼ pound Chinese snow peas trimmed

5 water chestnuts, sliced

½ cup cashews, preferably unsalted

½ teaspoon sesame oil

1. Preheat the oven to 375°F.

2. In a large skillet or wok, heat 1 tablespoon of the oil. Add the onion and sauté for 2 minutes over high heat until lightly browned. Spread the rice over the bottom of a shallow 2-quart casserole and top with the sautéed onion.

3. Cut the chicken crosswise into 1-inch slices. Add 1 tablespoon of the remaining oil to the skillet. Add the chicken and sauté for 1 minute over high heat until lightly browned. Arrange the chicken in the casserole on top of the onion.

4. Combine the soy sauce, sherry, oyster sauce, garlic, ginger, cornstarch, mushrooms, snow peas, and water chestnuts in a medium bowl. Add the remaining 1 tablespoon oil to the skillet and then the soy sauce mixture. Cook, stirring, over high heat for 2 minutes until thickened. Pour evenly over the chicken in the casserole.

5. Cover and bake for 25 minutes, or until bubbly and the chicken is cooked through. Sprinkle with the cashews and drizzle with sesame oil.

CHICKEN, POLENTA, AND MOREL CASSEROLE

Dried morels are the most aromatic of mushrooms! Here chicken breasts and asparagus are baked in a creamy morel sauce atop sliced polenta. Add a salad of baby spinach leaves, a crusty bread, and fresh berries for dessert to round out the meal.

SERVES 8

1 ounce dried morel mushrooms (about 1½ cups)

2 tablespoons butter

½ cup minced shallots

2 tablespoons all-purpose flour

1 cup dry sherry

1 cup homemade (page 25) or prepared chicken broth

1 cup heavy cream

2 packages (1 pound each) prepared polenta

8 boneless, skinless chicken breast halves (about 2½ pounds total)

16 asparagus spears, tough ends trimmed

8 thin slices prosciutto

1 cup shredded Asiago or Gruyère cheese

1. Preheat the oven to 400°F.

2. Put the morels in a heat-proof bowl and add 2 cups boiling water. Let stand until softened, about 15 minutes. Gently squeeze the mushrooms while in the water to remove any grit. Remove from the water, but do not throw out the soaking water. Squeeze out most of the liquid from the mushrooms. Set the mushrooms aside, and let the grit settle to the bottom of the bowl of water. Then pour the soaking water into a measuring cup, and discard the grit remaining in the bowl.

3. Heat the butter in a large skillet and add the shallots. Cook over high heat for 2 minutes, until soft. Add the flour and stir until light golden brown, about 2 minutes.

4. Remove the pan from the heat and whisk in the soaking water, sherry, broth, and cream; then add the morels. Stir over high heat until the sauce is reduced to 2½ cups, 20 to 25 minutes.

5. Meanwhile, slice the polenta and place in a shallow 9-by-13-inch baking pan. Rinse the chicken and pat dry with paper towels. Wrap a chicken breast half and 2 pieces of asparagus with 1 slice of prosciutto. Place on top of the polenta. Repeat with the remaining chicken, asparagus, and prosciutto.

6. Pour the sauce evenly over the chicken. (The casserole can be made a day ahead up to this point, covered, and refrigerated. Bake for an additional 10 minutes.)

7. Bake, covered, for 30 to 45 minutes, until the chicken breasts are cooked through. Uncover and sprinkle with cheese. Bake 5 minutes longer, or until the cheese melts.

CHICKEN WITH MUSHROOMS AND ARTICHOKES

Serve this homey casserole with an arugula and basil salad, toasted focaccia, and fresh berries and cream for dessert.

SERVES 4

2 tablespoons butter, plus extra for the dish

2 Roma (plum) tomatoes, thinly sliced

2 cups cooked rice

4 boneless, skinless chicken breast halves (about 1 pound total)

Salt

Pepper

1 jar (6 ounces) marinated artichoke hearts, drained

½ pound mushrooms, sliced

5 green onions, chopped (white and green parts)

2 tablespoons all purpose flour

½ cup homemade (page 25) or prepared chicken broth

½ cup light cream or half-and-half

2 tablespoons dry sherry

1. Preheat the oven to 350°F. Butter a shallow 2-quart casserole.

2. Spread the tomato slices and rice over the bottom of the dish. Rinse the chicken breast halves and pat dry with paper towels. Sprinkle with salt and pepper to taste, and place them in the casserole dish. Cut the drained artichokes in half and place on top of the chicken breasts.

3. Heat the 2 tablespoons butter in a skillet. Add the mushrooms and green onions and sauté for 5 minutes over medium heat, stirring. Sprinkle the flour over all and stir to mix. Gradually add the chicken broth, cream, and sherry and cook until thickened, about 3 minutes. Pour over the chicken in the casserole. (The dish can be prepared ahead to this point, covered, and refrigerated until ready to bake. Add about 10 minutes to the baking time.)

4. Bake, uncovered, until bubbly and the chicken is cooked through, about 45 to 55 minutes.

CHICKEN BREASTS WITH WILD RICE AND RAISINS

Wild rice is a natural favorite in Minnesota. It's the seed of a grass that grows in shallow lakes and swamps in our state and is harvested in the fall. The Native Americans called it *mahnomen,* or "the good berry." Depending on how it's processed (that is, how dry the grain has been made), cooking time can vary from 25 to 45 minutes.

SERVES 6

2 tablespoons butter, plus extra for the dish

1 cup wild rice

2½ cups water

½ cup golden raisins

½ cup orange juice

2 cups frozen mixed vegetables

6 boneless, skinless chicken breast halves (about 1½ pounds total)

¼ cup all-purpose flour

1 teaspoon dried basil

½ teaspoon paprika

1 teaspoon salt

⅛ teaspoon white pepper

2 tablespoons canola oil

1 cup heavy cream

½ cup milk

1. Lightly butter a shallow 2-quart casserole.

2. Rinse the wild rice in 3 changes of hot tap water, or until the water is no longer cloudy. Put the rice and water in a medium saucepan and cover. Bring the water to boil, lower the heat, and simmer for 45 minutes, or until the rice is tender. Drain any extra water from the rice.

3. In a small saucepan, combine the raisins and orange juice. Bring to a boil, reduce the heat, and simmer for 5 minutes. Combine with the vegetables in a bowl and set aside.

4. Wash the chicken and pat dry with paper towels. On a plate, mix the flour, basil, paprika, salt, and white pepper. Roll the chicken in the flour mixture until evenly coated. Reserve the remaining flour mixture.

5. Preheat the oven to 350°F.

6. In a large heavy skillet, heat the 2 tablespoons butter and the oil. Add the chicken pieces and brown quickly over medium-high heat. Remove the chicken and set aside. Stir the reserved seasoned flour into the drippings in the skillet. Stir in the cream and milk and bring to a boil, stirring constantly. Boil for 1 minute. Stir in the raisin, orange, and vegetable mixture.

7. Arrange the rice in the buttered casserole. Cover with half of the sauce and lay the chicken on top. Cover with the remaining sauce. (The casserole can be made to this point, covered, and refrigerated. Bake for an additional 10 minutes.)

8. Bake, uncovered, for about 45 minutes, or until the chicken is cooked through.

CHUNKY CHICKEN CHILI

Sometimes called a "white chili," this chunky chicken chili is colorful as well as tasty when served with a fresh tomato salsa and cilantro.

SERVES 8

1½ pounds boneless, skinless chicken breasts

5 tablespoons olive oil

2 cups chopped onions

4 garlic cloves, minced

1 tablespoon ground cumin

¼ teaspoon cayenne pepper, or more to taste

1 teaspoon dried oregano

1 teaspoon salt, or more to taste

2 fresh or canned jalapeño peppers, seeded and minced

2 cups homemade (page 25) or prepared chicken broth

1 can (15 ounces) cannellini beans, rinsed and drained

2 cups frozen corn kernels, thawed

2 cups shredded white Cheddar cheese

Sour cream for serving

Tomato salsa for serving

Chopped fresh cilantro for serving

1. Preheat the oven to 350°F.

2. Wash the chicken breasts, pat dry with paper towels, and trim any fat. Cut crosswise into ½-inch strips.

3. Heat 3 tablespoons of the olive oil in a 3- to 4-quart Dutch oven. Add the chicken and cook, stirring, over high heat until almost cooked through, about 5 minutes. Remove to a dish.

4. Add the remaining 2 tablespoons oil to the pot and sauté the onions, garlic, cumin, and cayenne and cook, stirring, over medium heat for 5 minutes. Add the oregano, salt, jalapeño peppers, chicken broth, beans, corn, and the partly cooked chicken.

5. Cover and bake for 30 to 45 minutes, until hot and bubbly. Stir in the cheese and serve with the sour cream, salsa, and chopped cilantro.

COUNTRY CAPTAIN CASSEROLE

Stewed Country Captain is said to have originated in India. The name was supposedly inspired by the British army officer who brought the recipe to England. It was probably brought to the United States by British immigrants. The fact that there are so many versions of this recipe indicates that it has become an American classic.

SERVES 6

6 boneless, skinless chicken breast halves (1½ to 2 pounds total)

1 teaspoon salt

1½ tablespoons paprika

1 large onion, halved and sliced

1 green bell pepper, cut into 1-inch pieces

⅓ cup raisins

1 tablespoon vegetable oil

2 cloves garlic, minced

1 tablespoon curry powder

1 can (14½ ounces) diced tomatoes with their juice

2 tablespoons cornstarch

3 cups hot cooked rice for serving

Chopped fresh parsley for garnish

½ cup slivered almonds, toasted, for garnish (see Note)

1. Preheat the oven to 350°F. Butter a 9-by-13-inch casserole.

2. Rinse the chicken breast halves and pat dry with paper towels. Arrange in the casserole and sprinkle with salt and paprika. Top with the onion, pepper pieces, and raisins.

3. Heat the oil in a small skillet and add the garlic. Cook for 15 seconds over medium heat and add the curry powder. Cook, stirring, for 1 minute. Mix the tomatoes in their juice with the cornstarch in a small bowl and add to the skillet. Bring to a boil and cook, stirring, until thickened.

4. Pour the tomato mixture over the chicken pieces. Cover and bake for about 1 hour, or until the chicken is cooked through.

5. Serve the chicken over hot cooked rice and spoon some of the sauce over each serving. Garnish with the parsley and slivered almonds.

○ ○ ○ ○ ○

NOTE: To toast the almonds, spread out on a baking sheet and place into the 350°F oven. Toast for 5 to 10 minutes, stirring often, until aromatic and lightly browned.

CURRIED CHICKEN BREAST CASSEROLE

A simple curry sauce flavors the chicken as it bakes. Serve with additional toppings, and it will taste as if you've spent the whole day preparing this delicious curry.

SERVES 6

1½ cups basmati or another long-grain rice

1½ cups homemade (page 25) or prepared chicken broth

1½ pounds boneless, skinless chicken breast halves

4 tablespoons flour, divided

¾ teaspoon salt

¼ teaspoon pepper

2 tablespoons butter

½ cup chopped green onions (white and green parts)

2 teaspoons curry powder

2 cloves garlic, minced

1 can (14 ounces) unsweetened coconut milk

1 teaspoon sugar

2 tablespoons fresh lemon juice

1 cup pitted ripe olives, quartered

Toasted coconut for serving

Raisins for serving

Dry-roasted peanuts for serving

Mango chutney for serving

1. Preheat the oven to 350°F. Spread the rice evenly in the bottom of a 9-by-13-inch baking dish and pour the chicken broth over the rice.

2. Cut the chicken breasts into 2-inch pieces and dust with 2 tablespoons of the flour. Arrange the pieces on top of the rice and sprinkle with salt and pepper.

3. Heat the butter in a large nonstick skillet and add the green onions, curry powder, and garlic. Cook over medium heat for 3 to 4 minutes. Stir the remaining 2 tablespoons flour into the pan and slowly add the coconut milk, whisking to keep the sauce smooth. Cook until thickened. Add the sugar and lemon juice.

4. Pour the sauce over the chicken. Cover and bake 30 to 40 minutes, until the chicken is cooked through and the rice is done. Sprinkle with the olives.

5. Put the coconut, raisins, peanuts, and chutney in small serving dishes and pass at the table.

GINGER CHICKEN BREASTS BAKED WITH RICE AND MANGO-TOMATO SALSA

A few years ago I was a judge for my local newspaper's recipe contest. My category was chicken and poultry recipes. About half of the entries turned out to be exactly the same recipe with slightly different names, such as "My Own Original Chicken Casserole" and "My Mother's Favorite Chicken Casserole." Every recipe called for rice, chicken breasts, and various combinations of canned soup. Well, this recipe is along the same lines, minus the canned soup. I usually have homemade chicken broth on hand, which I cook up and freeze in 2-cup portions, ready to use whenever I need it.

—————— SERVES 4 ——————

1 cup basmati rice

½ cup chopped onion

2 cups boiling-hot homemade (page 25) or prepared chicken broth

4 boneless, skinless chicken breast halves (about 1¼ pounds total)

1 cup tomato salsa (mild or medium)

1 mango, peeled, pitted, and diced

1 tablespoon grated fresh ginger

Salt

Pepper

1. Preheat the oven to 350°F.

2. Mix the rice and onion and transfer to a shallow 2-quart casserole. Pour the boiling chicken broth evenly over the rice. Rinse the chicken breast halves, pat dry with paper towels, and lay over the rice. Mix the salsa, mango, and fresh ginger and spoon over the chicken. Sprinkle with salt and pepper to taste.

3. Cover and bake for 45 to 55 minutes, or until the chicken breasts are cooked through and the rice has absorbed the broth.

GRANDMA'S "GOURMET" CHICKEN BREASTS

This is an adaptation of an old-fashioned casserole that remains popular today. The original was probably designed by Campbell's ages ago, and it still hangs around in the card files of grandmothers. It suggested baking the casserole for 1½ hours. No wonder the chicken breasts were dry!

SERVES 4

4 boneless, skinless chicken breast halves (about 1 pound)

4 slices (¼ pound total) Swiss or Jarlsberg cheese

1 recipe Basic Mushroom Sauce (page 22), or 1 can (10¾ ounces) cream of mushroom soup

¼ cup dry sherry

1 cup prepared crisp croutons

2 tablespoons butter, melted

1. Preheat the oven to 325°F.

2. Rinse the chicken breasts, pat dry with paper towels, and place in a shallow 8- or 9-inch square baking dish. Arrange a cheese slice on top of each piece of chicken.

3. Combine the sauce or soup with the sherry and pour over the cheese.

4. In a medium bowl, mix the croutons with the melted butter and sprinkle over the top. Bake, uncovered, for 30 to 35 minutes, until the chicken breasts are cooked through.

RASPBERRY-GLAZED CHICKEN BREASTS

Inspired when our raspberry patch was red with berries, I added fresh raspberries as a garnish for these quickly baked chicken breasts glazed with raspberry jam. If you don't have a berry patch, it's worth splurging on raspberries just to scatter some on this dish.

SERVES 6

1 cup medium-grain rice

1½ cups homemade (page 25) or prepared chicken broth

Pinch of saffron threads

6 boneless, skinless chicken breast halves (1½ to 1¾ pounds total)

3 tablespoons fresh thyme leaves, or 2 teaspoons dried thyme

¾ teaspoon sweet Hungarian paprika

Salt

Pepper

FOR THE GLAZE:

3 tablespoons seedless raspberry jam

2 tablespoons red wine vinegar

2 tablespoons light or dark brown sugar

2 cloves garlic, minced

1 teaspoon olive oil

¼ teaspoon ground cumin

½ cup raspberries for garnish

2 tablespoons pine nuts for garnish

1. Preheat the oven to 375°F. Butter a shallow 2-quart casserole.

2. Sprinkle the rice into the dish evenly. Mix the chicken broth and saffron and pour over the rice. Rinse the chicken and pat dry with paper towels. Lay over the rice and sprinkle with thyme, paprika, salt, and pepper. (You can assemble the dish in advance up to this point. Refrigerate for up to 1 day, and add 10 extra minutes to the covered baking time.)

3. Cover the casserole and bake for 15 minutes. Uncover and bake for 20 minutes longer, or until the chicken is cooked through.

4. *Meanwhile, make the glaze:* Mix the raspberry jam, vinegar, brown sugar, garlic, olive oil, and cumin and brush over the chicken.

5. Bake for 10 minutes longer, garnish with the raspberries and pine nuts, and serve.

SOUTH INDIAN BIRYANI WITH BASMATI RICE

The deep flavors and piquant aromas of southern Indian cooking come to life in this recipe. The chicken bakes in a yogurt and tomato sauce rich with herbs and spices.

SERVES 4

2½ tablespoons vegetable oil

1 cardamom pod

1 whole clove

1 cinnamon stick

4 medium onions (about 1 pound total), chopped

3 tablespoons chopped garlic

3 tablespoons chopped fresh ginger

1 pound boneless, skinless chicken breast halves, cut into 1-inch cubes

1 tablespoon chili powder

1½ medium tomatoes, chopped

2 cups plain yogurt

1½ cups plus 3 tablespoons water

1 cup basmati rice

Salt

1 to 2 tablespoons fresh lemon juice

1 teaspoon butter

1 bunch fresh mint, chopped

1 bunch fresh cilantro, chopped

1. Preheat the oven to 400°F.

2. Heat the oil in a large flame-proof casserole or a Dutch oven over medium heat. Add the cardamom pod, clove, and cinnamon stick, and sauté for 1 minute until aromatic. Stir in the chopped onions, and sauté until golden brown. Stir in the garlic and ginger and the chicken pieces, and fry for about 3 minutes. Stir in the chili powder, and cook for 3 or 4 minutes. Stir in the tomatoes, and cook for about 5 minutes. Mix the yogurt with 3 table-spoons water in a small bowl, and stir into the sauce.

3. Cover the pot, and bake until the sauce is somewhat thick-ened and concentrated, about 15 minutes.

4. Put the remaining water in a medium saucepan. Rinse the rice well and add to the water. Heat the water to boiling, lower the heat, and simmer the rice for about 7 minutes; it will be only partly cooked.

5. Stir the rice with the water into the chicken and sauce. Taste and add salt. Stir in the lemon juice and butter, cover the pot, and bake for 30 min-utes. Discard the cardamom pod, clove, and cinnamon stick before serving. Sprinkle with chopped mint and cilantro.

VIETNAMESE CURRIED CHICKEN BREASTS

The basic recipe for this curry sounded good to me, so I decided to put everything together in a casserole. The potatoes broke down into a nice thickener for the juices, which we sopped up with some crusty French bread.

SERVES 6

2 tablespoons peanut oil

2 cloves garlic, minced

1 medium onion, chopped

2 tablespoons curry powder

1 teaspoon red or green Thai curry paste (see Note)

3 large potatoes, peeled and shredded

2 carrots, peeled and shredded

1 stalk fresh lemongrass, cut up (see Note)

2 stalks celery, chopped

6 boneless, skinless chicken breast halves, cut into eighths (about 1½ pounds total)

1 can (14 ounces) Thai unsweetened coconut milk

1 cup homemade (page 25) or prepared chicken broth

1 teaspoon salt

1 teaspoon pepper

Fresh chopped cilantro for garnish

1. Preheat the oven to 350°F.

2. Place a Dutch oven over medium-high heat, warm the peanut oil, and add the garlic, onion, curry powder, curry paste, potatoes, carrots, lemongrass, and celery. Cook, stirring, until aromatic.

3. Add the chicken breast pieces and stir to coat well. Pour the coconut milk and chicken broth over all and stir to coat the chicken. Sprinkle with salt and pepper.

4. Cover and bake for 1 hour, or until the chicken breasts are cooked through. Sprinkle generously with chopped fresh cilantro.

NOTES: Thai curry paste is available in the Asian section of most large supermarkets as well as in Asian markets.

Lemongrass has long, thin, gray-green leaves and a woody base. It lends food a sour-lemon flavor and fragrance similar to the citrus oil that is in lemon zest. Lemongrass also goes by the name "citronella root." To trim the lemongrass, cut the leaves off of the woody base. Then peel away the papery leaves wrapped tightly around the base and use the white core.

ALMOND CHICKEN WITH BROCCOLI AND CREAM SAUCE

This make-ahead casserole is perfect for easy entertaining. Chicken breasts bathed with a lemon and sherry cream sauce are topped with crunchy cornflakes and almonds. Add sliced tomatoes and a green salad to the menu. A cake topped with fresh strawberries would be a lovely dessert.

SERVES 6

3 tablespoons butter, plus extra for the dish

6 boneless, skinless chicken breast halves (about 2 pounds total)

2 cups water

2 teaspoons salt

1 large bunch (about 2 pounds) fresh broccoli, trimmed, stems peeled

3 tablespoons all-purpose flour

1 cup milk

3 tablespoons dry sherry

½ cup mayonnaise

1 teaspoon fresh lemon juice

1 teaspoon dried tarragon

½ cup whipping cream, whipped until soft peaks form

1 cup grated Parmesan cheese, divided

½ cup cornflakes

2 tablespoons melted butter

¼ cup sliced almonds

1. Preheat the oven to 400°F. Butter a shallow 9-by-13-inch baking dish.

2. Place the chicken breasts into a skillet and add the 2 cups water and the salt. Bring to a boil, reduce the heat, and simmer for 25 minutes, or until the chicken is cooked through. Set aside in the water.

3. Put the broccoli into a saucepan, add water to cover, and heat to boiling. Continue boiling for 6 to 8 minutes, until just tender. Drain and arrange the broccoli in a single layer in the baking dish.

4. Remove the chicken from the skillet and strain the broth. Lay the chicken over the broccoli. Return the strained broth to the pan and boil until reduced to 1 cup.

5. In a saucepan, melt the 3 tablespoons butter and stir in the flour. Whisk in the reduced broth and the milk and cook until the sauce is thickened. Whisk in the sherry, mayonnaise, lemon juice, and tarragon. Fold in the whipped cream and ½ cup of the Parmesan cheese.

6. Spread the sauce over the chicken and top with the remaining ½ cup Parmesan cheese. (The dish can be assembled ahead up to this point and refrigerated for up to 1 day. After adding the topping, bake for an additional 10 minutes.)

7. Toss the cornflakes in the melted butter and sprinkle over the casserole. Top with the almonds. Bake for 20 minutes, or until heated through and the top of the casserole is lightly browned.

CHICKEN BAKED WITH ORZO

Orzo looks like rice but cooks quickly like pasta, which is what it is. It's available in both white and mixed vegetable colors.

1 cup orzo, white or colored, cooked according to package directions

1 recipe Basic Mushroom Sauce (page 22), or 1 can (10¾ ounces) cream of mushroom soup

½ cup milk

2 cups cooked chicken, or 1 can (13 ounces) chicken or turkey breast, drained and cut up

¼ cup chopped green bell pepper

1 tablespoon chopped fresh basil leaves, or 1 teaspoon dried

½ cup breadcrumbs

2 tablespoons butter, melted

1. Preheat the oven to 350°F. Coat a shallow 2-quart casserole with cooking spray.

2. In a large bowl, combine all ingredients except for the breadcrumbs and butter. Turn into the casserole dish. Mix the breadcrumbs and melted butter and top the casserole with the crumbs. (At this point the dish can be covered and refrigerated for up to 1 day. Bake for an additional 10 minutes.) Bake, uncovered, for 25 to 30 minutes, until the crumbs are browned and the casserole is bubbly.

CHICKEN COBBLER

Pastry crisscrossed over a savory mixture of chicken and onions makes this a soul-satisfying casserole.

5 tablespoons butter

1 large sweet onion, diced

¼ cup all-purpose flour

1 can (12 ounces) evaporated milk

1 tablespoon chicken broth base

½ cup dry white wine

¼ teaspoon pepper

3 cups coarsely chopped cooked chicken

3 tablespoons chopped fresh parsley

½ cup finely chopped pecans, toasted (see Note)

½ cup grated Parmesan cheese

1 recipe Flaky Pastry (page 32)

1. Preheat the oven to 425°F. Grease a shallow 2-quart casserole using about 2 teaspoons of the butter.

2. In a large skillet, melt the remaining butter over medium heat and add the onion. Sauté for 20 minutes, or until caramel-colored. Add the flour and cook, stirring constantly, for 1 minute. Stir in the evaporated milk, chicken broth base, wine, and pepper. Cook, stirring, for 5 minutes, or until thickened. Remove from the heat and stir in the chicken and parsley. Spread out in the casserole and sprinkle with the pecans and Parmesan cheese.

3. Prepare the pastry, refrigerate for 30 minutes, and roll out to ¼-inch thickness. Cut into 1-inch-wide strips and arrange them in a lattice design over the filling. Reserve any scraps and roll out into additional strips.

4. Bake the casserole for 35 to 40 minutes, or until golden brown. Put any extra rolled-out strips on a cookie sheet and bake during the last 10 to 12 minutes. Serve with the cobbler.

○ ○ ○ ○ ○

NOTE: To toast the pecans, preheat the oven to 350°F. Spread out the nuts on a baking sheet and bake, stirring occasionally, for 5 to 10 minutes, until aromatic and lightly browned.

CHICKEN NOODLE CASSEROLE

This is an "assemble ahead and bake later" dish. In Minnesota, where we call casseroles "hot dishes," it's a convenient choice for hockey moms, who spend the last minutes before dinnertime providing taxi service for their kids.

SERVES 6

½ cup (1 stick), plus 2 tablespoons butter, plus extra for the dish

1 package (8 ounces) egg noodles, cooked according to package directions and drained

½ cup flour

2 cups homemade (page 25) or prepared chicken broth

2 cups light cream or half-and-half

2 teaspoons salt

Dash of pepper

½ teaspoon dried sage

2 cups frozen peas, thawed

¼ pound mushrooms, sliced

½ cup chopped red bell pepper

2 cups diced cooked chicken

2 cups shredded Cheddar or Monterey Jack cheese

½ cup fine dry breadcrumbs

1. Preheat the oven to 350°F. Butter a 3-quart casserole. Spread out the cooked noodles evenly over the bottom of the casserole.

2. In a medium saucepan, melt the ½ cup butter and add the flour. Cook, stirring, until the mixture is bubbly and slowly add the chicken broth and cream. Cook, stirring, until thickened and smooth. Add the salt, pepper, sage, peas, mushrooms, bell pepper, and chicken.

3. Pour the mixture evenly over the noodles. Sprinkle with the cheese. Mix the breadcrumbs and the 2 tablespoons melted butter and sprinkle over the casserole. (At this point the dish can be covered and refrigerated for several hours. Add 10 minutes to the baking time.)

4. Bake, uncovered, for 40 to 45 minutes, until bubbly.

CHICKEN WITH BROCCOLI AND WHOLE-WHEAT NOODLES

Cream cheese is the basis of the sauce in this creamy noodle casserole. We like this with a marinated cucumber and tomato salad and freshly baked Rosemary and Parmesan Casserole Bread (page 82).

─── SERVES 6 ───

1 package (8 ounces) cream cheese

2 cups shredded sharp Cheddar cheese

1 cup milk

½ cup sour cream

2 cups chopped cooked chicken or turkey

3 cups broccoli florets, cooked until crisp-tender

1 package (8 ounces) whole-wheat egg noodles, cooked according to package directions and drained

1 tablespoon chopped fresh chives

1. Preheat the oven to 350°F. Butter a 3-quart casserole.

2. In a medium saucepan over low heat, combine the cream cheese, Cheddar cheese, milk, and sour cream. Cook, stirring, until the sauce is smooth, but do not let it boil.

3. Add the chicken, broccoli, and noodles and mix well. Pour into the casserole dish and sprinkle with the chives.

(At this point the casserole can be covered and refrigerated for for up to 1 day. Add 10 extra minutes to the oven time.)

4. Bake, uncovered, for 35 to 40 minutes, or until the center of the casserole is heated through and the edges are lightly browned and bubbly.

CHICKEN, MUSHROOM, AND RICE CASSEROLE

This is so easy to put together; you just mix all the ingredients, then bake. It's a great recipe for using leftover chicken or turkey.

SERVES 6 TO 8

2 cups cooked rice

2½ cups chopped cooked chicken

1 recipe Basic Mushroom Sauce (page 22), or 1 can (10¾ ounces) cream of mushroom soup

1 can (8 ounces) sliced water chestnuts, drained

½ pound mushrooms, sliced

2 small stalks celery, finely chopped

¾ cup mayonnaise

¾ cup grated Parmesan cheese, divided

Shredded Cheddar cheese

1. Preheat the oven to 350°F. Butter a shallow 9-by-13-inch baking dish.

2. In a large bowl, stir together the rice, chicken, sauce or soup, water chestnuts, mushrooms, celery, mayonnaise, and ¼ cup of the Parmesan cheese. Mix well to combine. Spread out in the prepared baking dish and sprinkle with the remaining ½ cup Parmesan cheese.

3. Bake, uncovered, for 25 to 30 minutes, or until hot and bubbly. Sprinkle with shredded Cheddar cheese and bake for 5 minutes, or until the cheese is melted.

CHICKEN WITH SUN-DRIED TOMATOES AND BROWN RICE

Sun-dried tomatoes add color, texture, and flavor to this simple casserole. Toss a green salad together and buy a crusty bread for a quick and easy meal.

─── SERVES 6 TO 8 ───

3 tablespoons butter, plus extra for the dish

1 large onion, thinly sliced

1 cup sliced mushrooms

½ cup julienned sun-dried tomatoes

2 cups cooked brown rice

1 cup homemade (page 25) or prepared chicken broth

4 cups diced or shredded cooked chicken

1 cup heavy or light cream

1. Preheat the oven to 350°F. Butter a 9-by-13-inch baking dish.

2. Melt the 3 tablespoons butter in a skillet and add the onion and mushrooms. Sauté until tender, about 4 minutes, but do not brown. Stir in the sun-dried tomatoes and remove from the heat.

3. Spread out the rice in the baking pan, and pour the chicken broth over the rice. Add the chicken, onion, mushrooms, sun-dried tomatoes, and cream. (At this point the dish can be covered and refrigerated for up to 8 hours. Add 10 minutes to the baking time.)

4. Cover tightly with lightly greased aluminum foil and bake for 35 to 40 minutes, until the rice is done.

CREAM OF CHICKEN HOT DISH

This is about as classic as a hot dish gets! (At least, that's what it's called in Minnesota.) To make this healthier, substitute white sauce for the cream of chicken soup.

2 quarts boiling water

1½ teaspoons salt

2 cups rainbow rotini pasta

¼ cup chopped sun-dried tomatoes (not oil-packed)

2 cups diced cooked chicken

1 recipe Basic White Sauce (page 18), or 1 can (10¾ ounces) cream of chicken soup

1 cup sour cream

2 cups frozen peas, thawed

1 cup finely crushed butter crackers, such as Ritz crackers

1. In a large pot, bring the water to a boil, add the salt, and cook the pasta for 7 minutes. Add the sun-dried tomatoes and cook for 2 minutes longer. Drain and transfer to a large bowl.

2. Preheat the oven to 350°F. Coat a shallow 2½- to 3-quart casserole with cooking spray.

3. Add the chicken, sauce or soup, sour cream, and peas to the pasta. Mix lightly, and transfer to the casserole. Top with the cracker crumbs. Bake, uncovered, for 30 minutes, or until crumbs are browned and the casserole is bubbly.

GINGER-CASHEW CHICKEN CASSEROLE

My late mother-in-law would have loved this—she was such a fan of what she called "Chinese food." I look at this as a way to give leftover chicken an Asian flair. You can assemble the casserole a few hours ahead of time and refrigerate it. Just before serving, pop it in the oven.

SERVES 6

1 tablespoon sesame oil

1 medium onion, halved and thinly sliced

1 stalk celery, thinly sliced on the diagonal

1 medium red bell pepper, seeded and cut into 1-inch pieces

1 cup sliced mushrooms

Pinch of red pepper flakes

1 can (20 ounces) pineapple chunks in juice

1 tablespoon cornstarch

1 tablespoon soy sauce

1 tablespoon grated fresh ginger

2 cups cooked rice

2 cups diced cooked chicken

½ cup cashew nuts for garnish

Chopped fresh cilantro for garnish

1. Preheat the oven to 350°F. Coat a deep 2½-quart casserole with cooking spray.

2. In large wok or nonstick skillet, heat the sesame oil. Add the onion, celery, bell pepper, and mushrooms and sauté over high heat, stirring, for about 2 minutes, until the vegetables are crisp-tender. Add the red pepper flakes.

3. Drain the pineapple over a small bowl to catch the juice. Add the cornstarch, soy sauce, and ginger to the juice. Pour the sauce into the wok, heat to boiling, and cook, stirring, until thickened.

4. Spread out the rice in the casserole. Add the chicken and pineapple chunks to the vegetables in the wok. Mix well and pour over the rice. (The casserole can be prepared 1 day in advance up to this point, covered, and refrigerated. Add 10 minutes to the baking time.)

5. Bake, uncovered, for 20 to 25 minutes, until hot. Sprinkle with the cashews and cilantro.

ITALIAN CHICKEN PIE

Get the table ready with a Chianti bottle "candlestick" and a red-checkered tablecloth while this casserole cooks. Add a Caesar salad and Italian bread to complete the menu.

SERVES 6

⅓ cup grated Parmesan cheese

2 cups diced cooked chicken (½-inch dice)

½ cup shredded mozzarella cheese

½ teaspoon dried oregano

½ teaspoon dried basil

2 cloves garlic, minced

1 can (14½ ounces) diced tomatoes with their juice

FOR THE TOPPING:

½ cup all-purpose flour

1 teaspoon baking powder

1 teaspoon salt

¼ cup vegetable oil

1 cup nonfat, 2%, or whole milk

2 large eggs

½ cup shredded mozzarella cheese

1. Preheat the oven to 400°F. Coat a 9-inch round pie pan with cooking spray and sprinkle the Parmesan cheese evenly over the bottom.

2. Scatter the chicken over the cheese. Top with the ½ cup shredded mozzarella cheese, the oregano, and basil. Mix the garlic with the diced tomatoes with their juice and spread evenly over all.

3. *To make the topping:* In a small bowl, mix together the flour, baking powder, and salt.

Whisk in the oil, milk, and eggs and continue whisking until the mixture is smooth like pancake batter.

4. Pour the batter over the chicken mixture in the pan. Bake, uncovered, for 35 minutes, or until set. Remove from the oven and immediately sprinkle with the ½ cup mozzarella. Let stand about 10 minutes before serving.

PASTA AND CHICKEN ALFREDO

Fettuccine Alfredo is a classic pasta dish. I've converted it into a casserole and included chicken or turkey meat; it's a great way to use leftovers. I often make this on Friday after Thanksgiving with almost any kind of pasta I happen to have on hand. Alfredo sauce is made with butter, Parmesan, and cream. Quick Alfredo Sauce deviates from that recipe but produces a creamy sauce that is easily made and better than the bottled variety you can buy.

SERVES 6

3 tablespoons butter, melted, plus extra for the dish

1 recipe Quick Alfredo Sauce (page 24), or 2 jars (10 ounces each) prepared sauce

8 ounces farfalle, fettuccine, or your favorite pasta

2 cups diced cooked chicken or turkey, or 1 can (13 ounces) chicken or turkey breast, drained

1 bunch green onions, thinly sliced (white and green parts)

2 cups frozen peas, thawed

1 teaspoon poultry seasoning

½ cup seasoned fine dry breadcrumbs

½ cup grated Parmesan cheese

1. Preheat the oven to 400°F. Butter a deep 3-quart casserole. Prepare the Alfredo sauce and have it ready.

2. Cook the pasta in a large pot of boiling water for 12 minutes, or until just tender but still firm to bite. Drain and transfer to a large bowl. Mix in the Alfredo sauce, chicken, green onions, peas, and poultry seasoning.

3. In a small bowl, mix the breadcrumbs, Parmesan, and 3 tablespoons melted butter.

4. Transfer the pasta mixture to the baking dish. Sprinkle with the crumb mixture. (At this point the casserole can be covered and refrigerated. overnight. Add about 10 extra minutes to the oven time.) Bake, uncovered, until the pasta is hot and the topping is golden brown, about 25 minutes.

KING RANCH CHICKEN

In the Southwest every cook has his or her own favorite version of this casserole. It always contains corn tortillas or tortilla chips and other Southwestern flavors. The problem with many of these recipes is that they call for so much canned soup that the resulting casserole is extremely salty. Here's my take on the idea.

SERVES 8

12 corn tortillas (6 inches)

Corn oil for brushing

1 tablespoon butter

2 large cloves garlic, minced

2 medium onions, chopped

1 poblano pepper, seeded and chopped

2 teaspoons ground cumin

1 can (14½ ounces) diced tomatoes and green chiles with their juice

1½ pounds boneless, skinless chicken breast halves, halved lengthwise and cut into ½-inch slices

⅓ cup all-purpose flour

3 cups homemade (page 25) or prepared chicken broth

1 cup heavy cream

4 cups shredded Colby Jack cheese (see Note, facing page)

¼ cup chopped fresh cilantro, divided

Salt

Pepper

2 cups salted tortilla chips, crushed

1. Preheat the oven to 450°F.

2. Spread out the tortillas on 2 baking sheets and brush both sides with corn oil. Bake for 12 minutes, shifting the pans around halfway through baking, until the tortillas are crisp. Remove from the oven, cool, and break into pieces (about 1½ to 2 inches wide).

3. Reduce the oven temperature to 350°F. Coat a 9-by-13-inch baking dish with cooking spray and spread half of the toasted tortilla pieces over the bottom. Set aside the rest.

4. In a heavy nonstick skillet over medium heat, melt the butter and add the garlic, onions, poblano pepper, and ground cumin. Sauté for 2 or 3 minutes, until the mixture

is aromatic and the onions are softened. Add the tomatoes and chiles with their juice and the chicken and cook, stirring, until the chicken is no longer pink. Stir in the flour and slowly add the chicken broth, stirring to remove any lumps. Cook for 3 minutes.

5. With a slotted spoon, remove the chicken and cooked vegetables from the skillet and spread evenly over the tortilla pieces in the baking dish.

6. Add the cream to the liquid in the skillet and cook, stirring, until the sauce has thickened, 3 to 4 minutes. Season with salt and pepper to taste and set aside.

7. Sprinkle the chicken and vegetables with half of the cheese and half of the chopped cilantro. Pour the thickened sauce over evenly. Top with the reserved toasted tortillas, then with the remaining cheese, and finally with the crushed tortilla chips.

8. Bake, uncovered, until the filling is bubbling, about 30 minutes. Sprinkle with the remaining cilantro.

NOTE: Colby Jack cheese is a blend of Monterey Jack and colby. If it is not available in your stores, use a blend of half Monterey Jack cheese and half mild Cheddar.

PUERTO RICAN CREAMED CHEESE CHICKEN

If you have cooked chicken on hand, you can skip step 1. You'll need about 3 cups of cooked chicken for this recipe.

SERVES 8

2 pounds boneless, skinless chicken breasts or thighs

4 cups water

½ teaspoon salt

2 cups Basic White Sauce (page 18)

1 can (16 ounces) creamed corn

8 saltine crackers, crumbled

2 cups shredded mild Cheddar cheese

1. Wash the chicken and pat dry with paper towels. Put into a large saucepan and add water to cover. Add the salt. Cover and simmer for 20 minutes, or until the chicken is cooked through. Remove from the heat and cool the chicken in the liquid (see Note). Dice the meat.

2. Preheat the oven to 350°F. In another saucepan, prepare the white sauce.

3. Pour the canned corn into a deep 3-quart casserole. In layers, add half of the crumbled crackers, all the diced chicken, all the white sauce, and the remaining crackers. Top with the cheese. (At this point, the casserole can be covered and refrigerated for up to 1 day. Add 10 minutes to the oven time.)

4. Bake the dish, uncovered, for 30 minutes, or until the cheese is melted and the casserole is bubbly around the edges.

○ ○ ○ ○ ○

NOTE: The liquid can be used in the sauce, if desired, or saved for another use.

SIMPLE CHICKEN AND RICE CASSEROLE

When you have extra meat from a roasted or barbecued chicken on hand, this casserole will put it to good use in no time. Coleslaw is a perfect accompaniment, followed by apple pie for dessert.

SERVES 4

2 cups diced cooked chicken, or 1 can (13 ounces) chicken breast, drained and chopped

1½ cups cooked brown rice

2 tablespoons butter

1 cup diced celery

2 tablespoons minced green onions (white and green parts)

3 tablespoons all-purpose flour

1½ cups homemade (page 25) or prepared chicken broth

Salt

Pepper

Buttered fine breadcrumbs

1. Preheat the oven to 375°F. Coat a 2-quart casserole with cooking spray.

2. In a large bowl, mix the chicken and rice. Melt the butter in a large skillet or saucepan over medium heat and add the celery and onions. Sauté, stirring, for 2 minutes. Stir in the flour, coating the vegetables. Add the broth and cook, stirring, until thickened and smooth.

3. Combine the sauce with the chicken and rice mixture and season with salt and pepper to taste. Transfer to the casserole and top with buttered breadcrumbs. Bake, uncovered, for about 25 minutes, or until heated through.

BAKED CHICKEN CHOWDER

Before this casserole is assembled, a whole chicken is poached with herbs in a slow oven. To save time, you can purchase a rotisserie chicken from the supermarket and skip step 1.

SERVES 6

FOR THE CHICKEN:

1 chicken (3½ to 4 pounds), cut up

1 bay leaf

1 carrot, peeled and chopped

1 clove garlic

Handful of celery leaves

1 to 2 sprigs fresh parsley

1 tablespoon salt

½ teaspoon dried sage

4 cups water

FOR THE CHOWDER:

2 tablespoons butter

1 medium onion, diced

4 medium potatoes, peeled and diced

2 cups half-and-half

½ teaspoon dried thyme

Salt

Pepper

1. *To make the chicken:* Wash the chicken pieces. Put in a Dutch oven and add the bay leaf, carrot, garlic, celery leaves, parsley, salt, and sage. Add the water, cover, and bring to a boil. Lower the heat and simmer for 2 hours, or until the chicken is done. Cool in the broth.

2. Remove the meat from the bones and cut into chunks. You should have about 3½ cups of meat. Discard the bones and skin. Strain the broth and discard the residue. Skim the fat from the broth and boil until reduced to 2 cups.

3. *To make the chowder:* Preheat the oven to 300°F. Clean out the pot, and melt the butter. Add the onion and potatoes and sauté for 5 minutes, or until the onion is tender. Add 2 cups of the chicken broth. Add the chicken, half-and-half, and thyme, and season with salt and pepper. Place the pot in the oven, and bake, covered, until the potatoes are tender and the flavors have developed, about 45 minutes to 1 hour more. Serve hot.

ROASTED CHICKEN CASSEROLE WITH GARLIC AND ROSEMARY

What an effortless and delicious way to roast a whole chicken! This is an adaptation of a recipe from Julia Child's *Mastering the Art of French Cooking*.

SERVES 6

1 chicken (3½ to 4 pounds)

Salt

Pepper

4 tablespoons butter, divided

2 tablespoons dried rosemary leaves, crushed

4 sprigs fresh rosemary

6 cloves garlic, peeled

1 large onion, sliced

2 medium carrots, peeled and sliced

¼ cup all-purpose flour

2 cups homemade (page 25) or prepared chicken broth

1 tablespoon Madeira or port

Fresh herbs for garnish, such as tarragon, rosemary, parsley, or whatever is in season

1. Preheat the oven to 325°F. Rinse the chicken inside and out and pat dry with paper towels.

2. Sprinkle the chicken inside and out with salt and pepper to taste. Rub the skin with 1 tablespoon of the butter and the dried rosemary leaves. Put 1 tablespoon of the remaining butter in the cavity and stuff the rosemary sprigs and 3 cloves of the garlic inside the cavity. Tie the legs of the chicken together and turn the wings so that the tips are under the back of the chicken.

3. Put the remaining 2 tablepoons butter into a deep, heavy Dutch oven and place over medium-high heat. Add the onion, carrots, and remaining 3 cloves garlic and stir until they are coated with butter. Push most of the vegetables to the sides of the pot and place the chicken, breast side up, in the center of the pot. Cover the pot.

4. Roast the chicken and vegetables for 1 hour and 15 minutes, or until the vegetables are tender, you can easily wiggle a chicken leg, and the juices run clear when a thigh is pierced with a knife. Remove the chicken to a serving platter and surround it with the vegetables. Keep warm.

5. Place the pot over medium heat and whisk the flour into the drippings. Whisk in the chicken broth to make a smooth gravy. Taste for salt and pepper and add the Madeira.

6. To serve, spoon some of the sauce over the chicken and surround with fresh herbs.

CASSOULET WITH CHICKEN AND SAUSAGE

Like baked beans in New England, there are many versions of this dish in France. Usually it contains a variety of meats, but there are always beans. Serve this with a steamed vegetable and a loaf of bread.

SERVES 6

4 slices bacon, diced

4 sweet Italian sausages, cut crosswise into chunks

1 chicken (3½ pounds), cut up

1½ cups chopped onion

1 clove garlic, minced

2 cups chopped fresh parsley

1 can (15 ounces) tomato sauce

1 cup dry white wine

1 teaspoon salt

½ teaspoon coarsely ground pepper

1 bay leaf

6 cups cooked white beans (see page 30)

1. Preheat the oven to 375°F.

2. Place a large Dutch oven or heavy cast-iron casserole over medium heat. Cook the bacon until crisp and transfer to paper towels to drain. Crumble the bacon when cool. Reserve 2 tablespoons of the drippings in the pot.

3. Add the sausages and chicken pieces, raise the heat to medium-high, and brown, turning once. Push to the sides of the pot, and add the onion, garlic, and parsley. Lower the heat to medium and cook until the onion softens, 5 to 7 minutes. Add the tomato sauce, wine, salt, pepper, bay leaf, and beans. Cover and bake for 45 minutes, or until the chicken is done. Sprinkle with the cooked bacon.

CHICKEN, ARTICHOKE, AND MUSHROOM CASSEROLE ON POLENTA

As the polenta cooks beneath the chicken and vegetables, it rises up to almost encase the chicken. Serve with a platter of roasted red and yellow bell peppers.

SERVES 6

1 cup stone-ground or coarse cornmeal

4 cups hot homemade (page 25) or prepared chicken broth or water

1 to 2 teaspoons salt

1 whole chicken (3 to 3½ pounds), cut up into 8 pieces

½ teaspoon paprika

¼ teaspoon pepper

4 tablespoons butter

1 package (10 ounces) frozen artichoke hearts, cooked

½ pound mushrooms, sliced

2 tablespoons all-purpose flour

3 tablespoons dry sherry

1 teaspoon fresh rosemary leaves, or ½ teaspoon dried, crushed

1. Preheat the oven to 350°F. Coat a 9-by-13-inch baking dish with cooking spray.

2. Spread the cornmeal over the bottom of the dish and pour chicken broth or water over it. Add 1 teaspoon salt if using water rather than chicken broth.

3. Remove the skin and visible fat from the chicken and sprinkle with 1 teaspoon salt, the paprika, and pepper.

4. Melt the butter in a heavy skillet over medium-high heat and brown the chicken pieces, a few at a time. Place the chicken on top of the cornmeal and broth mixture in the baking dish. Arrange the artichoke hearts between the chicken pieces.

5. Add the mushrooms to the skillet and sauté for 3 to 5 minutes, or until lightly browned. Add the flour to the pan, stir until the flour is very lightly browned, and stir in the sherry and rosemary leaves. Spoon the mushroom mixture evenly over the chicken and artichokes.

6. Bake, uncovered, for 45 minutes, or until the chicken is cooked through and the polenta is done.

CHICKEN MARENGO

A dear friend, Harriet Viksna, a Latvian refugee, gave wonderful dinner parties and often served Chicken Marengo. Her table held eight, but she always invited twelve. The extra four sat at the corners of the table and ate off salad plates. One of the evening's delightful moments was when Harriet dramatically told the story of Napoleon and Chicken Marengo (see page 180).

Here is what Harriet served with Chicken Marengo: First, an apéritif of vermouth or Asti Spumante. Then a salad of potatoes and aïoli. We washed that down with an excellent red Barolo wine. For dessert, *spumone alla piemontese*, a mousse of mascarpone cheese and rum, was a sweet finale. We ended the evening with an espresso and an Italian liqueur.

SERVES 6

1 chicken (3 to 3½ pounds), cut into serving pieces

1 teaspoon salt

Pepper

¼ cup olive oil

½ cup dry white wine

1 small clove garlic

10 small mushrooms

2 cups diced tomatoes

1 white truffle, sliced, or 3 dried morels, crushed

A few tablespoons water or chicken broth as needed

FOR GARNISH:

6 slices bread

6 small eggs

Butter for frying eggs

Minced fresh parsley

1. Preheat the oven to 350°F. Have ready a 3-quart casserole with a cover.

2. Wash the chicken pieces, pat dry with paper towels, and sprinkle with salt and pepper. Heat the oil in a skillet and brown the chicken pieces. Remove to the baking dish.

3. Add the wine, garlic, mushrooms, tomatoes, and sliced truffle or crushed morels to the skillet. Simmer for 5 to 6 minutes, adding a little water or chicken broth if the sauce gets too dry.

4. Pour over the chicken, cover, and bake for 1½ hours, or until the chicken is cooked through.

5. *Meanwhile, make the garnishes:* Cut each slice of bread into a heart shape using a cookie cutter if you have one, or a round one if you don't. Toast on both sides. Fry the eggs in a small amount of butter until still runny in the middle and trim with a round cookie cutter. Arrange the eggs on top of the toasts.

6. To serve, arrange the chicken on a platter, pour the sauce over the chicken, and sprinkle with parsley. Arrange the egg-topped toasts around the edge of the platter.

THE STORY OF CHICKEN MARENGO

○ ○ ○ ○ ○

The city of Marengo, in the northwest Italian province of Piedmont, is south of Turin. It was at Marengo that Napoleon defeated the Austrians in June 1800, in a battle that he regarded as the most brilliant of his career. Napoleon had led his army in a march across the Alps, through the Saint Bernard Pass, into the Po Valley. His army clashed with the Austrians at Marengo on June 14, 1800. Napoleon's troops would have been defeated had reinforcements not arrived. Napoleon pursued his enemy with such vigor that he left the commissary—but not his cook, Dunand—far behind.

Napoleon, as was his habit, had not eaten before the battle and was certain to be famished. When he called for a meal, he demanded immediate service (and bolted it down in a few minutes when he got it). Dunand was desperate. Foragers were sent out and turned up a meager booty—a scrawny chicken, some tomatoes, a few eggs, a few crayfish, a little garlic, and a skillet. Dunand was without his cooking utensils. They had been unable to find butter, but had managed to get some olive oil.

Dunand cut up the chicken with a saber and fried it in oil. Next he made a sauce with crushed garlic and water, which he had made more palatable with a little Cognac filched from Napoleon's own canteen. Then he fried the eggs in olive oil and placed them on top of some emergency-ration bread supplied by one of the soldiers. They became the garnish along with the crayfish, which he also fried in oil. A measure of Dunand's desperation was the unholy combination of chicken and crayfish; he must really have felt that all the food he could scrape together would be barely enough.

Napoleon found the dish excellent and ordered that Chicken Marengo be served after every battle. On the next occasion Dunand tried to improve the dish by substituting white wine for water, adding mushrooms, and leaving out the crayfish. Napoleon noted their disappearance and demanded that they be restored to the dish, but not for gastronomic reasons. Napoleon was highly superstitious and chicken with crayfish was associated in his mind with victory.

Today, French cooks leave out the crayfish, but in the Piedmont, restaurants abide by the tradition of including crayfish for historical reasons. Sometimes they add what Dunand's foragers might have found in the area, but did not—white truffles.

SOUTH AFRICAN SPICED CHICKEN BIRYANI

Some sources claim Pakistan is the originator of this classic rice dish. Others credit northern India, and still others say that it was first created in South Africa. So it's not surprising that there are many different recipes for this richly spiced preparation. My version blends Indian influence with South Africans' love for chicken.

SERVES 6

1 chicken (3½ pounds), cut into 8 pieces

Pinch of saffron threads, soaked in 2 teaspoons hot water

2 cloves garlic

1 tablespoon fresh mint leaves

1 piece fresh ginger, about 2 inches thick and 2 inches long

1 teaspoon ground cumin

½ teaspoon ground turmeric

½ teaspoon cinnamon

1 teaspoon cardamom seeds, crushed, divided

1 cup plain yogurt

1 can (4 ounces) green chiles, drained

1 can (14½ ounces) diced tomatoes with their juice

1 cup dried lentils

3 cups water

1 teaspoon salt

1 cinnamon stick

2 medium onions, thinly sliced

2 tablespoons vegetable oil

1 cup long-grain rice

Chopped fresh parsley or mint for garnish

1. Preheat the oven to 350°F. Wash the chicken pieces, pat dry with paper towels, and put in a large bowl.

2. In a blender, combine the saffron threads, garlic, mint leaves, ginger, cumin, turmeric, cinnamon, ½ teaspoon of the cardamom seeds, the yogurt, green chiles, and tomatoes with their juice. Process briefly, so the marinade has a little texture and is not quite smooth. Pour over the chicken and stir to coat all the pieces evenly. Cover and marinate at room temperature for 1 hour, or cover and refrigerate for at least 4 hours or overnight.

3. Combine the lentils, water, salt, cinnamon stick, and remaining ½ teaspoon cardamom seeds in a medium saucepan. Heat to boiling, lower the heat, and simmer for 10 minutes. Remove the cinnamon stick.

4. Meanwhile, in a medium skillet, sauté the onions in the vegetable oil for about 7 minutes over medium heat until tender.

5. Transfer the sautéed onions to the bottom of a 3-quart casserole. Add the lentils and their simmering liquid and the rice and stir to mix. Arrange chicken pieces over the top and pour the marinade over all.

6. Cover the casserole and bake for 1 hour, or until the chicken is cooked through. Garnish with parsley and serve directly from the dish.

CHICKEN WITH FORTY CLOVES OF GARLIC

When garlic is cooked, it melts down to a sweet, less pungent paste, which adds a delicious, rich flavor to the whole dish. If everybody partakes of it, nobody has to worry about "garlic breath."

SERVES 6

1 chicken (3 to 3½ pounds), cut up

40 cloves garlic, peeled

¾ cup dry white wine

¼ cup olive oil

4 stalks celery, cut into 1-inch pieces

2 teaspoons dried basil

1 teaspoon dried oregano

½ cup minced fresh parsley

Pinch of red pepper flakes

Juice of 1 lemon

1 teaspoon salt

½ teaspoon freshly ground pepper

1. Preheat the oven to 375°F. Place the chicken pieces close together in a single layer in a shallow 9-by-13-inch baking dish. Distribute the garlic cloves over the chicken.

2. Drizzle with the wine and olive oil. Distribute the celery on top of the chicken. Sprinkle with the basil, oregano, parsley, red pepper flakes, lemon juice, salt, and pepper.

3. Cover with aluminum foil coated with cooking spray and bake for 40 minutes. Uncover and bake for 15 minutes longer, or until the chicken is cooked through.

CURRIED CHICKEN CASSEROLE

This is comfort food for a chilly evening. You just throw all the ingredients into the casserole—no browning is required first. And it tastes even better the next day.

SERVES 6

1 chicken (3 to 3½ pounds)

¼ cup all-purpose flour

1 large onion, thinly sliced

¼ cup raisins

2 tablespoons chopped green onions (white and green parts)

1½ teaspoons curry powder

½ teaspoon salt

½ teaspoon dried thyme

Pinch of red pepper flakes

1 red bell pepper, seeded and cut into ½-inch pieces

1 green bell pepper, seeded and cut into ½-inch pieces

1 clove garlic, minced

1 can (14½ ounces) diced tomatoes with their juice

3 cups hot cooked rice, for serving

¼ cup slivered almonds, toasted, for garnish (see Note)

2 tablespoons chopped fresh parsley for garnish

1. Preheat the oven to 350°F.

2. Cut the chicken into 6 serving pieces. Rinse and pat dry with paper towels. Remove the skin and visible fat from the chicken pieces. Rub with the flour and place in a heavy 4-quart casserole with a tight-fitting lid.

3. Add the onion, raisins, green onion, curry powder, salt, thyme, red pepper flakes, red and green bell peppers, garlic, and tomatoes with their juice.

4. Cover and bake 2 hours, or until the chicken is cooked through. Serve hot over rice. Spoon the pan juices over the chicken, and sprinkle with almonds and parsley.

○ ○ ○ ○ ○

NOTE: To toast the almonds, spread them out on a baking sheet and bake in a 350°F oven for 5 to 10 minutes, or until lightly browned, stirring occasionally. Watch carefully so they do not burn.

FRENCH CASSEROLE OF CHICKEN COOKED IN WINE

This is an adaptation of coq au vin. An old classic perhaps quite overlooked today, coq au vin is probably the most famous of all French chicken dishes. Although the recipe might appear involved, there are periods of unattended cooking as the chicken simmers in wine. The saving grace of this recipe is that it is even better when made a day ahead, so it's a great choice for a casual dinner party. I like to use a dry white wine rather than the traditional red.

SERVES 6

1 chicken (3 to 3½ pounds), cut up

2 tablespoons all-purpose flour

3 tablespoons butter or olive oil, divided

1 small yellow onion, chopped

3 cups dry white wine

3 cups homemade (page 25) or prepared chicken broth

1 bay leaf

1 sprig fresh parsley

1 teaspoon dried marjoram

1 teaspoon dried thyme

2 cloves garlic, peeled

12 small white onions, peeled and simmered until tender (see Note, facing page)

½ pound mushrooms, stemmed

Cooked baby potatoes, rice, or noodles for serving

1. Preheat the oven to 350°F. Wash the chicken and pat dry with paper towels. Cut the legs and thighs apart. Rub the chicken parts with flour and set aside.

2. Melt 1½ tablespoons of the butter in a heavy 3- to 4-quart Dutch oven. Add the yellow onion and sauté for 3 minutes over medium heat until translucent. Add the chicken pieces, a few at a time, and brown on all sides, removing the browned pieces to a plate as they are done.

3. When all the pieces are browned, return them to the casserole. Add the wine and broth. Add the bay leaf, parsley, marjoram, thyme, and garlic cloves. Bake, covered, for 45 minutes, or until the chicken is tender. Remove and discard the bay leaf and parsley sprig.

4. While the chicken cooks, melt the remaining 1½ tablespoons butter in a skillet. Add the small white onions and mushrooms and cook over high heat for 4 or 5 minutes, until lightly browned. Add to the casserole. **5.** Drain off the excess liquid from the casserole into the skillet; bring to a boil and boil until reduced by half. Pour the reduced juices over the chicken and serve with cooked baby potatoes, rice, or noodles.

○ ○ ○ ○ ○

NOTE: Small whole onions are available frozen and are a great time-saver. (They are also called pearl onions.) But, for the freshest and best flavor, buy them in the produce department of your market. Trim them and cut an X in the bottom of each one. Drop them into boiling water for 1 minute. Drain and peel. Return to the pan, add about ½ inch of water, and simmer slowly for 25 to 30 minutes, until the onions are tender.

FRUITED GINGER CHICKEN ON COUSCOUS

There is a great combination of flavors here. Garam masala, a blend of dry-roasted ground spices from India, adds complexity but not heat to this casserole. If you don't have any, you can substitute curry powder. The couscous makes a tender base for the chicken as it bakes.

SERVES 4

1 cup whole-wheat couscous

2 cups homemade (page 25) or prepared chicken broth

1 chicken (3 to 3½ pounds), quartered

Salt

Pepper

2 tablespoons olive oil

1 medium onion, chopped

2 cloves garlic, minced

2 teaspoons ground cumin

1 teaspoon garam masala or curry powder

½ cup chopped dried apricots

½ cup raisins

1 tablespoon grated orange zest

2 teaspoons minced fresh ginger

Chopped fresh cilantro for garnish

1. Preheat the oven to 375°F. Put the couscous in the bottom of a deep, heavy 3- to 4-quart casserole or Dutch oven. Pour 1 cup of the chicken broth over it and set aside.

2. Rinse the chicken pieces and pat dry with paper towels. Remove the visible fat and the skin, if desired. Sprinkle the chicken with salt and pepper.

3. Place a large heavy skillet over medium-high heat and add the oil. Add the chicken pieces and cook until golden brown over medium-high heat, about 5 minutes per side. Place on top of the couscous as the pieces are browned.

4. Add the onion, garlic, cumin, and garam masala to the skillet and cook, stirring, until the spices are aromatic, 2 to 3 minutes. Transfer to the casserole. Add the remaining 1 cup chicken broth, the apricots, raisins, orange zest, and ginger to the casserole.

5. Cover tightly and bake for about 40 minutes, until the chicken is cooked through. Garnish with the chopped fresh cilantro.

ROSEMARY CHICKEN AND RICE

Rosemary and garlic is a wonderful combination for cooking almost anything, but especially chicken. Serve this with a salad and crusty French bread to sop up the juices.

SERVES 6

1 chicken (about 3 pounds), cut up, or 3 pounds chicken legs and thighs

1 cup long-grain brown rice or basmati rice

3 cloves garlic, minced

2½ cups homemade (page 25) or prepared chicken broth

1 teaspoon salt

1 tablespoon dried rosemary

2 tablespoons fresh lemon juice

¼ cup mayonnaise

¼ cup fine dry breadcrumbs

½ cup grated Parmesan cheese

1. Preheat the oven to 350°F. Coat a 9-by-13-inch casserole with cooking spray. Wash the chicken pieces and pat dry with paper towels. Cut the legs and thighs apart.

2. Spread out the rice evenly in the bottom of the casserole. Sprinkle the garlic over the rice and pour the broth over all.

3. Arrange the chicken pieces on top of the rice. Sprinkle with salt, rosemary, and lemon juice.

Brush or spread mayonnaise over the chicken pieces and sprinkle with the breadcrumbs.

4. Bake, uncovered, for 1 to 1¼ hours, or until the chicken and rice are tender. Sprinkle with Parmesan cheese before serving.

SWEET-AND-SOUR CHICKEN AND RICE

It's okay to remove the skin from the chicken before cooking. This reduces the fat in the final dish, while the sauce keeps the chicken moist and juicy. If you are cooking for company, you might start the meal with a Thai pumpkin soup and serve an Asian eggplant dish on the side. Fresh fruits or berries are always a perfect dessert.

SERVES 4

1 chicken (2½ to 3 pounds), cut up

1 cup long-grain rice

2 cups homemade (page 25) or prepared chicken broth

1 can (8 ounces) crushed pineapple with its juice

¼ cup packed dark or light brown sugar

1 tablespoon cornstarch

2 tablespoons fresh lemon juice

1 tablespoon Dijon mustard

2 tablespoons soy sauce

1. Preheat the oven to 350°F. Coat a 2-quart casserole with cooking spray. Wash the chicken and pat it dry.

2. Put the rice in the casserole. Pour the broth over the rice, and top with the chicken pieces.

3. Mix the pineapple and juice, brown sugar, cornstarch, lemon juice, mustard, and soy sauce in a medium bowl and pour over the chicken.

4. Cover and bake for 1½ to 2 hours, or until the chicken is cooked through.

WEST AFRICAN CHICKEN WITH PEANUTS

In Africa, chicken is served very often, especially for company meals. Because the chickens are free-range, they are a little less tender, but more flavorful, than our supermarket variety. For the most authentic flavor, buy organic free-range chicken from your local farmers' market.

SERVES 4 TO 6

1 chicken (3 to 3½ pounds) quartered

2 tablespoons all-purpose flour

2 tablespoons peanut or vegetable oil

2 medium onions, chopped

1 cup homemade (page 25) or prepared chicken broth

½ cup crunchy peanut butter

Salt

Pepper

Pinch of cayenne pepper

1 tomato, chopped

Chopped peanuts for garnish

Chopped fresh cilantro for garnish

Hot cooked rice or millet for serving

1. Preheat the oven to 350°F. Rinse the chicken pieces and pat dry with paper towels. Remove any visible fat. Dust with the flour and shake off any excess.

2. In a large skillet, heat the oil. Add the chicken pieces, a few at a time, and brown on all sides. Remove the chicken to a heavy 4-quart casserole.

3. Add the onions to the skillet, reduce the heat to low, and sauté for 5 minutes, or until the onions are softened. Add the chicken broth, peanut butter, salt and pepper to taste, and the cayenne and mix until well blended. Spread the sauce over the chicken and sprinkle with chopped tomato.

4. Cover and bake for 1½ to 2 hours, or until the chicken is cooked through. Garnish with peanuts and chopped cilantro and serve with the hot cooked rice or millet.

ANCHO CHICKEN BREASTS WITH CORN

Oven-simmered in beer, and spiced with the slightly fruity flavor of ancho chile powder, this is a really simple casserole. It's a good one to keep in mind when you're looking for a one-dish meal. Bone-in chicken breasts are often huge—about 2 servings each.

SERVES 8

4 cups fresh or frozen corn kernels

4 bone-in chicken breasts (about 3½ to 4 pounds total), split in half

2 teaspoons ancho chile powder

1 can (6 ounces) tomato paste

1 bottle (12 ounces) beer

2 tablespoons all-purpose flour

1 teaspoon salt

½ teaspoon pepper

1 green or red bell pepper, seeded and diced

Hot cooked rice for serving

1. Preheat the oven to 350°F. Coat a shallow 2- to 3-quart casserole with cooking spray. Spread the corn over the bottom of the casserole in an even layer.

2. Wash the chicken breasts and pat dry with paper towels. Sprinkle with the chile powder and arrange in the casserole on top of the corn.

3. Mix the tomato paste, beer, flour, salt, and pepper in a small bowl and pour the sauce over the chicken.

4. Sprinkle the chicken with the bell pepper. Spray a sheet of aluminum foil with cooking spray and cover the casserole. Bake for 1½ to 2 hours, or until the chicken is tender. Serve with hot cooked rice.

CHICKEN THIGHS WITH SPINACH NOODLES AND AVOCADOS

This cheesy chicken and noodle casserole is topped with avocado just before serving. The avocado makes a creamy counterpoint to the mild heat from the green chiles.

SERVES 6

6 bone-in chicken thighs

4 cups water

2 teaspoons salt

1 can (4 ounces) whole green chiles, coarsely chopped

6 ounces broad spinach noodles

4 tablespoons butter

¼ cup all-purpose flour

Dash of cayenne pepper

2 cups half-and half

1 cup shredded Cheddar cheese

1 large ripe avocado, peeled and sliced

2 tablespoons fresh lime juice

1. Coat a 9-by-13-inch baking dish with cooking spray.

2. Put the chicken thighs in a deep pot and add the water and 1 teaspoon of the salt. Heat to simmering and simmer the chicken for 30 minutes, or until the thighs are cooked through. Remove from the heat and cool in the pot. Remove and discard the skin and bones. Put the meat in the baking dish and distribute the chiles over the chicken.

3. Cook the noodles according to package directions, drain, and set aside. Preheat the oven to 350°F.

4. Melt the butter in a medium saucepan over low heat. Stir in the flour, the remaining 1 teaspoon salt, and the cayenne. Add the half-and-half slowly, and cook, stirring constantly, until the mixture thickens. Add the cheese and stir until melted. Reserve 1 cup of this sauce. Mix the remaining sauce with the noodles, spoon into the casserole, and top with the chicken. Top with the reserved cup of sauce.

5. Bake the chicken, uncovered, for 35 minutes. Meanwhile, drizzle the avocado slices with lime juice and set aside.

6. Remove the chicken from the oven and top with the avocado slices.

CHICKEN, ROSEMARY, AND POTATO BAKE

There isn't a lot of sauce and creaminess to this casserole, but it is a fresh-tasting one-dish meal. This is my favorite dinner for those days when I don't really have time to make sauces or to even think!

SERVES 4

1½ pounds bone-in chicken legs and thighs

4 large potatoes, peeled and cut into 6 wedges each

2 medium carrots, peeled and cut into 1-inch lengths

¼ pound mushrooms

2 tablespoons olive oil

1 tablespoon balsamic vinegar

1 tablespoon chopped fresh rosemary, or 1 teaspoon dried, crushed

1 teaspoon kosher salt

¼ cup grated Parmesan cheese

1. Preheat the oven to 400°F.

2. Arrange the chicken, potato wedges, carrots, and mushrooms in a single layer in a 9-by-13-inch baking dish. Drizzle with the olive oil and vinegar. Sprinkle with the rosemary and salt.

3. Bake, uncovered, for 55 minutes to 1 hour, or until the chicken is cooked through and the potatoes are tender. Sprinkle with the cheese and let stand for 5 minutes, until the cheese softens.

CHICKEN THIGHS AND RICE

Here's a fresh-tasting, easily assembled dish that is low in fat. Add a salad if you like, and for dessert, a fruit sorbet or homemade cookies.

SERVES 4

¾ cup long-grain rice

1½ cups homemade (page 25) or prepared chicken broth

1 pound boneless, skinless chicken thighs

Salt

Pepper

2 tablespoons all-purpose flour

½ cup chopped onions

½ cup sliced celery

2 cups sliced mushrooms

4 cups broccoli florets

½ cup shredded Gruyère or Swiss cheese

Paprika for sprinkling

1. Preheat the oven to 350°F. Butter a 9-by-13-inch baking dish.

2. Sprinkle the rice evenly over the bottom of the baking dish. Pour the chicken broth over the rice. Rinse the chicken thighs and pat dry with paper towels. Season with salt and pepper and place on the rice. Sprinkle with the flour and scatter the onions, celery, mushrooms, and broccoli on top.

3. Coat a sheet of aluminum foil with cooking spray and cover the casserole. Bake for 1 hour. Uncover and bake for about 20 minutes, or until the chicken is cooked through. Sprinkle with the shredded cheese and a pinch of paprika. Return to the oven just long enough to melt the cheese.

ROASTED GARLIC AND LEMON CHICKEN THIGHS

If you like skin on chicken, leave it on. Otherwise, to cut fat and calories, remove it for this recipe. Real baby carrots are very tender, immature vegetables. However, the baby carrots commonly available in supermarkets are just big carrots cut small. Use whichever you can get your hands on!

SERVES 4

4 large bone-in chicken thighs (about 1 ¼ pounds total)

Juice of ½ lemon

3 to 4 cloves garlic, chopped

1 teaspoon kosher salt

3 tablespoons olive oil

1 teaspoon dried oregano

12 baby potatoes, scrubbed

12 baby carrots, or 4 large carrots, peeled and cut into 1-inch chunks

1. Preheat the oven to 400°F. Coat a 9-by-13-inch baking dish with cooking spray.

2. Rinse the chicken thighs and pat dry. Remove the skin unless you prefer it on. Arrange the chicken in the baking dish in a single layer, skin side up. Squeeze lemon juice over the thighs and sprinkle with the garlic, salt, 2 tablespoons of the olive oil, and the oregano.

3. In a medium bowl, toss the potatoes and carrots with the remaining 1 tablespoon olive oil. Scatter over the chicken.

4. Bake, uncovered, for 50 to 55 minutes, or until the chicken is cooked through and the potatoes and carrots are tender.

GREEK CHICKEN

Flavored with lemon, garlic, and olives, this is a light but satisfying chicken casserole that is actually quite low in fat. Mop up the tasty juices with crusty bread.

SERVES 6

6 bone-in chicken thighs, skin removed

2 tablespoons olive oil

6 baking potatoes, scrubbed and cut into 1-inch cubes (leave skins on)

2 cups baby carrots

6 cloves garlic, peeled

Juice of 1 lemon

½ cup pitted kalamata olives

3 lemons, cut into wedges

1 teaspoon kosher salt

1 teaspoon pepper

2 tablespoons chopped fresh oregano

2 tablespoons cold butter, cut into small pieces

Crumbled feta cheese for garnish

Crusty bread for serving

1. Preheat the oven to 375°F.

2. Wash the chicken thighs and pat dry with paper towels. Arrange the thighs in a single layer in a 9-by-13-inch baking dish. Drizzle with 1 tablespoon of the olive oil.

3. Toss the potatoes, carrots, and garlic with the remaining 1 tablespoon olive oil and squeeze the lemon juice over them. Arrange around the chicken in the dish. Arrange the olives and lemon wedges around the chicken. Sprinkle the chicken with salt and pepper. Cover and bake for 45 minutes.

4. Uncover and sprinkle the chicken with the chopped oregano and butter. Bake, uncovered, for 15 minutes longer, or until the potatoes are tender and the chicken is cooked through. Sprinkle with the feta cheese. Serve hot with chunks of crusty bread.

JALAPEÑO CHICKEN LEGS

Serve this Southwestern casserole with salsa and a steamed vegetable on the side. It goes well with a light Mexican beer or a chilled crisp white wine, such as Johannisberg Riesling.

6 bone-in chicken legs with thighs attached

2 tablespoons vegetable oil

2 cups sour cream

1 teaspoon salt

½ teaspoon pepper

2 tablespoons all-purpose flour

1 clove garlic, minced

1 to 2 jalapeño peppers, seeded and chopped

1 large onion, sliced

1 can (4 ounces) diced green chiles

Tomato salsa for serving

1. Preheat the oven to 350°F. Wash the chicken and pat dry with paper towels. Heat the oil in a heavy skillet. Add the chicken pieces, a few at a time, and brown on both sides. Arrange in a shallow 9-by-13-inch baking dish as they are done.

2. In a food processor fitted with the steel blade or in a blender, combine the sour cream, salt, pepper, flour, garlic, and jalapeño pepper. Process until smooth.

3. Pour the sour cream mixture over the chicken. Top with the onion and green chiles. Bake, uncovered, for 40 minutes, or until the chicken is cooked through. Serve with the tomato salsa.

OVEN-SIMMERED CHICKEN THIGHS WITH WINE, MUSHROOMS, AND HERBS

When chicken thighs are on sale at the market, I buy a dozen and make this recipe, which is similar to coq au vin, but with a little less fuss. If the mahogany color of red wine bothers you, this dish is equally tasty cooked with a dry white wine.

SERVES 6

6 slices bacon, cut into ½-inch pieces

12 bone-in chicken thighs, skinned and excess fat trimmed

1 teaspoon salt, plus more to taste

½ teaspoon pepper, plus more to taste

¼ cup all-purpose flour

¾ cup chopped sweet red onion

3 cloves garlic, minced

1 bag (16 ounces) frozen baby boiling onions

½ pound mushrooms, trimmed

2 tablespoons chopped fresh marjoram

1 cup dry red or white wine

1 cup homemade (page 25) or prepared chicken broth

2 tablespoons butter at room temperature

2 tablespoons all-purpose flour

¼ cup chopped fresh chives for garnish

1. Preheat the oven to 350°F.

2. In a large skillet over medium-high heat, cook the bacon until crisp. Remove the bacon and drain on paper towels. Drain all but 1 tablespoon of the fat from the pan.

3. Wash the chicken and pat dry with paper towels. Sprinkle with the salt and pepper and coat with the flour. Brown the chicken in the bacon fat over medium-high heat and arrange in a 9-by-13-inch shallow baking dish.

4. Add the red onion and garlic to the skillet. Sauté for 1 minute and add the baby onions, mushrooms, and marjoram. Sauté over medium-high heat until the onions begin to brown, about 10 minutes. Spread over the chicken in the casserole. Add the wine to the skillet and bring to a boil, scraping up the browned bits on the bottom of the pan. Add the chicken broth and boil for 5 minutes. Pour the mixture over the chicken in the baking dish.

5. Cover the dish tightly with aluminum foil coated with cooking spray and bake until the chicken is cooked through, about 1 hour.

6. Transfer the chicken to a serving platter. Strain the liquid from the baking dish into a heavy saucepan. Transfer the onion mixture to the platter with the chicken and keep warm.

7. Mix the butter and flour in a small dish. Bring the cooking liquid in the saucepan to a boil. Whisk in the flour mixture and boil until the sauce is thickened and reduced to about 2½ cups, 8 minutes or so. Season with salt and pepper and ladle the sauce over the chicken and onions. Sprinkle with chives and serve.

CHILI PIE WITH CORNMEAL CRUST

A buttery cornmeal crust tops this chili pie, which is made with ground turkey. Serve it with fresh salsa.

1 tablespoon vegetable oil

1 pound ground turkey breast

2 cloves garlic, minced

1 small red bell pepper, seeded and chopped

1 can (14½ ounces) diced tomatoes with basil, garlic, and oregano with their juice

1 tablespoon chili powder

1 teaspoon ground cumin

1 teaspoon dried oregano

½ teaspoon salt

Cayenne pepper

1 can (about 15 ounces) pink or red kidney beans, rinsed and well drained

FOR THE PASTRY:

1 cup all-purpose flour, plus extra for dusting

½ cup yellow cornmeal

½ teaspoon salt

½ cup (1 stick) cold butter, thinly sliced

¼ cup ice water

1. Preheat the oven to 400°F. Coat a shallow 1½- to 2-quart casserole with cooking spray.

2. In a large nonstick skillet, heat the oil and brown the turkey with the garlic and bell pepper, breaking up the meat with a spoon as it browns.

3. Add the tomatoes with their juice, chili powder, cumin, oregano, salt, and a dash of cayenne pepper and cook for 5 minutes, or until the mixture has thickened slightly.

4. Reduce the heat to low and add the beans. Cook for 5 minutes longer, stirring frequently. Spoon the mixture into the casserole and let it cool while you prepare the crust.

5. *To make the pastry:* In a large bowl, stir the flour, cornmeal, and salt together. Cut in the butter until the mixture resembles coarse crumbs. Add the water and stir with a fork until dough begins to come together.

6. Gather the dough together into a ball, then press it into a disk and dust very lightly with flour. Place between sheets of waxed paper or plastic wrap and roll out until it is about ¼ inch thick and slightly larger than the top of the casserole.

7. Remove one of the sheets of paper or plastic from the pastry and place the pastry, covered side up, over the contents of the casserole. Remove the top sheet of paper or plastic. Turn under and flute the edges of the pastry. Cut large slits in the crust to let the steam escape. Bake for 30 to 35 minutes, or until the crust is nicely browned and the casserole is bubbly.

CRAB-STUFFED TURKEY BREASTS

Turkey breast is mild-flavored, so the taste of the crab really comes through here. Serve this with freshly cooked wild rice and steamed asparagus.

SERVES 6

4 tablespoons butter

2 pounds turkey breast tenderloins

½ cup sliced green onion (white and green parts)

¼ pound thinly sliced mushrooms

3 tablespoons all-purpose flour

2 teaspoons dried thyme, divided

½ cup homemade (page 25) or prepared chicken broth

½ cup light cream or half-and-half

½ cup dry white wine

Salt

Pepper

¾ pound fresh crabmeat, or 2 packages (6 ounces each) frozen crabmeat, thawed and drained

½ cup chopped fresh parsley

1 cup shredded Swiss cheese

1. Preheat the oven to 350°F. Grease a shallow 3-quart casserole with about 2 teaspoons of the butter.

2. Wash the turkey and pat dry with paper towels. Cut each piece in half crosswise. Place between sheets of plastic wrap and pound with the flat side of a meat mallet until thin and about tripled in size.

3. Melt the remaining butter in a nonstick skillet. Add the green onion and mushrooms and sauté for 5 minutes, or until soft. Stir in the flour and 1 teaspoon of the thyme. Whisk in the broth, cream, and wine and bring to a boil, whisking constantly. Cook until thickened and season with salt and pepper to taste. Remove from the heat.

4. In a small bowl, combine ¼ cup of the sauce, the crabmeat, parsley, and remaining 1 teaspoon thyme. Divide the mixture between the turkey breast slices. Roll up into tight bundles and place, seam side down, in the buttered casserole. Spoon the remaining sauce over the turkey bundles and sprinkle with the cheese. (At this point the dish can be covered and refrigerated for up to 1 day. Add 10 minutes to the baking time.)

5. Cover the casserole with a sheet of aluminum foil coated with cooking spray. Bake for 30 minutes, or until the turkey is cooked through.

TURKEY AND BROCCOLI CASSEROLE

It seems people are always looking for another way to serve cooked turkey on the day after Thanksgiving. Serve this dish with any leftover baked sweet potatoes and cranberry sauce.

○——————————— SERVES 6 ———————————○

4 tablespoons butter, plus extra for the dish

¼ cup all-purpose flour

2 cups homemade (page 25) or prepared chicken broth

1 cup light cream

1 teaspoon salt

¾ cup grated Parmesan cheese, divided

½ cup shredded Swiss cheese

Dash of cayenne pepper

1 large head broccoli (about 2 pounds), tough ends trimmed, and cut into spears

¼ pound thinly sliced cooked ham

1 pound sliced cooked turkey breast

1. Preheat the oven to 350°F. Butter a 9-by-13-inch casserole.

2. In a medium saucepan, melt the 4 tablespoons butter and stir in the flour until smooth. Cook over low heat for 3 minutes, stirring. Whisk in the chicken broth and cream. Bring to a boil and cook, whisking constantly, until thickened and smooth. Stir in the salt, ½ cup of the Parmesan cheese, the Swiss cheese, and the cayenne pepper.

3. In a large saucepan, cook the broccoli in boiling salted water for about 12 minutes or until crisp-tender. Drain and arrange in the casserole, covering the bottom. Top with the sliced ham, then the turkey.

4. Pour the cheese sauce evenly over all and sprinkle with the remaining ¼ cup Parmesan cheese. (At this point the dish can be covered and refrigerated for up to 1 day. Add 10 minutes to the baking time.)

5. Bake, uncovered, for 25 minutes, or until bubbly.

TURKEY AND CURRIED RICE CASSEROLE

Here's another delicious casserole to try on the day after Thanksgiving, especially if you have leftover stuffing as well as turkey.

3 tablespoons butter, divided, plus extra for the dish

2 medium onions, chopped

½ pound mushrooms, sliced

2 cups diced cooked turkey

½ cup diced cooked ham

1 cup crumbled leftover stuffing or toasted and seasoned bread cubes

2 tablespoons chopped fresh parsley

Pinch of dried thyme

Salt

Pepper

1 tablespoon curry powder

1 cup rice

2 cups hot turkey or chicken broth

1. Preheat the oven to 375°F. Butter a 2- to 3-quart casserole.

2. In a large skillet, melt 2 tablespoons of the butter and add the onions and mushrooms. Sauté over medium heat for 5 minutes, or until the vegetables are softened.

3. Transfer the onions and mushrooms into the casserole and add the turkey, ham, stuffing, parsley, and thyme, and season with salt and pepper.

4. Melt the remaining 1 tablespoon of butter in the skillet and add the curry powder and rice, stirring. Add the broth, stir well, and pour over the ingredients in the casserole.

5. Bake, uncovered, for 25 minutes, or until the rice has absorbed all of the liquid.

TURKEY AND MUSHROOM CASSEROLE

This casserole is made with ground turkey breast, which I prefer over turkey labeled simply "ground turkey." Turkey breast is leaner and higher in protein. Plain ground turkey often includes turkey skin in the mix, which adds fat.

SERVES 6

1 package (8 ounces) wide egg noodles

3 slices bacon, diced

1 pound ground turkey breast

1 pound mushrooms, sliced

1 medium onion, chopped

Salt

Pepper

2 teaspoons poultry seasoning or dried thyme

½ cup dry white wine

1 cup homemade (page 25) or prepared chicken broth

½ cup heavy cream

½ teaspoon freshly ground nutmeg

2 cups shredded Gruyère cheese

1 cup plain breadcrumbs

2 to 3 tablespoons chopped fresh parsley

1. Preheat the oven to 350°F. Coat a 3-quart casserole with cooking spray.

2. Cook the noodles as directed on the package until al dente (firm to the bite). Drain and transfer to the casserole.

3. In a large, deep skillet, brown the bacon over medium-high heat until crisp; remove the bacon and set aside. Add the turkey and sauté until the turkey is no longer pink. Push the turkey to the side and add the mushrooms and onion. Sauté for 3 to 5 minutes over medium-high heat until the vegetables are softened.

4. Mix the meat, onions, and mushrooms together and season with salt, pepper, and poultry seasoning. Cook for 5 minutes over medium heat, and stir into the noodles in the casserole.

5. Add the wine, broth, and heavy cream to the skillet and heat to boiling, stirring. Boil the sauce until reduced to about 1 cup and add the nutmeg.

6. Pour the sauce over the turkey and noodles in the casserole and mix in. Top with the cheese and breadcrumbs. Bake, uncovered, until the cheese is melted, about 5 minutes. Sprinkle with parsley and serve.

TURKEY AND WILD RICE AU GRATIN

This hearty casserole is a tasty way to use leftover turkey, but leftover rotisserie chicken from the supermarket works, too.

SERVES 4

4 tablespoons butter, divided

3 tablespoons all-purpose flour

1 teaspoon dried basil

1 cup homemade (page 25) or prepared chicken broth

1 cup milk

2 cups diced cooked turkey or chicken

¼ teaspoon salt

Pepper

2 cups Cooked Wild Rice (page 29), or 2 cups cooked brown rice

1 cup frozen peas

2 tablespoons grated Parmesan cheese

1 tablespoon seasoned breadcrumbs

1. Preheat the oven to 400°F. Coat a shallow 1½-quart casserole with cooking spray.

2. Melt 3 tablespoons of the butter in a saucepan over medium heat. Blend in the flour and basil and cook for 1 minute without browning. Gradually whisk in the chicken broth and milk and cook until thickened and smooth. Stir in the turkey, salt, and pepper to taste.

3. Spread out the rice in the bottom of the casserole and top with the peas. Spread the chicken mixture over the top. Dot with the remaining 1 tablespoon butter. Sprinkle with the Parmesan cheese and breadcrumbs. Bake, uncovered, for 20 minutes, or until bubbly.

TURKEY BREAST MOLE

The word *Mole* comes from a Nahuatl word meaning "concoction." But the word actually refers to a rich, dark-reddish-brown Mexican sauce usually served with poultry. There are many versions of this sauce, depending mainly on what there is in the cook's kitchen. Usually, though, it is a blend of onion, garlic, several varieties of spices and chiles, and a small amount of chocolate.

SERVES 6 TO 8

2 pieces boneless turkey breast (about 5 pounds total)

2 tablespoons vegetable oil

2 large onions, chopped

3 cloves garlic, minced

4 cups homemade (page 25) or prepared chicken broth or water, divided

1 square (1 ounce) unsweetened chocolate

2 to 3 tablespoons chili powder

3 tablespoons all-purpose flour

1 teaspoon ground cinnamon

¼ teaspoon ground cloves

¼ teaspoon anise seeds, crushed

2 teaspoons salt

½ teaspoon pepper

¼ cup chopped peanuts for garnish

¼ cup toasted sesame seeds for garnish

Chopped fresh cilantro for garnish

1. Preheat the oven to 350°F.

2. Rinse the turkey and pat dry with paper towels. Heat the oil in a 3- or 4-quart Dutch oven. Add the onions and garlic and sauté over medium-high heat for 3 minutes, stirring. Remove with a slotted spoon and set aside. Add more oil if needed. Add the turkey breasts and brown on both sides. Remove from the heat. Arrange the onions and garlic on top of the turkey in the Dutch oven.

3. Heat 1 cup broth or water to simmering. Transfer to a small bowl and add the chocolate; stir until melted. Stir in chili powder, flour, cinnamon, cloves, anise seeds, salt, and pepper and continue stirring until blended.

4. Pour the remaining 3 cups broth or water over the turkey in the casserole, then add the broth with the chocolate and seasonings. Cover and bake for 1¼ hours, or until the turkey is cooked through. Garnish with the peanuts, sesame seeds, and cilantro.

TURKEY CRUNCH CASSEROLE

Celery and water chestnuts add a pleasing crunch to this casserole. It's perfect for a weeknight meal because it goes together so quickly.

SERVES 6

½ cup slivered almonds

2 stalks celery, sliced

1 can (8 ounces) sliced water chestnuts, drained

2 cups diced cooked turkey

½ teaspoon salt

¼ teaspoon dried tarragon

2 teaspoons minced onion

2 tablespoons fresh lemon juice

1 cup mayonnaise

½ cup shredded Cheddar cheese

1 cup coarsely crumbled potato chips

1. Preheat the oven to 350°F. While the oven preheats, toast the almonds on a baking sheet. Be careful not to burn them; it will take about 5 minutes. Remove the almonds from the oven. Coat a 2½-quart casserole with cooking spray.

2. In a large bowl, combine the almonds with the celery, water chestnuts, turkey, salt, tarragon, onion, lemon juice, and mayonnaise. Blend thoroughly and transfer to the casserole.

3. Top the turkey mixture with the cheese and potato chips and bake, uncovered, for 20 to 30 minutes, until heated through and the cheese is melted.

TURKEY TETRAZZINI

Chicken tetrazzini was reportedly created in the early 1900s in honor of an Italian opera singer, Luisa Tetrazzini, who lived from 1871 to 1941. James Beard thought the dish was created in San Francisco, but there seems to be no documentation to support that theory. I use strips of shredded leftover turkey, rather than chicken. The turkey bakes with spaghetti in a rich sherry-and-Parmesan-cheese sauce.

SERVES 6 TO 8

6 tablespoons butter, divided, plus extra for the dish

5 tablespoons all-purpose flour

2½ cups homemade (page 25) or prepared chicken broth

1½ cups half-and-half or light cream

½ cup dry sherry

1½ cups grated Parmesan cheese, divided

¾ pound mushrooms, sliced

1 package (12 ounces) vermicelli or spaghetti

4 cups shredded cooked turkey

Salt

Pepper

1. Preheat the oven to 375°F. Lightly butter a 2½- to 3-quart casserole.

2. In a medium saucepan, melt 2 tablespoons of the butter. Stir in the flour until smooth. Whisk in the broth, half-and-half, and sherry. Bring to a boil, whisking constantly until thickened and smooth. Stir in ½ cup of the Parmesan cheese.

3. Transfer 1 cup of the sauce to a small bowl and stir in ½ cup of the remaining Parmesan cheese.

4. In a large skillet, melt the remaining 4 tablespoons butter. Add the mushrooms and sauté until lightly browned. Remove from the heat. Set aside ½ cup of the mushrooms in a small bowl.

5. Cook the vermicelli according to the package directions until tender but firm to the bite, and drain.

6. In a large bowl, combine the sauce from the saucepan, the mushrooms from the skillet, the hot vermicelli, and the turkey and season with salt and pepper to taste. Transfer to the buttered casserole. Spoon the reserved 1 cup sauce evenly over the surface. Sprinkle with the remaining ½ cup Parmesan cheese and top with the reserved cooked mushroom slices.

7. Bake the casserole, uncovered, for 15 to 20 minutes, or until heated through and bubbly.

8. Preheat the broiler and broil the casserole 5 inches from the heat until lightly browned.

CASSOULET OF DUCK WITH GREAT NORTHERN BEANS AND HAM HOCKS

This is a simplified version of the French dish cassoulet. The classic dish is traditionally made with preserved duck legs, known as duck confit. Of course, one could make them, but I get tired just thinking of such a time-consuming preparation when it isn't really necessary today. Confit was probably something of a necessity in old French farmhouses in order to preserve the slaughtered fowl. I don't suggest doing away with the duck completely, though. I have tried substituting chicken, but the flavor just isn't the same. Traditionally, an earthenware pot is used for this dish, but any heavy, ovenproof casserole is suitable for this dish. This takes 8 hours to bake at a low temperature, so plan accordingly. Long, slow baking simply improves the flavors.

SERVES 8

1 pound Great Northern or pea beans

1 package (12 ounces) salt pork, skin removed

1½ pounds smoked ham hocks

1 large sweet onion, quartered

1 carrot, peeled and cut into chunks

1 clove garlic, quartered

2 pounds pork spareribs, cut into 2 slabs

1 teaspoon kosher salt

1 duckling (4 to 5 pounds), excess fat removed

1. Wash the beans and pick over, removing any pebbles or dirt. Put in a large pot and add cold water to cover. Soak overnight and drain.

2. Preheat the oven to 300°F. Transfer the beans to a large 6- to 8-quart earthenware pot and add water to cover. Place the salt pork in the center of the beans and add the ham hocks, onion, carrot, and garlic. Top with the spareribs and sprinkle with salt.

3. Bake the beans for 3 hours, uncovered. Check the moisture and add water if necessary.

4. Split the duck in half and place on a foil-covered baking pan. Roast, skin side up, right along with the cassoulet, for 3 hours. The duck should be very tender. Remove the skin and bones from the breast, cut up the meat, and place on top of the bean casserole. Push the duck legs and thighs into the beans. Remove the meat from the ham hocks, chop, and add to the beans.

5. Bake the beans for 2 hours longer, or until most of the liquid has been absorbed.

Chapter 6
BEEF CASSEROLES

⸻ ○○○○○ ⸻

I have a dog-eared little 4½-by-5½-inch mimeographed booklet that belonged to my mother. It is titled simply "Hot Dishes," and it was assembled by members of the Bethany Guild of the Lutheran Church in Floodwood, Minnesota. Each recipe bears the name of the contributor. Most of them are based on ground beef and have names like "Mary's Hot Dish," "1-2-3 Casserole," "Delicious Hot Dish,"

and "Tillie Rosendahl's Casserole." Undoubtedly, all of these appeared time and again at funeral lunches.

That booklet explains why, when I think of beef casseroles, the first thing that comes to mind is a casserole made with ground beef. In this chapter, however, I also include other cuts of beef that do very well with long, slow, moist cooking.

These casseroles include the chile-spiced flavors of the Southwest, the hearty beans

of South America and the Caribbean, and the garlic and herbs of Italy and France, as well as favorites from around the United States. Many of them provide the convenience people associate with a slow cooker: You put them in the oven and forget about them. Oven-simmered stews, for example, turn out succulent and tasty. They are cooked covered, so the flavors stay right in the pot!

FIESTA CASSEROLE

With its old-fashioned flavors of the Southwest, this is a casserole to please the kids. Grown-ups enjoy it, too, especially when it's served with ice-cold beer.

SERVES 6

1 pound extra-lean ground beef

1 large onion, chopped

1 green bell pepper, seeded and diced

1 red bell pepper, seeded and diced

2 cups chunky tomato salsa (mild, medium, or hot)

1 can (14½ ounces) diced tomatoes with their juice

2 cups fresh or frozen corn kernels

12 flour tortillas (6 inches)

1½ cups shredded Cheddar cheese

Sour cream for serving

Chopped avocados for serving

Chopped fresh cilantro for serving

1. Preheat the oven to 375°F. Brown the meat in a large non-stick skillet over medium-high heat. Add the onion and green and red bell peppers and sauté until the meat is no longer pink, about 10 minutes. Drain off any excess fat. Stir in the salsa, tomatoes with their juice, and corn, bring to a boil, and remove from the heat.

2. Spread out 1 cup of the meat mixture in the bottom of a shallow 9-by-13-inch baking dish. Top with 6 tortillas, overlapping them. Spoon half of the remaining meat mixture over the tortillas. Top with half of the cheese. Layer with the remaining tortillas and then the meat mixture. Cover with lightly greased aluminum foil and bake for 25 minutes, or until heated through.

3. Uncover the casserole, sprinkle with the remaining cheese, and let stand for 5 minutes, or until the cheese is melted. Serve with sour cream, chopped avocados, and cilantro.

FINNISH CABBAGE CASSEROLE (KAALILAATIKKO)

When our Finnish friend Tello Anttila served this classic dish on our recent visit to Finland, she made its name, *Kaalilaatikko,* into a song. We all joined in, repeating the word over and over again as we raised the pitch, so that eventually we were singing "KAA-LEE-LAA-TIK-KO" in eight-part harmony! (A hint for those who don't know Finnish— all of the letters in a word are pronounced. The first syllable is always accented, and where there are double letters, they are pronounced twice, giving them emphasis.)

Aside from the fun, this is a delicious, hearty casserole. The hint of corn syrup gives the cabbage a sweet, fresh taste, and the marjoram lends an authentic Finnish flavor.

─── MAKES 6 TO 8 SERVINGS ───

2 tablespoons butter, plus extra for the dish

1 small head cabbage, shredded

2 tablespoons dark corn syrup

2 teaspoons salt

¼ teaspoon ground marjoram

1 pound lean ground beef

1 cup fresh breadcrumbs (see Note)

½ cup milk

2 large eggs, beaten

1. Preheat the oven to 350°F. Butter a 3-quart shallow casserole.

2. Put the cabbage in a deep pot and add enough boiling water to cover. Simmer for about 5 minutes, until crisp-tender; drain and transfer to a large bowl. Add the 2 tablespoons butter, the corn syrup, salt, and marjoram.

3. In another bowl, mix the ground beef, breadcrumbs, milk, and eggs.

4. Spread half the cabbage in the bottom of the casserole. Top with an even layer of the ground beef, and then with the remaining cabbage. Bake, uncovered, for 1 hour, or until the casserole is browned and the casserole is set.

∘ ∘ ∘ ∘ ∘

NOTE: To make fresh breadcrumbs, tear 1 or 2 slices of fresh bread into pieces and put in a food processor with the steel blade in place. Process with on/off pulses until the bread is broken down into crumbs.

MEAL-IN-ONE-DISH HAMBURGER CASSEROLE

This dish falls somewhere between a casserole and a meat loaf. The meat mixture bakes on the bottom layer while the vegetables cook on top.

SERVES 6

1 pound lean ground beef

1 cup chopped onions

1 can (14½ ounces) diced tomatoes with their juice

2 teaspoons Worcestershire sauce

½ teaspoon chili powder

2 teaspoons salt

3 medium potatoes, peeled and sliced

1½ cups fresh or frozen corn kernels

1½ cups frozen peas, thawed

1 green bell pepper, seeded and chopped

⅓ cup all-purpose flour

1½ cups shredded Cheddar cheese

1. Preheat the oven to 375°F. Coat a 9-by-13-inch baking dish with cooking spray.

2. In a large bowl, mix the ground beef, onions, tomatoes with their juice, Worcestershire, chili powder, and salt. Pat the mixture into a smooth layer in the casserole. Spread the potatoes over the meat layer.

3. Combine the corn, peas, and green pepper in a medium bowl, add the flour, and toss to coat the vegetables. Spread in an even layer over the potato layer.

4. Coat a sheet of aluminum foil with cooking spray and cover the casserole tightly. Bake for 45 minutes. Uncover, sprinkle with cheese, and bake for 10 minutes longer, or until the potatoes are tender. Cut into squares and serve.

RICE AND BURGER CASSEROLE

There are a zillion variations on this basic casserole, and almost every one has a different name. I found this one in several church cookbooks, entitled "Cherokee Casserole." I don't know where the name came from, but it's definitely simple!

SERVES 6

1 pound ground beef

1 medium onion, chopped

1 teaspoon salt

½ teaspoon pepper

Pinch of dried oregano

Pinch of dried thyme

1 can (14½ ounces) diced tomatoes with their juice

1 recipe Basic Mushroom Sauce (page 22), or 1 can (10¾ ounces) cream of mushroom soup

1 cup long-grain rice

1 cup water

6 stuffed green olives, sliced

¼ pound (about 4 slices) Cheddar cheese, cut into strips

1. Preheat the oven to 350°F. Coat a shallow 2-quart casserole with cooking spray.

2. In a nonstick skillet over medium heat, brown the beef with the chopped onion. Add the salt, pepper, oregano, thyme, tomatoes with their juice, sauce or soup, rice, water, and olives.

3. Transfer to the casserole dish and bake, uncovered, for 30 minutes, or until the rice is cooked. Top with the cheese and return to the oven for a few minutes until the cheese melts.

SIX-LAYER CASSEROLE

One popular name for this dish is "shipwreck casserole." Nobody seems to know where this rather off-the-wall name came from; there is nothing in the ingredients that comes from the sea. I suppose that leaves it open, so we can make up our own story.

SERVES 6

2 large potatoes, peeled and sliced

2 cups diced celery

1 pound lean ground beef

½ cup diced onions

1 to 2 teaspoons salt

¼ teaspoon pepper

1 red, yellow, or green bell pepper, seeded and diced

1 can (14½ ounces) diced tomatoes with their juice

½ cup chopped fresh herbs—parsley, basil, cilantro, marjoram, or thyme, or a combination—for garnish

Sour cream for serving

1. Preheat the oven to 350°F. Coat a 2-quart casserole with cooking spray.

2. Arrange the potatoes in the bottom of the casserole. In layers, add the celery, ground beef, and onions. Sprinkle all with the salt and pepper. Next, add a layer of bell peppers and pour the tomatoes with their juice over all.

3. Bake the casserole, uncovered, for 2 hours, or until the meat is cooked and the vegetables are tender. Garnish with chopped fresh herbs and serve with sour cream.

BEEF AND ARTICHOKE BAKE

Serve this earthy, richly flavored casserole with French Potato Gratin (page 423) and a crisp green salad for a satisfying meal you can proudly serve guests.

— SERVES 8 —

1 package (9 ounces) frozen artichoke hearts, thawed

3 tablespoons butter

2 cloves garlic, minced

3 pounds sirloin or top round beefsteak, cut into 1½-inch cubes

2 large onions, sliced

½ cup dry red wine

1 can (8 ounces) tomato sauce

Chopped fresh parsley for garnish

1. Preheat the oven to 325°F. Cook the artichoke hearts according to package directions, drain, and set aside.

2. In a heavy skillet, melt the butter over medium-high heat. Add the garlic and the beef cubes, a few at a time, and brown the beef on all sides. Remove to a 2- to 3-quart heavy casserole. When all the meat is browned, add the onions to the skillet and sauté over low heat for about 10 minutes, or until very tender. Remove the onions to casserole.

3. Pour the wine into the skillet and bring to a boil, stirring constantly and scraping up the browned bits on the bottom of the pan. Pour over the meat mixture in the casserole. Add the artichoke hearts and tomato sauce.

4. Bake, uncovered, for about 30 minutes, or until the beef is tender. Garnish with parsley before serving.

BEEF, BEAN, AND BACON CASSEROLE

Hardly a potluck goes by without a casserole that's something like this one. Ground beef is, of course, the old-time favorite, but ground turkey, pork, venison, or a combination are equally suitable. Of all the canned foods available, canned beans are one of the best because they are such a great time-saver. But if you have more time than money, cook your own beans (see page 30).

SERVES 6

1 pound extra-lean ground beef

6 slices bacon, diced

1 large onion, chopped

1 green bell pepper, seeded and chopped

1 tablespoon white vinegar

1 tablespoon prepared mustard

½ cup tomato ketchup

1 tablespoon packed brown sugar

2 cups cooked kidney beans, drained (see page 30)

2 cups cooked pinto beans, drained

1 can (15½ ounces) whole corn kernels, drained

2 cups shredded mild Cheddar cheese

1 cup crushed tortilla chips

1. Preheat the oven to 375°F. In a large nonstick skillet over medium-high heat, brown the beef, bacon, onion, and pepper together until the beef is cooked. Drain the accumulated fat.

2. Transfer the mixture to a 3-quart casserole. Add the vinegar, mustard, ketchup, sugar, beans, and corn and stir to blend well. Bake, uncovered, for 30 to 40 minutes, or until bubbly.

3. Remove from the oven and spread the cheese and chips evenly over the top. Return to the oven and bake for about 10 minutes longer, or until the cheese is melted and chips are crisp.

JUNIPER BEEF

Juniper berries, which we associate with the flavor of gin, are astringent, blue-black berries that grow wild in Europe and America. Although in many preparations they are crushed, I like to add them whole to meat dishes. The resulting flavor is much more subtle. Assemble this casserole and set it to bake at a low temperature over a long period of time. Choose this recipe when you are really busy but don't want to settle for take-out fare. It might take a little bit of planning, but the result is worth it!

SERVES 8

⅓ cup all-purpose flour

1 teaspoon salt

½ teaspoon allspice

½ teaspoon pepper

2½ to 3 pounds beef stew meat, cut into 1-inch chunks

2 tablespoons olive oil

4 carrots, peeled and cut diagonally into 1-inch lengths

4 large onions, cut into eighths

4 cloves garlic, bruised and peeled

8 whole juniper berries

1 teaspoon dried rosemary, crushed

1 bottle (12 ounces) dark beer

Chopped fresh parsley for garnish

Crumbled crisply cooked bacon for garnish

Hot buttered noodles or boiled potatoes for serving

1. Preheat the oven to 275°F. Combine the flour, salt, allspice, and pepper in a plastic bag. Add the meat to the bag and shake until all the pieces are coated with flour.

2. In a heavy skillet, heat the olive oil. Add the floured beef chunks, a few at a time, and brown on all sides. Remove to a deep 3-quart casserole. When all meat is browned, add the carrots, onions, garlic, and juniper berries to the casserole. Sprinkle the meat and vegetables with the rosemary.

3. Pour the beer into the skillet and bring to a boil, stirring constantly to scrape up the browned bits on the bottom of the pan. Pour over the meat mixture in casserole.

4. Bake, covered, for 4 to 5 hours, or until the beef is very tender. Garnish with chopped parsley and cooked bacon. Serve over hot buttered noodles or boiled potatoes.

BEER-BAKED IRISH BEEF

Busy day? This stew cooks slowly at a low temperature, untended, until the beef is succulently tender.

SERVES 6 TO 8

⅓ cup all-purpose flour

1 teaspoon salt

1 teaspoon ground allspice

½ teaspoon pepper

2½ to 3 pounds beef stew meat, cut into 1- to 1½-inch cubes

6 slices bacon, diced

4 carrots, peeled and cut diagonally into 1-inch lengths

4 large onions, cut into eighths

2 cloves garlic, bruised and peeled

¼ cup minced fresh parsley, plus chopped fresh parsley for garnish

1 teaspoon dried rosemary, crushed

1 teaspoon dried marjoram

1 bay leaf

1 bottle (12 ounces) Irish stout or dark beer

Hot boiled potatoes for serving

1. Preheat the oven to 275°F.

2. Combine the flour, salt, allspice, pepper, and beef cubes in a plastic bag. Shake until all the meat is evenly coated with flour.

3. In a large nonstick skillet, cook the bacon over medium heat until crisp. Remove the bacon and set aside, leaving the drippings in the pan.

4. Add the floured pieces of meat, a few at a time, and quickly brown them on all sides. Transfer to a deep 2½- to 3-quart casserole with a cover.

Add the carrots, onions, garlic, minced parsley, rosemary, marjoram, and bay leaf to the meat.

5. Pour the beer into the skillet and bring to a boil, scraping up the browned bits from the bottom of the pan. Pour over the meat in the casserole.

6. Cover and bake for 4 hours, or until the beef is very tender. Remove and discard the bay leaf. Sprinkle the dish with the chopped fresh parsley and cooked bacon. Serve over hot boiled potatoes.

CARAWAY BEEF AND MUSHROOM BAKE

Beef, beer, and caraway seeds have a natural affinity for each other. This succulent stew simmers for several hours, and if you'd like to extend the cooking time even longer, reduce the oven temperature to 275°F and double the cooking time. The dish will be all the better for it.

SERVES 8

¼ cup all-purpose flour

1½ teaspoons salt

2 pounds beef stew meat, cut into 1½-inch cubes

2 tablespoons vegetable oil

2 teaspoons caraway seeds

1 can (12 ounces) dark beer

6 carrots, cut into 1-inch lengths

½ pound small mushrooms

10 small white onions, peeled (see Note), or frozen baby onions, thawed

½ cup chopped fresh parsley, plus extra for garnish

1. Preheat the oven to 325°F. Combine the flour and salt in a plastic bag and put the meat into the bag. Shake until the pieces are coated.

2. In a cast-iron 3-quart Dutch oven, heat the oil over medium-high heat. Add the beef chunks, a few at a time, and brown on all sides. When all the meat is browned, add the caraway seeds, beer, carrots, mushrooms, onions, and the ½ cup parsley.

3. Bake, tightly covered, for 2½ to 3 hours, or until the beef is very tender. Garnish with additional parsley.

○ ○ ○ ○ ○

NOTE: To peel small onions, trim them and cut an X in the bottom of each one. Drop them into boiling water for 1 minute. When they're cool enough to handle, slip off the skins.

COVER-AND-FORGET-IT BEEF AND VEGETABLE STEW

You don't need to brown the beef for this tasty stew; just mix up everything in a heavy casserole and let it bake while you take off for up to 3 hours. Be sure to cover the casserole tightly to prevent the liquid from evaporating. If you would like even more time off for other activities, cook the beef at the lower suggested temperature for an extra hour or two.

SERVES 6 TO 8

2 pounds boneless beef chuck, cut into 1-inch cubes

4 large baking potatoes, peeled and cut into 1-inch chunks

6 carrots, peeled and cut into ½-inch chunks

2 parsnips, peeled and cut into ½-inch chunks

1 medium onion, chopped

2 cups tomato sauce

1 cup water

1 teaspoon sugar

2 teaspoons salt

½ teaspoon pepper

3 tablespoons quick-cooking tapioca

1. Preheat the oven to 325°F (or 300°F for a longer cooking time). Coat a heavy 3-quart casserole with oil.

2. Put the meat in the casserole, and top with the potatoes, carrots, parsnips, and onion.

3. In a small bowl, mix together the tomato sauce, water, sugar, salt, pepper, and tapioca and pour over the meat and vegetables.

4. Cut a piece of parchment paper large enough to overhang the top of the casserole by 2 inches all around. Press the paper onto the top of the beef and vegetable mixture and tuck it down around the sides of the contents. Cover the whole thing, using the cover of the casserole or aluminum foil.

5. Bake for 2½ to 3 hours at 325°F or 4 to 5 hours at 300°F.

FIVE-HOUR BEEF AND RUTABAGA STEW

We all know how challenging it is to balance many activities and chores in a day and end up with a decent meal at the end of it. Root vegetables have an affinity for long, slow cooking, and this casserole is a perfect example. The ingredient list is long, but don't let that deter you. The assembly and cooking are incredibly simple!

SERVES 8

2 pounds beef stew meat, cut into 1½-inch cubes

5 stalks celery, cut into ½-inch-thick slices

1 parsnip, peeled and diced

1 medium rutabaga, peeled and diced

4 large potatoes, peeled and cubed

1 large onion, chopped

2 cloves garlic, minced

½ cup quick-cooking tapioca

1 teaspoon salt

½ teaspoon pepper

1 can (28 ounces) whole tomatoes with their juice, crushed

1. Preheat the oven to 275°F. Combine all of the ingredients in a heavy 3-quart casserole, pouring the tomatoes with their juice over all last.

2. Place a heavy cover on top of the casserole so that the liquids will not evaporate. If the casserole has no lid, seal the top with aluminum foil, but do not press the foil down on top of the contents of the casserole because foil tends to discolor foods.

3. Bake for 5 hours. Remove the cover and serve. It's as simple as that!

HUNGARIAN BEEF GOULASH WITH SPAETZLE

In Hungary, goulash is called *gulyas*. This stew of beef and vegetables, flavored with paprika, is delicious over spaetzle—fresh noodles or dumplings made with flour and eggs, which are popular in Eastern Europe and Germany.

— SERVES 6 —

2 tablespoons vegetable oil

1 large onion, thinly sliced

2 bell peppers, green or yellow, seeded and cut into ½-inch dice

2 tablespoons sweet Hungarian paprika

1½ pounds beef stew meat, cut into 1-inch cubes

2 teaspoons salt

⅛ teaspoon cayenne pepper

4 medium potatoes, peeled and cubed

4 cups homemade (page 26) or prepared beef broth

FOR THE SPAETZLE:

1 cup all-purpose flour

1 teaspoon salt

3 large eggs, lightly beaten

1 teaspoon caraway seeds for garnish

Shredded fresh carrots for garnish

1. Preheat the oven to 300°F. In a heavy 2- to 3-quart Dutch oven, heat the oil and add the onion. Sauté the onion over medium heat for 3 minutes; add the bell peppers and paprika and continue cooking until the vegetables are tender.

2. Push the vegetables to the side and add the meat. Sprinkle with the salt and cayenne and stir the meat cubes until they are coated with the seasonings. Cover tightly and place in the oven. Bake for 1 to 1½ hours, or until the meat is tender.

3. Meanwhile, cook the potatoes in the beef broth until tender. Remove the cooked potatoes with a slotted spoon and transfer to the pot with the meat. Heat the broth to simmering again.

4. *To make the spaetzle:* Mix the flour and salt in a large bowl. Make a well in the center and add the eggs. Stir the flour into the eggs gradually to make a stiff dough. Alternatively, combine the flour and salt in a food processor with the steel blade in place. Add the eggs and process until the dough is formed. Roll and stretch the dough to make a rope about 12 inches long. Cut into ½-inch pieces. Drop into the simmering broth to cook. When the spaetzle rise to the top, in about 1 minute, they are done.

5. Add the spaetzle and the cooking broth to the goulash, stir to blend, and garnish with the caraway seeds and shredded fresh carrot.

MOROCCAN BEEF TAGINE

Traditionally served over couscous, a tagine is a Moroccan stew. It can be made from meat or poultry and is seasoned with sweet spices like cinnamon and cumin.

SERVES 6

2 pounds beef stew meat, cut into 1-inch cubes

1½ teaspoons salt

½ teaspoon freshly ground pepper

3 tablespoons olive oil

2 medium onions, chopped

1 teaspoon ground cumin

½ teaspoon ground turmeric

½ teaspoon ground ginger

Pinch of cayenne pepper

1 cinnamon stick, 3 inches long

½ cup chopped fresh parsley

4 tomatoes, chopped

3 tablespoons tomato paste

¾ cup water

1 pound green beans, halved lengthwise

1 tablespoon toasted sesame seeds

Couscous, cooked according to package directions, for serving

1. Preheat the oven to 350°F. Pat the meat dry with paper towels and sprinkle with salt and pepper.

2. In a heavy, flameproof 3-quart casserole, such as cast iron, heat the oil. Add the meat chunks, a few at a time, and brown on all sides over medium heat; remove to a bowl or plate.

3. Add the onions to the pot and sauté for about 3 minutes, or until lightly browned; add the cumin, turmeric, ginger, cayenne, cinnamon stick, parsley, tomatoes, tomato paste, and water to the pot. Return the meat to the pot and stir to combine.

4. Bake, covered, for 2 hours, or until the meat is tender. Add more water during cooking if necessary.

5. When the meat is almost done, parboil the green beans by dropping them into a pot of boiling water for a few minutes. Add to the casserole and bake, covered, for 15 minutes longer. Remove and discard the cinnamon stick. Sprinkle with sesame seeds and serve over hot couscous.

BEEF WITH MUSHROOMS

For this casserole, I like to brown the beef chunks quickly in a hot oven, saving time and mess. To augment the flavor of the fresh mushrooms, I sometimes add dried morels that we've harvested ourselves. In recent years, morels have become more abundant in Minnesota, perhaps because of global warming. Dried morels are incredibly aromatic and add an exotic flavor to soups, sauces, and stews.

SERVES 6

2 pounds beef stew meat, cut into 1½-inch cubes

2 teaspoons salt

About ½ cup all-purpose flour

1½ cups water

6 carrots, peeled and cut into 1-inch chunks

1 pound fresh mushrooms, whole or quartered

4 dried morel mushrooms, crushed (optional)

10 small whole onions, peeled (see Note), or frozen baby onions, thawed

½ cup chopped fresh parsley, plus extra for garnish

1. Preheat the oven to 500°F. Line a baking sheet with heavy-duty foil and coat with cooking spray.

2. Pat the meat chunks dry with paper towels. Combine the salt and flour in a plastic bag. Add the meat chunks and shake until coated with flour, then shake off the excess. Arrange the meat chunks in a single layer on the baking sheet with a little space in between the chunks so they brown properly. Bake for 20 minutes until browned. Reduce the oven to 350°F.

3. Remove the beef from the oven and transfer to a heavy 3-quart Dutch oven. Pour a small amount of water into the pan and, with a rubber spatula, stir to scrape up the browned bits. Pick up the edges of the foil and carefully pour over the beef. Add the remaining water, carrots, fresh mushrooms, dried morels, onions, and ½ cup chopped parsley to the pot.

4. Cover and bake for 2½ to 3 hours, until the meat is very tender. Remove from the oven and sprinkle with parsley before serving.

ο ο ο ο ο

NOTE: To peel small onions, trim them and cut an X in the bottom of each one. Drop them into boiling water for 1 minute. When they're cool enough to handle, slip off the skins.

CARBONNADE FLAMANDE

This is a classic stew that originated in Flanders, Belgium. Traditionally it includes beer, beef, onions, garlic, and brown sugar. Like any classic, it has many variations. For example, sometimes it's made with bacon instead of vegetable oil. Once assembled, this casserole can be left to cook, unattended, at a low temperature for a long period of time. The juices are thickened with dumplings, which you can easily make at the last minute.

SERVES 8

2 pounds lean shoulder or top round beefsteaks, cut into ¼-inch-thick slices

½ cup all-purpose flour

½ cup vegetable oil, or more as needed

2 large sweet onions (about 2 pounds total), thickly sliced

6 cloves garlic, minced or pressed with a garlic press

3 tablespoons light or dark brown sugar

2 tablespoons red wine vinegar

½ cup chopped fresh parsley

2 bay leaves

2 teaspoons fresh thyme leaves, or 1 teaspoon dried

1 tablespoon salt

Pepper

4 cups homemade (page 26) or prepared beef broth

2 bottles (12 ounces each) dark beer

FOR THE DUMPLINGS:

2 cups all-purpose flour

2 teaspoons baking powder

½ teaspoon salt

½ cup milk

1 large egg

2 tablespoons butter, melted

1. Preheat the oven to 325°F. Put the beef slices and flour in a plastic bag and shake well until the meat is coated with flour.

2. Heat the oil in a heavy nonstick skillet over medium heat. When the oil is very hot, add the beef slices, a few at a time. Brown quickly on both sides and remove to a deep 4- or 6-quart Dutch oven.

3. Add the onions and garlic to the pan and brown them lightly, adding more oil if necessary.

Drain out the fat and stir in the sugar, vinegar, parsley, bay leaves, thyme, salt, and pepper to taste. Add the beef broth to the skillet and bring to a boil, scraping up any browned bits from the bottom. Pour over the meat mixture in the casserole and add the beer.

4. Cover and bake for 2 hours. Transfer the casserole to the stove top and heat until the juices bubble. Maintain at a simmer while you make the dumplings.

5. *To make the dumplings:* In a medium bowl, mix the flour, baking powder, salt, milk, egg, and melted butter. Drop the batter by teaspoonfuls into the simmering stew. Cover and cook for 15 minutes, until fluffy.

STUFFED BEEF ROLLS

In Germany, this dish is often served with sweet-and-sour red cabbage. For an authentic German menu, accompany it with some pumpernickel bread and offer apple strudel for dessert.

SERVES 4

1¼ pounds top round beefsteak, cut into ½-inch-thick slices

4 slices bacon

Salt

Pepper

2 tablespoons minced fresh parsley, plus extra for garnish

1 large dill pickle, halved, and each half cut lengthwise into 2 strips

2 tablespoons all-purpose flour

2 tablespoons butter

1 cup homemade (page 26) or prepared beef broth

½ cup heavy cream

1 tablespoon whole-grain mustard

1. Preheat the oven to 325°F. Cut the beef into 4 equal squares.

2. Place the squares of beef between sheets of plastic wrap. With the flat side of a mallet, pound the meat until thin and about tripled in size.

3. Place a bacon slice diagonally across a piece of beef, and sprinkle with salt, pepper, and minced parsley. Place a piece of pickle on one end of the meat. Roll up tightly, starting on the end with the pickle. Repeat for the remaining 3 pieces of meat. Secure the rolls with toothpicks and dust the rolls lightly with flour.

4. Melt the butter in a heavy Dutch oven and add the beef rolls. Brown them over medium heat all over. Arrange them in a single layer and pour the broth over them. Cover tightly and bake for 1 hour, or until the meat is very tender.

5. Strain the cooking juices into a skillet. Bring to a boil and whisk in the cream and mustard. Boil until the juices are reduced to a glossy sauce, about a third of its original amount. Pour over the beef rolls and garnish with the additional parsley.

GREEK BEEF WITH CUMIN AND CURRANTS

Serve this with Bulgur Baked with Raisins and Cranberries (page 334) and a salad.

Serve this with Bulgur Baked with Raisins and Cranberries (page 334) and a salad.

SERVES 8

3 pounds boneless beef chuck, cut into 1½-inch cubes

1 teaspoon salt

½ teaspoon pepper

4 tablespoons butter

1 pound small white onions, peeled (see Notes), or frozen baby onions, thawed

1 can (8 ounces) tomato sauce

1 tablespoon mixed pickling spices (see Notes)

½ cup dry red wine

2 tablespoons red wine vinegar

1 clove garlic, minced

1 bay leaf, crumbled

1 stick cinnamon, 3 inches long

½ teaspoon whole cloves

½ teaspoon ground cumin

½ cup currants or raisins

1. Preheat the oven to 300°F. Sprinkle the beef with salt and pepper.

2. In a heavy 5- to 6-quart Dutch oven, melt the butter. Add the beef and stir to coat with butter, but do not brown. Add the onions, tomato sauce, and pickling spices.

3. In a small bowl, combine the wine, vinegar, and garlic; pour over the meat in the casserole. Add the bay leaf, cinnamon stick, cloves, cumin, and currants.

4. Cover and bake for 2½ hours, or until the meat is very tender. If the stew becomes dry and the juices separate during cooking, skim off the fat and whisk in about 1 cup broth or water to thicken the juices.

○ ○ ○ ○ ○

NOTES: To peel small onions, trim them and cut an X in the bottom of each one. Drop them into boiling water for 1 minute. When they're cool enough to handle, slip off the skin.

Pickling spices can include allspice, bay leaves, cardamom, cinnamon, cloves, coriander, ginger, mustard seeds, and peppercorns. They can be purchased prepackaged in most supermarkets. The proportions of the spices vary from one company to the next.

BURGUNDY BEEF

Make this a day ahead and reheat before serving. The flavor actually improves overnight! The Burgundy provides a deep, rich color to the gravy.

SERVES 8

1 pound small white onions, peeled (see Note), or 1 pound frozen baby onions, thawed

6 slices bacon, diced

4 pounds boneless beef chuck, cut into 1½-inch cubes

¼ cup brandy

1 ½ teaspoons salt

¼ teaspoon pepper

2 cups Burgundy wine

2 cloves garlic, bruised and peeled

1 pound small mushrooms

2 sprigs fresh parsley, plus chopped parsley for garnish

Leafy top from 1 celery stalk

1 carrot, peeled and quartered

1 bay leaf

1 teaspoon dried thyme

3 tablespoons cornstarch

½ cup cold water

1. Preheat the oven to 350°F. In a medium, nonstick heavy skillet, brown the onions and bacon over medium heat and set aside. Add the beef chunks to the skillet, a few at a time, and brown on all sides, transferring them to a bowl as they are done.

2. When all the meat is browned, return the meat to the skillet. In a small saucepan, warm the brandy over low heat until warm to the touch. Ignite the brandy with a match and pour over the meat. Stir gently until the flame goes out.

3. Put the beef, bacon, and onions into a deep 3-quart casserole. Sprinkle with salt and pepper. Pour about ½ cup of the Burgundy into the skillet; bring to a boil, stirring constantly to scrape up the browned bits of meat. Pour over the meat in the casserole. Add the remaining Burgundy, the garlic, mushrooms, parsley sprigs, celery, carrot, bay leaf, and thyme to the meat mixture. Bake, tightly covered, for 2 hours, or until the beef is very tender.

4. Using a slotted spoon, remove the beef, bacon, mushrooms, and onion to a large bowl. Strain the cooking liquid into skillet and discard the solids. Boil the cooking liquid until reduced by half. In a small bowl, blend the cornstarch and water and whisk into the hot cooking liquid. Cook over medium heat until thickened, whisking constantly. Return the meat, mushrooms, and onions to the casserole. Pour the thickened cooking liquid over the beef mixture. Garnish with the chopped parsley and serve.

○ ○ ○ ○ ○

NOTE: To peel small onions, trim them and cut an X in the bottom of each one. Drop them into boiling water for 1 minute. When they're cool enough to handle, slip off the skins.

BURGUNDY BEEF

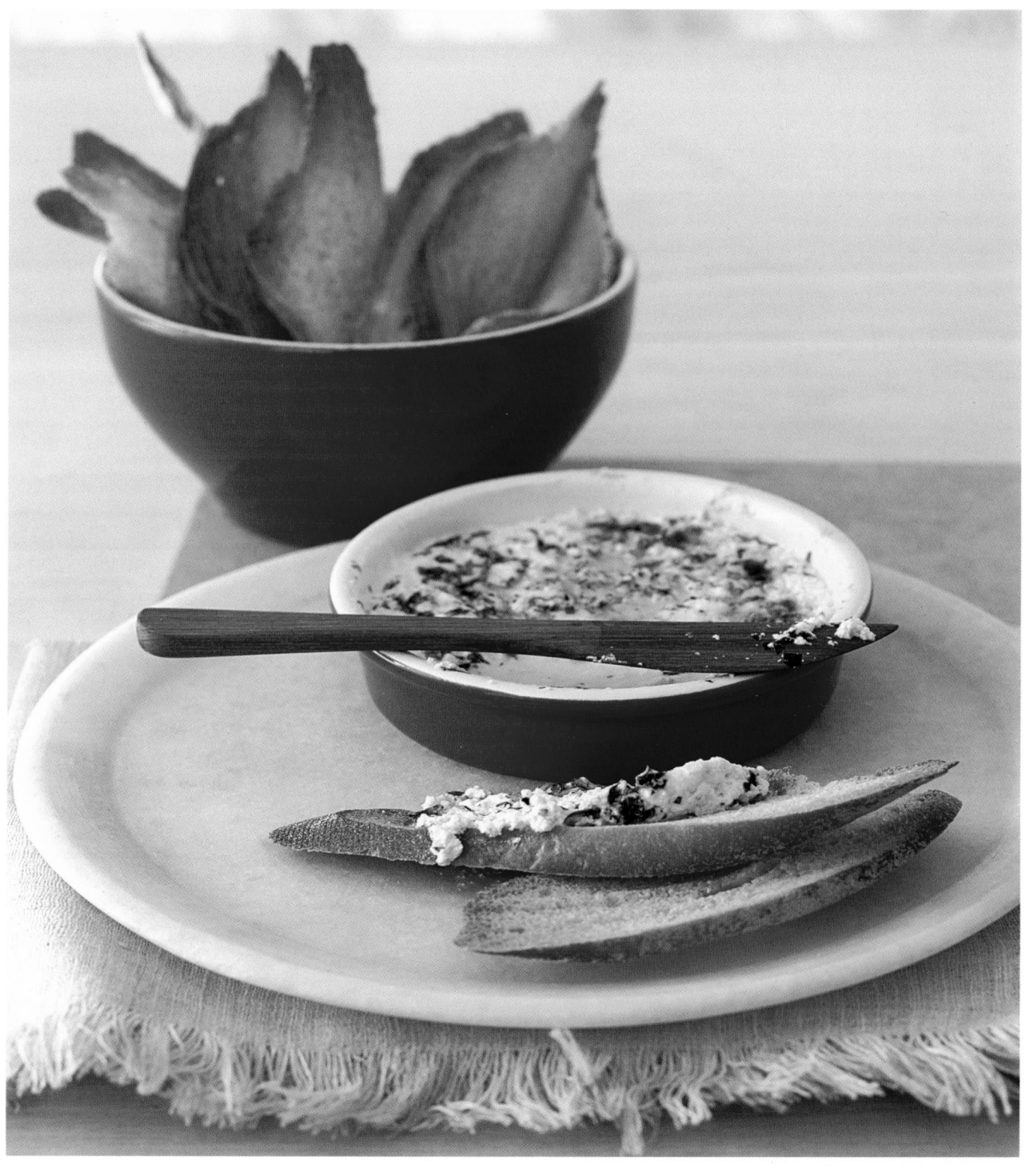

BAKED RICOTTA WITH GARLIC AND HERBS, PAGE 58
OPPOSITE PAGE: PUFFY OVEN APPLE PANCAKE, PAGE 133

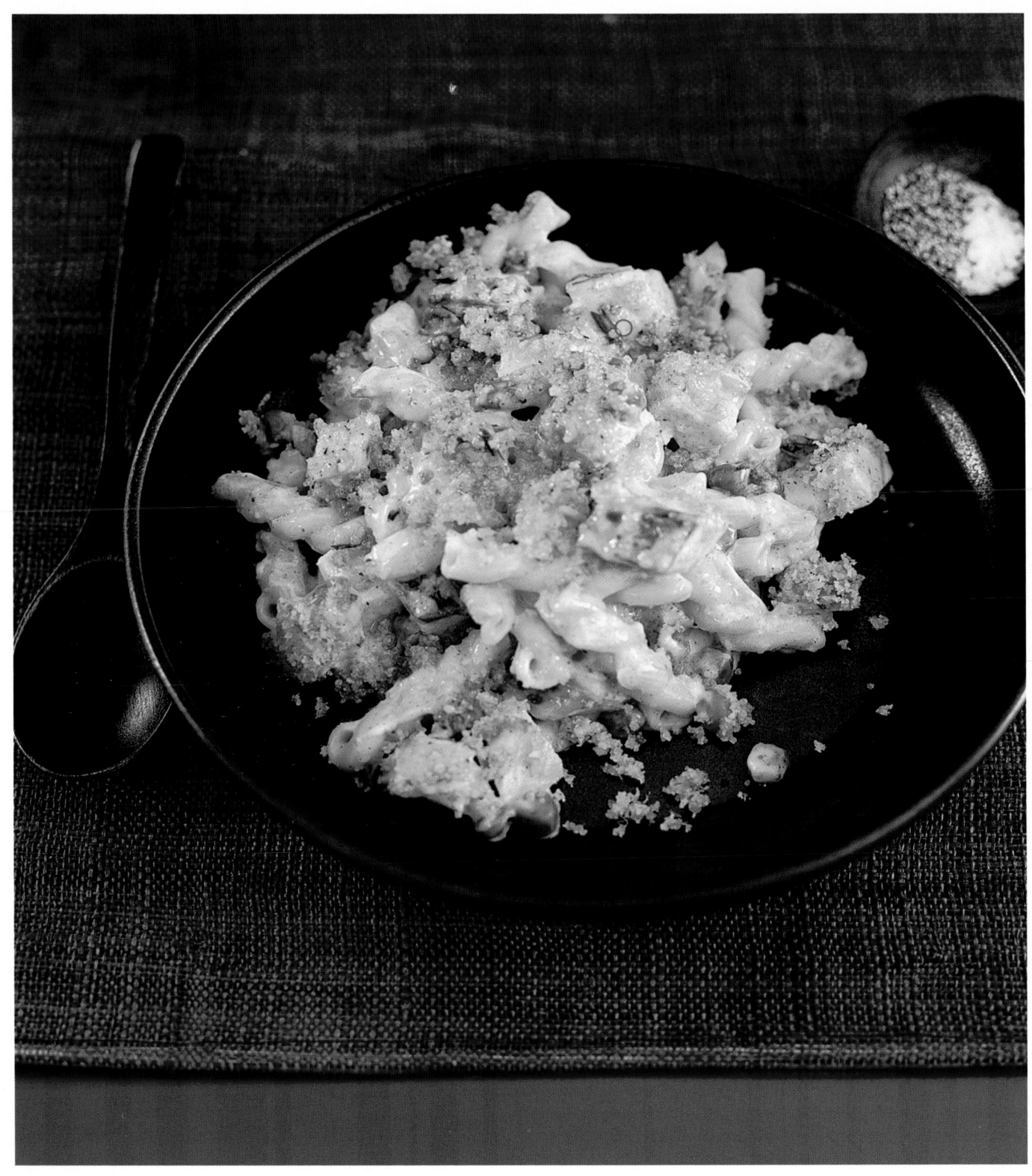

PASTA AND CHICKEN ALFREDO, PAGE 169
OPPOSITE PAGE: TOURTIÈRE, PAGE 283

MOROCCAN LAMB CASSEROLE WITH MINT DRESSING, PAGE 294
OPPOSITE PAGE: MASHED POTATO—CRUSTED PORK PIE, PAGE 266

GREEK BEEF CASSEROLE WITH ONIONS

GREEK BEEF CASSEROLE WITH ONIONS (STIFADO)

Here's an authentic-tasting Greek dish, certified by our Greek family friend. It is easy to put together, and through long and slow cooking, it melds into a succulent casserole.

¼ cup olive oil

2½ pounds top round beefsteak, cut into 1½-inch cubes

3 tablespoons red wine vinegar

½ cup dry red wine

1 cup water

1 sprig fresh rosemary

2 tablespoons tomato puree

2 teaspoons salt

1 teaspoon pepper

1 cinnamon stick

5 whole allspice berries

4 to 6 tablespoons vegetable oil

¾ pound small white onions, peeled (see Note), or frozen baby onions, thawed

1 teaspoons sugar

Chopped fresh parsley for garnish

1. Preheat the oven to 325°F. Heat the olive oil in a large skillet. Add the beef chunks, a few at a time, and brown quickly on both sides. Remove the beef to a heavy Dutch oven.

2. Pour the vinegar and wine over the beef. Add the water, rosemary, tomato puree, salt, pepper, cinnamon stick, and allspice berries. Cover and bake for 1 hour, or until the meat is tender.

3. Heat the vegetable oil in a large skillet and add the onions in one layer. Sauté them gently for about 15 minutes, shaking and turning them over until they brown lightly. Sprinkle the sugar over the onions, cover, and cook very gently for 30 minutes, until the onions are soft but not disintegrating. Lift them out with a slotted spoon and spread them over the meat, distributing them evenly. Do not stir once the onions have been added to the casserole.

4. Sprinkle with chopped fresh parsley just before serving.

○ ○ ○ ○ ○

NOTE: To peel small onions, trim them and cut an X in the bottom of each one. Drop them into boiling water for 1 minute. When they're cool enough to handle, slip off the skin.

BEEF CHUCK WITH VEGETABLES AND HERBS

This is really a slow-cooked oven pot roast. Simple to put together, it is wonderful on a chilly autumn or winter day. Add a salad and biscuits to make it a complete meal. In the fall, apple pie makes a perfect dessert.

SERVES 6 TO 8

1 boneless beef chuck roast (3 to 4 pounds)

12 small red potatoes

1 pound baby carrots

½ pound fresh green beans, trimmed

1 medium red onion, cut into wedges

1 whole head garlic, cloves separated and peeled

2 or 3 sprigs fresh rosemary

1 teaspoon dried thyme

1 teaspoon salt

1 teaspoon coarsely ground pepper

½ cup homemade (page 26) or prepared beef broth

1. Preheat the oven to 350°F. Arrange the meat in a deep 3-quart casserole. Arrange the potatoes, carrots, green beans, onion, garlic cloves, and rosemary around the meat.

2. Sprinkle with the thyme, salt, and pepper and pour the beef broth over everything. Cover and bake for 2 to 2½ hours, or until the beef and vegetables are tender. Serve with the pan juices.

POT ROAST AND POTATOES

In a casserole, beef cooks evenly without much tending. For a stress-free dinner party, all you need to add to the menu is a green salad. I like to toss baby spinach leaves with dried cranberries and chopped pecans, and coat with a simple vinaigrette. In autumn, Cranberry Pears (page 587) makes a perfect and simple dessert.

─────────────── SERVES 8 ───────────────

1 boneless beef chuck roast (4 to 4½ pounds)

½ teaspoon salt

¼ teaspoon pepper

4 tablespoons canola or olive oil, divided

2 large onions, sliced

3 tablespoons cider vinegar

½ cup tomato sauce or ketchup

2 pounds Yukon Gold or white potatoes, peeled and cut into 1-inch dice

1 pound carrots, peeled and cut into 1-inch pieces

Chopped fresh parsley for garnish

1. Preheat the oven to 325°F. Rub the meat on both sides with the salt, pepper, and 1 tablespoon of the oil.

2. Heat the remaining 3 tablespoons oil in a Dutch oven or a flameproof casserole. Brown the meat, turning to brown both sides. Add the onions and sauté, stirring. Add the vinegar, tomato sauce, potatoes, carrots, and enough water to come three-quarters of the way up the meat (1½ to 2 cups). Bring to a boil.

3. Cover the pot and bake in the oven for 2 hours, or until the meat and vegetables are tender.

4. Remove the meat from the pan and slice thinly across the grain. Put the meat and vegetables on a serving platter, spoon the pan gravy on top, and sprinkle with chopped parsley.

BARBECUED BRISKET

Perfect for a country lunch, this barbecue is easy to serve. Thinly slice the cooked meat and serve the slices in buns. The flavor improves if you make the brisket a day ahead.

SERVES 10

½ cup cider vinegar

1 clove garlic, minced

1 tablespoon vegetable oil

3 tablespoons Worcestershire sauce

Few drops of hot pepper sauce

2 tablespoons brown sugar

1 tablespoon mixed pickling spices

½ cup tomato ketchup

1 teaspoon whole-grain mustard

1 teaspoon salt

1 boneless beef brisket
(4 to 4½ pounds)

Buttered buns for serving

Mustard for serving

1. Preheat the oven to 350°F.

2. In a medium saucepan, combine the vinegar, garlic, oil, Worcestershire sauce, hot pepper sauce, brown sugar, pickling spices, ketchup, mustard, and salt. Simmer, covered, for 10 to 15 minutes over medium heat.

3. Put the meat in a 3-quart heavy Dutch oven. Pour the sauce over the beef, cover, and bake for 2½ hours, or until the meat is very tender. Cool.

4. Slice the meat thinly and return to the sauce. Cover and bake for 1 hour longer. Serve the slices in buttered buns and offer mustard.

SHORT RIBS AND ONIONS

After a couple of hours in the oven, beef short ribs are baked to tenderness. Serve with coleslaw to round out the meal.

⅓ cup all-purpose flour

1 teaspoon salt

1 teaspoon paprika

3 pounds beef short ribs, cut into 2½-inch pieces

2 cups hot homemade (page 26) or prepared beef broth

2 large onions, sliced

Hot noodles, cooked according to package directions, for serving

Chopped fresh parsley for garnish

1. Preheat the oven to 450°F. Line a 10-by-15-inch jelly-roll pan or baking sheet with aluminum foil. In a plastic bag, mix the flour, salt, and paprika. Add the short ribs and shake to coat them with the flour mixture.

2. Place the ribs in the prepared pan so there is space between them. Bake, uncovered, for 20 minutes, turning 3 times during the baking to brown on all sides. Remove from the oven and reduce the temperature to 325°F.

3. Transfer the ribs to a 2-quart casserole. Pour the hot broth over the ribs and top with the onions. Bake, covered, for 1½ to 2 hours, or until the meat is very tender. Transfer the ribs to a warm serving platter.

4. Toss the cooked noodles in the hot juices in the casserole. Garnish everything with parsley and serve the ribs and noodles together.

SPICED CHUCK WITH VEGETABLES

This chuck steak marinates for at least 2 hours, or overnight, so plan accordingly. The marinade lends the beef a flavor reminiscent of a German sauerbraten.

SERVES 6

½ cup cider vinegar

1½ cups water

2 teaspoons whole allspice

1 boneless beef chuck roast, about 2 inches thick (about 3 to 4 pounds)

3 tablespoons canola or vegetable oil

3 medium onions, cut into eighths

2 teaspoons salt

1 teaspoon dried sage

6 medium thin-skinned potatoes, peeled

6 carrots, peeled and cut into chunks

1. In a small saucepan, combine the vinegar, water, and allspice and bring to a boil. Put the meat in a deep bowl and pour the marinade over it. Cover and refrigerate for at least 2 hours or overnight, turning once or twice. Drain, reserving the marinade.

2. Preheat the oven to 350°F.

3. Place a heavy Dutch oven over medium-high heat and heat the oil. Brown the meat and onions, turning the meat several times. Remove from the heat and add the reserved marinade, salt, and sage.

4. Cover and bake for 1½ hours. Add the potatoes and carrots, and bake for another 30 minutes, or until the vegetables are tender and the meat is done. Slice the meat thinly and serve with the vegetables.

CORNMEAL-TOPPED TAMALE PIE

Plan to have leftover roast beef or pork—which we call doing a "planover"—so you can make this pie. Serve with ice-cold Mexican beer.

SERVES 6

4 tablespoons butter, divided, plus extra for the dish

1 large onion, finely chopped

1 zucchini, chopped

2 cups chopped cooked beef or pork roast

1 can (4 ounces) chopped green chiles

1 can (15 to 16 ounces) kidney beans, rinsed and drained

2 cups fresh or frozen corn kernels

1 can (8 ounces) tomato sauce

1 cup chopped ripe olives

1 teaspoon chili powder

2 cups cold water

¾ cup yellow cornmeal

½ teaspoon salt

¼ teaspoon paprika

1. Preheat the oven to 375°F. Butter a 2½- to 3-quart casserole.

2. In a large skillet, melt 3 tablespoons of the butter and add the onion and zucchini. Sauté, stirring, for 3 to 4 minutes, until the onion is tender. Stir in the meat, chiles, beans, corn, tomato sauce, olives, and chili powder. Transfer the mixture to the casserole and set aside.

3. In a medium saucepan, stir the water, cornmeal, and salt together and cook over medium-high heat until thickened. Add the remaining 1 tablespoon butter.

4. Spread the cornmeal mixture over the meat mixture and sprinkle with the paprika. Bake, uncovered, for 1 hour or until the cornmeal crust is lightly browned and the filling bubbles up around the edges. Let stand for 5 to 10 minutes before serving.

FINNISH LIVER AND RICE CASSEROLE

It isn't Christmas in Finland without this classic casserole. Liver doesn't appeal to many Americans, but it is really delicious served with melted butter and lingonberry preserves.

SERVES 6

2 tablespoons butter, plus extra for the dish

3 cups cooked rice

2½ cups milk

1 large egg, beaten

1 medium onion, chopped

¼ cup dark corn syrup

3 teaspoons salt

½ teaspoon white pepper

½ teaspoon ground marjoram

1 cup raisins

1 pound liver, sliced, then finely chopped

Melted butter for serving

Lingonberry preserves for serving

1. Preheat the oven to 350°F. Butter a shallow 2-quart casserole.

2. Mix the rice, milk, and egg in a large bowl.

3. Melt the 2 tablespoons butter in a skillet and brown the onion in it. Add to the rice and milk mixture. Stir in the corn syrup, salt, pepper, marjoram, and raisins. Add the liver and pour into the buttered casserole.

4. Bake, uncovered, for 1 hour, or until the casserole is set. Serve hot with melted butter and lingonberry preserves.

BAKED STEAK AND MUSHROOMS

Less tender cuts of beef, such as eye of round beefsteaks, cook to delicious succulence over a long and slow baking time. This is a great meal for a day when there is no time for attending to last-minute cooking.

SERVES 6

1 tablespoon vegetable oil

6 eye of round beefsteaks
(3 to 4 ounces each)

2 large onions, sliced

1 pound mushrooms, sliced

1 pound baby carrots

2 pounds potatoes, peeled and quartered

½ pound green beans

1 large can (28 ounces) cut tomatoes with their juice

2 cups homemade (page 26) or prepared beef broth

1 bay leaf

1 clove garlic, minced

1. Preheat the oven to 300°F. Place a nonstick skillet over medium-high heat and add the oil. Brown the steaks quickly on both sides and set aside.

2. Put the onions in the bottom of a deep 3-quart casserole in one layer. In layers, scatter the mushrooms, carrots, potatoes, and green beans over the onions. Place the steaks on top.

3. Pour the tomatoes with their juice, and then the beef broth, over the steaks. Add the bay leaf and sprinkle with garlic.

4. Cover the casserole tightly and bake for 8 hours, or until the beef is very tender. Add extra water during cooking if the casserole seems dry. Drain the juices into a saucepan and boil until reduced and thickened. Pour the gravy over the meat and vegetables and serve.

BEEF AND MOSTACCIOLI CASSEROLE

In this recipe, tube-shaped mostaccioli are layered with beef and topped off with a white sauce before baking. For extra nutrition I like to use whole-wheat pasta.

SERVES 6

FOR THE BEEF LAYER:

2 tablespoons olive oil

1 medium onion, chopped

1 clove garlic, chopped

3 to 4 cups chopped cooked beef

¼ teaspoon ground cinnamon

1 can (8 ounces) tomato sauce

FOR THE SAUCE:

3 tablespoons butter

¼ cup all-purpose flour

2 cups milk, heated

½ teaspoon salt

Dash of white pepper

Pinch of nutmeg

½ cup grated Parmesan cheese

FOR THE PASTA LAYER:

½ pound whole-wheat mostaccioli or elbow macaroni

2 large eggs

2 cups coarsely shredded Cheddar cheese

1. Preheat the oven to 375°F. Coat a 2½-quart casserole with cooking spray.

2. *To make the beef layer:* Heat the olive oil in a large skillet and add the onion and garlic. Sauté over low heat for 5 minutes, or until the onions are soft. Stir in the beef, cinnamon, and tomato sauce and set aside.

3. *To make the sauce:* Melt the butter in a medium saucepan and stir in the flour. Gradually whisk in the milk and cook, stirring, until thickened. Season with salt, pepper, and nutmeg, and stir in the Parmesan cheese.

4. *To make the pasta layer:* Cook the mostaccioli in a large pot of boiling salted water according to package directions; drain well and return to the pot. Whisk in the eggs.

5. Spread half the mostaccioli in the bottom of the casserole, all of the meat mixture, and then half the Cheddar cheese. Top with the remaining mostaccioli, and then all of the white sauce. Sprinkle the remaining Cheddar cheese on top. (At this point the casserole can be covered and refrigerated for up to to 1 day. Add 10 minutes to the baking time.)

6. Coat a sheet of aluminum foil with cooking spray and cover the casserole. Bake for 30 minutes. Uncover and bake for 30 minutes longer, or until the cheese is melted and lightly browned around the edges.

BEEF AND POTATO CASSEROLE

This homey casserole begins with cut-up leftover roast beef and gravy, which are topped with leftover mashed potatoes and a shower of Cheddar cheese. Think of it as comfort food in a casserole.

SERVES 6

2½ to 3 cups finely chopped roast beef

½ cup finely chopped onion

1 cup roast beef gravy or prepared brown gravy

2 tablespoons dry white wine

¼ teaspoon dried thyme, crumbled

¼ teaspoon dried rosemary, crumbled

½ to 1 teaspoon salt, or more to taste

¼ teaspoon pepper

Beef broth or water, if needed

2 cups cooked mashed potatoes, seasoned with salt and pepper

2 tablespoons butter

1 large egg

½ to 1 cup shredded Cheddar cheese

1. Preheat the oven to 350°F.

2. In a large bowl, combine the beef, onion, gravy, wine, thyme, rosemary, salt, and pepper. Stir in beef broth or water if the mixture seems dry (it should have the texture of a meat loaf mixture before it is shaped and baked).

3. Put the beef mixture in a shallow 2-quart casserole. Combine the mashed potatoes with the butter and egg in a medium bowl. Mix well and then spread over the meat mixture. Sprinkle with the cheese. Bake, uncovered, for 30 minutes, or until browned and bubbly.

CORNED BEEF AND CABBAGE CASSEROLE

Make this St. Patrick's Day classic with either leftover corned beef that you've cooked yourself or the canned variety. This is perfect served with thinly sliced Irish Wheat and Oatmeal Bread (page 69) and, for dessert, Mixed Fruit Clafouti (page 595).

SERVES 8

4 tablespoons butter

4 cups chopped cabbage

1 cup sliced celery

½ cup chopped onion

½ pound mostaccioli or rotini pasta, cooked according to package directions and drained

2 cups cooked corned beef, diced, or 1 can (16 ounces) corned beef, crumbled

1 cup sour cream

½ teaspoon dry mustard

½ teaspoon caraway seed

⅛ teaspoon pepper

1 cup shredded Swiss cheese

1. Preheat the oven to 350°F. Coat a 2½- to 3-quart casserole with cooking spray.

2. In a large nonstick skillet, melt the butter and add the cabbage, celery, and onion. Sauté over medium heat for about 10 minutes, stirring occasionally, until the vegetables have cooked down. Add the remaining ingredients, except for the cheese, and mix well. Spoon into the casserole and top with the cheese.

3. Coat a sheet of aluminum foil with cooking spray and cover the casserole. (At this point the dish can be covered and refrigerated for up to 1 day. Add 10 minutes to the baking time.) Bake for 45 to 50 minutes, until heated through.

EASIEST-EVER BEEF AND WINE CASSEROLE

When I found this recipe in my late mother-in-law's collection, I kind of doubted that it could be good. But then I thought, if you use good ingredients, it can't be all that bad. So I tried it. We thought it was fantastic! This recipe requires no more effort than piling all the ingredients into a casserole dish, covering it, and sticking it in the oven. Serve it with cooked noodles or mashed potatoes and a salad.

SERVES 4

1 pound lean beef stew meat

½ cup red wine

1 can (14 ounces) beef broth

1 teaspoon salt

Freshly ground pepper (about 7 turns of the grinder)

2 cloves garlic, minced

1 medium onion, sliced

¼ cup all-purpose flour

¼ cup fine dry breadcrumbs

1. Preheat the oven to 275°F if you prefer to let the casserole bake for 6 hours, or 300°F if you'd like it to be done in 3 hours.

2. Combine all of the ingredients in a 2-quart casserole.

3. Bake, covered, for 3 or 6 hours, depending on the oven temperature, or until the beef is tender.

MOUSSAKA

Made with ground beef or ground lamb, this hearty casserole is a popular dish throughout the Middle East. There are many variations. The version on page 000, for example, is made with potatoes instead of the more traditional eggplant featured here. Sometimes moussaka is topped with a plain béchamel sauce, but here the sauce is thickened with eggs to make a custard-like sauce.

— SERVES 8 —

2 tablespoons olive oil

2 tablespoons butter, melted

2 large eggplants (about 1½ pounds each), cut crosswise into ½-inch-thick slices

2 pounds ground beef or lamb

2 large onions, chopped

2 cloves garlic, minced

2 tablespoons all-purpose flour

1 teaspoon ground cinnamon

1 teaspoon dried oregano

1 teaspoon salt

½ teaspoon ground nutmeg

½ teaspoon pepper

1 can (8 ounces) tomato sauce

¾ cup dry red wine

1 can (14½ ounces) diced tomatoes with their juice

½ cup minced fresh parsley

1 recipe Béchamel Sauce (page 21)

6 large eggs

1. Preheat the oven to 400°F.

2. In a small dish, mix the olive oil and butter and spread equally between 2 rimmed baking sheets. Arrange the eggplant slices on top of the oil and butter mixture, dividing the slices between the baking sheets. Turn the slices over to coat both sides of the eggplant. Place in the oven and bake for 15 minutes. Turn the slices over and bake for another 15 minutes, or until the

eggplant is soft. Remove from the oven and cool on the baking sheets.

3. Reduce the oven temperature to 350°F. Coat a 9-by-13-inch baking dish with cooking spray.

4. Place a large nonstick skillet over medium-high heat and add the meat. Cook the meat, stirring and breaking it up, until it's crumbled. Add the onions and garlic and cook, stirring often, for 10 minutes, or until the onions are soft. Discard any extra fat. Stir in the flour, cinnamon, oregano, salt, nutmeg, and pepper. Slowly stir in the tomato sauce, wine, diced tomatoes with their juice, and parsley. Cook, stirring, for 15 minutes, or until thick, and set aside.

5. Prepare the Béchamel Sauce and whisk in the eggs. Set aside.

6. Arrange half the cooked eggplant slices in the prepared baking dish. Spread with the meat sauce. Top with remaining eggplant. Pour the Béchamel Sauce over all. (The casserole can be covered and refrigerated at this point for up to 1 day. Add 10 minutes to the baking time.)

7. Bake, uncovered, for 50 minutes, or until the casserole is bubbly around the edges and the center is firm. Let stand for 15 minutes before cutting into squares.

CORNED BEEF CASSEROLE

This is a great way to give leftover roast beef a fresh new taste. For a quick meal, however, keep a can of corned beef in your cupboard.

SERVES 4

2 cups chopped roast beef, or 1 can (15 ounces) corned beef, chopped

1 can (14½ ounces) stewed tomatoes with their juice

5 tablespoons all-purpose flour, divided

2 tablespoons butter

¼ teaspoon salt

¼ teaspoon chili powder

½ cup milk

1 cup shredded Cheddar cheese

2 large eggs, separated

1. Preheat the oven to 325°F. Coat a 1½-quart casserole with cooking spray.

2. Combine the chopped beef or canned corned beef, tomatoes with their juice, and 3 tablespoons of the flour in a medium bowl. Spread out evenly in the bottom of the casserole and set aside.

3. In a medium saucepan over medium heat, melt the butter and stir in the remaining 2 tablespoons flour. Stir in the salt and chili powder. Gradually stir in the milk and cook, stirring constantly, until thickened. Add the cheese, stirring until melted and the sauce is well blended. Remove the sauce from the heat.

4. Beat the egg yolks in a small bowl and stir in a few tablespoons of the sauce. Add the tempered eggs to the saucepan, stirring well.

5. Beat the egg whites in a large bowl until stiff, and fold the cheese mixture into the egg whites. Pour the egg mixture over the beef mixture in the casserole dish. Bake, uncovered, for 35 to 40 minutes, until lightly browned. Remove from the oven and let stand for about 10 minutes before serving.

ROUND STEAK CASSEROLE

This is an easy, everyday kind of dish. You can put it together and refrigerate it to bake the next day, or bake it slowly right away while you do other things. Add a broccoli coleslaw and freshly baked biscuits to complete the meal.

SERVES 4

1 pound top round beefsteak, cut into 1-inch cubes

1 large sweet onion, thinly sliced

½ cup cider vinegar

1 cup water

1 teaspoon salt

½ teaspoon pepper

¼ cup tomato ketchup

2 tablespoons olive oil

¼ cup dry seasoned breadcrumbs

1. Preheat the oven to 325°F. Coat the bottom of a heavy 2-quart casserole with cooking spray.

2. Put the meat in the bottom of the casserole and top with the onion. Pour the vinegar and water over all and sprinkle with salt and pepper. Mix the ketchup and olive oil together and pour evenly over all as well.

3. Sprinkle with the breadcrumbs, cover, and bake for 2 hours, or until the meat is very tender.

Chapter 7
PORK CASSEROLES

Although wild pigs were found in Mexico by the Spanish conqueror Hernán Cortés in the early 1500s, swine have probably been domesticated since the Stone Age. It is said that Hernando de Soto brought a herd of thirteen pigs to Florida in the mid-1500s.

The pork we know today is a far cry from those strong-muscled animals. Although pigs are no longer muscular, they are much leaner than they were a few decades ago. In fact, they are one of the leanest meats available. Pork producers responded to consumers who were worried about all the fat. In this chapter we use a variety of cuts, including loin chops, tenderloin, ham, ribs, sausage, and ground pork.

BLUE CHEESE AND PORK TENDERLOIN CASSEROLE

Nestled on top of egg noodles, the pork tenderloin slices cook really quickly, and they get an interesting flavor boost from blue cheese and green chiles. Serve with roasted asparagus and slices of rye bread for a standout meal.

SERVES 6

6 ounces egg noodles

6 slices pork tenderloin, 1 inch thick

¾ teaspoon salt

¾ teaspoon pepper

3 tablespoons butter

3 tablespoons all-purpose flour

2½ cups milk

¾ cup crumbled blue cheese

1 can (4 ounces) chopped green chiles

1. Preheat the oven to 350°F.

2. Cook the noodles according to package directions and drain. Transfer to a shallow 2-quart casserole.

3. Season the tenderloin with the salt and pepper. Heat 1 tablespoon of the butter in a nonstick skillet and brown the meat on both sides over moderately high heat. Place on top of the noodles.

4. Add the remaining 2 tablespoons butter to the pan. Add the flour and stir until the flour is lightly browned, about 5 minutes. Add the milk and bring to a boil, whisking constantly. Add the cheese and stir until smooth. Add the chiles. Pour the sauce over the meat and noodles.

5. Bake, uncovered, for about 30 minutes, until bubbly.

CHILI PORK STEW

Serve this casserole, with its south-of-the-border flavors, over rice.
For a refreshing dessert, offer fresh mango or papaya slices sprinkled
with coarse salt.

SERVES 8

2 pounds boneless pork shoulder, cut into 1½-inch cubes

¼ cup all-purpose flour

2 tablespoons vegetable oil

1 clove garlic, minced

1 medium onion, chopped

2 cups water

1½ teaspoons salt

1½ teaspoons chili powder

¼ pound pepperoni or chorizo sausage, peeled and sliced

3 tomatoes, diced

½ teaspoon dried oregano

Sour cream for serving

Diced avocado for serving

Chopped fresh cilantro for serving

Diced tomatoes for serving

1. Preheat the oven to 350°F.

2. Toss the pork cubes with the flour until the cubes are coated. Heat the oil in a heavy Dutch oven. Add the pork and brown quickly over medium-high heat, stirring and turning the cubes constantly. Add the garlic and onion and stir until heated through. Add the water, salt, chili powder, pepperoni, tomatoes, and oregano.

3. Cover and bake for 45 minutes, or until the meat is cooked through. Serve with sour cream, avocado, cilantro, and tomatoes.

ENCHILADA CASSEROLE

In this piquant dish, the tortillas absorb the flavors, which meld together when refrigerated overnight. Serve watermelon sorbet for dessert.

———————————— SERVES 8 ————————————

8 flour tortillas (7 inches)

¾ pound cooked ham

1 small onion, chopped

1 small green bell pepper, seeded and chopped

1 small tomato, chopped

2 cups shredded Cheddar cheese

2 cups heavy cream

1 tablespoon all-purpose flour

1 can (4 ounces) diced green chiles

4 large eggs

Picante sauce for serving

1. Coat a 9-by-13-inch baking dish with cooking spray.

2. On one side of a tortilla, spread about ¼ cup ham, 1 tablespoon onion, 1 tablespoon bell pepper, 1 tablespoon tomato, and 1 tablespoon cheese. Roll up, enclosing the filling. Repeat with the remaining tortillas and set the remaining cheese aside. Place the tortilla rolls in the baking dish, seam side down.

3. In a medium bowl, combine the cream, flour, green chiles, and eggs. Pour the mixture over the enchiladas. Coat a sheet of aluminum foil with cooking spray and cover the baking dish with the foil. Refrigerate overnight.

4. Preheat the oven to 350°F. Remove the casserole from the refrigerator, uncover, and bake for 45 to 50 minutes, or until the egg mixture is set. Sprinkle with the remaining cheese and return to the oven for 5 minutes, or until the cheese is melted. Serve hot with picante sauce.

POTATO AND SAUSAGE CASSEROLE

This recipe comes from my friend Esa Anttila in Finland. Instead of making a casserole, however, he forms the same potato and pork mixture into patties to make potato sausage. This casserole looks like a meat loaf. It makes an excellent first course, served cold over a bed of crisp lettuce with whole-grain mustard and lingonberry preserves on the side.

— SERVES 6 —

½ cup quick-cooking rolled oats

1 cup water

5 medium Yukon Gold potatoes

2 onions

1 pound lean ground pork

1 teaspoon salt

1 teaspoon ground allspice

Lingonberry preserves for serving

Strong Finnish or brown whole-grain mustard for serving

1. Preheat the oven to 350°F. Butter a 5-by-9-inch ceramic loaf pan.

2. In a small saucepan, cook the rolled oats in the water until the water is absorbed, about 5 minutes.

3. Peel and shred the potatoes into a bowl, or shred in a food processor with a shredding disk in place. Peel the onions, slice thinly from top to bottom, and add to the potatoes. Stir in the cooked rolled oats, ground pork, salt, and allspice.

4. Press the mixture into the prepared loaf pan. Bake, uncovered, for 1 to 1½ hours, or until the loaf is cooked through and registers 165°F on an instant-read thermometer. Cool, slice, and serve with lingonberry preserves and mustard.

HAM AND CABBAGE CASSEROLE

Cabbage, ham, and caraway seeds blend together to make a casserole reminiscent of old-fashioned farmhouse food. Serve with a rustic loaf of bread.

SERVES 8

3 tablespoons butter, plus extra for the dish

½ medium cabbage (about 1½ pounds)

1 package (8 ounces) whole-wheat extra-wide egg noodles

3 cups cooked ham cubes, ground in the food processor

3 cups milk, scalded

3 large eggs

½ teaspoon caraway seeds

1. Preheat the oven to 350°F. Butter a 9-by-13-inch casserole. Shred the cabbage into 2-inch pieces and set aside.

2. Cook the noodles according to package directions until tender but firm to the bite; drain.

3. In a large heavy skillet or wok, melt the 3 tablespoons butter. Add the cabbage and sauté over medium-high heat for 5 minutes, or until wilted.

4. Put half of the cooked noodles in the bottom of the casserole. Top with half of the sautéed cabbage in an even layer, and then with all of the ham. Cover with the remaining cabbage, and then with the remaining noodles.

5. In a medium bowl, beat the scalded milk and eggs and add the caraway seeds. Pour over the cabbage mixture in the casserole. Coat a sheet of aluminum foil with cooking spray and cover the casserole. Bake for 1 hour, or until set.

HAM AND CHEESE CASSEROLE

Whether for breakfast, brunch, or supper, this satisfying, puffy casserole requires just a few minutes of preparation. Serve with a salad of sliced tomatoes set on a bed of crisp lettuce and sprinkled with feta cheese. Cinnamon Bubble Bread (page 71) goes well with this dish.

SERVES 6

6 large eggs

1 cup milk

½ cup sour cream

2 cups frozen chopped broccoli, thawed and drained

2 cups crisp seasoned croutons

1 teaspoon poultry seasoning

2 cups chopped boiled ham

½ cup shredded Swiss cheese

½ cup shredded Cheddar cheese

1. Preheat the oven to 375°F. Coat a shallow 2-quart casserole with cooking spray.

2. In a large bowl, whisk the eggs, milk, and sour cream until blended. Add the broccoli, croutons, seasoning, ham, and Swiss cheese and mix well. Spread out the mixture evenly in the casserole. Coat a sheet of aluminum foil with cooking spray and cover the casserole.

3. Bake for 1 hour. Uncover, sprinkle with the Cheddar cheese, and bake for 5 minutes, or until the cheese is melted and the mixture is cooked through.

HAM AND CHICKEN PIE

To make leftover bits of ham and chicken into a new creation, combine them with a quickly made sauce, cover the mixture with a pastry crust, and *voilà*–a delightful dish for lunch or supper!

SERVES 4 TO 6

1 cup diced cooked ham

1 cup diced cooked chicken or turkey

1 cup cooked fresh or frozen peas

2 green onions, minced (white and green parts)

½ cup finely diced celery

2 tablespoons butter

3 tablespoons all-purpose flour

2 cups milk

½ to 1 teaspoon salt

¼ teaspoon pepper

1 teaspoon dried marjoram, thyme, or basil

1 recipe Flaky Pastry (page 32)

1. Preheat the oven to 350°F.

2. Combine the ham, chicken, and peas in a 9-inch quiche pan or a shallow 1½-quart oval casserole.

3. In a skillet over medium heat, sauté the green onions and celery in the butter for 2 minutes. Add the flour, stirring until blended, and slowly add the milk. Cook, stirring, until thickened. Season with the salt, pepper, and herb. Pour the sauce over the ham and turkey mixture.

4. Prepare the pastry, refrigerate for 30 minutes, and roll it out so it is slightly larger than the top of the dish. Lay it across the casserole and crimp the edges to seal. With the tip of a knife, cut a few slits into the top of the pastry to allow steam to escape during baking.

5. Bake for 30 minutes, or until the pastry is golden.

HAM AND SCALLOPED POTATOES

We always seem to have sliced ham left over from Easter dinner, so sometime during the following week, I make these scalloped potatoes with a layer of ham in the center.

SERVES 6

6 medium potatoes, preferably russets, peeled and sliced

½ cup finely chopped green onions (white and green parts)

2 tablespoons all-purpose flour

½ teaspoon salt

½ teaspoon pepper

About 1 pound thinly sliced or diced cooked ham, or as much or as little as you wish

1 can (12 ounces) undiluted evaporated milk

½ cup cream or milk

1 tablespoon butter, cut up

1. Preheat the oven to 325°F. Coat a shallow 2-quart casserole with cooking spray.

2. Layer half of the potatoes in the baking dish, and sprinkle with the green onions, 1 tablespoon of the flour, ¼ teaspoon of the salt, and ¼ teaspoon of the pepper. Top with the ham in one layer, and cover with the remaining potatoes. Sprinkle with the remaining 1 tablespoon flour, ¼ teaspoon salt, and ¼ teaspoon pepper.

3. Mix the evaporated milk and cream together and pour evenly over the casserole. Dot with the butter.

4. Coat a sheet of aluminum foil with nonstick cooking spray. Cover the casserole and bake for 1 hour, uncover, and continue baking 30 minutes to 1 hour longer, or until the potatoes are cooked and the top is lightly browned.

HAM AND SWEET ONIONS

Sautéed sweet onions form the top and bottom crusts, enclosing a ham-and-spinach layer in the middle. This savory dish is better yet on the second day, when the flavors have had a chance to blend together and develop.

SERVES 8

3 slices thick-cut smoked bacon, coarsely diced, plus 1 slice for greasing the baking dish

3 large sweet white onions (2½ to 3 pounds total), cut into ½-inch-thick rounds

1 teaspoon salt

1½ pounds smoked ham, cut into ½-inch dice

1 bag (9 ounces) fresh baby spinach, or 1 package (10 ounces) chopped frozen spinach

2 large cloves garlic, pressed with a garlic press

2 teaspoons fennel seeds, crushed

Pepper

½ cup heavy cream

1 tablespoon grated lemon zest

¾ pound fontina cheese, cut into ½-inch cubes

¼ cup grated Parmesan cheese

1 tablespoon seasoned fine dry breadcrumbs

1. Preheat the oven to 350°F. Rub a large oval gratin dish or baking dish with a piece of bacon.

2. In a large skillet over medium-high heat, cook the diced bacon until the fat has rendered and the bacon is crisp. Lower the heat to medium-low, add the onions, and cook until softened and golden, but not browned, stirring occasionally, about 20 to 25 minutes. Sprinkle with the salt. Remove the onions and bacon from the pan and set aside.

3. Add the ham, spinach, garlic, fennel seeds, and pepper to taste to the skillet and sauté for 3 minutes. Stir the cream and lemon zest into the ham mixture.

4. Spread out half of the onions in the bottom of the dish. Cover with the ham mixture and top with the remaining onions. Press the fontina cheese into the onions, leaving a margin of onions without cheese near the edges of the dish. Mix the Parmesan and breadcrumbs in a small bowl and sprinkle over the casserole. (You can assemble the dish up to this point, cover, and refrigerate overnight. Add 10 minutes to the baking time.)

5. Bake the casserole, uncovered, for 45 to 55 minutes, until the top is golden brown. Let stand for 15 minutes before serving.

ASIAN OVEN-LACQUERED BONELESS PORK RIBS

What used to be called "glazed" is now "lacquered" in the realm of Asian foods. It simply means the food is coated with a mixture of honey or molasses and various Asian flavorings, such as Chinese five-spice powder, hoisin sauce, and citrus. Here the ribs are first cooked until tender, and then brushed with this rather heavy glaze. Wonderful for those who like gooey, sticky ribs!

SERVES 6

3 pounds boneless country-style pork ribs

2 teaspoons salt

½ cup low-sodium soy sauce

Zest of 2 oranges, cut into ½-inch strips

2 tablespoons light molasses

2 teaspoons honey

2 tablespoons hoisin sauce

2 pinches red pepper flakes

1 tablespoon Chinese five-spice powder

Cooked brown rice for serving

1. Preheat the oven to 325°F. Cut the ribs into 3- or 4-inch-wide pieces.

2. Sprinkle the salt into a large heavy skillet or wok and place over high heat. Add as many pieces of ribs as will fit into the pan without crowding and brown them, turning them occasionally.

3. In a small saucepan, combine the soy sauce, orange zest, molasses, honey, hoisin sauce, red pepper flakes, and five-spice powder. Simmer over medium-low heat for 5 minutes. Remove from the heat and set aside.

4. Line a 9-by-13-inch baking pan with foil and coat with cooking spray. Arrange the ribs in the pan. Bake, uncovered, for 1½ hours, or until the ribs are tender, basting 3 or 4 times with the sauce during baking.

○ ○ ○ ○ ○

NOTE: Five-spice powder is a mixture of equal parts of cinnamon, cloves, fennel seed, star anise, and Szechwan peppercorns. You can find it with other spices in the baking sections of most supermarkets.

MASHED POTATO–CRUSTED PORK PIE

This casserole is a great way to use what's left of Sunday's pork roast, including the pan juices. In fact, I purposely cook a large enough roast so that there will be enough left over to make this homey casserole.

SERVES 6

7 tablespoons butter, divided

1 medium onion, finely chopped

1 clove garlic, minced

3 tablespoons all-purpose flour

1½ cups roast pork pan juices or beef broth, heated to boiling

2 cups chopped cooked lean roast pork (gristle and fat removed before chopping)

1 teaspoon Dijon mustard

1 teaspoon dried thyme

¼ cup chopped fresh parsley

3 large baking potatoes (about 1½ pounds total), peeled and cubed

½ cup milk, heated

1 teaspoon salt

3 tablespoons fine dry breadcrumbs

1. Preheat the oven to 400°F.

2. In a large skillet, melt 2 tablespoons of the butter and add the onion and garlic. Sauté for 15 minutes over medium heat, stirring often, until the onion is soft and aromatic. Sprinkle the flour evenly over the onion and garlic, whisk in the hot pan juices or broth, and boil until thickened. Add the pork, mustard, thyme, and parsley and set side.

3. For the potato crust, put the potatoes into a deep large saucepan, cover with water, and boil until fork-tender, about 20 minutes. Remove from the heat and drain. With a hand mixer, beat in 4 tablespoons of the butter, the hot milk, and salt.

4. Spread out about a third of the potato mixture evenly in the bottom of a shallow 2- to 2½-quart casserole. Top with the pork mixture, and pipe the remaining potato mixture around the edges with a pastry bag or use a spoon.

5. Melt the remaining 1 tablespoon butter in a small saucepan and mix with the breadcrumbs. Sprinkle on the center of the casserole. Bake, uncovered, for 20 minutes, or until the potatoes are lightly browned.

OVEN-BARBECUED COUNTRY-STYLE RIBS

Meaty pork ribs cook until they reach falling-off-the-bone tenderness. Serve this with a pile of mashed potatoes, and you have a perfect meal for a chilly day.

SERVES 6

3 pounds boneless country-style pork ribs

2 teaspoons salt

½ teaspoon pepper

1 large onion, chopped

¼ cup cider vinegar

¼ cup packed light or dark brown sugar

1 cup tomato ketchup

3 tablespoons fresh lemon juice

1 tablespoon prepared mustard

A few drops Tabasco sauce

A few drops liquid-smoke flavoring (optional)

½ cup water

1. Preheat the oven to 325°F. Separate the ribs into 3- to 4-inch pieces.

2. Sprinkle the salt into a large heavy skillet or wok and place over high heat. Add as many pieces of ribs as will fit in the pan without crowding and brown them, turning them occasionally.

3. Remove the ribs to a 9-by-13-inch baking dish. Pour off all but 2 tablespoons of the fat from the skillet.

4. Add onions to the skillet and sauté over medium-high heat for 5 minutes, or until tender. Add the remaining ingredients and bring to a boil, stirring constantly. Cook until the sauce is slightly thickened and the consistency of ketchup. Spoon over the ribs in the baking dish.

5. Bake, uncovered, for 1½ hours, or until the ribs are tender, basting 2 or 3 times during baking. Serve directly from the baking dish.

PORK AND BROCCOLI

Got leftover bits of pork? Here is one quick and easy way to turn them into a fresh new main dish.

SERVES 6

2 packages (10 ounces each) frozen broccoli spears or chopped broccoli, or 1 pound fresh broccoli

1½ to 2 cups diced cooked pork (gristle and fat removed before dicing)

2 cups seasoned toasted croutons

1 cup mayonnaise

½ cup sour cream

¼ cup grated Parmesan cheese

1. Preheat the oven to 350°F. Butter a 2-quart casserole.

2. If using frozen broccoli, cook according to package directions and drain. If using fresh broccoli, cut off and discard tough ends from stalks. Peel the remaining stems if the skin is tough. Cook in boiling water for 10 minutes, or until tender, and drain. Chop the broccoli.

3. Spread the pork evenly over the bottom of the casserole. Top with the broccoli and half the toasted croutons.

4. Mix the mayonnaise and sour cream in a small bowl. Spread over the top of the croutons and sprinkle with the Parmesan cheese. Bake, uncovered, for 30 minutes, or until bubbly and hot.

PORK CASSEROLE STEW WITH BEER AND JUNIPER BERRIES

This stew simmers slowly in the oven for several hours, unattended, while the flavors of pork, garlic, herbs, juniper, and beer meld together and their aromas fill your kitchen.

SERVES 6 TO 8

2 tablespoons vegetable oil

3 pounds lean boneless pork, cut into 1½-inch cubes

Salt

Pepper

1 tablespoon chopped fresh garlic

2 cups sliced onions

1 bay leaf

2 cups peeled and chopped carrots

1 cup chopped celery

2 tablespoons all-purpose flour

1 bottle (12 ounces) dark beer

2 whole cloves

1 teaspoon fresh thyme leaves, or ½ teaspoon dried

10 juniper berries, crushed with the side of a knife

Mashed potatoes for serving

1. Preheat the oven to 300°F. Heat the oil over medium-high heat in a heavy flameproof casserole or a Dutch oven. Brown the pork cubes, a few at a time, turning the cubes over to brown on all sides and transferring them to a plate as they are done. Return the cubes and their juices to the casserole and sprinkle with salt, pepper, and garlic.

2. Spread the onions over the top and bury the bay leaf among the onions. Top with the carrots and celery, sprinkle evenly with the flour, and pour the beer over all. Add the cloves, thyme leaves, and juniper berries, pressing them into the mixture.

3. Cover tightly and bake for 3 to 4 hours, or until the pork is very tender. Serve with mashed potatoes.

PORK CHOP AND APPLE BAKE WITH CARAWAY NOODLES

Pork has a natural affinity for apples. In this dish, their flavors blend as the dish bakes. Serve with a salad of shredded cabbage, carrots, and onions with a vinaigrette dressing.

SERVES 4

6 tablespoons butter, plus extra for the dish

¼ cup all-purpose flour

½ teaspoon salt

½ teaspoon dry mustard

⅛ teaspoon pepper

⅛ teaspoon ground allspice

4 bone-in pork chops, 1 inch thick

2 tablespoons brown sugar

1½ cups apple cider

1 package (8 ounces) egg noodles, cooked according to package directions

1 teaspoon caraway seeds

2 apples, cored, peeled, and sliced

⅓ cup raisins

½ teaspoon ground cinnamon

1. Preheat the oven to 350°F. Lightly butter a shallow 2-quart casserole or 8-inch square baking dish.

2. In a small bowl, mix the flour, salt, mustard, pepper, and allspice. Coat the pork chops with the flour mixture. Set aside the remaining seasoned flour.

3. In a heavy skillet, melt 2 tablespoons of the butter, add the pork chops, and brown on both sides. Place in the buttered casserole.

4. Stir the brown sugar and reserved flour into the meat drippings in the skillet to make a thick paste. Over moderately high heat, gradually whisk in the apple cider and continue whisking until thickened and smooth. Remove from the heat.

5. Toss the noodles with the remaining 4 tablespoons butter and add the caraway seeds. Spread in the casserole. Arrange the apple slices over the pork chops and place on top of the noodles in the casserole, sprinkle with the raisins, and pour the sauce over all. Sprinkle with cinnamon. Bake, covered, for 1 hour or until the chops are tender. Serve hot.

PORK CHOP AND APRICOT CASSEROLE

Scalloped Mushrooms and Potatoes (page 435) makes a great accompaniment for this casserole. Pork is always tasty when cooked with fruit and a bit of sweetener. Here the molasses adds flavor and color to the mixture of orange and apricots.

SERVES 4

4 boneless pork chops, 1½ inches thick

½ teaspoon salt, plus extra for seasoning

½ teaspoon poultry seasoning

¾ cup orange juice

½ cup chopped dried apricots

2 tablespoons light molasses

2 tablespoons apple cider vinegar

⅓ cup water

2 tablespoons all-purpose flour

Salt

Pepper

1. Preheat the oven to 350°F. Sprinkle the pork chops on both sides with the ½ teaspoon salt and the poultry seasoning and place in a shallow 2-quart casserole.

2. Combine the orange juice and apricots in a saucepan. Add the molasses and vinegar and heat the mixture to a boil. Pour over the chops, cover the dish with foil, and bake until the chops are tender and cooked through, about 45 minutes.

3. Remove the chops to a serving platter and keep warm. Pour cooking liquid from the casserole dish into a saucepan. Mix the water and flour to make a smooth paste and add to the saucepan. Heat to boiling, stirring constantly. Boil, stirring, for 1 minute. Season to taste with salt and pepper. Pour the sauce over the chops and serve.

PORK CHOP, APPLE, AND GINGER CASSEROLE

Boneless pork chops are very lean and it is easy to overcook them, which makes them dry. Here they cook on a bed of sliced apples, which helps preserve their moisture.

SERVES 6

2 tablespoons butter, cut into small pieces, plus extra for the dish

6 boneless pork chops, about 1½ inches thick

Salt

Pepper

1 tablespoon vegetable oil or butter

3 tart apples, such as Granny Smith, cored and sliced (leave peel on)

¼ cup light or dark brown sugar

2 tablespoons finely chopped candied ginger

½ teaspoon ground cinnamon

1. Preheat the oven to 350°F. Lightly oil or butter a 9-by-13-inch baking dish.

2. Sprinkle the pork chops with salt and pepper on both sides.

3. Heat the oil in a heavy non-stick skillet over moderately high heat. Add the pork chops and brown on both sides, about 1 minute per side.

4. Arrange the sliced apples in the baking dish. Sprinkle with the sugar, ginger, and cinnamon and dot with the 2 tablespoons butter. Top with the pork chops.

5. Coat a sheet of aluminum foil with nonstick spray and cover the dish. Bake for 45 minutes to 1 hour, until the pork chops are cooked through.

PORK CHOPS ON APPLE STUFFING

In this recipe, pork chops bake on top of a stuffing, which absorbs all the wonderful juices. Personally, I think bone-in pork chops have a lot more flavor than boneless, although you could use boneless chops in this recipe if that's what you have on hand.

SERVES 4

5 tablespoons butter, melted, plus extra for the dish

4 bone-in pork chops, 1 inch thick

Salt

Pepper

1½ cups seasoned stuffing mix

1 large apple, cut into chunks (leave peel on)

2 stalks celery, chopped

1 small onion, thinly sliced

1. Preheat the oven to 325°F. Butter a shallow 2-quart casserole.

2. Trim the fat off the pork chops and sprinkle both sides with salt and pepper.

3. In a large bowl, mix the 5 tablespoons butter into the stuffing. Add the apple, celery, and onion.

4. Spoon a layer of stuffing onto the bottom of the prepared casserole. Stand the chops on edge on the top of the stuffing layer with the fat side up. Spoon the remaining stuffing around, between, and over the chops. Cover and bake for 1½ hours, or until the pork chops are cooked through and the stuffing is lightly browned around the edges.

PORK CHOPS WITH POTATOES AND MUSHROOMS

So simple! Just layer everything in a casserole and bake it. Add a shredded carrot salad to the menu, and if you're up to it, bake a pan of biscuits right along with the casserole.

— MAKES 4 SERVINGS —

Olive oil for brushing

4 large baking potatoes, scrubbed and thinly sliced (leave skin on)

2 cups sliced mushrooms

2 small onions, sliced

2 teaspoons salt

1 teaspoon dried sage leaves

1 cup heavy cream

4 boneless pork chops, 1½ inches thick

¼ cup seasoned fine dry breadcrumbs

1. Preheat the oven to 400°F. Brush a 9-by-13-inch baking dish with olive oil.

2. Layer the sliced potatoes, mushrooms, and onions in the dish. Sprinkle with the salt and sage leaves and pour the cream over evenly.

3. Brush the pork chops with olive oil (just enough to coat very lightly), and rub the breadcrumbs onto both sides of each pork chop (about 1½ teaspoons per side). Place pork chops on top of the vegetables in the casserole.

4. Bake, uncovered, for 45 minutes to 1 hour, or just until the pork chops are cooked through and the potatoes are tender.

PORK TENDERLOIN CASSEROLE WITH GARLIC AND ROSEMARY

Here, pork tenderloin bakes on top of scalloped potatoes and onion. The dish is an example of country comfort food at its best and simplest. Add steamed carrots to complete a winter menu.

3 teaspoons butter, divided

3 medium potatoes, peeled and thinly sliced

1¼ cups milk

1 teaspoon salt

½ teaspoon pepper

1½ cups fine dry breadcrumbs

1 pork tenderloin (about 1 pound)

1 small onion, thinly sliced

2 cloves garlic, minced

2 tablespoons fresh rosemary, or 1 tablespoon dried, crushed

1. Preheat the oven to 350°F. Spread 1 teaspoon of the butter evenly in a 2-quart shallow casserole. Arrange the potatoes in the casserole in an even layer. Pour the milk over the potatoes and sprinkle with the salt and pepper. Bake for 30 minutes, or just until the potatoes are tender.

2. Melt the remaining 2 teaspoons butter in a small saucepan and transfer to a shallow dish. Put the breadcrumbs in another shallow dish. Dip the pork tenderloin slices in the butter, and then coat with breadcrumbs. Place on top of the partially cooked potato layer in the casserole. Spread out the sliced onion over the pork and dribble any remaining melted butter over the onion. Sprinkle with the garlic cloves and rosemary.

3. Coat a sheet of aluminum foil with nonstick cooking spray. Cover the casserole with the foil and bake for another 30 minutes, or until the potatoes are completely tender and the pork is cooked through.

QUICK CASSOULET

Traditional cassoulet is a classic French dish of white beans and various meats baked long and slow to meld their flavors. This version comes together quickly because it includes canned beans and precooked sausage.

SERVES 6 TO 8

2 pounds precooked French garlic sausage or Polish kielbasa, cut into 2-inch chunks

2 cups chopped onion

9 cloves garlic, minced

2 cups dry white vermouth

2 cups sliced carrots

1 tablespoon sugar

1 can (15 ounces) red kidney beans, rinsed and drained

1 can (15 ounces) white beans, rinsed and drained

1 can (14½ ounces) stewed tomatoes with their juice

5 bay leaves

2 tablespoons chopped fresh parsley

1 tablespoon dried thyme

1 teaspoon whole allspice

4 slices bacon

1. Preheat the oven to 350°F.

2. Cook the sausage in a large heavy skillet over medium heat until heated through. Add the onion, garlic, and vermouth and simmer until the vermouth has evaporated, turning the sausage several times. Remove from the heat.

3. Put the carrots in a saucepan with water to cover. Add the sugar and cook until the carrots are tender. Drain.

4. Transfer the sausage and onion mixture to a deep 2-quart casserole. Top with the cooked carrots, the beans, tomatoes with their juice, bay leaves, parsley, thyme, and allspice. Stir to evenly distribute the ingredients. Lay the bacon slices over the top.

5. Bake, covered, for 45 minutes, or until the bacon is browned and the casserole is bubbly. Remove and discard the bay leaves.

SPAM AND BROCCOLI CASSEROLE

Spam was first sold in 1937 and became an important item in the military food rations during World War II. It is made of pork and ham with salt, water, and sodium nitrite (a preservative) added. There are many varieties of Spam on the market today, including Spam with cheese and Spam made with turkey. You can use any variety in this casserole.

SERVES 6

½ pound elbow macaroni

2 cups frozen chopped broccoli, thawed and drained

1 can (12 ounces) Spam luncheon meat, cubed

½ cup chopped red bell pepper, seeded and deribbed

2 cups milk

4 large eggs

1 teaspoon Tabasco sauce

1 cup shredded Cheddar cheese

¾ cup panko or fine dry bread-crumbs (see Note)

2 tablespoons butter, melted

1. Preheat the oven to 350°F. Coat a 3-quart casserole with cooking spray.

2. Cook the macaroni according to package directions, drain, and transfer to the casserole. Mix in the broccoli, Spam, and red bell pepper.

3. Mix the milk, eggs, Tabasco, and cheese in a medium bowl and pour over the Spam mixture.

4. Combine the panko and melted butter and sprinkle over the top. Bake, uncovered, for 25 to 35 minutes until the topping is lightly browned.

○ ○ ○ ○ ○

NOTE: Panko are Japanese breadcrumbs. They are coarser than regular breadcrumbs and create a crunchier crust. Panko can be purchased in Asian markets or in the Asian sections of large supermarkets.

SAUSAGE AND CABBAGE CASSEROLE

Eastern European country-style flavors blend together in this casserole. Serve this with a hearty pumpernickel or rye bread. To save time, you can substitute a packaged coleslaw mix for the shredded cabbage. The shredded carrots and red cabbage in the mix add a bit of color to the casserole.

SERVES 6

4 slices bacon, diced

1 medium onion, chopped

2 cloves garlic, minced

½ pound smoked Polish kielbasa, cut into 1-inch pieces

¼ pound cooked ham, cut into ½-inch cubes

1 pound lean ground pork

2 tablespoons sweet Hungarian paprika, plus more to taste

2 teaspoons caraway seeds, crushed with a mortar and pestle or ground in a coffee grinder

2 large red-skinned potatoes, scrubbed and cut into ¼-inch-thick slices

1 small cabbage, shredded (about 6 cups), or 1 package (1 pound) coleslaw mix

1 package (2 pounds) sauerkraut, rinsed and squeezed dry

1 pint sour cream

Pepper

1. Preheat the oven to 350°F. Butter a 4-quart casserole.

2. In a large heavy skillet, cook the bacon over medium heat for about 5 minutes, or until browned. Add the onion and garlic and sauté for 3 to 4 minutes, or until tender but not browned. Add the sausage, ham, and pork and cook, stirring occasionally, until the meat is no longer

pink. Drain off the fat and return the skillet to the heat. Add the 2 tablespoons paprika and the caraway seeds. Cook for 2 minutes longer and remove from the heat.

3. Arrange half of the potatoes in a layer in the buttered casserole. Top with half of the shredded cabbage and half of the sauerkraut, and then cover with the meat mixture.

4. Top with ½ cup of the sour cream. Add the remaining potato slices in one layer, and then the remaining cabbage and sauerkraut. Spread the top with the remaining 1½ cups sour cream, and sprinkle generously with pepper to taste and additional paprika. (At this point the casserole can be covered and refrigerated for up to 1 day, or frozen for up to 2 weeks. If frozen, thaw in the refrigerator overnight. Add 10 to 15 minutes to the baking time.)

5. Cut a sheet of aluminum foil and coat with cooking spray. Cover and bake 1 hour or until browned around the edges. Cool for 15 minutes before serving.

PORK RIBS, RICE, AND CHICKPEA CASSEROLE

Select meaty ribs for this casserole. Baked on top of a bed of rice and chickpeas, they become juicy and tender.

SERVES 6

2½ pounds boneless country-style pork ribs, cut into 3-inch pieces

Salt

Pepper

1 tablespoon vegetable oil or butter

1 large onion, chopped

4 large cloves garlic, chopped

2 cans (14½ ounces each) beef broth

1 cup long-grain white rice

2 cans (15 ounces each) chickpeas (garbanzo beans), drained

⅓ cup red wine vinegar

1 tablespoon paprika

1 tablespoon dried oregano, crumbled

½ teaspoon red chili flakes

1 roasted red bell pepper, freshly roasted (see page 35) or from a jar, sliced

2 tablespoons chopped fresh cilantro

1. Preheat the oven to 350°F. Season the ribs with salt and pepper. Brown, a few pieces at a time, in a heavy nonstick skillet. Set aside.

2. Place a large, heavy Dutch oven over medium-high heat and add the oil or butter. Add the onion and garlic and sauté until the onion is translucent, about 5 minutes. Add the beef broth, rice, chickpeas, vinegar, paprika, and oregano, and red chili flakes. Top with the browned ribs and the roasted red bell pepper. Sprinkle with salt and pepper.

3. Cover the pot and bake for 1 to 1½ hours, or until the meat is cooked through, the rice is tender, and all the liquids are absorbed. Sprinkle with the chopped fresh cilantro.

SPARERIBS WITH POTATOES

Marinate the ribs with the dry rub for at least an hour for the best flavor. This is a really easy one-dish meal. Add a salad or lightly steamed vegetables and hearty bread to complete the meal.

SERVES 4

2 pounds pork spareribs, cut into 2 slabs

2 teaspoons kosher salt

2 tablespoons pepper

2 tablespoons chili powder

1 tablespoon paprika

1 tablespoon dried oregano

1 tablespoon dried thyme

3 medium potatoes, scrubbed and diced (leave peel on)

4 medium carrots, peeled and cut into 1-inch chunks

1 tablespoon olive oil

1 clove garlic, minced

1. Cut the spareribs into serving pieces. In a small dish, combine the salt, pepper, chili powder, paprika, oregano, and thyme and rub into the spareribs, coating both sides. Place the ribs in a shallow pan, cover, and refrigerate for at least 1 hour and up to 1 day.

2. Preheat the oven to 400°F. Coat a 9-by-13-inch shallow baking dish with cooking spray.

3. Toss the potatoes and carrots with the olive oil in a medium bowl and spread out in the bottom of the casserole. Top with the ribs and sprinkle with the minced garlic.

4. Bake for 20 minutes. Turn the ribs over and bake for another 20 minutes, or until the potatoes and carrots are tender.

SWEET-AND-SOUR COUNTRY-STYLE RIBS

These are truly finger-lickin' good! Provide lots of extra napkins or hot washcloths to relieve sticky fingers.

SERVES 6

1 teaspoon salt

3 pounds bone-in country-style pork ribs or pork back ribs

¼ cup soy sauce

¼ cup sherry

¼ cup packed light or dark brown sugar

⅓ cup cider vinegar

2 teaspoons grated fresh ginger

½ cup juice from drained canned pineapple, or water

1 to 2 teaspoons Szechwan peppercorns, or 1 teaspoon red pepper flakes

1 green bell pepper, seeded and diced

1 can (8 ounces) whole water chestnuts, drained

1 can (8 ounces) pineapple chunks, drained

2 teaspoons cornstarch

2 teaspoons cold water

½ teaspoon sesame oil

Hot cooked rice for serving

1. Preheat the oven to 350°F.

2. Sprinkle the salt in a large heavy skillet. Cut the ribs into 3- or 4-rib sections. Brown on all sides in the skillet over medium to medium-high heat. Remove to a shallow 9-by-13-inch baking dish.

3. Add the soy sauce, sherry, sugar, vinegar, ginger, pineapple juice or water, and peppercorns or flakes to the skillet in which the pork was browned. Bring to a boil, stirring constantly to scrape up the browned bits of meat.

4. Pour the mixture over the pork in the casserole. Bake, covered, for 1 hour. Scatter the green pepper, water chestnuts, and pineapple over all. Bake, covered, for 30 minutes longer.

5. Drain the juices from the casserole into a small saucepan. In a small bowl, blend the cornstarch, 2 teaspoons cold water, and the sesame oil. Stir into the meat juices, bring to a boil, and cook, stirring constantly, for 1 to 2 minutes, or until thickened.

6. Pour the sauce over the meat in the casserole. Bake, uncovered, for 15 minutes longer or until the meat is tender and the juices are clear and thickened. Serve over hot cooked rice.

TOURTIÈRE

This classic French Canadian pork pie is traditionally served on Christmas Eve and on New Year's Eve. It can be made ahead and frozen for up to 2 months. Start with hot spiced cider and serve with a chopped salad and your favorite relish.

SERVES 8

Double recipe Flaky Pastry (page 32) to make a double crust

2 pounds lean ground pork

1 medium onion, finely chopped

2 cloves garlic, minced

1 thin-skinned potato, peeled and shredded

¼ teaspoon ground cinnamon

¼ teaspoon ground allspice

¼ teaspoon ground nutmeg

¼ teaspoon pepper

1½ teaspoons salt

1 tablespoon cornstarch

1 to 1½ cups homemade (page 25) or prepared chicken broth

1 large egg yolk, beaten with 1 tablespoon water

1. Prepare the pastry, refrigerate for 30 minutes, and divide into 2 balls. Roll out one ball into a circle 12 inches in diameter and transfer to a 9-inch pie pan. Refrigerate the second ball.

2. In a large skillet over medium-high heat, combine the pork, onion, garlic, potato, cinnamon, allspice, nutmeg, pepper, and salt. Cook over medium-high heat, uncovered, until the pork is cooked and the onion and potato are soft. Mix the cornstarch and chicken broth together and add to the skillet. Cook, stirring until the mixture is thickened. Cool, taste, and adjust the seasonings. Transfer the mixture to the pastry-lined pan.

3. Preheat the oven to 375°F.

4. Roll out the top crust into a circle 10 inches in diameter and arrange over the filling. Brush the edges with water and crimp them to seal. With a fork or the tip of a small knife, make a few slashes to allow steam to escape. Brush with the egg glaze and bake for 40 to 50 minutes, or until the crust is browned.

SANTA FE TAMALE PIE

Tamales were first prepared by the Aztecs, who served them to the Spanish conqueror Hernán Cortés when he arrived in Mexico City. A traditional tamale consists of a vegetable or meat filling enclosed in masa harina and wrapped in a dry corn husk that has been soaked in water. Tamale pies are made with similar ingredients, but they are baked in a casserole lined with just masa harina instead of corn husks. (Masa harina is made from masa, a flour that is like fine cornmeal.) I enjoyed this version of tamale pie in Santa Fe, where Mexican-style cooking abounds. A salad made with baby spinach and peppered fresh orange slices makes a refreshing accompaniment.

─────────────────── SERVES 8 GENEROUSLY ───────────────────

FOR THE CRUST:

5 cups water

2 cups yellow cornmeal

1 tablespoon salt

4 tablespoons butter

FOR THE FILLING:

1 tablespoon corn or vegetable oil

1 large onion, diced

1 clove garlic, minced or pressed

1 cup chopped celery

1 pound lean ground pork

1½ pounds chorizo sausage, crumbled

1 can (4 ounces) chopped green chiles

1 can (15 ounces) kidney beans, rinsed and drained

1 can (15 ounces) whole corn kernels, drained, or 2 cups fresh corn kernels

1 can (8 ounces) tomato sauce

1 cup sliced ripe olives

1 tablespoon chili powder

2 teaspoons salt

½ cup whole ripe olives for garnish

½ cup raisins for garnish

2 cups (8 ounces) shredded Monterey Jack or Cheddar cheese for garnish

1. Preheat the oven to 350°F. Coat a 3½-quart casserole with cooking spray.

2. *To make the crust:* Boil the water in a medium saucepan, stir in the cornmeal and salt, and cook, stirring, until

thickened. Stir in the butter. Spread half of the cooked cornmeal over the bottom and sides of the casserole and set aside the rest.

3. *To make the filling:* In a heavy, nonstick skillet, heat the oil. Add the onion, garlic, and celery. Sauté over low heat for 5 minutes. Increase the heat to high and add the pork and chorizo. Brown the meat, stirring constantly. Add the green chiles, beans, corn, tomato sauce, olives, chili powder, and salt. Lower the heat and simmer for 10 minutes, stirring often.

4. Spread out the filling in the cornmeal-lined casserole. Spread the remaining half of the cooked cornmeal over the top. (At this point the casserole can be wrapped well and refrigerated for up to 1 day, or frozen for up to 2 weeks. If frozen, thaw in the refrigerator overnight. Add 10 to 15 minutes to baking time.)

5. Bake for 45 minutes, or until heated through. Before serving, garnish with the whole ripe olives, raisins, and shredded cheese.

Chapter 8
LAMB, VEAL & GAME CASSEROLES

To be called "lamb" the animal must be less than a year old. Between one and two years, it is labeled "yearling lamb." If it's any older, it is technically referred to as "mutton." Mutton has a stronger flavor than lamb, which makes it popular in some places, such as England, and distinctly unpopular in others, including the United States.

Many Americans shy away from eating lamb, too. My husband, Dick, was once one of those people. When we were first married, he insisted he did not like lamb. He was a PhD student at Stanford, and I was an editor at *Sunset* magazine in Menlo Park. We were working on a lamb story, and every day for a couple of weeks we cooked just about every cut available. My kind coworkers knew that we were on a very restricted student budget, so I got to take home the results. I didn't tell Dick what kind of meat it was at first, and he devoured every bite. When I finally told him, he laughed, and he has been eating lamb ever since.

Lamb is more popular in Mediterranean countries than it is in the United States, and several recipes in this chapter hail from that region. Veal, on the other hand, is especially popular in Italy, the home of the classic dish made with veal shanks, osso buco (page 300).

There is no meat more delicate in flavor than true milk-fed veal. I grew up on a farm with dairy cattle. We usually butchered the bull calves, but only after they had been fed a diet of mother's milk for up to three months. At that point, the cow went on to produce milk, which we sold, and the veal we enjoyed was heavenly. We also enjoyed fresh venison because my father liked to hunt. "Venison" refers to the meat of elk, moose, reindeer, caribou, antelope, and of course, deer. Like all game, venison is lean and requires moist cooking.

In the pages that follow you can choose from among robust game dishes, Middle Eastern–inspired lamb casseroles, and even a Hungarian veal stew (page 301).

CASSEROLE-BRAISED LAMB SHANKS

When you cook lamb shanks with moisture, long and slow, they become meltingly tender. If you like, add Rice and Tomato Pilaf (page 341) to the menu and bake it at the same time.

MAKES 4 SERVINGS

4 lamb shanks, cracked (about 4 pounds total)

¼ cup all-purpose flour

1 teaspoon salt

½ teaspoon pepper

2 cups dry red or white wine

1 clove garlic, minced

1 teaspoon dried basil

1 teaspoon dried oregano

3 or 4 sprigs fresh rosemary, about 4 inches long

1. Preheat the oven to 300°F. Rinse the lamb shanks and pat dry with paper towels.

2. In a paper bag, combine the flour, salt, and pepper. Add the lamb shanks and shake until the meat is coated evenly.

3. Put the lamb shanks in a heavy 2- to 3-quart Dutch oven. Add the wine, garlic, basil, oregano, and rosemary sprigs. Place a piece of parchment paper or waxed paper over the top of the lamb shanks and press down to tuck the edges in around the meat. Cover tightly with the lid.

4. Bake for 3½ hours, or until the meat is very tender. Transfer the lamb to a serving plate, spoon the cooking juices over the meat, and serve.

LAMB STEW WITH POTATOES AND THYME

In this casserole, layers of potatoes, onion, and chunks of lamb, flavored with herbs and bacon, bake slowly into a succulent stew.

— 6 SERVINGS —

12 medium red-skinned potatoes (leave skins on)

4 large onions, quartered

3 pounds lamb stew meat, cut into 1-inch cubes

½ pound bacon, diced

1 teaspoon dried thyme

3 tablespoons minced fresh parsley

2 teaspoons salt

1 teaspoon pepper

3 cups beef or lamb broth

1 bay leaf

1. Preheat the oven to 350°F.

2. Slice the potatoes and layer half of them in the bottom of a deep 3-quart Dutch oven or casserole. Slice the onions ½ inch thick and layer half over the potatoes. Arrange the lamb and bacon over the onions. Sprinkle with the thyme, parsley, ½ teaspoon of the salt, and ½ teaspoon pepper. Cover with the remaining onions and potatoes and pour the broth over all. Sprinkle with the remaining 1½ teaspoons salt and ½ teaspoon pepper. Tuck the bay leaf into the center.

3. Bake, covered, for 2½ hours, or until the meat is very tender and the potatoes on the bottom have cooked down into a sauce. Remove and discard the bay leaf.

LAMB AND ARTICHOKE STEW

This stew is reminiscent of Greek *avgolemono* because the juices in this casserole are thickened with egg yolks and lemon juice. (*Avgolemono* is a Greek soup or sauce made with chicken broth, egg yolks, and lemon.) Serve the stew with a Greek salad made with cucumbers, tomatoes, peppers, black olives, and feta on a bed of lettuce. Offer some pita bread, too.

SERVES 4

1 pound lean boneless lamb, cut into 1½-inch chunks

2 tablespoons olive oil

1 teaspoon salt

½ teaspoon pepper

1 medium onion, thinly sliced

1 clove garlic, minced

1 teaspoon dried dill weed

½ cup water

1 package (8 ounces) frozen artichoke hearts, thawed

1 tomato, diced

3 large egg yolks

3 tablespoons fresh lemon juice

Chopped fresh parsley for garnish

Cooked rice for serving

1. Preheat the oven to 350°F.

2. In a heavy 2-quart casserole, brown the lamb over medium heat in 1 tablespoon of the olive oil. Sprinkle with the salt and pepper. Push the meat to one side and add the onion, the remaining olive oil, and garlic. Cook, stirring, until the onion is limp, about 5 minutes.

3. Mix the onion, garlic, and meat together and stir in the dill and water. Cover and bake for 1 hour, or until the meat is very tender. Add the artichokes and tomato. Bake, covered, for another 20 minutes. Remove from the oven.

4. In a small bowl, beat the egg yolks with the lemon juice until foamy. Whisk in about 3 tablespoons of the broth from the casserole to temper the eggs, and then stir the egg mixture into the casserole juices. Sprinkle with parsley and serve over cooked rice.

LAMB AND EGGPLANT MOUSSAKA

There are lots of variations to this popular dish, which is originally from Greece. Some include a variety of vegetables, such as the one on page 471. This recipe includes just eggplant and onion.

SERVES 8

4 large eggplants, peeled and sliced ½ inch thick

2 teaspoons salt, plus extra for sprinkling

2 tablespoons butter

1 large onion, chopped

2 pounds lean ground lamb

1 teaspoon paprika

Pepper

1 teaspoon dried oregano

About ¼ cup olive oil

4 tomatoes, sliced

1 cup plain yogurt

4 large egg yolks

½ cup all-purpose flour

1. Sprinkle the eggplant slices lightly with salt. Place on a double layer of paper towels and let stand for 1 hour to release their bitter liquid.

2. Preheat the broiler.

3. In a large heavy skillet, melt the butter over low heat. Add the onion and sauté for 10 minutes until soft. Increase the heat to medium-high and add the lamb, the 2 teaspoons salt, the paprika, pepper to taste, and the oregano. Cook, stirring, for 5 to 10 minutes, or until the meat is crumbly and no longer pink.

4. Pat the eggplant slices dry, place on a baking sheet, and brush with olive oil. Broil about 3 inches from the heat until lightly browned on one side. Turn over and broil on the other side.

5. Preheat the oven to 350°F. Rub a shallow 9-by-13-inch baking dish with olive oil. Spread half the meat mixture in the casserole. Top with half the eggplant, and then the remaining meat mixture and remaining eggplant. Top with the tomato slices. Bake, uncovered, for 1 hour.

6. Meanwhile, in a small bowl, blend the yogurt, egg yolks, and flour. Pour over the tomato layer in the casserole. Bake, uncovered, for 15 minutes longer, or until the custard is golden. Let stand for 15 minutes before serving.

LAMB CHOP AND VEGETABLE CASSEROLE

Shoulder lamb chops need to be cooked longer than loin chops, and this is a homey and flavorful way to cook them. Toss some potato wedges with olive oil and roast in a pan alongside the casserole.

SERVES 4

4 shoulder lamb chops (about 1½ pounds total)

6 carrots, peeled and cut into 2-inch pieces

4 medium onions, peeled and quartered

1 bay leaf

½ teaspoon dried thyme

½ teaspoon dried oregano

⅛ teaspoon pepper

1 cup homemade (page 26) or prepared beef broth

1. Preheat the oven to 375°F. Coat a shallow 2-quart casserole with cooking spray.

2. In a heavy nonstick skillet, brown the lamb chops over high heat for about 1 minute on each side. Arrange the chops in the casserole and add the carrots, onions, bay leaf, thyme, oregano, pepper, and beef broth.

3. Coat a sheet of aluminum foil with cooking spray and cover the casserole. Bake for 45 minutes, uncover, and drain off the fat. Bake for 20 minutes longer, or until the lamb is cooked to your liking.

4. Pour the juices into the skillet, bring to a boil, and continue boiling, stirring often, until reduced by half. Pour the juices over the lamb and vegetables and serve hot.

LAMB AND POTATO MOUSSAKA

Who says moussaka has to be made with eggplant? Well, maybe the Greeks do. But in this version, it is made with potatoes. This is true comfort food.

— SERVES 6 —

3 tablespoons butter, plus extra for the dish

4 large potatoes, peeled and cut into ½-inch-thick slices

¾ cup minced onion

1 pound ground lamb

2 tablespoons minced fresh parsley

1 can (8 ounces) tomato sauce

½ cup water

1 teaspoon salt

½ teaspoon pepper

About ½ cup fine dry breadcrumbs

2 cups sour cream

1. Preheat the oven to 350°F. Butter a shallow 2½-quart casserole.

2. Put the potatoes in a large saucepan, add water to cover, and bring to a boil. Boil the potatoes for 6 or 7 minutes, or just until they can be easily pierced with a toothpick, and drain.

3. In a large skillet, sauté the onion in the 3 tablespoons butter over medium heat until softened. Add the ground lamb, and cook, stirring and breaking up the meat, for 5 minutes. Add the parsley, tomato sauce, water, salt, and pepper and simmer for 15 minutes.

4. Sprinkle the bottom of the casserole with some of the breadcrumbs. Arrange all of the meat on top. Cover with the potatoes. Spread the sour cream over the potatoes and sprinkle with the remaining breadcrumbs. Bake, uncovered, for 30 minutes or until the top is browned and bubbly around the edges.

MOROCCAN LAMB CASSEROLE WITH MINT DRESSING

This is one of my favorites because you simply marinate the meat overnight in the casserole, then put it into the oven and bake it for many hours at a low temperature. This gives you time to cook the couscous (which only takes 5 minutes) and prepare the mint sauce. We have mint-gone-wild all around our house, and this is a wonderful way to use it. The marinade contains harissa, a fiery hot sauce often used to flavor couscous, soups, stews, and other dishes. If you can't find harissa, you can substitute Thai red or green curry paste, which isn't exactly the same flavor, but adds heat and some layers of flavor.

SERVES 8

4 pounds boneless leg of lamb, cut into 2-inch chunks

2 teaspoons kosher salt

1 teaspoon coarsely ground pepper

2 tablespoons olive oil

⅓ cup fresh lemon juice

1 tablespoon lemon zest

2 tablespoons minced garlic

1 tablespoon harissa or Thai green or red curry paste, or more to taste

1 teaspoon whole coriander seeds, toasted and crushed (see Note, facing page)

½ teaspoon ground cumin

1 large onion, coarsely chopped

FOR THE MINT SAUCE:
2 cups tightly packed fresh mint leaves, washed and dried

2 tablespoons chopped shallots

1 small clove garlic, minced

2 teaspoons red wine vinegar

½ cup olive oil

Kosher salt and pepper to taste

Cooked couscous for serving

Dry-roasted peanuts for garnish

Raisins for garnish

Sweetened shredded coconut for garnish

1. Put the lamb into a heavy 3-quart casserole. Sprinkle with the salt, pepper, olive oil, lemon juice, lemon zest, garlic, harissa, coriander seeds, and cumin. Mix well. Cover and refrigerate for at least 2 hours or overnight.

2. Preheat the oven to 300°F.

3. Remove the lamb from the refrigerator and spread the onions over the top of the meat. Press a piece of parchment paper or waxed paper onto the meat and tuck the edges around the sides of the casserole. Cover with the lid of the casserole.

4. Place the casserole in the oven and bake for 4 hours, or until the meat is very tender. Meanwhile, prepare the mint sauce.

5. *To make the mint sauce:* Combine all of the ingredients in a food processor with the steel blade in place and process until almost smooth. Taste and add salt and pepper.

6. When the meat is almost done, prepare the couscous according to the package directions. To serve, spoon the meat and juices over each serving of couscous. Top with the mint sauce, peanuts, raisins, and coconut, plus more harissa, if desired.

NOTE: To toast coriander seeds, put them in a small, dry skillet over medium-low heat. Toast, stirring occasionally, until aromatic, about 10 minutes.

TURKISH LAMB STEW AND SULTAN'S DELIGHT

Stewing is a popular method of cooking meat in Turkey for many reasons. First of all, roasting requires a lot of firewood, a scarce commodity there. Second, according to Islamic tradition, meats need to be cooked until they are no longer bloody. Third, meat stewed with vegetables results in a delicious sauce.

I tend to convert dishes such as this into casseroles because they are so much easier to handle. Traditionally, this lamb stew is served surrounded by eggplant cream, known as Sultan's Delight. We enjoyed this delicious dish the first night we were in Istanbul, only to have it served to us every night for two weeks! It was then that I found out I had developed a sensitivity to eggplant.

MAKES 6 SERVINGS

4 tablespoons butter

3 pounds boneless lamb stew meat, or boneless leg of lamb, cut into 1-inch cubes

3 medium onions, finely chopped

4 cloves garlic, minced

1 green bell pepper, seeded and finely chopped

6 tomatoes, chopped

1½ teaspoons salt

½ teaspoon pepper

1 teaspoon dried thyme

1½ cups water

FOR THE SULTAN'S DELIGHT:

2 large eggplants (about 1½ pounds each)

2 tablespoons fresh lemon juice

4 tablespoons butter

½ cup all-purpose flour

1½ cups milk, heated

Salt

Pepper

1 cup shredded kasseri or Gruyère cheese

¼ cup chopped fresh parsley

1. Preheat the oven to 300°F.

2. Melt the butter in a large cast-iron Dutch oven, and brown the lamb cubes in the butter over medium-high heat. Add the onions, garlic, bell pepper, tomatoes, salt, pepper, thyme, and water. Cover and bake for 3 hours, or until the lamb is tender and the sauce is thickened.

3. *Meanwhile, make the Sultan's Delight:* Pierce the eggplants with a fork and place over an open flame, such as a gas stove burner, or a hot charcoal fire. Cook, turning often, until the skin blisters on all sides and the eggplant is soft, 5 to 10 minutes. Cool, cut the eggplants in half lengthwise, and scoop out the pulp, transferring it to a medium bowl. Press out all the moisture with a spoon, tipping the bowl to drain away the liquid. Mash the eggplant with a fork. Mix in the lemon juice and set aside.

4. In a heavy large saucepan, melt the butter, add the flour, and cook over low heat for 2 to 3 minutes, until the flour is cooked but not browned. Slowly whisk in the milk and cook until the sauce is thickened. Add salt and pepper to taste. Mix the mashed eggplants into this sauce, add the cheese, and stir until well blended and the cheese has melted.

5. Pour the eggplant puree into a serving dish, make a hollow in the center, and arrange the meat in this hollow. Sprinkle with parsley.

MIDDLE EASTERN STEWED LAMB AND VEGETABLES

This casserole is based on a classic Turkish dish, *kuzu kapama,* which literally means "lamb stewed with vegetables." I bake it in two stages, first with the aromatic vegetables—onions, tomatoes, and peppers—and then with the potatoes, peas, and carrots. Serve it with a dollop of sour cream or yogurt and a lettuce salad.

SERVES 8

4 pounds boneless leg of lamb, cut into 1½-inch cubes

1 large onion, chopped

1 can (14½ ounces) diced tomatoes with their juice

1 green bell pepper, seeded and diced

1 red bell pepper, seeded and diced

2 tablespoons chopped fresh parsley

1 teaspoon paprika

1 teaspoon salt

½ teaspoon pepper

4 medium potatoes, peeled and cubed

2 cups peas, fresh or frozen

1 cup sliced carrots

1. Preheat the oven to 300°F. Put the lamb in the bottom of a large, heavy Dutch oven in one layer. Top with the onion, tomatoes with their juice, and green and red bell peppers. Cover tightly with the foil and then the lid of the Dutch oven. Bake for 2 hours, or until the lamb is aromatic and tender.

2. Remove from the oven, add the remaining ingredients, and cover. Bake for another hour, or until the potatoes are tender.

SHEPHERD'S PIE

The Farmer magazine first published a recipe for this classic Shepherd's Pie in January 1912, as a suggestion for using leftover roast lamb or beef. A young family that we know makes this their Christmas Eve meal every year.

SERVES 4

2 tablespoons butter at room temperature, plus extra for the dish

2 large russet potatoes, peeled and diced

¼ cup half-and-half, sour cream, or softened cream cheese

Salt

1½ cups ground cooked meat (see Note)

1 cup leftover gravy, or 1 cup hot homemade (page 26) or prepared beef broth, thickened (see Note)

1 small onion, sliced

1 medium carrot, peeled and cut into ¼-inch dice

½ cup frozen baby peas

Pepper

2 tablespoons chopped fresh parsley

1. Preheat the oven to 350°F. Butter a shallow 2-quart casserole.

2. In a medium saucepan, boil the potatoes in salted water until tender, about 12 minutes. Drain and transfer a medium bowl. With a hand mixer, mash the potatoes and add the half-and-half and the 2 tablespoons butter; beat until fluffy. Season with salt to taste.

3. While the potatoes boil, preheat a large skillet over medium-high heat. Add the meat, gravy or broth, onion, and carrot. Heat to simmering and continue to simmer for 5 minutes. Transfer to the casserole, stir in the peas, and season with salt and pepper to taste.

4. Spoon the potatoes over the meat evenly. Bake for 25 to 30 minutes, or until lightly browned.

○ ○ ○ ○ ○

NOTES: If you do not have leftover meat on hand, you can substitute 1 pound extra-lean ground lamb or ground beef. Season the meat with salt and pepper. Place a large nonstick skillet over medium-high heat. Add oil to the hot pan and brown the meat for 3 or 4 minutes, separating the clumps with a fork.

To thicken beef broth into a gravy, melt 2 tablespoons butter in a skillet or small saucepan and add 3 tablespoons flour. Gradually whisk in the hot beef broth and cook until thickened.

BRAISED VEAL SHANKS (OSSO BUCO)

Translated from the Italian, *osso buco* means "hollow bone." This Milanese classic is made with veal shanks, which are slowly braised until they reach fall-apart tenderness. One of the pleasures of eating it is spooning the rich marrow out of the center of the bone. It is traditionally served with a garlicky condiment called gremolata.

—— MAKES 4 SERVINGS ——

¼ cup all-purpose flour

½ teaspoon salt

¼ teaspoon pepper

4 veal shanks, 2 inches thick (about 4 pounds)

¼ cup olive oil

1 medium onion, quartered

1 medium carrot, cut into 1-inch chunks

1 stalk celery, cut into 2-inch pieces

1 clove garlic, bruised and peeled

½ cup dry white wine

½ cup homemade (page 26) or prepared beef broth

1 can (28 ounces) Italian plum tomatoes with their juice

½ teaspoon dried basil

½ teaspoon dried rosemary

½ teaspoon dried marjoram

FOR THE GREMOLATA:

6 cloves garlic, minced

2 tablespoons grated lemon zest

½ cup minced fresh parsley

1. Preheat the oven to 325°F. In a plastic bag, mix the flour, salt, and pepper. Add the veal shanks and shake until coated with the flour mixture.

2. In a large, heavy skillet, heat half of the oil. Add the veal, one piece at a time, and cook until browned and crusty; transfer to a 3-quart casserole.

3. Add the remaining oil to the skillet and then the onion, carrot, celery, and garlic; sauté until tender. Spoon the vegetables on top of the veal.

4. Pour the wine into the skillet and bring to a boil, stirring constantly to scrape up the browned parts from the bottom. Add the broth, tomatoes with their juice, and herbs, and bring to a boil. Pour the mixture over the veal and vegetables in the casserole.

5. Cover and bake for 2½ to 3 hours, or until the veal is very tender.

6. *While veal cooks, prepare the gremolata:* Combine the garlic, lemon zest, and parsley in a small serving bowl. Cover and set aside.

7. Transfer the veal shanks to serving plate and keep warm. Drain the juices from the casserole into the skillet and heat to boiling. Continue boiling until the juices are thickened and reduced to 1½ cups. Pour over the veal. Pass the gremolata so people can sprinkle some on their osso bucco if they wish.

PAPRIKA VEAL

Paprika from Hungary comes mild, medium, and hot and is available from specialty stores such as Penzeys and other spice markets. I like the hot variety, while my husband prefers the mild, so we settle on medium.

SERVES 4

1 tablespoon all-purpose flour

½ teaspoon salt

¼ teaspoon pepper

1 pound veal stew cubes

1 slice bacon, cut into ¼-inch strips

2 small onions, chopped

1 clove garlic, minced

½ pound mushrooms, quartered

1 tomato, peeled, seeded, and diced

1 tablespoon mild, medium, or hot Hungarian paprika

¾ cup homemade (page 25) or prepared chicken broth

2 tablespoons dry sherry

¼ cup plain yogurt

Chopped fresh parsley for garnish

Hot noodles, cooked according to package directions, for serving

1. Preheat the oven to 350°F. Combine the flour, salt, and pepper in a plastic bag. Add the veal, and shake the bag to coat it with the seasoned flour.

2. In a flameproof 1½- to 2-quart casserole, cook the bacon over medium-high heat until crisp and drain on paper towels. Add the veal cubes to the casserole, a few at a time, and brown on all sides, transferring them to a plate as they're done. Add the onions and garlic and sauté for 5 minutes, stirring. Add the mushrooms and sauté until browned. Return the beef to the pan, add the tomato, and sprinkle with the paprika. Pour the chicken broth and sherry into the pan and stir to blend well.

3. Cover tightly and bake for 1 hour. Drain the juices from the casserole into a nonstick skillet. Bring to a boil and cook, stirring, until the juices are reduced to a glaze, about ½ cup. Stir the yogurt into the juices and pour over the veal.

4. Sprinkle the veal with parsley and serve over hot noodles.

BAKED VENISON STEW

I grew up on venison. It is a dark red meat that is low in fat and cholesterol. When my father went hunting, he shunned the bucks with six-point antlers or more in favor of younger animals, because they were more tender and flavorful. Older animals have a stronger, gamey flavor. No matter what kind of venison you have, it will be delicious in this slow-baked stew. Allow a couple of hours for the meat to soak in the spicy marinade.

SERVES 8

2 cups dry red wine

1 bottle (12 ounces) dark beer, such as Guinness extra stout

½ cup olive oil

4 cloves garlic, coarsely chopped

2 teaspoons dried thyme

2 teaspoons coarsely cracked black peppercorns

12 juniper berries, crushed

1 bay leaf

3 pounds boneless venison shoulder, cut into 1½-inch cubes

½ pound bacon (about 6 slices), cut into 1-inch pieces

3 tablespoons all-purpose flour

1 rutabaga (about 2½ pounds), peeled and cut into ½-inch cubes

1 large onion, cut into 1-inch cubes

1. In a large bowl, combine the wine, beer, olive oil, garlic, thyme, peppercorns, juniper berries, and bay leaf. Add the venison, cover, and marinate at room temperature for 2 hours.

2. Preheat the oven to 300°F. Drain the venison and pat dry, reserving the marinade.

3. Place a 3- to 4-quart Dutch oven or flameproof casserole over medium heat. Add the bacon and cook until browned; drain on paper towels and set aside.

4. Add the venison to the casserole in batches and brown quickly over medium-high heat, transferring the cubes to a plate when they're done. Return all the meat to the casserole and sprinkle with the flour; stir to coat all the pieces. Add the reserved marinade and heat for 2 minutes. Add the rutabaga and onion.

5. Cover the casserole and place in the oven. Bake for 3 hours, or until the venison is very tender. Top with the cooked bacon.

VENISON SLOW-BAKED IN RED WINE

This venison stew simmers in the oven until it reaches tender succulence. Serve with a couple of vegetables to add contrasting colors, such as broccoli and baby carrots or Brussels sprouts and mashed potatoes. Cranberry sauce, lingonberry jam, or rowan jelly make great accompaniments, too.

SERVES 8

2 tablespoons all-purpose flour

2 pounds venison, cut into 2-inch cubes

4 tablespoons butter

1 cup red or dry white wine

1 to 2 cups water

Pinch of dried thyme

1 bay leaf

2 to 3 cloves of garlic

1 small celery root, peeled and cut into ½-inch dice

8 whole juniper berries

2 teaspoons salt

½ teaspoon pepper

2 large onions (about 1 pound total), chopped

½ pound small mushrooms

1 cup sour cream

1 tablespoon capers

½ cup sliced green olives

1. Preheat the oven to 300°F. Put the flour in a shallow dish or plastic bag. Wipe the venison cubes dry and toss with the flour until lightly coated.

2. In a heavy 3- to 4-quart Dutch oven, melt the butter and add the venison pieces; cook over medium-high heat until browned. Add the wine and water and heat to boiling.

3. Add the thyme, bay leaf, garlic, celery root, juniper berries, salt, and pepper. Stir to mix well, and top with the onions and mushrooms.

4. Cover tightly, place in the oven, and bake for 4 to 5 hours, until the venison is very tender. Stir in the sour cream and sprinkle with the capers and green olives.

VENISON STRIPS IN KOREAN MARINADE

If you have hunters in your family, it's likely that you'll have some frozen venison on hand. Venison can vary in tenderness, depending on the age of the animal. This recipe works for meats ranging from tough to tender because it is thinly sliced across the grain before cooking. The venison steaks are easier to cut into slices when partially frozen. The marinade is a classic Korean one used for beef. For a simple, authentic, and delicious meal, serve with steamed rice and stir-fried green beans seasoned with a touch of soy and sesame oil.

SERVES 4

2 tablespoons sesame seeds

1 pound venison steaks, partially frozen

2 tablespoons soy sauce

2 tablespoons water

2 tablespoons sliced green onion (white and green parts)

¼ teaspoon sesame oil

2 teaspoons sugar

1 clove garlic, minced

Dash of Tabasco sauce

1. Put the sesame seeds in a small heavy skillet and stir over medium heat for 5 to 10 minutes, or until golden brown. Crush with a mortar and pestle or process in a blender until pulverized.

2. Cut the partially frozen venison across the grain into ¼-inch-thick slices. In a shallow 2-quart casserole or an 8-inch square baking dish, arrange the venison slices in a single layer.

3. In a small bowl, combine the soy sauce, water, green onion, sesame seeds, sesame oil, sugar, garlic, and Tabasco. Pour over the meat. Marinate for 30 minutes to 1 hour at room temperature or in the refrigerator overnight, turning over the venison slices once.

4. Preheat the oven to 400°F. Bake, uncovered, for 10 to 15 minutes, or until the meat is tender. Tenderloin steaks will take 10 minutes to cook to rare.

WILD RICE VENISON CASSEROLE WITH CRANBERRIES

Simple to assemble, this casserole is a classic Minnesota hot dish. Wild rice isn't a rice at all, but rather the seed of a long-grained marsh grass native to some regions of the Great Lakes. It is now commercially grown and harvested, but the flavor of the hand-parched wild rice we buy from local Native Americans surpasses that of the commercial variety by far. Usually hand-parched rice cooks more quickly than the commercial rice because in the processing, less water is taken out of the grains. If you are lucky enough to be able to find hand-parched rice, reduce the cooking time by 10 minutes.

SERVES 6

1 cup wild rice

1½ cups water

¼ cup all-purpose flour

1 pound venison, cut into 2-inch cubes

3 tablespoons oil or butter

½ onion, chopped

1 clove garlic, minced

1 can (14½ ounces) stewed tomatoes with their juice

½ cup diced green bell peppers

1 teaspoon salt

½ teaspoon chili powder

¼ teaspoon curry powder

1½ cups fresh or dried cranberries

1. Preheat the oven to 350°F.

2. Rinse the rice in three changes of hot tap water and drain. In a saucepan, combine the rice with the water and bring to a boil; reduce the heat to low and cook for 25 minutes. Drain off any remaining liquid. (The rice should not be entirely cooked at this point.)

3. Put the flour in a shallow bowl or plastic bag and coat the venison with the flour. In a heavy nonstick skillet, heat the oil or melt the butter and brown the venison with the chopped onion.

4. Transfer to a heavy 3-quart heavy casserole and add the rice, garlic, tomatoes with their juice, peppers, salt, chili powder, curry powder, and cranberries. Cover tightly and bake for 1½ hours, or until the venison is tender and the rice is completely cooked, adding a little water if the casserole cooks dry.

Chapter 9
PASTA CASSEROLES

○○○○○

We often think of pasta as nothing more than an extender for other ingredients. Nutritionally, however, whole-grain pastas add complex carbohydrates and plant protein to our diets. Whole-grain dried pasta can be substituted for the white variety in any casserole calling for a dried pasta. Check out the exciting variety at well-stocked supermarkets and health food stores.

There are no really hard-and-fast rules about substituting one pasta for another. If a recipe calls for pasta shells, you can easily substitute elbow macaroni or any other small macaroni for the shells. Other choices would be rotini spirals, ziti, bow tie pasta, or wheels. It is not a good idea to substitute spaghetti or noodles for small pastas, but you can use noodles instead of spaghetti, even though the texture and appearance will be different. You may end up with a whole new creation!

Many of the casseroles in this chapter reflect global influences. Some of them, such as lasagna, are so well known in their country of origin that there are countless variations.

BAKED POLENTA WITH CHEESE AND SWISS CHARD

Swiss chard is a member of the beet family, which is not surprising, given the reddish stalks and chunky leaves of one variety. Although it is available year-round, Swiss chard is best in the summer. It is considered a cruciferous vegetable and a good source of vitamins A and C. In this dish the Swiss chard is cooked and layered with polenta and cheese, making it a healthy and tasty one-dish meal. *Polenta* is the Italian name for cornmeal, but often the finished dish is called "polenta," too.

SERVES 6

1 tablespoon olive oil

6 cloves garlic, minced

1 bunch red-stemmed Swiss chard, stems and leaves chopped separately

2 tablespoons water

FOR THE POLENTA:

2 cups low-fat or skim milk

1½ cups water

½ teaspoon salt

1 cup polenta, corn grits, or cornmeal

4 tablespoons grated Parmesan cheese, divided

1 tablespoon butter

1 cup shredded part-skim mozzarella cheese

⅓ cup sour cream

1. Preheat the oven to 400°F. Butter a shallow 2½- to 3-quart casserole.

2. Heat the oil in a large skillet or wok with a cover over medium heat. Add the garlic and cook for 30 seconds; stir in the Swiss chard stems. Add the 2 tablespoons water, cover the pan, and cook for 2 minutes. Add the Swiss chard leaves and cook, covered, until the leaves are wilted, about 3 minutes. Remove from the heat and let cool, uncovered.

3. *To make the polenta:* Combine the milk, water, and salt in a large saucepan and bring to a boil. Reduce the heat to medium-low and slowly whisk in the polenta. Cook, whisking, until the mixture is thickened to the consistency of mashed potatoes, about 5 minutes. Add 2 tablespoons of the Parmesan cheese, the butter, and the mozzarella cheese.

4. Spread half the polenta in the casserole dish and spoon the Swiss chard on top, distributing it evenly. Spread the sour cream over the Swiss chard. Spread the remaining polenta over the sour cream. Sprinkle with the remaining 2 tablespoons Parmesan cheese. (At this point up the casserole can be covered and refrigerated for up to 1 day. Add about 5 minutes to the baking time.)

5. Bake, uncovered, for 20 to 25 minutes, or until golden on top and sizzling. Do not overcook.

BOW TIES WITH BROCCOLI AND ALFREDO SAUCE

Although fettuccine is the classic pasta paired with Alfredo sauce—a rich sauce made with butter, Parmesan, and heavy cream—Alfredo is wonderful used in many different ways. Here the sauce is combined with bow tie pasta and vegetables.

SERVES 4

3 cups farfalle (bow tie pasta)

2 cups fresh broccoli stems and florets

1 roasted red bell pepper, peeled, seeded, and sliced (see page 35)

2 teaspoons chopped fresh basil, or 1 teaspoon dried

1½ cups Alfredo sauce, store-bought or homemade (page 24)

2 cups freshly shredded or grated Parmesan cheese

1. Preheat the oven to 350°F. Butter a 2-quart casserole.

2. Cook the pasta as directed on the package until al dente, or firm to the bite. Add the broccoli to the pasta for the last 3 minutes of cooking. Drain.

3. Combine all of the ingredients except the cheese. Transfer to the casserole, cover, and bake for 20 minutes. Uncover and sprinkle with the cheese. Bake for 5 to 10 minutes longer, until the cheese is melted.

Variation: Add 2 cups diced cooked chicken to the casserole along with the Alfredo Sauce for a satisfying one-dish casserole.

CHILI AND CHEDDAR BOW TIE CASSEROLE

Chipotle chiles are actually dried and smoked jalapeño chiles. They're easiest to find either whole or minced in an adobo sauce, which is a dark-red piquant sauce made from ground chiles, herbs, and vinegar. The can may be simply labeled "adobo sauce." You can use almost any tube-shaped pasta in this recipe, such as ziti, penne, rigatoni, or even macaroni.

SERVES 6

1 tablespoon butter

1 red bell pepper, seeded and chopped

4 green onions, thinly sliced (white and green parts)

1 tablespoon minced chipotle chiles in adobo sauce

2 tablespoons all-purpose flour

1 teaspoon chili powder

½ teaspoon salt

½ teaspoon ground cumin

2 cups milk

2 cups shredded sharp Cheddar cheese, divided

2 tablespoons chopped fresh cilantro

8 ounces farfalle (bow tie pasta) or other short pasta, cooked according to package directions

1. Preheat the oven to 400°F. Coat a shallow 2-quart casserole dish with cooking spray.

2. Melt the butter in a large skillet over medium-high heat. Add the bell pepper and sauté for 4 minutes, stirring. Add the green onions and sauté for 1 minute. Stir in the chipotle chiles in adobo sauce, flour, chili powder, salt, and cumin and cook for 1 minute. Gradually add the milk and cook, stirring constantly with a whisk, until thick and bubbly, about 4 minutes. Remove from heat. Gradually add 1½ cups of the cheese and the cilantro, stirring until the cheese melts. Add the pasta to the pan, and toss until blended.

3. Spoon the pasta mixture into the casserole dish and sprinkle with the remaining ½ cup cheese. Bake for 15 minutes, or until the cheese is melted and the casserole is heated through.

CREAMY EGG NOODLE AND SUN-DRIED TOMATO CASSEROLE

Without the sun-dried tomatoes, this is a classic fifties casserole. In those days, it was called noodles Romanoff, in honor of the Russian dynasty of the same name.

SERVES 6

1 package (8 ounces) egg noodles

½ cup julienned sun-dried tomatoes (not oil-packed)

1 cup grated Parmesan cheese, divided

2 cups cottage cheese

1 cup sour cream

3 green onions, minced (white and green parts)

2 teaspoons Worcestershire sauce

1 teaspoon paprika

½ teaspoon salt

⅛ teaspoon Tabasco sauce

1. Preheat the oven to 350°F. Butter a 2-quart casserole.

2. Heat a pot of salted water to boiling. Add the noodles and the sun-dried tomatoes. Bring to a boil, reduce the heat, and simmer for 10 minutes.

3. Drain the noodles and sun-dried tomatoes and transfer to the casserole. Add ½ cup of the Parmesan cheese, the cottage cheese, sour cream, green onions, Worcestershire sauce, paprika, salt, and Tabasco sauce.

4. Bake the casserole for 25 to 30 minutes, until bubbly. Sprinkle the top with the remaining ½ cup Parmesan cheese and bake for 5 minutes longer.

FARFALLE WITH GARLIC, ANCHOVIES, AND OLIVES

Bow tie pasta, or "farfalle," is served here in a sauce full of personality, which contains the classic Italian combination of garlic, anchovies, and black olives.

— SERVES 6 TO 8 —

3 tablespoons olive oil, divided, plus extra for the dish

1 pound farfalle (bow tie pasta)

3 cloves garlic, peeled and lightly smashed

3 to 6 anchovy fillets

2 cans (14½ ounces each) diced tomatoes with basil and garlic, with their juice

Salt

Pepper

½ cup pitted black kalamata olives

2 tablespoons capers

Red pepper flakes

½ cup grated Parmesan cheese

Chopped fresh parsley, oregano, marjoram, or basil for garnish

1. Preheat the oven to 350°F. Smear a shallow 2-quart casserole with a little olive oil.

2. Bring a pot of salted water to a boil, add the pasta, and cook until tender but not mushy, 8 to 10 minutes.

3. Meanwhile, heat 2 tablespoons of the olive oil in a skillet and add the garlic and anchovies. Cook over medium-low heat until the garlic is pale gold. Add the tomatoes with their juice, salt, and pepper to taste, and cook, stirring occasionally, until the tomatoes break down and the mixure becomes saucy, about 10 minutes. Stir in the olives, capers, and red pepper flakes to taste and simmer 3 minutes longer.

4. Drain the pasta and toss with the sauce and the remaining tablespoon of oil. Transfer to the prepared casserole and top with the Parmesan cheese. Bake for 15 to 20 minutes, until bubbly. Sprinkle with the chopped fresh herbs for garnish.

GIANT STUFFED PASTA SHELLS

Even though this dish is inexpensive and easy to make, it is colorful and very tasty. All you need is a salad and a loaf of bread to complete the meal.

———————— SERVES 6 ————————

2 packages (10 ounces each) frozen chopped spinach, thawed

2 green onions, finely chopped (white and green parts)

1 cup grated Parmesan cheese, divided

1 cup shredded mozzarella cheese

1 cup whole-milk or part-skim ricotta cheese

1 large egg, lightly beaten

¼ teaspoon pepper

⅛ teaspoon nutmeg

¼ pound (about 18) jumbo pasta shells

3 cups of your favorite marinara or spaghetti sauce

1. Preheat the oven to 350°F.

2. Put the thawed spinach in a sieve and use a large spoon to press out the moisture.

3. In a large bowl, combine the green onions, ½ cup of the Parmesan cheese, the mozzarella and ricotta cheeses, egg, pepper, nutmeg, and spinach.

4. Cook the pasta according to the package directions until al dente, or firm to the bite, and drain.

5. Spread 1 cup sauce over the bottom of a shallow 2-quart casserole. Stuff the shells with the spinach mixture and arrange them on top of the sauce. Ladle the remaining 2 cups sauce over the shells and sprinkle with the remaining ½ cup Parmesan. Spray a sheet of aluminum foil with cooking spray and cover the casserole. (At this point the dish can be covered and refrigerated for up to 1 day. Add 10 minutes to the baking time.)

6. Bake for 20 minutes, remove the foil, and continue baking until the casserole is heated through and the sauce is bubbly, about 10 to 20 minutes longer.

GNOCCHI WITH SPINACH AND MOZZARELLA

Gnocchi is the Italian word for "dumplings." They can be made from potatoes, flour, or farina. Of course homemade gnocchi are unbeatable, but in this recipe, bubbling cheeses and tender spinach elevate the flavor of store-bought gnocchi. You'll find them in the dried pasta section of the supermarket.

SERVES 4

1 package (1 pound) potato gnocchi

⅔ cup heavy cream

½ teaspoon all-purpose flour

½ teaspoon salt

½ teaspoon black pepper

⅛ teaspoon ground nutmeg

1 bag (1 pound) fresh baby spinach leaves

½ cup whole-milk or part-skim ricotta cheese

⅔ cup shredded part-skim mozzarella

1. Preheat the oven to 400°F. Butter a shallow 2-quart casserole.

2. Cook the gnocchi in a 5-quart pot of boiling salted water according to package instructions (they will float to the surface when done). Drain in a colander.

3. While the gnocchi are cooking, whisk together the cream, flour, salt, pepper, and nutmeg in a large nonstick skillet and bring to a boil over moderate heat, whisking constantly. Continue to boil, whisking frequently, until reduced by half, about 2 minutes. Add the spinach in handfuls, tossing with tongs, and cook until wilted, 2 to 4 minutes. Remove from the heat and stir in the gnocchi. Spread out in the casserole dish.

4. Spoon the ricotta over the gnocchi in 5 large dollops and sprinkle with the mozzarella. Bake, uncovered, for 15 to 20 minutes, until bubbly.

MACARONI AND FRESH MOZZARELLA

A delicious mixture of macaroni, butter, and fresh cheese, this is incredibly simple to make. Serve it in the summer with vine-ripened tomatoes sprinkled with olive oil, salt, and basil.

SERVES 8 TO 10

¾ pound elbow macaroni (about 3 cups)

4 tablespoons butter at room temperature

½ pound fresh mozzarella, sliced (see Note)

½ cup fine dry breadcrumbs

1. Preheat the oven to 350°F.

2. Cook the macaroni in boiling salted water for 6 to 7 minutes, until al dente, or firm to the bite.

3. Spread 1 tablespoon of the butter inside a shallow 2-quart casserole. Spread out 1 cup cooked macaroni in the bottom of the dish. Top with a layer of mozzarella slices. Top that with more cooked pasta, then with more mozzarella. Repeat the layers until the pasta and mozzarella are used up.

4. Melt the remaining 3 tablespoons butter in a small skillet, mix in the breadcrumbs, and sprinkle the mixture over the casserole. Bake, uncovered, for 25 to 30 minutes, until breadcrumbs are browned.

o o o o o

NOTE: An easy way to cut fresh mozzarella is with kitchen shears. Simply snip the log or ball into slices.

SPINACH AND RICOTTA LASAGNA ROLLS

Who doesn't like lasagna? To turn this into a vegetarian casserole, simply eliminate the sausage.

8 dried lasagna noodles

2 teaspoons olive oil

1 tablespoon canola oil

⅓ cup chopped onion

1 clove garlic, minced

¾ pound to 1 pound bulk Italian pork sausage (mild, medium, or hot)

1 can (14½ ounces) diced tomatoes with their juice

2 tablespoons tomato paste

½ teaspoon dried basil

¼ teaspoon sugar

1 package (10 ounces) frozen chopped spinach, thawed

¾ cup whole-milk or part-skim ricotta cheese

½ cup shredded part-skim mozzarella cheese

2 tablespoons grated Parmesan cheese

½ teaspoon dried basil

1 large egg, lightly beaten

1. Preheat the oven to 350°F. Coat an 8-inch square baking dish with cooking spray.

2. Cook the lasagna noodles according to package directions and drain. Drizzle with olive oil.

3. While the lasagna is cooking, heat the canola oil in a medium saucepan, and add the onion, garlic, and sausage. Sauté over medium-high heat until the meat is cooked through and the onion is tender. Add the tomatoes with their juice, the tomato paste, basil, and sugar. Bring to a boil over high heat; reduce the heat to low, and simmer, uncovered, for 5 to 6 minutes.

4. Put the thawed spinach in a sieve and, with a spoon, press out as much liquid as possible. In a medium bowl, combine the ricotta, mozzarella, Parmesan, and basil. Add the spinach and egg to the cheese mixture and mix thoroughly.

5. Lay the lasagna strips side by side on a work surface. Divide the filling equally between them and place it near one short end of each strip. Roll up the lasagna, beginning at the end with the filling so that the filling is enclosed.

6. Place the lasagna rolls, seam side down, in the casserole. Pour the tomato sauce over them and bake for 25 minutes, or until bubbly.

SAUSAGE AND MUSHROOM MANICOTTI

Manicotti are large tubes of pasta that are stuffed with a savory filling, covered with sauce, and baked. Although this may seem a little fussy to prepare, the result is certainly worth it.

———————— SERVES 8 ————————

16 manicotti

FOR THE MUSHROOM SAUCE:
2 tablespoons butter, plus extra for the dishes

½ pound mushrooms, sliced

1 can (12 ounces) evaporated milk

2 cups shredded Monterey Jack cheese

1 tablespoon minced fresh parsley

FOR THE FILLING:
1 pound bulk Italian pork sausage (mild, medium, or hot)

½ cup chopped green onion (white and green parts)

1 clove garlic, minced

½ pound mushrooms, sliced

¼ cup all-purpose flour

1½ cups half-and-half

¼ teaspoon white pepper

¼ teaspoon ground nutmeg

¼ teaspoon dried sage, crushed

2 tablespoons chopped fresh parsley, plus extra for garnish

1. Preheat the oven to 350°F. Butter two 9-by-13-inch baking dishes.

2. Cook the manicotti according to the package directions, until tender but firm to the bite. Drain, reserving ½ cup of the cooking water. Rinse the pasta with the cooking water to prevent the manicotti from sticking together.

3. *To make the sauce:* In a large skillet, melt the butter over medium-high heat. Add the mushrooms and sauté for 10 minutes, or until the liquid from the mushrooms has evaporated. Stir in the evaporated milk, cheese, and parsley and cook, stirring, until the cheese is melted. Set aside the sauce.

4. *To make the filling:* In a large skillet, cook the sausage until it is crumbly and no longer pink. Drain off the fat. Stir in the green onion, garlic, and mushrooms. Sauté over medium-high

heat for 10 minutes, or until the liquid from the mushrooms has evaporated. Add the flour, stirring until blended. Add the half-and-half and cook over medium heat, stirring constantly, until the filling is thickened. Stir in the white pepper, nutmeg, sage, and parsley.

5. *To assemble the manicotti:* Transfer the filling to a large, heavy-duty plastic bag with a zipper top. Cut a 1-inch triangle off a corner of the bottom of the bag. Press the sausage filling into the manicotti shells, and place the filled manicotti into the prepared baking dishes. Pour the sauce over the filled shells. (At this point the casseroles can be covered and refrigerated for up to 1 day. Add about 10 minutes to the baking time.)

6. Bake, uncovered, for 25 minutes, or until heated through. Garnish with additional chopped parsley.

VEGGIE MAC

This is perfect for a one-dish family meal. If your kids object to the suggested vegetables, substitute something they do like!

2 teaspoons butter, plus extra for the dish

½ pound elbow macaroni (about 2 cups)

1 tablespoon olive oil

6 tablespoons chopped green onions (white and green parts)

3 cloves garlic, minced

1 medium red bell pepper, seeded and chopped

1 tablespoon chopped fresh basil

½ teaspoon dried oregano

¼ teaspoon ground cumin

½ cup asparagus, cut into 2-inch lengths

1 cup halved cherry tomatoes

½ cup trimmed and halved snow peas

2 teaspoons all-purpose flour

1 cup milk

½ cup grated Parmesan cheese

½ teaspoon pepper

1. Preheat the oven to 400°F. Butter a 2½- to 3-quart casserole.

2. Cook the macaroni according to package directions, until tender but still firm to the bite. Drain and transfer to the casserole.

3. Warm the oil in the saucepan. Add the green onions, garlic, and bell pepper, and cook over medium-high heat until the vegetables are soft but not browned, 2 to 3 minutes. Add the basil, oregano, cumin, asparagus, tomatoes, and snow peas. Cook for another 2 to 3 minutes, stirring, until the asparagus and snow peas are tender but not overcooked. Mix the cooked vegetables with the macaroni in the casserole.

4. Melt the 2 teaspoons butter in the saucepan and stir in the flour; cook for 2 minutes. Gradually add the milk and cook, whisking until the sauce is thickened. Remove from the heat and stir in the grated Parmesan cheese and pepper. Stir the sauce into the pasta and vegetables.

5. Bake, uncovered, for 25 minutes, or until lightly browned and bubbly.

ZITI AND CAULIFLOWER GRATIN WITH SAFFRON AND PINE NUTS

Substitute any short pasta for the ziti, such as mostaccioli or penne. The word *ziti* means "bridegroom" in Italian, and describes relatively thin tubes ranging in length from 2 to 12 inches.

SERVES 8

6 quarts water

2 tablespoons kosher salt

1 medium head cauliflower, cut into large florets

1 teaspoon saffron

5 tablespoons extra-virgin olive oil, divided

6 cloves garlic, thinly sliced

3 salt-cured anchovy fillets, rinsed

1½ tablespoons pine nuts

1¼ pounds ziti

½ cup grated Pecorino Romano or Parmesan cheese

1 cup fine dry breadcrumbs

1. Preheat the oven to 375°F. Coat a deep 3-quart casserole with cooking spray.

2. In a large stockpot, bring 6 quarts water to a boil and add the salt. Add the cauliflower florets and cook for 5 to 7 minutes, until crisp-tender. Remove the cauliflower with a slotted spoon. Pour ¼ cup of the cauliflower cooking water into a small bowl, add the saffron, and set aside. Reserve the pot of cooking water.

3. In a medium skillet, heat 4 tablespoons of the olive oil over medium heat and add the garlic, cauliflower florets, and anchovy fillets and sauté for 2 minutes. Add the pine nuts and sauté for 1 minute more. Remove from the heat and set aside.

4. Return the cauliflower cooking water to a boil and add the ziti. Boil for 7 to 9 minutes, or until tender but not mushy, and drain.

5. Transfer the ziti to the casserole dish. Add the cauliflower mixture and half the cheese. Sprinkle with the saffron water and mix gently. Top with the remaining cheese and the breadcrumbs. Drizzle with the remaining 1 tablespoon olive oil. Bake for 15 minutes, or until the breadcrumbs are golden and the casserole is bubbly, and serve hot.

BAKED SPAGHETTI CASSEROLE

Think of this casserole on a busy day; it is so easy to throw together. Add a green salad and garlic bread and you have a real kid-pleaser here.

SERVES 6

½ pound spaghetti

1 pound ground beef

½ cup onion, chopped

¼ cup chopped green bell pepper

1 recipe Basic Mushroom Sauce (page 22), or 1 can (10¾ ounces) cream of mushroom soup

1 recipe Savory Tomato Sauce (page 23), or 1 can (10¾ ounces) cream of tomato soup

½ cup shredded mozzarella cheese

2 or 3 cloves garlic, minced

1. Preheat the oven to 350°F. Coat a 9-by-13-inch casserole with cooking spray.

2. Cook the spaghetti according to package directions and drain, but do not rinse.

3. Meanwhile, in a large skillet, cook the beef, onion, and pepper over medium-high heat just until the beef is no longer pink. Add all the remaining ingredients, mix well, and transfer to the prepared casserole. Cut a sheet of foil and coat with cooking spray. Cover the casserole and bake for 30 to 35 minutes, until bubbly.

PINTO BEANS AND PASTA

With the beans, corn, and whole-wheat pasta, you have a complete protein here. The dish is very low in fat and has an abundance of complex carbohydrates, making this a very healthy main dish.

SERVES 6

1 tablespoon vegetable oil

1 medium onion, chopped

1 large clove garlic, chopped

1 jalapeño pepper, seeded and minced, or ¼ teaspoon cayenne pepper

1 tablespoon chili powder

2 cans (14½ ounces each) stewed tomatoes with their juice

1 teaspoon dried oregano

½ teaspoon ground cumin

1 cup whole-wheat elbow macaroni or another small pasta

1½ cups fresh corn kernels, or frozen corn, thawed

1 can (12 ounces) pinto beans, rinsed and drained

⅓ cup sliced ripe olives

1 cup coarsely broken tortilla chips

1 cup shredded Jack cheese

1. Preheat the oven to 325°F.

2. In a heavy medium saucepan, heat the oil over medium-high heat and sauté the onion, garlic, and jalapeño pepper, if using, for 3 minutes to soften. Add the cayenne (if not using the jalapeño) and the chili powder, stir, and cook for about 1 minute. Add the tomatoes with their juice, oregano, and cumin and bring to a boil. Add the pasta and corn and simmer, uncovered, for 15 minutes, until the pasta is just tender. Stir in the pinto beans and olives. Transfer to a shallow 2-quart casserole and top with the broken tortilla chips and cheese. (The dish can be assembled up to 1 day in advance, covered, and refrigerated. Increase the baking time by 10 or 15 minutes, or until heated through.)

3. Bake the casserole for 10 minutes to melt the cheese.

GEMELLI PASTA CASSEROLE

Gemelli is the Italian word for "twins." In the culinary sense, it refers to short, 1½-inch twists that resemble two strands of spaghetti twisted together.

SERVES 8

1 package (1 pound) gemelli pasta

1 recipe Savory Tomato Sauce (page 23)

1 recipe Alfredo Sauce (page 24)

Grated Parmesan cheese for serving.

1. Preheat the oven to 350°F. Butter a 9-by-13-inch baking dish.

2. Cook the pasta according to package directions until al dente, or firm to the bite. Don't rinse. Transfer the pasta to the baking dish.

3. Prepare the tomato sauce and Alfredo sauce. Stir the tomato sauce into the pasta and top with the Alfredo sauce.

4. Bake, uncovered, until bubbly. Remove from the oven and let sit for about 5 minutes before serving. Sprinkle with Parmesan cheese.

MACARONI AND PARMESAN CHEESE

Macaroni and cheese was a popular dish in the early 1900s,
and it remains so today. Here Parmesan cheese replaces the traditional
Cheddar for a fresh twist.

7 tablespoons butter, plus extra for the dish

¾ pound elbow macaroni (about 3 cups)

2 tablespoons all-purpose flour

3 cups milk, heated

1 cup grated Parmesan cheese

1 cup fresh breadcrumbs (see Note)

2 tablespoons melted butter

1. Preheat the oven to 400°F. Butter a 3-quart casserole.

2. In a large pot, cook the macaroni in boiling salted water according to package directions until just tender. Drain, but don't rinse.

3. In a large saucepan, melt 4 tablespoons of the butter over medium heat and stir in the flour. Cook, stirring, until the flour is golden. Gradually stir in the milk, whisking to keep the sauce smooth. Simmer, stirring occasionally, for about 10 minutes, until thickened, and stir in ⅓ cup of the cheese.

Add the drained macaroni, the remaining 3 tablespoons butter, and the remaining ⅔ cup cheese. Mix well and transfer to the casserole dish.

4. Mix the breadcrumbs and melted butter and sprinkle over the casserole. Bake for 20 minutes, or until lightly browned.

○ ○ ○ ○ ○

NOTE: To make fresh breadcrumbs, tear 1 or 2 slices of fresh bread into pieces and put in a food processor with the steel blade in place. Process with on/off pulses until the bread is broken down into crumbs.

PASTA BAKED WITH CHEESE AND STOUT

The strong, bitter flavor of stout mixed with extra-sharp Cheddar transforms this mac and cheese into an adult dish. I used Irish blarney cheese and a vintage Irish Cheddar when I made it, but a sharp Vermont or English Cheddar would be good, too. Panko is a crispy Japanese breadcrumb, which makes a crunchy topping here.

SERVES 4 TO 6

3 teaspoons butter (1 tablespoon, cut into thirds), plus extra for the dish

½ pound pasta, gemellini, cavatelli, penne, or another small pasta

1 small red onion, minced

¾ cup stout or very dark beer

½ cup heavy cream

1 can (12 ounces) undiluted evaporated milk

1½ cups extra-sharp shredded Cheddar cheese

¼ cup grated Parmesan cheese

¾ cup seasoned panko or fine dry breadcrumbs

1. Preheat the oven to 350°F. Butter a shallow 2-quart casserole.

2. Cook the pasta in 2 quarts of boiling salted water according to package directions until al dente, or firm to the bite, and drain.

3. Meanwhile, melt 1 teaspoon of the butter in a large skillet and add the onion; cook over medium heat for 2 to 3 minutes, until the onion is soft. Add the stout, heat to boiling, and continue boiling for 5 minutes. Add the cream and evaporated milk and boil for another 5 minutes, or until reduced by half.

4. Mix the cooked pasta with the stout and cream sauce and add the Cheddar and Parmesan cheeses. Turn the mixture into the buttered casserole.

5. Melt the remaining 2 teaspoons butter in a small saucepan and mix in the breadcrumbs. Sprinkle over the top of the casserole. Bake for about 25 minutes, or until the breadcrumbs are lightly browned and the casserole is bubbly.

ooooo

NOTE: Panko are Japanese breadcrumbs. They are coarser than regular breadcrumbs and create a crunchier crust. Panko can be purchased in Asian markets, or in the Asian sections of large supermarkets.

RAVIOLI AND CHEESE BAKE

It takes just 5 minutes to put this casserole together, but you need to bake it for almost an hour, so assemble it ahead and refrigerate it overnight if you wish.

SERVES 6

2 cups prepared spaghetti sauce

1 can (14½ ounces) diced tomatoes with herbs, with their juice

1¼ cups homemade (page 26) or prepared beef broth

3 tablespoons olive oil

1 tablespoon balsamic vinegar

2 packages (9 ounces each) cheese-filled ravioli

1 tablespoon prepared pesto

1 cup shredded mozzarella cheese

1. Preheat the oven to 375°F.

2. Combine the spaghetti sauce, tomatoes with their juice, beef broth, olive oil, and balsamic vinegar together in a medium bowl.

3. Spread half of the sauce in a 9-by-13-inch baking dish. Top with the ravioli and spread with the remaining sauce.

4. Coat a sheet of aluminum foil with cooking spray. Cover the baking dish and bake for 45 to 50 minutes, until the ravioli are tender and the sauce is bubbly.

5. Stir in the pesto and top with the mozzarella cheese. Let stand for 5 minutes, or until the cheese melts.

RAVIOLI LASAGNA

Fresh ravioli take the place of lasagna noodles in this popular, easily prepared casserole. You'll find frozen ravioli in the freezer case of your local supermarket. Layer the ravioli with beef, mozzarella, and your favorite spaghetti sauce, flavored with herbs or other seasonings.

SERVES 6

1 pound extra-lean ground beef

3½ cups prepared spaghetti sauce

½ cup water

1 teaspoon dried oregano

1 teaspoon dried basil

40 frozen cheese raviolis, or a combination of cheese-, sausage-, and spinach-filled ravioli

2 cups shredded part-skim mozzarella cheese

1. Preheat the oven to 425°F. Coat a 9-by-13-inch baking dish with cooking spray.

2. In a skillet over medium-high heat, cook the beef until it is no longer pink.

3. Mix the spaghetti sauce with the water so you have a total of 4 cups sauce. Add the oregano and basil. Spread 1 cup of the sauce over the bottom of the baking dish.

4. Lay 20 frozen ravioli, puffy sides down, in the sauce. If you are using a combination of flavors, alternate the ravioli. Cover with half the cooked ground beef. Sprinkle 1 cup shredded mozzarella cheese over the beef. Cover with 1¼ cups sauce, the remaining ground beef, and then the remaining 20 ravioli. Top with the remaining 1¾ cups sauce, making sure it covers the ravioli.

5. Coat a sheet of aluminum foil with cooking spray. Cover tightly and bake for 35 minutes. Uncover and sprinkle with the remaining cup of mozzarella. Bake, uncovered, for 5 minutes longer.

SPINACH LASAGNA

You don't need to precook the noodles when assembling this lasagna, which will save you about 20 minutes of time and make cleanup easier. The noodles cook between the layers of filling, expanding to fill the pan.

SERVES 12

1 pound extra-lean ground beef

4 cups prepared spaghetti sauce

½ cup water

1 teaspoon salt

2 cups whole-milk or part-skim ricotta cheese or cottage cheese

1 large egg, lightly beaten

3 cups shredded mozzarella cheese, divided

½ cup grated Parmesan cheese, divided

1 package (10 ounces) frozen chopped spinach, thawed and drained

½ cup prepared basil pesto

1 tablespoon chopped fresh basil, or 1 teaspoon dried basil

12 lasagna noodles

1. Preheat the oven to 350°F.

2. In a large skillet over medium-high heat, cook the beef until it is no longer pink. Add the spaghetti sauce, water, and salt.

3. In a medium bowl, mix the ricotta cheese, the egg, 1 cup of the mozzarella cheese, and ¼ cup of the Parmesan cheese.

4. In a small bowl, mix the spinach, pesto, and basil.

5. Spread 1 cup of the meat sauce in the bottom of a 9-by-13-inch baking pan. Top with 4 of the uncooked lasagna noodles, then a third of the ricotta mixture, and half the spinach. Top with 4 more noodles, 1 cup of the sauce and another third of the ricotta mixture. Cover with the remaining spinach, and sprinkle with half the mozzarella. Top with the 4 remaining noodles and the remaining ricotta, sauce, and mozzarella.

6. Sprinkle with the remaining ¼ cup Parmesan cheese.

7. Coat a sheet of aluminum foil with cooking spray, cover the lasagna, and bake for 50 minutes to 1 hour, until bubbly. Remove the foil during the last 15 minutes of baking.

Chapter 10
GRAIN & LEGUME CASSEROLES

○○○○○

Grains and legumes are naturals for casseroles because they provide a simple backdrop for lots of flavorful ingredients. Barley, for example, pairs well with mushrooms, nuts, spices, and dried fruits to make appealing side dishes. Other casseroles include bulgur, cracked wheat, millet, quinoa, lentil, chickpeas, beans, white rice, or wild rice.

Pair almost any of these earthy, fiber-filled casseroles with simple grilled meats, fish, or poultry for lunch or dinner. Barley with Nuts and Dried Fruit (page 332), on the other hand, is a breakfast favorite. Southwestern Bean Casserole with Double-Corn Topping (page 342) can be the inspiration for a Southwestern-style picnic.

BARLEY AND MUSHROOM CASSEROLE

Earthy and richly flavored, this is great as a side dish for grilled meat or salmon. If you like, add a few drops of truffle oil to enhance the mushroom flavor.

SERVES 6

2 tablespoons butter at room temperature

A few drops truffle oil (optional)

1½ cups finely diced onion

1 carrot, finely chopped

1 rib celery, thinly sliced

¾ pound assorted mushrooms, such as white button, shiitake, baby portobellos, and oyster, thinly sliced

1½ cups pearl barley

1½ teaspoons minced fresh thyme, or ¾ teaspoon dried

¾ teaspoon salt

½ teaspoon pepper

4 cups boiling vegetable broth, homemade (page 27) or prepared

½ cup boiling water

1. Preheat the oven to 350°F. Brush a shallow 2½-quart casserole with 1 teaspoon of the butter.

2. Add the remaining butter and the truffle oil, if using, to a large nonstick skillet and place over medium-high heat. Add the onion, carrot, celery, mushrooms, barley, thyme, salt, and pepper to the pan and sauté, stirring, for 10 minutes, until the mixture is aromatic and the mushrooms are lightly browned.

3. Turn the mixture into the casserole dish. (You can assemble the casserole a day in advance to this point, cover, and refrigerate. Add 15 to 20 minutes to the baking time.)

4. Pour the boiling stock and water over the vegetables and barley evenly. Cover and bake for 1 hour to 1 hour and 15 minutes, or until all the liquid is absorbed.

BARLEY BAKED WITH PINE NUTS AND SUN-DRIED TOMATOES

Barley has a low glycemic index, which makes it valuable for those who are trying to lose weight. For the best flavor and texture, use regular whole barley rather than pearl barley, which has the bran removed. Avoid the quick-cooking 10-minute variety, which can have a sticky, starchy texture. The best source for whole barley is a food co-op or natural-foods store. Barley has another virtue—its pleasing taste. I love the flavor of barley!

SERVES 6

4 tablespoons butter

1 medium onion, chopped

1 cup whole barley

½ cup pine nuts

1 cup chopped fresh parsley, divided

4 green onions, thinly sliced (white and green parts)

½ cup thinly sliced sun-dried tomatoes

½ teaspoon salt

½ teaspoon pepper

3 cups beef or vegetable broth, homemade (page 26 or 27), or prepared

1. Preheat the oven to 350°F.

2. In a cast-iron Dutch oven, melt the butter over medium-heat and add the onion, barley, and pine nuts. Cook, stirring, until the onions are soft, about 10 minutes. Add ½ cup of the parsley, the green onions, sun-dried tomatoes, salt, and pepper. Pour in the broth and stir to blend.

3. Cover and bake for 1 hour and 15 minutes, or until the barley is tender and the broth is absorbed. Garnish with the remaining ½ cup chopped parsley.

BARLEY WITH NUTS AND DRIED FRUIT

Crunchy with almonds and pine nuts, this casserole is perfect served alongside baked ham or turkey.

2 tablespoons butter, plus extra for the dish

½ cup slivered almonds

2 tablespoons pine nuts

1 cup pearl barley

1 bunch green onions, sliced (white and green parts; about 1 cup)

4 cups homemade (page 25) or prepared chicken broth

½ cup diced dried apricots

½ cup golden raisins

¼ cup dried cranberries

1. Preheat the oven to 325°F. Butter a 3-quart casserole.

2. In a large skillet over medium-high heat, melt 1 tablespoon of the butter and toast the almonds and pine nuts until golden, 2 to 3 minutes. Remove to a small bowl. Add the remaining 1 tablespoon of butter to the pan and add the barley and green onions; cook for 3 to 4 minutes, until the green onions are soft, but not browned. Add the broth, bring to a boil, and remove from the heat. Transfer the barley mixture to the casserole dish and mix in the toasted nuts, the apricots, raisins, and cranberries.

3. Cover and bake for 1 hour to 1 hour and 20 minutes, or until the liquid is absorbed and the barley is tender.

BASMATI PILAF WITH SPICES, RAISINS, AND PISTACHIOS

You can throw this casserole together and bake it alongside roast pork, chicken, or turkey. Add Brussels sprouts to the menu in the winter, and some steamed asparagus in the spring.

SERVES 8

2 tablespoons butter

1 cup thinly sliced shallots, or ½ cup thinly sliced onions

2½ cups boiling water

1½ cups basmati rice

¾ cup frozen peas

¾ cup golden raisins

1½ teaspoons salt

¾ teaspoon fennel seeds, lightly crushed (see Notes)

¼ teaspoon freshly ground pepper

⅛ teaspoon crushed saffron threads

⅛ teaspoon ground cardamom

1 cinnamon stick, 1 inch long

1 bay leaf

½ cup chopped pistachios, toasted (see Notes)

1. Preheat the oven to 350°F.

2. Melt the butter in a large nonstick skillet over medium heat. Add the shallots and sauté for 8 minutes, or until softened. Remove from the heat and set aside.

3. Combine the water and rice in a deep 2- to 3-quart casserole. Stir in the peas, sautéed shallots, raisins, salt, fennel seeds, pepper, saffron threads, cardamom, cinnamon stick, and bay leaf. Cover and bake for 50 minutes to 1 hour, until the liquid is absorbed and the rice is tender. Discard the cinnamon stick and bay leaf and garnish with the pistachios.

NOTES: To crush fennel seeds, place them in a mortar and grind with a pestle. Or put them in a clean coffee grinder or spice grinder and grind for about 3 seconds.

To toast pistachios, spread out the nuts on a cookie sheet and place in a 350°F oven for 5 to 10 minutes, stirring occasionally, until the pistachios are aromatic and lightly browned.

BULGUR BAKED WITH RAISINS AND CRANBERRIES

Bulgur is made from cooked wheat berries, which are dried and then cracked. It is not the same as cracked wheat, which is made by cracking uncooked wheat berries. In this casserole you can use either, although bulgur tends to have a nuttier flavor. The toasty flavor of the wheat blends well here with fruit, a bit of butter, and nuts. Serve this as a base for curries or stews, or as a side with roasts and poultry dishes. It is also wonderful as a breakfast dish. Assemble the casserole the night before, if you wish, and bake it in the morning. I love it with cream poured over my serving. For breakfast I might eliminate the basil.

SERVES 6

2 teaspoons butter, plus extra for the dish

1 cup bulgur or cracked wheat

2 cups boiling water

1 teaspoon salt

1 teaspoon dried basil

½ cup golden raisins

½ cup dark raisins

½ cup dried cranberries

½ cup slivered almonds, toasted (see Note)

1. Preheat the oven to 300°F. Butter a 1½-quart casserole.

2. Combine the bulgur, water, salt, basil, raisins, cranberries, and the 2 teaspoons butter in the casserole and stir to blend well. Cover and bake for 30 to 45 minutes, or until the bulgur is tender and has absorbed all the liquid. Before serving, fluff with a fork and garnish with the toasted almonds.

NOTE: To toast the almonds, spread them out on a baking sheet and toast in a 350°F oven for about 10 minutes, stirring occasionally, until the nuts are fragrant and lightly browned.

CRACKED WHEAT CASSEROLE

I particularly like this grainy casserole with grilled or broiled salmon. Instead of cracked wheat, you can use kasha, which are roasted buckwheat groats.

SERVES 6

2 cups cracked wheat or kasha

1 large onion, minced

3 tablespoons butter

4 cups homemade (page 26) or prepared beef broth

1 pound mushrooms, sliced

Salt

Pepper

Sour cream for serving

1. Preheat the oven to 350°F. Coat a 2½-quart casserole with cooking spray.

2. Place a large, heavy, dry skillet over medium-high heat and add the cracked wheat or kasha. Stir and toast until fragrant and nutty. Transfer to the casserole.

3. In the same skillet, cook the onion in the butter until wilted and aromatic. Mix in with the cracked wheat in the casserole. Add the beef broth and mushrooms and cover the casserole.

4. Bake for 45 minutes, or until the liquid is absorbed and the grains are tender. Stir and season with salt and pepper to taste. Serve hot with sour cream spooned on top.

GARLICKY BULGUR, GREEN LENTIL, AND CHICKPEA CASSEROLE

This makes a lovely vegetarian main dish. If you like, you can assemble the casserole several hours ahead and bake it just before serving.

SERVES 4

¾ cup green lentils

3 cups homemade (page 25) or prepared chicken broth

1 teaspoon fresh rosemary leaves, or ½ teaspoon dried rosemary

1 teaspoon fresh tarragon leaves, or ½ teaspoon dried tarragon

1 bay leaf

2 tablespoons sesame oil

1 carrot, peeled and shredded

4 cloves garlic, minced

1 large onion, chopped

¾ cup bulgur

2 cups canned chickpeas (garbanzo beans)

Chile-garlic paste or red pepper flakes (optional)

1. Put the lentils and broth in a large saucepan, add the rosemary, tarragon, and bay leaf and bring to a boil. Reduce the heat to a simmer and cook, uncovered, until the lentils are tender but not mushy, about 25 minutes. Remove the bay leaf.

2. Preheat the oven to 350°F. Butter a 2-quart casserole.

3. Heat the sesame oil in a skillet and add the carrot, garlic, and onion; sauté for 5 minutes, until softened. Then add the bulgur and chickpeas and the chile-garlic paste or red pepper flakes to taste, if desired.

4. Transfer the mixture to the casserole dish. (At this point the casserole can be covered and refrigerated for several hours. Add 5 to 10 minutes to the baking time.) Bake, uncovered, for 20 minutes, or until heated through.

SPICED HAZELNUT BARLEY CASSEROLE

Hazelnuts (also called filberts) have an earthy flavor that goes well with barley. For the most flavor, texture, and fiber, I prefer to use whole barley, but in a pinch, pearl barley will do. (Quick-cooking barley, which has a pasty, starchy texture, does not work very well in casseroles.) Cumin and coriander enhance the flavor of the hazelnuts. This recipe is adapted from one from the Oregon Hazelnut Grower's Association.

SERVES 6

6 tablespoons butter

½ teaspoon ground cumin

½ teaspoon ground coriander

½ cup chopped hazelnuts (filberts)

1 cup whole or pearl barley

1 medium yellow onion, finely chopped

¼ cup thinly sliced green onions (white and green parts)

½ teaspoon Chinese five-spice powder

¼ teaspoon salt

¼ teaspoon pepper

3 cups vegetable, chicken, or beef broth, homemade (page 27, 25, or 26) or prepared, heated until boiling

3 tablespoons chopped crystallized ginger

Parsley for garnish

1. Preheat the oven to 350°F.

2. In a heavy skillet, melt 2 tablespoons of the butter and add the cumin, coriander, and nuts. Stir until lightly roasted and aromatic; remove nuts and set aside.

3. Melt the remaining 4 tablespoons butter in the skillet and add the barley and yellow onion. Sauté, stirring, until the onion is tender and the barley is lightly browned. Add the toasted nuts, green onions, five-spice powder, salt, and pepper. Pour in the broth and stir to blend.

4. Transfer the mixture to a 2-quart casserole. Cover and bake for 1 hour and 15 minutes, or until the liquid is absorbed and barley is cooked. Sprinkle with crystallized ginger and parsley.

HERBED BARLEY AND MUSHROOM CASSEROLE

I love the flavor combination of mushrooms, butter, and sage. In fact, when I have sage in the garden, I'll add a whole bunch more to this recipe because it is so fresh and aromatic.

SERVES 6

4 tablespoons butter

2 medium onions, chopped

½ pound mushrooms, sliced

¼ cup chopped fresh sage leaves, or 1 tablespoon dried sage

1 tablespoon fresh thyme leaves, or 1 teaspoon dried thyme

1½ cups whole or pearl barley

3 cups chicken or beef broth, homemade (page 25 or 26) or prepared

¼ teaspoon salt

¼ teaspoon pepper

Chopped fresh parsley for garnish

1. Preheat the oven to 350°F.

2. Melt the butter in a flameproof 2-quart casserole over medium heat. Add the onions, mushrooms, sage, and thyme and sauté for 5 to 7 minutes, until the vegetables are softened. Add the barley and stir until kernels are coated with butter. Add 2 cups of the broth, the salt, and pepper.

3. Cover the casserole, place in the oven, and bake for 45 minutes. Add the remaining 1 cup broth, return to the oven, and bake, covered, for 30 minutes longer. Stir and garnish with the chopped parsley.

MILLET WITH HERBS AND ROASTED RED PEPPER

Although we know millet primarily as a cereal grass seed used in bird feed, it is a staple for almost one-third of the world's population. Millet is rich in protein, with a mild flavor that takes to lots of different seasonings.

SERVES 6

2 roasted red bell peppers (see page 35)

1 tablespoon olive oil

Pinch of saffron threads

3 tablespoons butter

1 small onion, finely chopped

1 cup millet

2 cups water

½ teaspoon salt

2 tablespoons chopped fresh basil, or 2 teaspoons dried basil, plus extra for the garnish (optional)

1 tablespoon chopped fresh parsley, plus extra for the garnish (optional)

2 teaspoons chopped fresh marjoram, or ¾ teaspoon dried marjoram

Pepper

1. Roast the red peppers as directed, removing the skins, cores, seeds, and veins. Cut into small squares and put in a buttered 2-quart casserole.

2. In a small skillet, warm the oil and saffron threads over low heat for 1½ minutes. Remove from the heat and let stand for 5 minutes. Add the saffron to the roasted peppers.

3. Melt 1½ tablespoons of the butter in the skillet, add the onion, and cook until softened, about 5 minutes. Add the onion to the casserole.

4. Preheat the oven to 350°F.

5. Melt the remaining 1½ tablespoons butter in the skillet over medium heat, add the millet, and stir until the grains begin to color and pop, 3 to 4 minutes. Stir the millet into the ingredients in the casserole and add the water.

6. Cover and bake for 20 minutes, or until the millet is slightly chewy, but not crunchy. Stir in the salt, basil, parsley, marjoram, and pepper to taste. Garnish with additional chopped basil or parsley, if desired, and serve hot.

BAKED QUINOA CASSEROLE WITH BABY POTATOES AND CHEESE

Try this for lunch or a light supper. Quinoa is a staple grain in South America. It is high in protein and cooks in about half as much time as rice.

SERVES 4

1 pound organic baby potatoes (with skins on), cut into 1-inch dice

2 large leeks, trimmed and halved lengthwise (white and tender green parts)

2 tablespoons olive oil

2 cloves garlic, finely chopped

1 large green bell pepper, seeded and diced

1 large red bell pepper, seeded and diced

4 large eggs

½ cup low-fat milk

1 cup quinoa, cooked according to package directions

1½ cups shredded smoked Cheddar cheese

1½ teaspoons salt

½ teaspoon pepper

1 teaspoon dried thyme

1. Preheat the oven to 350°F. Coat a shallow 2-quart casserole with cooking spray.

2. Put the potatoes in a pot with just enough water to cover and cook until they are tender, about 15 minutes. Set aside. Wash the leeks, pat dry, and cut into 1-inch pieces.

3. Place a large skillet over medium heat and add the olive oil. Add the leeks and garlic and sauté for 5 minutes, or until the leeks and garlic are tender. Add the bell peppers and cook, covered, for 5 to 10 minutes, until peppers are crisp-tender. Remove from the heat and set aside.

4. In a large bowl, beat the eggs and milk together. Stir in the quinoa and add the cheese, potatoes, bell pepper mixture, salt, pepper, and thyme. Transfer to the casserole.

5. Bake, uncovered, for 35 to 45 minutes, until the top is golden brown. Let rest for 5 minutes before serving.

RICE AND TOMATO PILAF

I like this as a main course with a crisp green salad and freshly baked bread. For a heartier meal, this makes a perfect accompaniment for Casserole-Braised Lamb Shanks (page 288).

SERVES 4

3 tablespoons butter

¾ cup long-grain white rice

1 can (14½ ounces) diced tomatoes with their juice, or 2 large fresh tomatoes, peeled and diced

1½ cups water

½ teaspoon salt

1 tablespoon minced fresh basil, or 2 teaspoons dried

1 tablespoon crushed dried morel mushrooms (optional)

1. Preheat the oven to 300°F.

2. Combine all of the ingredients in a 1½-quart casserole.

3. Bake, covered, for 1 to 1¼ hours, until the rice is tender and has absorbed all the liquid. Before serving, fluff with a fork.

SOUTHWESTERN BEAN CASSEROLE WITH DOUBLE-CORN TOPPING

Don't let the list of ingredients intimidate you! If you wish, you can substitute a corn muffin mix for the muffin topping and add the corn kernels, cheese, and chiles to it.

SERVES 6

1 tablespoon butter, plus extra for the dish

½ cup chopped onion

1 pound lean ground beef

2 tablespoons Taco Seasoning Mix (page 34)

½ teaspoon salt

¼ teaspoon pepper

½ to 1 teaspoon red pepper flakes

2 cans (15 ounces each) pinto beans, rinsed and drained

1 can (16 ounces) diced tomatoes with their juice

FOR THE CORN MUFFIN TOPPING:

¾ cup yellow cornmeal

¼ cup all-purpose flour

2 teaspoons baking powder

½ teaspoon salt

¼ teaspoon pepper

1 large egg

½ cup sour cream

2 tablespoons butter, melted

1 cup frozen corn kernels, thawed

1½ cups coarsely shredded sharp Cheddar cheese, divided

¼ cup chopped canned green chiles

1. Preheat the oven to 400°F. Butter a 2-quart casserole.

2. In a skillet over medium-high heat, sauté the onion in the 1 tablespoon butter for 5 minutes. Add the ground beef and cook until browned. Drain off the fat. Stir in the Taco Seasoning Mix, salt, pepper, pepper flakes to taste, beans, and diced tomatoes with their juice. Transfer the mixture to the casserole.

3. *To make the corn muffin topping:* In a large bowl, stir the cornmeal, flour, baking powder, salt, and pepper together. In a medium bowl, whisk the egg and sour cream until smooth. Stir in the butter, corn, ½ cup of the cheese, and the chiles. Add the mixture to the dry ingredients and stir just until moistened.

4. Spoon the batter around the edges of the casserole, leaving the center uncovered. Sprinkle the remaining 1 cup cheese over all. Bake, uncovered, for 20 to 30 minutes, until the corn muffin topping is lightly browned and the meat and bean mixture is hot and bubbly.

SPICED AND HERBED MILLET

A staple in Asia and Africa, millet is high in protein and cooks quickly. You can use it in place of rice in almost any dish. Cumin, lemon juice, and parsley perk up millet's flavor here. Enjoy this as a vegetarian main-course dish with just a fresh salad on the side.

MAKES 6 SERVINGS

2 teaspoons olive oil

1 cup millet

½ teaspoon ground cumin

2 cups vegetable or chicken broth, homemade (page 27 or 25) or prepared, heated until boiling

Juice of ½ lemon

¼ cup chopped fresh parsley

2 tablespoons chopped fresh chives

2 tablespoons olive oil

1. Preheat the oven to 350°F.

2. Pour the olive oil into a heavy, flameproof 2-quart casserole and place over medium heat. Stir in the millet and cumin, and cook for 10 minutes, stirring frequently, until the grain toasts and becomes aromatic. Pour in the broth and stir.

3. Cover and bake for 30 minutes, or until the liquid is absorbed. Remove from the oven and stir in the lemon juice, parsley, chives, and olive oil, using a fork. Fluff the mixture with a fork.

TOASTED FOUR-GRAIN AND WILD MUSHROOM CASSEROLE

The flavors and textures of four grains, mushrooms, and vegetables blend into a satisfying one-dish meal. Lots of good fiber here!

¼ cup millet

¼ cup wheat berries

¼ cup whole or pearl barley

½ cup wild rice

⅓ cup (½ ounce) crushed dried morel mushrooms

2½ cups water

1 teaspoon olive oil

1 medium onion, coarsely chopped

2 cloves garlic, minced

1 stalk celery, coarsely chopped

1 small red bell pepper, seeded and chopped

1 carrot, peeled and chopped

1 can (14½ ounces) diced tomatoes with their juice

1 teaspoon curry powder

1 teaspoon salt

½ teaspoon pepper

¼ cup pine nuts, toasted (see Note)

½ cup feta cheese, crumbled

1. Place a dry heavy skillet over medium heat and add the millet, wheat berries, barley, and wild rice. Stir and toast about 5 minutes, or until the grains give off a nutty aroma. Add the crushed morels and water, bring to a simmer, cover, and cook over low heat for 40 minutes, or until the grains are softened. Transfer to a 2-quart casserole and wipe the skillet dry.

2. Preheat the oven to 350°F.

3. Add the oil to the skillet and raise the heat to medium-high. Add the onion, garlic, celery, bell pepper, and carrot and sauté until the onion is soft but not browned, about 5 minutes. Add to the grains and mushrooms in the casserole. Stir in the tomatoes with their juice, curry powder, salt, and pepper.

4. Cover and bake for 25 to 30 minutes, or until bubbly. Sprinkle with the pine nuts and feta cheese.

○ ○ ○ ○ ○

NOTE: To toast pine nuts, spread them out on a baking sheet and bake in a 350°F oven for 5 to 10 minutes, stirring occasionally, until aromatic and golden.

ASPARAGUS AND WILD RICE CASSEROLE

I love this as a main dish. Just add a green salad and a loaf of bread to fill out the menu for lunch or a light supper.

SERVES 6

1 tablespoon butter, plus extra for the dish

2 tablespoons chopped green onion (white and green parts)

1 tablespoon all-purpose flour

⅛ teaspoon salt

1 cup milk

½ cup light mayonnaise

2 cups cooked wild rice (see page 29)

2 pounds asparagus, cut into 2-inch pieces

¾ cup shredded Cheddar cheese

6 strips bacon, cooked until crisp and crumbled

¼ cup toasted chopped walnuts

1. Preheat the oven to 350°F. Butter a shallow 2-quart casserole.

2. Melt the 1 tablespoon butter in a small saucepan, add the green onion, and sauté until tender. Add the flour and salt, stir to coat the flour with the butter, and gradually stir in the milk. Cook over medium heat, stirring, until the mixture thickens. Cook for 1 minute longer without stirring. Remove from the heat and stir in the mayonnaise.

3. Put the wild rice in the bottom of the casserole dish and top with the asparagus. Cover with the sauce, and sprinkle with the cheese and then the bacon. Bake for 30 minutes, or until bubbly Sprinkle with the walnuts.

BAKED WILD RICE WITH MUSHROOMS

This recipe is based on a popular method for cooking wild rice in Minnesota—the overnight method. The rice and water are combined in a casserole, which goes into a cold oven. The oven is then briefly cranked up to 500°F and turned off. As the oven cools, the rice continues to cook slowly and can sit there overnight. It's simple, but you do need to plan ahead for this one! Some cooks I know always prepare wild rice this way. They portion it into freezer bags so they can add the wild rice to soups, salads, casseroles, and even breads.

SERVES 8

1 cup wild rice

2½ cups water

1 pound mushrooms, stemmed

3 tablespoons butter

2 tablespoons fresh lemon juice

1 cup homemade (page 25) or prepared chicken broth

1 tablespoon chopped fresh thyme, or 1 teaspoon dried thyme

Salt

Pepper

1. Wash the rice in 3 changes of hot tap water. Combine the rice with the 2½ cups water in a 3-quart casserole. Place the casserole into the cold oven, then heat it to 500°F. After 15 minutes, turn the oven off and leave the door closed. Keep the casserole in the oven for at least 6 hours, or overnight.

2. When the rice is about ready to come out of the oven, cut the mushroom caps into quarters. Melt the butter in a large skillet or saucepan, and add the mushrooms, along with the lemon juice and chicken broth. Bring to a boil over high heat. Reduce the heat and simmer for 5 minutes.

3. Remove the wild rice casserole from the oven and preheat the oven to 350°F.

4. Stir the mushroom mixture into the rice, add the thyme, and season with salt and pepper. Cover and bake for 15 minutes, or until heated through.

WILD RICE BUFFET CASSEROLE

Sometimes people are wary of cooking wild rice. This method is foolproof and is a delicious alternative to the overnight method offered in the previous recipe. This is a perfect casserole for a buffet. I like to serve it with roasted salmon and a salad platter.

SERVES 6

⅔ cup wild rice

1 cup chopped green onions (white and green parts)

1½ cups chopped fresh celery

½ pound mushrooms, sliced

2 cups homemade (page 26) or prepared beef broth

2 cups water

1 teaspoon dried thyme

½ teaspoon dried rosemary, crushed

1 tablespoon cornstarch

2 tablespoons dry sherry or water

½ cup heavy cream

1. Preheat the oven to 325°F.

2. Wash the rice in 3 changes of hot tap water and put in a 2½-quart casserole. Add the green onions, celery, mushrooms, broth, water, and herbs. Stir to combine. In a small bowl, blend the cornstarch and sherry or water, and pour over the mixture. Add the heavy cream and stir.

3. Cover and bake for 2 to 2½ hours, until the rice has absorbed the liquid.

WILD RICE CASSEROLE WITH PEPPERS AND SUN-DRIED TOMATOES

This casserole is a perfect side dish for roasts and grilled meat, chicken, or fish. If you're entertaining, you can assemble it ahead of time and bake it before serving.

SERVES 6

1 tablespoon butter, plus extra for the dish

½ cup chopped onion

1 red or yellow bell pepper, seeded and diced

¼ cup julienned sun-dried tomatoes

1 cup wild rice

2 teaspoons Worcestershire sauce

1 tablespoon minced fresh parsley

2 cups homemade (page 25) or prepared chicken broth

½ cup dry white wine or apple juice

1 cup cubed sharp Cheddar cheese

1. Preheat the oven to 350°F. Butter a 1½-quart casserole.

2. In a saucepan or skillet, melt the 1 tablespoon butter and add the onion, bell pepper, and sun-dried tomatoes. Stir and cook over medium heat for 4 minutes, or until the onion is soft but not browned. Transfer the mixture to the casserole.

3. Wash the rice in 3 changes of hot tap water. Add the rice to the casserole along with the Worcestershire sauce, parsley, chicken broth, and wine.

4. Cover and bake for 1 hour or until the rice has absorbed all of the liquid. Stir in the cheese cubes and return to the oven just long enough for the cheese to melt, about 5 minutes.

Chapter 11
FISH & SHELLFISH CASSEROLES

Fish and seafood—whether fresh, frozen, or canned—have always been important in casserole cuisine. Even today, when good-quality frozen seafood is easy to find, I like to stock our pantry shelves with the ingredients for satisfying seafood hot dishes. In the summertime, when we head to our cabin, where refrigeration is minimal, canned tuna, salmon, and crab can come to the rescue if the fishing has been lousy. On the other hand, if the fishing has been good, I might turn to a recipe for Walleye and Green Chile Casserole (page 377), an updated version of an old favorite.

Below are a wide variety of fish and shellfish casseroles, from Poor Man's Lobster (page 353), which is a local name for cod, to a classic Finnish Salmon Casserole (page 361). One recipe that beautifully illustrates the ability of a casserole to "stretch" flavors is the Lobster Mac and Four Cheeses (page 366), which elevates classic mac and cheese to a new level.

BAKED BAY SCALLOPS

Fresh bay scallops are generally found only on the East Coast, although they can be found frozen in other parts of the country. The scallops are very tiny, about ½ inch across, and average about 100 per pound. They have a very sweet flavor and are expensive because they are not plentiful. In other parts of the country, calico scallops are sold as bay scallops, and can be about 1½ inches across (about 30 to the pound). Although not as tender, calico scallops are still sweet and moist. Either variety is wonderful cooked this way.

SERVES 4

6 tablespoons butter, divided, plus extra for the pan

½ cup fresh breadcrumbs (see Note)

3 cloves garlic, minced

2 tablespoons minced onion

¼ cup chopped fresh parsley

2 tablespoons white wine or sherry

2 tablespoons fresh lemon juice

½ teaspoon salt

¼ teaspoon pepper

2 tablespoons diced onion (¼-inch dice)

1½ pounds fresh bay scallops

½ pound mushrooms, sliced

1. Combine 4 tablespoons of the butter, the breadcrumbs, garlic, minced onion, parsley, wine, lemon juice, salt, and pepper. Chill until the mixture is firm, at least 1 hour.

2. Preheat the oven to 450°F. Lightly butter a 1½-quart shallow casserole or au gratin pan and set aside.

3. Heat the remaining 2 tablespoons butter in a large skillet. Add the diced onion and sauté over medium heat until soft, but not browned. Add the scallops, and mushrooms, and sauté briefly.

4. Arrange the scallop mixture in the casserole dish. Slice the chilled garlic butter–breadcrumb mixture and arrange evenly over the scallops. Bake until the butter is hot and bubbly, about 5 to 10 minutes. Serve immediately.

○ ○ ○ ○ ○

NOTE: To make fresh breadcrumbs, tear 1 or 2 slices of fresh bread into pieces and put in a food processor with the steel blade in place. Process with on/off pulses until the bread is broken down into crumbs.

POOR MAN'S LOBSTER (BUTTER-BAKED COD)

I recall being served this cod casserole many years ago, when it was all the rage among Norwegian Americans. It was served with boiled buttered potatoes and pickled beets (for color).

SERVES 4

1½ pounds fresh cod fillets, or frozen fillets, thawed

1 cup (2 sticks) butter, melted

1 teaspoon kosher salt

½ teaspoon pepper

⅛ teaspoon paprika

Fresh parsley sprigs for garnish

Lemon slices for serving

1. Preheat the oven to 375°F.

2. Arrange the fish in a shallow casserole. Pour half of the melted butter over the fillets. Sprinkle with salt, pepper, and paprika.

3. Place the fish in the oven and bake, uncovered, basting occasionally, until the fish flakes with a fork, about 15 to 20 minutes. Garnish with parsley. Serve with lemon slices and the remaining melted butter for dipping.

CLAM CHOWDER CASSEROLE

All the comforting flavors of clam chowder are in this hearty casserole. To round out the meal, serve a roasted vegetable salad and hot cornmeal muffins.

SERVES 6

6 tablespoons butter, plus extra for the dish

2 cups chopped onions (about 1 large onion)

2 cups diced celery (2 stalks)

4 cups peeled and diced boiling potatoes (about 8 potatoes)

1½ teaspoons minced fresh thyme, or ½ teaspoon dried

1 teaspoon salt

½ teaspoon pepper

3 cups chopped fresh clams (littleneck, pismo, or whatever clams are available) or canned clams, including juices

½ cup milk or cream

1 tablespoon cornstarch

¼ cup fine dry breadcrumbs

1. Preheat the oven to 350°F. Butter a 9-by-13-inch baking dish.

2. In a nonstick skillet, melt 4 tablespoons of the butter over medium-high heat. Add the onions and celery and sauté for 10 minutes, or until the vegetables are soft, and transfer to a large bowl.

3. Meanwhile, put the potatoes in a pot with just enough water to cover and cook until they are tender, about 15 minutes. Drain the potatoes and add to the onions and celery. Add the thyme, salt, pepper, and clams. In a measuring cup, mix the milk and cornstarch, then stir into the potato mixture.

4. Transfer the potato mixture to the prepared casserole. (At this point the casserole can be covered and refrigerated for up to 1 day. Add 10 to 15 minutes to the baking time.) In a small bowl, mix the remaining 2 tablespoons of the butter and the breadcrumbs and sprinkle over the casserole. Bake, uncovered, for 30 to 35 minutes, until bubbly.

COD AND PLANTAIN CASSEROLE

This Peruvian recipe combines the rather bland flavors of cod and plantains with spicy chiles. Choose any red chile, from a relatively mild cherry pepper to a fiery habanero if you really like the hot stuff. Start the meal with pisco sours, which are made with pisco, a regional Peruvian brandy, and follow with a pumpkin soup. For dessert, serve a creamy cheesecake.

SERVES 4

2 tablespoons butter

2 ripe plantains, thinly sliced

2 green jalapeño peppers, seeded and finely chopped

1 red chile, seeded and finely chopped

1 can (14½ ounces) diced tomatoes with their juice

2 tablespoons chopped cilantro

1 pound cod fillets, skinned

1 tablespoon fresh lime or lemon juice

1 teaspoon salt

¼ teaspoon pepper

Brown rice for serving

1. Preheat the oven to 375°F. Coat a shallow 1½-quart casserole with cooking spray.

2. In a nonstick skillet, melt the butter. Add the plantain slices and cook over medium-high heat for 5 minutes, turning the slices once. Add the jalapeño and red chiles and stir-fry for 1 minute. Add the tomatoes with their juice along with the cilantro. Heat to simmering and transfer to the prepared casserole.

3. Sprinkle the fish with the lime or lemon juice, salt, and pepper and nestle the fillets in the tomato mixture in the casserole. Cover and bake for 20 minutes, or until the fish is just cooked through. Serve with brown rice.

CRAB AND HOMINY CASSEROLE

Hominy is dried white or yellow corn kernels, from which the hull and germ have been removed. It is sold canned, ready to eat or dried, in which case it must be reconstituted before using. Hominy is often served as a side dish or as part of a casserole. Here we're blending it with crab.

SERVES 6

6 tablespoons butter

1 large can (29 ounces) whole hominy, drained

¾ pound fresh crabmeat, or 2 packages (6 ounces each) frozen crabmeat, thawed and drained

1 cup sliced ripe olives

2 tablespoons diced red bell peppers

2 tablespoons diced canned green chiles

1 recipe Basic White Sauce (page 18)

Salt

Pepper

½ cup fine dry breadcrumbs

1. Preheat the oven to 350°F. Lightly coat a shallow 2½-quart casserole with cooking spray.

2. Melt 3 tablespoons of the butter in a heavy skillet and add the drained hominy. Cook over medium-high heat until golden. Add the crabmeat, olives, bell peppers, and green chiles. Mix in the white sauce. Season with salt and pepper to taste.

3. Melt the remaining 3 tablespoons of butter in a small pan and stir in the breadcrumbs. Sprinkle over the casserole. Bake for 20 minutes, or until lightly browned.

CRAB AND MUSHROOM CASSEROLE

Make two of these casseroles, freeze one, and you've got a tasty meal left over for a busy day. Add a crisp green salad and cut a crusty loaf of French bread into thick slices to sop up the juices.

SERVES 6

½ cup (1 stick) butter, divided, plus extra for the dish

1 pound mushrooms, sliced

⅓ cup all-purpose flour

1½ cups clam or chicken broth

1½ cups light cream or half-and-half

Salt

Pepper

1½ pounds fresh crabmeat, or 4 packages (6 ounces each) frozen crabmeat, thawed

1 cup fresh breadcrumbs (see Note)

1 cup shredded Swiss cheese

1. Preheat the oven to 350°F. Butter a shallow 1½-quart casserole.

2. In a large nonstick skillet, melt 2 tablespoons of the butter over medium-high heat and add the mushrooms. Sauté for 5 minutes, stirring, until the mushrooms are tender and the liquid has been absorbed. Transfer the mushrooms to the buttered casserole.

3. Melt 4 tablespoons of the remaining butter in the skillet over medium heat. Stir in the flour until blended. Remove from the heat and whisk in the broth and cream. Season with salt and pepper to taste. Return to the heat and cook over medium-high heat until thickened and smooth.

4. Spread the crabmeat over the mushrooms in the casserole and pour the sauce over all. Melt the remaining 2 tablespoons butter in a small saucepan and mix in the breadcrumbs. Sprinkle over the sauce and top with the cheese. (The dish can be assembled up to this point and frozen for up to 2 months.)

5. Bake the casserole until browned and bubbly, 30 to 35 minutes. (If frozen, do not defrost. Bake in a 325°F oven for 45 minutes to 1 hour.)

○ ○ ○ ○ ○

NOTE: To make fresh breadcrumbs, tear 1 or 2 slices of fresh bread into pieces and put in a food processor with the steel blade in place. Process with on/off pulses until the bread is broken down into crumbs.

CRABMEAT AND SHRIMP LASAGNA

Although the list of ingredients looks intimidating, this lasagna really comes together easily. Note that you don't need to cook the noodles. There are special noodles on the market, called "no-boil noodles," that are designed to go straight into a baking dish. But I've had good luck with regular dried lasagna noodles, too.

SERVES 12

4 tablespoons butter

¼ cup all-purpose flour

3 cups milk

1 cup fish or chicken broth or water

¾ cup grated Parmesan cheese

1 package (10 ounces) frozen chopped spinach, thawed and drained

1 cup part-skim ricotta cheese or low-fat cottage cheese

1 cup shredded part-skim mozzarella cheese, divided

⅛ teaspoon ground nutmeg

1 package (9 ounces) no-boil lasagna noodles (12 noodles)

1 package (12 ounces) frozen cooked shrimp (about 50 count), thawed

2 packages (6 ounces each) frozen crabmeat, thawed, drained, and flaked

1. Preheat the oven to 350°F.

2. In a large saucepan, melt the butter over medium heat. Add the flour, and stir until blended. Gradually whisk in the milk and broth, and bring to a boil, stirring constantly. Reduce the heat to low and simmer for 3 to 5 minutes, stirring constantly, until thickened. Remove from the heat, stir in ½ cup of the Parmesan cheese, and set aside.

3. In a medium bowl, combine the spinach, ricotta, ⅔ cup of the mozzarella cheese, and the nutmeg.

4. Spread out a quarter of the sauce in the bottom of a 9-by-13-inch baking dish. Cover with a third of the lasagna noodles, overlapping them if necessary.

Top with half of the shrimp, half of the crabmeat, half of the spinach mixture, and a third of the remaining sauce. Repeat the layers once, starting with half of the remaining noodles, using all of the remaining shrimp, crabmeat, and spinach mixture, and half of the remaining sauce. Top with the remaining noodles, sauce, and ⅓ cup mozzarella cheese. Coat a sheet of aluminum foil with cooking spray and cover the casserole.

5. Bake for 35 minutes, uncover, and bake for an additional 15 to 20 minutes, or until bubbly. Sprinkle with the remaining ¼ cup Parmesan cheese. Let stand for 10 minutes. Cut into 12 pieces and serve.

CREAMY POTATO AND GRAVLAX CASSEROLE

Gravlax is a Scandinavian specialty made with raw salmon, which is cured with a sugar and salt mixture. Typically, it is served thinly sliced as an open-faced sandwich. Gravlax is also a fine ingredient in creamy soups as well as casseroles such as this one.

SERVES 6

1 tablespoon butter, melted, plus extra for the dish

6 medium thin-skinned potatoes

2 large onions

½ cup chopped fresh dill, or 2 tablespoons dried

¼ pound gravlax, julienned

1 to 1½ cups heavy cream

2 tablespoons fine dry breadcrumbs

1. Preheat the oven to 425°F. Butter a shallow 2-quart casserole.

2. Peel and rinse the potatoes. Cut the potatoes into ¼-inch-thick slices and cut the slices into ¼-inch strips. Peel the onions and trim off the ends. Cut in half lengthwise. With the cut side down, cut each half lengthwise into ¼-inch strips.

3. Spread out the onions, dill, and gravlax in the prepared dish. Cover with the potato strips. Add just enough cream to cover the potatoes. Mix together the breadcrumbs and the 1 table-spoon melted butter, then sprinkle over the potato layer.

4. Bake for 45 to 50 minutes, until the potatoes are tender and the top of the casserole is browned.

EASY TILAPIA CASSEROLE

Tilapia is a very lean fish that is aqua cultured around the world. This white, rather thin fish cooks quickly. Here, we've placed it on top of potato gnocchi, another convenience food that you can find in shelf-stable packages. If you are not bothered by the MSG and other ingredients in cream of shrimp soup, go ahead and use it. I prefer heavy cream for a delicious alternative.

SERVES 4

2 tablespoons butter, melted, plus extra for the dish

1 pound frozen tilapia fillets, thawed

Salt

Pepper

1 package (1 pound) potato gnocchi

2 dashes Tabasco sauce

1⅓ cups heavy cream, or 1 can (10¾ ounces) cream of shrimp soup

¼ cup grated Parmesan cheese

¼ cup panko (see Note) or fine dry breadcrumbs

1. Preheat the oven to 350°F. Butter a shallow 2-quart casserole.

2. Rinse the tilapia and pat dry. Sprinkle with salt and pepper.

3. Spread the gnocchi in an even layer in the casserole. Add the Tabasco to the cream or soup and drizzle half over the gnocchi. Top with the fish fillets in one layer, overlapping if necessary. Spread the remaining cream over the fish. Mix the Parmesan, panko, and 2 tablespoons melted butter in a small dish and sprinkle over the fish evenly.

4. Bake, uncovered, for 30 to 35 minutes, until the casserole is bubbly and the fish flakes.

○ ○ ○ ○ ○

NOTE: Panko are Japanese breadcrumbs. They are coarser than regular breadcrumbs and create a crunchier crust. Panko can be purchased in Asian markets, or in the Asian sections of large supermarkets.

FINNISH SALMON CASSEROLE

Fish is a summertime food in Finland, and Finns have many ways to serve it. We have been served this casserole in Helsinki along with a lovely salad of fresh garden lettuce and sour rye buns.

SERVES 4

2 tablespoons butter, plus extra for the dish

1 pound salmon or rainbow trout fillet, skinned

3 medium potatoes (about 1 pound)

2 medium onions

1 cup heavy cream

½ cup milk

⅓ cup fine dry breadcrumbs

Salt

Pepper

1. Preheat the oven to 425°F. Butter a shallow 2-quart casserole.

2. Remove any bones from the fish and cut into 1-inch cubes. Peel the potatoes and cut into matchsticks. Peel the onions and trim off the ends. Cut the onions in half lengthwise. With the cut sides down, cut each half lengthwise into matchsticks.

3. Put the fish, potatoes, and onions in the casserole and pour the cream and milk over all. Sprinkle with the breadcrumbs, dot with the 2 tablespoons butter, and sprinkle with salt and pepper to taste.

4. Bake for 45 minutes to 1 hour, until the potatoes are tender and the breadcrumbs are golden.

FLORENTINE FISH CASSEROLE

"Florentine" designates a dish made in the style of Florence. Usually it consists of fish or eggs presented on a bed of spinach and topped with a sauce.

SERVES 8

2 tablespoons butter, plus extra for the dish

3 packages (10 ounces each) frozen chopped spinach

3 cups sour cream

4½ tablespoons all-purpose flour

¾ cup chopped green onions (white and light green parts)

Juice of 1½ lemons

3 teaspoons salt

3 pounds thin fillets of sole or flounder

Paprika for sprinkling

1. Preheat the oven to 375°F. Butter a shallow 2-quart casserole.

2. Cook the spinach according to package directions. Drain, let cool a little, and squeeze dry.

3. Blend the sour cream with the flour, green onions, lemon juice, and salt. Combine half of this mixture with the spinach and spread over the bottom of the casserole.

4. Arrange the fish fillets on top of the spinach and dot with the 2 tablespoons butter. Spread the remaining sour cream mixture evenly over the fillets, leaving a border to show the spinach. Dust lightly with paprika. (The casserole can be covered and refrigerated at this point for up to 1 day. Add 10 minutes to the baking time.)

5. Bake for 25 minutes, or until the fish flakes when probed with a fork.

FLORIDA SEAFOOD CASSEROLE

I received this recipe from a cousin, Marilyn Magee, who admitted that she substitutes a carton of cream of mushroom soup for the sauce. I tried it both ways and prefer the homemade sauce below.

SERVES 6

4 tablespoons butter

⅓ cup minced onion

¼ cup all-purpose flour

1 cup milk, heated

1 cup light cream, heated

½ teaspoon salt

½ teaspoon pepper

1 tablespoon chopped pimientos

1 can (8 ounces) sliced water chestnuts, drained

2 tablespoons fresh lemon juice

1 tablespoon minced fresh parsley

1 package (6 ounces) frozen crabmeat, thawed, drained, and flaked

1 package (12 ounces) frozen small cooked shrimp, thawed

3 cups cooked basmati rice

1 cup shredded sharp Cheddar cheese, divided

1. Preheat the oven to 350°F. Coat a 2½-quart casserole with cooking spray.

2. In a heavy medium saucepan, melt the butter and sauté the onion over medium heat until tender, about 5 minutes. Add the flour and stir until blended. Gradually whisk in the milk and cream, reduce the heat to low, and cook, stirring, until thickened and smooth. Remove from the heat. Stir in the salt, pepper, pimientos, water chestnuts, lemon juice, parsley, crabmeat, shrimp, rice, and half of the cheese. Transfer the mixture to the prepared casserole. (At this point the casserole can be covered and refrigerated overnight. Add 10 minutes to the baking time.)

3. Bake for 25 minutes, or until heated through. Sprinkle with remaining cheese just before serving.

FLOUNDER FILLET CASSEROLE

If you can get fresh flounder, it is wonderful! I am often forced to buy it frozen. Some of the better known species of flounder are dab, English sole, and plaice. In the United States, if you see something labeled "fresh fillet of sole," you know it is probably flounder, because sole is only caught in Europe. Some sole is apparently shipped here frozen.

SERVES 4

2 pounds boneless flounder fillets

1 tablespoon fresh lemon juice

2 tablespoons butter, melted

1 cup heavy cream or undiluted evaporated skim milk

2 tablespoons dry sherry

½ cup shredded Gruyère or Swiss cheese

2 tablespoons chopped fresh parsley for garnish

Paprika for garnish

1. Preheat the oven to 400°F.

2. Arrange the fish fillets in a shallow 9-by-13-inch baking dish and sprinkle with the lemon juice. Brush with the melted butter.

3. Bake for 15 minutes and lower the oven temperature to 300°F.

4. In a small bowl, mix the cream and sherry, and pour over the fish. Sprinkle with the cheese and continue baking for another 15 minutes. Garnish with the parsley and paprika.

JANSSON'S TEMPTATION (CREAMY POTATO AND ANCHOVY CASSEROLE)

You will always find Jansson's Temptation on a smorgasbord in Sweden, and it is often served as a luncheon dish or midnight snack. Its popularity has spread to Finland and Norway as well. To get the right flavor in this dish, you must use Swedish anchovies, which are cured in a slightly sweet brine and are therefore not as salty as Spanish anchovies. You can find them in Scandinavian specialty food stores and even in some IKEA stores in jars and flat tins. Buy the fillets rather than the whole little fish, or you'll have to clean and fillet them yourself. If you cannot find Swedish anchovies, substitute a package of lightly smoked salmon or lox, but of course, the flavor will not be the same.

There are many theories about the identity of the Jansson who inspired the dish. Some say he was Erik Jansson, an eighteenth-century religious zealot, while others guess it was Pelle Janzon, an early-twentieth-century Swedish opera singer. In any case, this is a popular and very delicious Swedish casserole.

SERVES 6

1 tablespoon butter, melted, plus extra for the dish

6 medium thin-skinned potatoes

2 large onions

1 tin (4½ ounces) Swedish anchovies (14 to 16 fillets)

1 to 1½ cups heavy cream

2 tablespoons fine dry breadcrumbs

1. Preheat the oven to 425°F. Butter a shallow 2-quart casserole.

2. Peel and rinse the potatoes and cut into matchsticks ¼ inch or less. Peel the onions and trim off the ends. Cut the onions in half lengthwise. With the cut side down, cut each half lengthwise into ¼-inch matchsticks.

3. Spread out the onions and anchovies in the prepared dish. Cover with the potatoes. Add just enough cream to cover the potatoes. Mix together the breadcrumbs and the 1 table-spoon melted butter in a small dish, then sprinkle over the potato layer.

4. Bake for 45 to 50 minutes, until the potatoes are tender and the top of the casserole is browned.

LOBSTER MAC AND FOUR CHEESES

When I first made this several years ago, my sister, Nancy, asked for the recipe. It has since become one of her family's favorites. Nancy usually freezes half for days when there isn't time to cook. Although it contains only 1 pound of lobster meat, the lobster flavor permeates the whole dish, which serves at least 6 people.

SERVES 6 TO 8

1 pound fresh lobster meat or frozen lobster meat, thawed

½ pound elbow macaroni

2 cups shredded sharp Cheddar cheese

1½ cups grated Parmesan cheese, divided

1 cup shredded Gruyère cheese

½ package (4 ounces) cream cheese

2 cups heavy cream or milk

1 tablespoon butter

2 cloves garlic, minced

2 shallots, minced

Salt

Pepper

½ cup panko (see Note, facing page) or fine dry breadcrumbs

1. Preheat the oven to 350°F. Lightly coat a shallow 3-quart casserole with cooking spray. Chop the lobster meat and set aside.

2. Cook the macaroni according to package directions. Drain and set aside, reserving about 1 cup of the cooking water.

3. In a medium skillet, bring about 2 inches of water to a boil. Combine the Cheddar cheese, 1 cup of the Parmesan cheese, the Gruyère, and cream cheese in a metal bowl. Place the bowl over the water, but not touching it, and melt the cheeses, stirring. Gradually stir in the cream. Remove from the heat and keep warm.

4. Pour out the boiling water and melt the butter in the skillet. Over medium-high heat, cook the garlic and shallots for 2 minutes; add the lobster meat and cook until opaque. Remove from the heat.

5. Pour the reserved cooking water over the macaroni to loosen it, and drain. Add the macaroni to the lobster mixture. Add the cheese sauce, season with salt and pepper to taste, and mix well. Turn into the casserole. Sprinkle with the remaining ½ cup Parmesan cheese and the breadcrumbs. (At this point the casserole can be covered and refrigerated for up to 1 day or wrapped well and frozen for up to 2 months. Thaw in the refrigerator before baking. Add 10 to 15 minutes to the baking time.)

6. Bake, uncovered, for about 10 minutes, or until the breadcrumbs are golden brown.

○ ○ ○ ○ ○

NOTE: Panko are Japanese breadcrumbs. They are coarser than conventional breadcrumbs and yield a crunchier crust. Panko can be purchased in Asian markets, or in the Asian sections of large supermarkets.

NORWEGIAN FISH PUDDING

In Norway, a cook's reputation is determined by the smoothness of the fish pudding she or he prepares. This makes a tasty luncheon or supper dish, especially when served with a cucumber salad. If you prefer, serve this with hollandaise sauce (see page 121) or melted butter rather than the dill sauce.

SERVES 6

6 tablespoons butter, plus extra for the dish

6 tablespoons all-purpose flour

2 cups milk, heated

2 teaspoons salt

Pepper

1½ pounds boneless fish, such as halibut, snapper, or flounder, cut into 2-inch cubes

6 large eggs, separated

FOR THE DILL SAUCE (OPTIONAL):

1 cup sour cream

1 cup mayonnaise

1 tablespoon fresh dill, or 1 teaspoon dried

1 teaspoon fresh lemon juice

1. Preheat the oven to 350°F. Butter a 1½-quart casserole or soufflé dish. Have at hand a larger pan in which the dish can be set. Heat a few cups of water to boiling.

2. In a medium saucepan, melt the 6 tablespoons butter over medium heat and add the flour; stir until blended, and gradually whisk in the milk. Reduce the heat to low and simmer, stirring, until thickened. Add the salt and pepper to taste and remove from the heat.

3. Put half the sauce and the fish into a food processor with the steel blade in place and process until the mixture is smooth. Transfer to a large bowl and add the remaining sauce from the saucepan.

4. Beat the egg yolks in a medium bowl with an electric mixer until thick and add to the fish mixture. In another bowl, beat the egg whites with an electric mixer until stiff and fold into the fish mixture.

5. Transfer the mixture to the prepared casserole. Set into the larger pan and add 1 inch of boiling water. Bake for 1 hour, or until set and lightly browned.

6. *Meanwhile, make the dill sauce, if desired:* Stir all the ingredients together in a bowl.

7. Serve the casserole with the dill sauce or with hollandaise sauce (see page 121) or melted butter.

NOT MY MOTHER-IN-LAW'S TUNA HOT DISH

This is a fresh, updated version of tuna-noodle casserole,
a 1950s classic. It sparkles with the flavor of herbs, mushrooms,
fresh tuna, and a dash of sherry.

SERVES 6

5 tablespoons butter, divided

1 pound tuna steaks, sliced on the diagonal

1 sweet onion, sliced

1 pound mushrooms, such as shiitake, button, or portobello, sliced (about 4 cups)

2 tablespoons chopped fresh rosemary, or 1 tablespoon dried, crushed

1 tablespoon chopped fresh thyme, or 1½ teaspoons dried

2 teaspoons Worcestershire sauce

¼ cup dry sherry

¼ cup all-purpose flour

2 cups clam juice or chicken broth

1 cup milk

2 teaspoons fresh lemon juice

3 cups egg noodles, cooked in boiling salted water

1½ cups fresh breadcrumbs (see Note)

1 cup grated Parmesan cheese

1. Preheat the oven to 375°F. Coat a shallow 2-quart casserole with cooking spray.

2. In a large nonstick skillet, melt 1 tablespoon of the butter over medium heat. Add the tuna steaks and sauté quickly for about 2 minutes on each side. Remove the tuna from the pan and set aside. Put the onion into the pan and sauté for 4 to 5 minutes, until the onion is wilted. Add the mushrooms and herbs and cook for 5 minutes longer. Add the Worcestershire sauce and sherry. Cook for 2 minutes longer and set aside.

3. Melt 3 tablespoons of the butter in a heavy saucepan over medium heat and add the flour; stir until blended. Whisk in the clam juice, milk, and lemon juice and cook, stirring, until thickened. Stir the sauce into the mushroom mixture and add the tuna. Stir in the noodles and transfer the mixture to the casserole dish.

4. Melt the remaining 1 tablespoon butter in a small skillet and mix in the breadcrumbs. Sprinkle over the noodle mixture and top with the cheese. Bake for 25 minutes, or until the casserole is bubbly and the topping is browned.

○ ○ ○ ○ ○

NOTE: To make fresh breadcrumbs, tear 1 or 2 slices of fresh bread into pieces and put in a food processor with the steel blade in place. Process with on/off pulses until the bread is broken down into crumbs.

SALMON AND GREEN OLIVE CASSEROLE

Green olives perk up the taste of canned salmon, making this a very flavorful casserole you can even serve to company.

SERVES 6

6 tablespoons butter, plus extra for the dish

2 tablespoons chopped green onions (white and green parts)

¼ cup all-purpose flour

Pepper

1 can (14¾ ounces) red or pink salmon

Light cream or half-and-half, as needed

½ cup stuffed green olives, sliced

2 teaspoons chopped fresh dill, or 1 teaspoon dried

Salt (optional)

3 tablespoons sliced almonds

3 tablespoons fine dry breadcrumbs

1. Preheat the oven to 400°F. Butter a shallow 1½-quart casserole.

2. Melt 4 tablespoons of the butter in a saucepan and sauté the green onions over medium heat until wilted, about 4 to 5 minutes. Stir in the flour and pepper to taste until evenly blended.

3. Drain the juices from the salmon into a 2-cup measure and add enough cream to measure 2 cups. Whisk the liquid into the green onion mixture. Cook over medium heat, stirring, until thickened and smooth and remove from the heat. Add the olives and dill. Taste and add salt if desired.

4. Remove the skin and bones from the salmon and break the salmon into large chunks. Put in the bottom of the prepared casserole. Pour the sauce over the salmon.

5. Melt the remaining 2 tablespoons butter in a small skillet. Stir in the almonds and breadcrumbs and sprinkle on top of the casserole.

6. Bake for 15 minutes, or until heated through and lightly browned.

SALMON AND POTATO CASSEROLE

Canned salmon is not only a good source of calcium, but also a flavorful convenience food. Goat cheese gives this casserole a contemporary spin. Serve it with mango salsa and a romaine salad.

SERVES 6

1 can (14 ¾ ounces) pink or red salmon, drained, juices reserved

2 ½ pounds medium russet potatoes (about 4), peeled and cut into 1-inch slices

1 cup milk

¼ pound soft fresh goat cheese

3 tablespoons grated Parmesan cheese, divided

Salt

Pepper

2 large eggs

½ cup chopped green onion (white and green parts)

1. Preheat the oven to 400°F. Coat a 2-quart casserole with cooking spray.

2. Separate the salmon into chunks, leaving the bones intact (they are high in calcium, soft, and will disappear in the casserole). Remove and discard the skin.

3. Cook the potatoes in a large pot of boiling salted water until tender, about 20 minutes, and drain.

4. Transfer the potatoes to a large bowl and add the milk, salmon juices, goat cheese, and 2 tablespoons of the Parmesan cheese. With a hand mixer, beat until almost smooth. Taste and add salt and pepper. Beat in the eggs. Stir in the salmon and green onions. Transfer the mixture to the dish and sprinkle with the remaining 1 tablespoon Parmesan cheese. (At this point the casserole can be covered and refrigerated for up to 1 day. Add 10 minutes to the oven time.)

5. Bake until golden and heated through, about 45 minutes.

SUMMER SALMON CASSEROLE

Vary the vegetables for this casserole, depending on what is in season, and adjust their cooking times as needed. For instance, snap peas, whole baby garden carrots, and small chunks of zucchini or yellow squash all are lovely when fresh and in season.

SERVES 4

1½ pounds new potatoes, scrubbed and halved

½ pound green beans, trimmed

½ pound yellow beans, trimmed

½ pound asparagus, trimmed

½ pound cherry tomatoes

¼ cup extra-virgin olive oil

Zest and juice of 1 lemon

Salt

Pepper

½ cup chopped fresh basil

4 salmon fillets (½ pound each)

1. Preheat the oven to 500°F.

2. Bring a large pan of salted water to a boil. Add the new potatoes and cook for 10 to 12 minutes, until they can be pierced with a skewer, but are not quite done. Add the green and yellow beans and cook for 2 minutes. Add the asparagus and cook for another 2 minutes.

3. Drain the vegetables and put in a shallow 3-quart casserole. Sprinkle with the cherry tomatoes. Drizzle with a little bit of the olive oil, lemon zest, and lemon juice. Sprinkle with salt and pepper and half of the chopped basil.

4. Pat the salmon fillets dry and slash the skin sides in 3 places. Drizzle with more of the olive oil, lemon zest, and lemon juice, and sprinkle lightly with salt and pepper. Place the salmon, skin side down, on top of the vegetables. Drizzle with the remaining olive oil, lemon zest, and lemon juice, and sprinkle with the remaining fresh basil.

5. Place the casserole in the oven and bake for 10 to 15 minutes, until the salmon flakes when probed with a fork. Serve hot.

TUNA AND WILD RICE CASSEROLE

Large chunks of tuna distinguish this casserole. If you cannot find fresh tuna steaks (and that's not unusual in many parts of the country), use canned tuna and add it to the mixture along with the corn and peas.

— SERVES 6 —

3 tablespoons butter, plus extra for the dish

¾ cup wild rice

2½ cups water

1 cup finely chopped onion

1 cup sliced mushrooms

1 pound fresh tuna steaks, sliced, or 2 cans (6 ounces each) water-packed tuna

5 tablespoons all-purpose flour

1 teaspoon salt

3 cups milk, heated

1 cup frozen corn kernels, thawed

1 cup frozen peas, thawed

2½ cups shredded mild or medium-sharp Cheddar cheese

¼ cup seasoned fine dry breadcrumbs

¼ cup grated Parmesan cheese

1. Preheat the oven to 350°F. Butter a shallow 2½-quart casserole.

2. In a medium saucepan, combine the wild rice and water. Heat to boiling, cover, lower the heat, and simmer for about 30 minutes, until the rice is cooked and the water has been absorbed.

3. In a medium skillet, melt the 3 tablespoons butter. Add the onion and mushrooms and sauté, stirring, for about 3 minutes over medium-high heat. If using tuna steaks, add them and continue to sauté until the tuna is cooked, about 3 minutes. If using water-packed tuna, drain and separate into large chunks. Add to the onion and

mushrooms and cook until just heated through. Add the flour and salt, stirring constantly, and gradually add the hot milk. Lower the heat and cook, stirring, until thickened, about 10 minutes. Add the corn, peas, and half the Cheddar cheese. Blend in the cooked wild rice.

4. Transfer the mixture to the casserole dish. Sprinkle with the remaining Cheddar cheese. Mix the breadcrumbs and Parmesan together and sprinkle over the casserole. (At this point you can cover the casserole and refrigerate for up to 1 day. Add 10 minutes to the baking time.)

5. Bake for 20 to 30 minutes, or until the cheese has melted.

CRAB OR TUNA MELT CASSEROLE

One of our favorite sandwiches is transformed into a casserole that is great for lunch or a light supper and special enough for company.

SERVES 8

8 slices whole-wheat bread, toasted and crusts removed

½ cup mayonnaise

¼ cup minced red onion

¼ cup chopped fresh parsley

½ Granny Smith apple, peeled, cored, and finely diced

A few drops Tabasco sauce, or more to taste

Salt

Pepper

1 pound lump crabmeat, or 3 cans (6 ounces each) water-packed tuna, drained

1½ cups shredded Gruyère cheese

1. Preheat the oven to 400°F. Butter a shallow 9-by-13-inch baking dish.

2. Line the bottom of the baking dish with the whole-wheat toast.

3. In a small bowl, mix the mayonnaise, onion, parsley, and apple together. Taste and add Tabasco sauce, salt, and pepper to taste. Blend in the crabmeat or tuna and spread over the bread. Top with the cheese.

4. Bake for 15 to 20 minutes, or until heated through and cheese is melted. Cut into squares to serve.

TUNA NOODLE CASSEROLE WITH MUSHROOMS AND FRESH HERBS

Instead of using "cream of" soup, make your own white sauce. It really doesn't take that long to prepare especially if you have the necessary ingredients on hand. I usually have fresh mushrooms, onions, and celery in the refrigerator. If you don't have shiitake mushrooms, just double the amount of button mushrooms in the recipe.

SERVES 4

1 recipe Basic White Sauce (page 18), or 1 can (10½ ounces) cream of mushroom soup

2 tablespoons butter

1 cup sliced stemmed fresh shiitake mushrooms

1 cup sliced button mushrooms

½ cup chopped green onions (white and green parts)

¼ cup chopped celery

1 tablespoon chopped fresh rosemary, or 1 teaspoon dried

1 tablespoon chopped fresh thyme, or 1 teaspoon dried

1 package (8 ounces) egg noodles

2 cans (6 ounces each) water-packed tuna, drained well

Salt

Pepper

½ cup fine dry breadcrumbs or panko (see Note)

1. Preheat the oven to 350°F. Coat an 8-inch square baking pan with cooking spray.

2. Prepare the white sauce if using. Put the sauce or mushroom soup in a large bowl.

3. In a skillet, melt the 1 tablespoon butter over medium-high heat. Add the mushrooms, green onions, and celery. Sauté until the mushrooms are tender, about 5 minutes. Add the rosemary and thyme. Stir the mushroom mixture into the sauce or soup.

4. Cook the noodles in a large pot of boiling salted water until tender but still firm to the bite. Drain well and add to the sauce. Using a fork, flake the tuna into bite-size pieces. Add to the noodles and sauce and toss to coat. Season with salt and pepper and transfer the mixture to the prepared dish. (At this point you can cover and refrigerate the casserole for up to 1 day. Add 10 minutes to the baking time.)

5. Melt the remaining 1 tablespoon butter in a medium skillet and add the breadcrumbs. Stir until golden brown, about 10 minutes. Sprinkle the breadcrumbs over the casserole. Bake until it bubbles around the edges, about 30 minutes. Serve hot.

○ ○ ○ ○ ○

NOTE: Panko are Japanese breadcrumbs. They are coarser than conventional breadcrumbs and create a crunchy crust. Panko can be purchased in Asian markets, or in the Asian sections of large supermarkets.

TUNA, PESTO, AND VEGGIE CASSEROLE

A mixture of sour cream, milk, and pesto becomes a tasty sauce that moistens this casserole. To add some sparkle to your menu, serve a salad of baby spinach, topped with sliced strawberries and dressed with equal parts of cider vinegar and honey.

SERVES 6

1 package (8 ounces) medium egg noodles

½ cup low-fat sour cream

½ cup low-fat or skim milk

⅓ cup basil pesto

1 can (6 ounces) water-packed tuna, drained and flaked

1 package (10 ounces) frozen peas and carrots, thawed

1 cup roasted red bell peppers, diced (see page 35)

¼ cup pitted black olives, halved

2 tablespoons grated Parmesan cheese

1. Preheat the oven to 350°F.

2. Cook the noodles according to package directions and drain. Transfer to a 3-quart casserole coated with cooking spray.

3. Mix the sour cream, milk, and pesto in a small dish. Stir into the noodles and add the tuna, peas, bell peppers, and olives; mix lightly. Top with the Parmesan cheese. Coat a sheet of aluminum foil with cooking spray and cover the dish loosely.

4. Bake for 25 to 30 minutes, or until thoroughly heated and bubbly around the edges.

WALLEYE AND GREEN CHILE CASSEROLE

Walleye is a popular sport fish with a rather mild flavor. I had my doubts when I paired it with green chiles, but the result was a very fine casserole!

SERVES 4

2 tablespoons butter

1 pound mushrooms, sliced

½ cup chopped onion

1 can (4 ounces) diced green chiles

1 to 1¼ pounds walleye fillets

2 tablespoons all-purpose flour

1 cup clam broth or vegetable broth

½ cup sour cream

1 tablespoon fresh lime juice

Salt

Pepper

Chopped fresh cilantro or parsley for garnish (optional)

1. Preheat the oven to 400°F. Butter a shallow 1½-quart casserole with 1 tablespoon of the butter.

2. Melt the remaining 1 table-spoon butter in a large skillet over high heat. Add the mushrooms, onion, and green chiles and cook for 10 to 12 minutes, stirring often, until the mushrooms are tender and dry. Transfer to the buttered casserole dish and spread out evenly. Top with the walleye fillets, spreading them evenly over the mushroom layer.

3. Add the flour to the pan in which the mushrooms were cooked and place over medium heat. Whisk in the broth and cook, whisking constantly, until thickened. Whisk in the sour cream and lime juice and season with salt and pepper.

4. Spoon the sauce over the fish, coating the fillets evenly. (The dish may be covered and refrigerated at this point for up to 1 day. Add 10 minutes to the oven time.)

5. Bake for 12 to 15 minutes, or just until the fish flakes when probed with a fork. Sprinkle with the chopped cilantro or parsley, if desired, and serve.

Chapter 12
SIDE-DISH CASSEROLES

Vegetables and starches have been historically short-changed in our country. This is especially true when it comes to side-dish casseroles, which are often overcooked and poorly seasoned. But with the wide variety of vegetables available to us today, there's lots to choose from. This includes convenient, partially prepared fresh produce, such as packaged sliced mushrooms and bags of mixed cut-up vegetables. Just browse the colorful produce departments in supermarkets, green grocers, and farmer's markets.

Casseroles provide a way for the home cook to do pre-preparation—that is, assemble a whole vegetable dish ahead of time, cover it, and refrigerate it until just before the meal. Here we have a variety, from cut-up vegetables baked in casseroles to custards, gratins, and even soufflés. These recipes are mainly side dishes, though. For vegetarian main dishes, see the next chapter.

CONTINUED ON NEXT PAGE...

ACORN SQUASH CASSEROLE

I think winter squash tastes best in the fall and winter. Think of this casserole when planning holiday menus. The pecans give it a nice crunch.

SERVES 6 TO 8

4 tablespoons butter, plus extra for the dish

2 acorn or 1 butternut squash (4 to 4½ pounds total)

2 tablespoons finely chopped green onion (white and green parts)

1 teaspoon dried rosemary, crushed

½ teaspoon salt

¼ cup coarsely chopped pecans

1. Preheat the oven to 400°F. Butter a shallow 1½-quart casserole.

2. Cut the squash (or squashes) in half and remove the seeds. Place, cut side down, in the casserole and pour in boiling water to a depth of ¼ inch.

3. Bake for 30 to 35 minutes, or until tender. Scoop out the squash and put in a large bowl. Drain any liquid remaining in the casserole dish. Beat until smooth and then beat in the 4 tablespoons butter, green onion, rosemary, and salt. Transfer to the casserole and sprinkle with the chopped pecans. (At this point you can cover and refrigerate for up to 1 day. Add 5 to 10 minutes to the baking time.)

4. Bake, uncovered, for 15 to 20 minutes, or until thoroughly heated.

ALMOND, CARROT, AND CAULIFLOWER CASSEROLE

Sliced almonds add a crunchy top to this casserole, and also a bit of class. Serve this with meat loaf or a casserole made with chicken breast. They can bake at the same time.

SERVES 8

1 small head cauliflower, broken into florets

3 cups sliced carrots

5 tablespoons butter, divided

¼ cup all-purpose flour

½ teaspoon salt

1½ cups milk, heated

1 cup shredded sharp Cheddar cheese

¾ cup fresh breadcrumbs (see Note)

½ cup sliced almonds

1. Preheat the oven to 350°F. Coat a shallow 2½-quart casserole with cooking spray.

2. Cook the cauliflower and carrots separately in boiling salted water to cover until just tender. Drain and transfer to the casserole.

3. In a small saucepan, melt 2 tablespoons of the butter over medium heat. Whisk in the flour and stir until blended. Gradually whisk in the salt and milk and continue whisking until thickened. Bring to a boil, lower the heat and simmer, stirring constantly, until thickened. Stir in the cheese, whisking until blended, and pour over the vegetables.

4. Melt the remaining 3 tablespoons butter in a small skillet and combine with the breadcrumbs. Sprinkle over the top of the casserole. Sprinkle the almonds evenly over the crumbs. Bake, uncovered, for 25 minutes until golden.

○ ○ ○ ○ ○

NOTE: To make fresh breadcrumbs, tear 1 or 2 slices of fresh bread into pieces and put in a food processor with the steel blade in place. Process with on/off pulses until the bread is broken down into crumbs.

APPLE AND CARROT CASSEROLE

Think of this as an autumn casserole, when apples are abundant in the orchards and carrots are sweet from the garden. You might even add this casserole to your Thanksgiving menu.

SERVES 6

1 tablespoon butter, cut up, plus extra for the dish

6 large carrots

5 large Rome or York apples

5 tablespoons sugar

5 tablespoons all-purpose flour

½ teaspoon ground nutmeg

½ cup orange juice

1. Preheat the oven to 350°F. Butter a shallow 2-quart casserole.

2. Cut the carrots into thin slices, cook in boiling salted water to cover for 5 minutes, and drain. Slice the apples and put in a clean saucepan. Cover with water, bring to a simmer, and continue simmering for 5 minutes. Drain the apples.

3. Place the carrots in the casserole in a single layer and top with the apples. Mix the sugar, flour, and nutmeg in a small dish and sprinkle over the top. Dot with the 1 tablespoon butter and pour the orange juice over all. (At this point you can cover and refrigerate the casserole for up to 1 day. Add 10 minutes to the baking time.) Bake, uncovered, for 30 to 40 minutes.

APPLE, YAM, AND PECAN CASSEROLE

This casserole is perfect with roasts and poultry dishes all winter long—not just for Thanksgiving. It is important to rinse the raw yams or sweet potatoes in cold water to prevent them from darkening. This doesn't take long, just a minute or two.

SERVES 6

2 large yams or sweet potatoes

3 Granny Smith apples, peeled, cored, and sliced

3 tablespoons butter, melted

Dash of ground nutmeg

½ cup chopped pecans

1. Preheat the oven to 325°F. Coat a 2-quart casserole with cooking spray.

2. Peel and slice the yams or sweet potatoes and place them in a bowl of cold water; let sit for a few minutes, then drain.

3. Layer the drained potatoes in the bottom of the casserole and cover with the apples.

Drizzle with the melted butter and sprinkle with the nutmeg and pecans.

4. Cover and bake for 30 minutes, or until the potatoes and apples are tender.

ARTICHOKE AND TOMATO CASSEROLE

Assemble this casserole ahead of time, and cover and refrigerate it. Then pop it in the oven while you heat up the grill. It makes a tasty side dish for grilled fish.

SERVES 8

2 cups fresh breadcrumbs (see Note)

½ cup olive oil

¾ cup grated Parmesan or Romano cheese

2 cloves garlic, minced

1 teaspoon salt

½ teaspoon pepper

3 packages (9 ounce each) frozen artichoke hearts, thawed and cooked

8 Roma (plum) tomatoes, sliced

1. Preheat the oven to 350°F. Coat a shallow 2-quart casserole with cooking spray.

2. In a small bowl, combine the breadcrumbs, oil, cheese, garlic, salt, and pepper.

3. Layer the artichokes on the bottom of the casserole dish, cover with the tomatoes, and top with the crumb mixture. (At this point you can cover and refrigerate the casserole for up to 1 day. Add 10 minutes to the baking time.)

4. Cover and bake for 30 minutes, remove the cover, and continue baking for 10 to 15 minutes longer, or until bubbly and the crumbs are lightly browned.

○ ○ ○ ○ ○

NOTE: To make fresh breadcrumbs, tear 1 or 2 slices of fresh bread into pieces and put in a food processor with the steel blade in place. Process with on/off pulses until the bread is broken down into crumbs.

ROASTED BACON AND POTATO CASSEROLE

Here is a really simple and delicious recipe to add to your repertoire. The potatoes are cut into cubes and topped with bacon; then the casserole is roasted to golden goodness.

SERVES 4

1½ pounds boiling potatoes (3 or 4 medium)

2 teaspoons olive oil

1 teaspoon finely chopped fresh rosemary

½ teaspoon salt

¼ teaspoon pepper

5 slices bacon, cut into 1-inch pieces

1. Preheat the oven to 450°F. Coat a shallow 3-quart casserole with cooking spray.

2. Peel the potatoes and cut into ¾-inch cubes. In a large bowl, toss the potatoes with the olive oil, rosemary, salt, and pepper.

3. Spread out the potatoes in the casserole dish in an even layer and scatter the bacon pieces on top.

4. Bake for 35 minutes, or until the bacon is crisp and the potatoes are cooked through and golden around the edges.

BAKED BEANS WITH APPLES AND ONIONS

Serve this with grilled burgers or hot dogs, of course. It is also good with Oven-Barbecued Country-Style Ribs (page 267). Add a loaf of Caraway and Cheddar Casserole Bread (page 75) to the menu, too!

○———————————— SERVES 8 ————————————○

1 tablespoon butter or vegetable oil

1 cup diced onions

1 can (28 ounces) Boston-style baked beans

1 cup diced tart cooking apples, such as Granny Smith

1 tablespoon prepared mustard

¼ cup light or dark brown sugar

1 teaspoon salt

5 strips bacon, cut into ½-inch pieces

1. Preheat the oven to 350°F. Coat a deep 2-quart casserole with cooking spray.

2. In a medium skillet, heat the butter or oil. Add the onions and sauté until softened, about 4 minutes.

3. Transfer the onions to a large bowl, and add the beans, apples, mustard, brown sugar, and salt. Transfer to the casserole and lay the raw strips of bacon on top.

4. Cover and bake for 45 minutes, or until thick and bubbly. Uncover and bake for 5 minutes longer.

BAKED EGGPLANT WITH FETA

Eggplant, tomatoes, and feta cheese are a classic Mediterranean combination. Serve this with shish kebabs or another grilled meat.

SERVES 6

1 eggplant (about 1 pound)

1 tablespoon salt

Olive oil for frying, plus extra for the dish

1 sweet onion, thinly sliced and separated into rings

2 cloves garlic, minced

2 cups diced fresh tomatoes, or 1 can (14½ ounces) diced tomatoes with their juice

Salt

Pepper

1 pound crumbled feta cheese

½ cup grated Parmesan cheese

½ cup fine dry breadcrumbs

1. Peel the eggplant, slice crosswise, and sprinkle with salt. Let sit for 30 minutes, rinse well, and pat dry.

2. Preheat the oven to 400°F. Coat a shallow 2- or 3-quart casserole with oil.

3. Heat ¼ inch of olive oil in a heavy nonstick skillet. (Be careful not to add too much oil, as the eggplant wants to absorb it all.) Sauté the eggplant slices, turning once, until lightly browned.

4. Brown the onion and garlic in the remaining oil. Add the tomatoes and simmer for 10 minutes. Season with salt and pepper.

5. Spread a third of the sauce in the bottom of the casserole. Top with half the eggplant, then half the feta cheese. Cover with half of the remaining sauce, the remaining eggplant, and the remaining feta cheese. Pour the remaining sauce on top.

6. Mix the Parmesan and breadcrumbs in a small dish and sprinkle over the casserole. Bake for 20 minutes, uncovered, until bubbly and lightly brown on top. Let rest for 15 minutes before serving.

BAKED GREEN TOMATOES

At the end of the summer, when the first frost hits our garden, we sometimes have green tomatoes on the vine. And when we have green tomatoes, we have a lot of them! This is truly a seasonal dish.

SERVES 6 TO 8

3 tablespoons butter, melted

8 medium green tomatoes

1 cup fine fresh breadcrumbs (see Note), toasted

1 teaspoon salt

1/8 teaspoon pepper

1/3 cup grated Parmesan cheese

1. Preheat the oven to 350°F. Spread 1 tablespoon of the butter in a shallow 2-quart casserole.

2. Core the tomatoes and cut into ½-inch-thick slices. Arrange half the tomato slices in a single layer in the casserole dish. Sprinkle with half the breadcrumbs, half the salt and pepper, and 1 of the remaining tablespoons butter. Repeat, using the remaining tomatoes, breadcrumbs, salt and pepper, and butter.

3. Sprinkle the cheese on top of the casserole. Bake for 35 to 40 minutes, until the tomatoes are done.

○ ○ ○ ○ ○

NOTE: To make fresh breadcrumbs, tear 1 or 2 slices of fresh bread into pieces and put in a food processor with the steel blade in place. Process with on/off pulses until the bread is broken down into crumbs.

CHEESY BAKED SPINACH

It's good news that fresh baby spinach is so widely available today. The not-so-good news for cookbook authors is that it comes in so many different package sizes, ranging from 5-ounce to 1-pound bags, which makes it difficult to standardize a recipe. Here we use two 9-ounce bags. The fresh spinach leaves are layered with beaten eggs and cheese, and then baked. If you like, assemble this casserole ahead of time and refrigerate it up to 1 day before baking.

SERVES 6

4 tablespoons butter, melted

2 packages (9 ounces each) fresh baby spinach leaves

¼ cup all-purpose flour

1 cup shredded Cheddar cheese

1 teaspoon salt

½ teaspoon pepper

⅛ teaspoon ground nutmeg

4 large eggs, beaten

1 cup milk

½ cup plain or seasoned fine dry breadcrumbs

1. Preheat the oven to 350°F. Butter a shallow 1½-quart casserole with 1 tablespoon of the melted butter. Put the spinach leaves into a large colander and pour boiling water over the leaves to wilt. Drain well.

2. In a large bowl, toss the wilted spinach leaves with the flour, cheese, salt, pepper, and nutmeg and pack into the casserole dish. Mix the eggs and milk together and pour over the spinach and cheese.

3. Bake, uncovered, for 25 to 30 minutes until set. Blend the breadcrumbs with the remaining 3 tablespoons butter and sprinkle over the casserole, then continue baking until the breadcrumbs are crispy, another 5 to 10 minutes.

FRESH BEET AND BLUE CHEESE CASSEROLE

Anneli Johnson, a Finnish friend who gives food demonstrations at the University of Massachusetts, passed this recipe on to me. It's an unusual combination of baked shredded beets, onions, and blue cheese.

———— SERVES 6 ————

1 bunch raw beets (1 pound)

1 medium onion, chopped

1 cup crumbled blue cheese

½ teaspoon salt

¼ teaspoon pepper

1 tablespoon chopped fresh basil

1 tablespoon chopped fresh tarragon

1 cup light cream, or homemade (page 27) or prepared vegetable broth

1. Preheat the oven to 350°F.

2. Peel the beets and shred them. Transfer to a 1½-quart shallow casserole and mix in the onion, cheese, salt, pepper, and herbs. Pour the cream or vegetable broth over all.

3. Bake for 1 hour, or until the beets are tender.

BROCCOLI AND CAULIFLOWER BAKE

Broccoli and cauliflower, though rather homely vegetables, look really pretty together in this casserole. And they are so tasty, too. Tote this to a potluck and use your artistic eye to arrange the vegetables and garnish.

SERVES 4 TO 5

6 cups combined broccoli and cauliflower florets

1½ cups shredded Monterey Jack cheese

1 cup sour cream

¼ to ½ teaspoon red pepper flakes

1 teaspoon salt

2 tablespoons butter, melted

½ cup seasoned fine dry breadcrumbs

2 tomatoes, diced

2 tablespoons chopped fresh basil

1. Preheat the oven to 350°F. Coat a 2½-quart casserole with cooking spray.

2. Pour 1 inch of water into a Dutch oven or deep pot. Bring to a boil and add the broccoli and cauliflower. Cover and cook for 5 to 6 minutes, or until crisp-tender, and drain.

3. In a large bowl, combine the cheese, sour cream, red pepper flakes, and salt.

4. Fold the vegetables into the cheese mixture. Transfer to the casserole dish and spread out evenly. Mix the butter with the breadcrumbs and sprinkle evenly over the vegetables. (At this point you can cover and refrigerate for up to 1 day. Add 10 minutes to the baking time.)

5. Bake, uncovered, for 20 to 25 minutes, or until the breadcrumbs are browned and the vegetables are heated through. Before serving, sprinkle with the tomatoes and chopped fresh basil.

HOT ROASTED BROCCOLI, ONION, AND BELL PEPPER SALAD

Serve this roasted vegetable salad hot from the oven or at room temperature. It's especially good alongside a simple roast chicken, broiled salmon, or grilled hamburger.

SERVES 6

6 cups broccoli florets

2 red bell peppers, cut into ¼-inch-thick slices

1 small red onion, cut into ¼-inch-thick slices

1 small sweet onion, cut into ¼-inch-thick slices

1½ teaspoons olive oil

1 tablespoon Dijon mustard

1 tablespoon balsamic vinegar

½ teaspoon red pepper flakes

½ teaspoon salt

½ cup grated Parmesan cheese for garnish

¼ cup chopped fresh basil leaves for garnish

1. Preheat the oven to 350°F.

2. Combine the broccoli, bell peppers, onions, and olive oil in a 3-quart casserole. Toss to coat the vegetables with oil.

3. Bake for 25 minutes, stirring occasionally.

4. Meanwhile, whisk together the mustard, vinegar, pepper flakes, and salt in a small bowl.

With a rubber spatula, stir the mixture into the hot cooked vegetables. Return to the oven for another 20 to 25 minutes, until the vegetables are tender.

5. Garnish with the Parmesan cheese and basil leaves. Serve hot or cooled to room temperature.

BROCCOLI, RED BELL PEPPER, AND MUSHROOM CASSEROLE

If you are looking for a colorful casserole to accompany a baked ham, leg of lamb, or roast beef, look no further. This is a great company dish that can easily be doubled for a big party. Just be careful not to overbake the casserole, or the vegetables will lose their appealing color and texture.

SERVES 6

3 tablespoons butter, divided, plus extra for the dish

6 cups loosely packed broccoli florets

½ pound mushrooms, sliced

1 red bell pepper, seeded and diced

3 tablespoons all-purpose flour

1½ to 1¾ cups milk, heated (use the larger quantity if not using wine)

¼ cup dry white wine (optional)

1 teaspoon Dijon mustard

1 teaspoon salt

1 cup shredded Cheddar cheese

1. Preheat the oven to 375°F. Butter a shallow 2-quart casserole.

2. Blanch the broccoli in the boiling salted water for 3 to 4 minutes, or until crisp-tender. Drain and transfer to the casserole.

3. Heat 1 tablespoon of the butter in a 10-inch skillet, add the mushrooms and bell pepper, and sauté until the mushrooms are lightly browned, about 4 minutes. Add to the casserole and distribute evenly.

4. Melt the remaining 2 tablespoons butter in the pan and stir in the flour until well blended. Gradually whisk in the milk and bring to a boil, stirring. Add the wine (if using), the mustard, and salt. Lower the heat and simmer until thickened. Pour the sauce over the vegetables and sprinkle with the Cheddar cheese. (At this point you can cover and refrigerate for up to 1 day. Add 5 to 10 minutes to the baking time.)

5. Bake, uncovered, for 15 to 20 minutes, until the casserole is hot and bubbly and the cheese is melted.

HOT BROCCOLI SLAW

Shredded broccoli stems, carrots, and cabbage can be purchased in 1-pound bags labeled "broccoli coleslaw" in supermarkets' produce departments. The combination is a convenient base for this tasty side-dish casserole.

SERVES 6

3 tablespoons butter, plus extra for the dish

1 medium onion, thinly sliced

1 package (1 pound) broccoli coleslaw

½ cup light mayonnaise

½ cup light sour cream

½ cup grated Parmesan cheese

3 tablespoons seasoned fine dry breadcrumbs

1. Preheat the oven to 350°F. Butter a shallow 2-quart casserole.

2. Melt the 3 tablespoons butter in a skillet over high heat. Add the onion and sauté, stirring, for 2 minutes, or until aromatic. Add the broccoli slaw and continue sautéing and stirring until the vegetables are wilted, about 5 minutes. Remove from the heat and transfer to the casserole.

3. Mix the mayonnaise and sour cream together and spread over the top of the vegetables. Sprinkle with the Parmesan cheese and breadcrumbs.

4. Bake, uncovered, for 20 to 25 minutes, until the crumbs are lightly browned.

BROWN SUGAR AND CARROT CASSEROLE

Try this for a holiday meal. The flavor of the carrots may remind you of sweet potatoes. For good color contrast, serve this with steamed broccoli or Brussels sprouts.

SERVES 6

2 pounds carrots, peeled and cut into ¼-inch-thick slices

⅓ cup light or dark brown sugar

1 cup shredded mild Cheddar cheese

¼ cup crushed saltine crackers

2 tablespoons butter, melted

1. Preheat the oven to 350°F. Coat a 2½-quart casserole with cooking spray.

2. Put the carrots in a large pot and add water to cover. Boil for about 10 minutes, until crisp-tender. Drain well and arrange in the casserole dish in an even layer. Sprinkle with the brown sugar and the cheese. Mix the crushed crackers with the butter and sprinkle over the carrots.

3. Bake for 20 to 25 minutes, or until the topping is lightly browned and the carrots are bubbly.

BUTTERNUT SQUASH AND RED PEPPER CASSEROLE

Butternut squash is incredibly hard, so you need a heavy cleaver to hack it in half. Then remove the skin with a peeler, and cut the flesh into cubes. It is worth the effort, because the roasted result is so flavorful.

SERVES 6

2½ pounds butternut squash, peeled, seeded, and cut into 1-inch cubes

1 large red bell pepper, seeded and cut into 1-inch pieces

2 tablespoons olive oil

2 large cloves garlic, minced

2 tablespoons minced fresh parsley

2 teaspoons minced fresh rosemary leaves

½ cup grated Parmesan cheese

1. Preheat the oven to 400°F. Coat a shallow 3-quart casserole with cooking spray.

2. In a large bowl, toss everything together but the cheese.

Transfer to the casserole dish and sprinkle with the Parmesan cheese.

3. Bake for 55 minutes to 1 hour, or until the squash is tender.

CABBAGE AND MUSHROOM GRATIN

The cabbage is baked in cream, making it sweet and flavorful. The term "gratin" simply means that a dish is covered with cheese, like this one, or with breadcrumbs, or both, and then browned in the oven. Serve this with grilled bratwurst or Polish sausage and rye bread or buns.

SERVES 6

1 medium head cabbage, coarsely chopped

1½ cups heavy cream, divided

¼ teaspoon ground nutmeg

2 tablespoons butter

½ pound mushrooms, sliced

1 teaspoon salt

½ teaspoon pepper

2 tablespoons grated Parmesan cheese

1. Preheat the oven to 375°F. Coat a shallow 2½-quart casserole or gratin dish with cooking spray.

2. In a large saucepan, bring about 2 quarts salted water to a boil. Add the cabbage, return to a boil, and continue boiling for 3 minutes. Drain well. In a medium bowl, combine the cooked cabbage with 1 cup of the cream and transfer to the casserole. Cover and bake for 25 minutes, or until the cabbage has absorbed the cream. Sprinkle with the nutmeg.

3. Meanwhile, in a large skillet, melt the butter and add the mushrooms and the remaining ½ cup cream. Simmer, stirring, for 3 minutes, or until the cream has been absorbed and the mushrooms are dry. Add the salt and pepper.

4. Mix the mushrooms into the cabbage in the casserole and sprinkle with the Parmesan cheese. (At this point you can cool the casserole, and cover and refrigerate overnight. Add 5 to 10 minutes to the baking time in step 5.)

5. Bake the casserole, uncovered, for 15 to 25 minutes more, or until heated through and the cheese is melted.

CARROT AND PARSNIP GRATIN WITH PARMESAN

Choose small to medium-size parsnips for this recipe—they are sweeter and nuttier. This makes a perfect side for a roast turkey or pork dinner. If you like, you can make it ahead and refrigerate it for several hours.

SERVES 6

4 tablespoons butter, plus extra for the dish

1 pound carrots, peeled and shredded

1 pound parsnips, peeled and shredded

6 tablespoons all-purpose flour, divided

1 cup grated Parmesan cheese, divided

2 cups milk

½ cup heavy cream

2 large eggs

2 teaspoons salt

¼ teaspoon pepper

⅛ teaspoon ground nutmeg

⅛ teaspoon cayenne pepper

1. Preheat the oven to 350°F. Butter a 9-by-13-inch baking dish.

2. In a large bowl, combine the carrots and parsnips. Add 2 tablespoons of the flour, 2 tablespoons of the butter, and ½ cup of the Parmesan cheese and mix well.

3. In a saucepan, melt the remaining 2 tablespoons butter and add the remaining 4 tablespoons flour. Cook over medium-high heat, stirring, until well blended. Gradually whisk in the milk and cook, stirring continuously, until the sauce begins to bubble and thickens; remove from the heat.

4. In a small bowl, whisk together the cream, eggs, salt, pepper, nutmeg, and cayenne. Mix a small amount of the hot mixture into the egg mixture to temper, then stir the remaining mixture into the hot milk mixture. Whisk until combined.

5. Pour the sauce over the carrot and parsnip mixture, mix well, and transfer all to the baking dish. Sprinkle with the remaining ½ cup Parmesan cheese. (At this point you can cover and refrigerate for 4 or 5 hours. Add 5 to 10 minutes to the baking time.)

6. Bake, uncovered, for about 50 minutes, or until the vegetables are tender.

CARROT, CAULIFLOWER, AND BROCCOLI CASSEROLE

Sunflower seeds provide the crunch for this easy casserole. To save time, buy a 1-pound bag of cut-up vegetables in the produce section. Assemble this casserole ahead, as much as 1 day in advance, if you are short on last-minute preparation time.

SERVES 4

5 cups mixed cut-up broccoli and cauliflower florets, red peppers, and sweet onion

1 cup shredded carrots

1 tablespoon butter, melted

1 cup sour cream

½ cup mayonnaise

½ cup shredded sharp Cheddar cheese

1 cup sunflower seeds

1. Preheat the oven to 400°F.

2. Heat a pot of water to boiling and add the vegetables; cook for 5 minutes, or just until crisp-tender, and drain.

3. Spread out the melted butter in the bottom of a shallow 3-quart casserole. Add the vegetables and toss them in the butter until they are coated.

4. Mix the sour cream, mayonnaise, and cheese in a small bowl and pour evenly over the vegetables. (At this point you can cover and refrigerate for up to 1 day in advance. Add 5 to 10 minutes to the baking time.)

5. Top the casserole with the sunflower seeds and bake for 20 minutes, or until heated through and the top is lightly browned.

CAULIFLOWER AND BROCCOLI CUSTARD

Cruciferous vegetables (vegetables in the cabbage family) are said to have special cancer-fighting characteristics. But that's not the only reason to enjoy this casserole, which is comfort food at its best. Serve it with a homemade meat loaf or pot roast. To save time, you can use a 1-pound bag of fresh mixed cauliflower and broccoli florets.

MAKES 6 SERVINGS

2 tablespoons butter, plus extra for the dish

6 cups combined cauliflower and broccoli florets

3 tablespoons all-purpose flour

1 teaspoon salt

¼ teaspoon freshly ground white pepper

1 tablespoon minced fresh parsley

2 cups milk

3 large eggs

1. Preheat the oven to 350°F. Butter a shallow 2-quart casserole.

2. Cook the cauliflower and broccoli in boiling salted water to cover for 5 to 7 minutes, until crisp-tender. Drain and arrange in the casserole.

3. Melt the 2 tablespoons butter in a saucepan over medium heat and add the flour, salt, pepper, and parsley, stirring until blended. Gradually whisk in 1 cup of the milk, bring to a boil, lower the heat, and simmer, stirring, until thickened. Beat the eggs in a medium bowl and beat in the remaining 1 cup milk. Whisk about 1 cup of the hot mixture into the egg mixture to temper the eggs. Then whisk the eggs and milk into the pan. Heat through, and pour over the cauliflower and broccoli.

4. Bake for 30 to 35 minutes, or until the custard is set.

CAULIFLOWER AND BROWN RICE CASSEROLE

Cauliflower is one vegetable that's available pretty much year-round. This casserole takes it beyond raw or simply steamed. Brown rice and toasted walnuts complement its flavor and texture.

MAKES 6 SERVINGS

1 small head cauliflower, trimmed and cut into florets

½ cup cooked brown rice

3 large eggs, beaten

1 cup milk

½ teaspoon salt

Dash of allspice

Chopped fresh parsley for garnish

Chopped toasted walnuts for garnish (optional)

1. Preheat the oven to 350°F. Coat a 2-quart casserole with cooking spray.

2. Cook the cauliflower florets in boiling salted water to cover until crisp-tender, 5 to 10 minutes, and drain.

3. Arrange the florets in the casserole. In a medium bowl, combine the rice with the eggs, milk, salt, and allspice and pour over the cauliflower.

4. Bake for 30 to 35 minutes, or until the custard has set. Garnish with the parsley and the toasted walnuts, if desired.

OLD-FASHIONED SCALLOPED POTATOES

As a young farm girl I learned to prepare scalloped potatoes without a recipe. My mother told me to plan on 1 large potato per person. To determine the size of the casserole dish, we estimated 1 quart for 4 large potatoes. Eight potatoes would therefore require a 2-quart casserole.

SERVES 4

2 tablespoons cold butter, cut up, plus extra for the dish

4 to 5 large potatoes, peeled and sliced

2 tablespoons all-purpose flour

1 teaspoon salt

¼ teaspoon pepper

1 small onion, chopped

Milk or cream or undiluted evaporated milk as needed (see Note)

1. Preheat the oven to 325°F. Butter a 1½-quart shallow casserole.

2. Place a layer of potatoes in the bottom of the casserole dish and sprinkle with a little of the flour. Sprinkle with salt, pepper, and some of the chopped onion. Continue layering the potatoes, flour, seasonings, and onion in this way until the ingredients come within ½ inch of the top. Dot wih the 2 tablespoons butter.

3. Pour in enough milk to reach the top layer.

4. Bake for 1½ hours, or until the potatoes are tender. Check with a fork or a wooden skewer.

○ ○ ○ ○ ○

NOTE: New potatoes tend to be more acidic, causing milk to curdle, so if using them, use cream or undiluted evaporated milk, rather than regular milk.

CHEESY SCALLOPED POTATOES

This is pure comfort food, and so easy to make. You can assemble it on a Sunday night and then bake it on a busy Monday evening for a quick side dish. If you are making the casserole ahead, be sure to rinse the potatoes in cold water to prevent them from turning color. The last time I made this, we had about a cupful left over. The next day, I put it into the blender with some broth and milk and whirled it into a delicious, cheesy, smooth potato soup!

SERVES 6

6 medium baking potatoes, peeled and thinly sliced

1 small onion, thinly sliced

2 cups shredded low-fat Cheddar cheese

Salt

Pepper

1 recipe Basic White Sauce (page 18), or 1 can (10¾ ounces) cream of mushroom soup

½ cup water

1. Preheat the oven to 350°F. Coat a 9-inch square baking dish with cooking spray.

2. Rinse the sliced potatoes in cold water to prevent browning. Pat dry with paper towels.

3. Place a layer of potatoes in the bottom of the baking dish and sprinkle with the onion, cheese, salt, and pepper. Continue layering the potatoes, onion, cheese, and seasonings in this way, ending with a layer of cheese.

4. Mix the sauce or soup and the water in a small bowl and pour over the casserole. (At this point you can cover and refrigerate for up to 1 day. Add 5 to 10 minutes to the baking time.)

5. Bake for 1½ to 2 hours, or until the potatoes are tender.

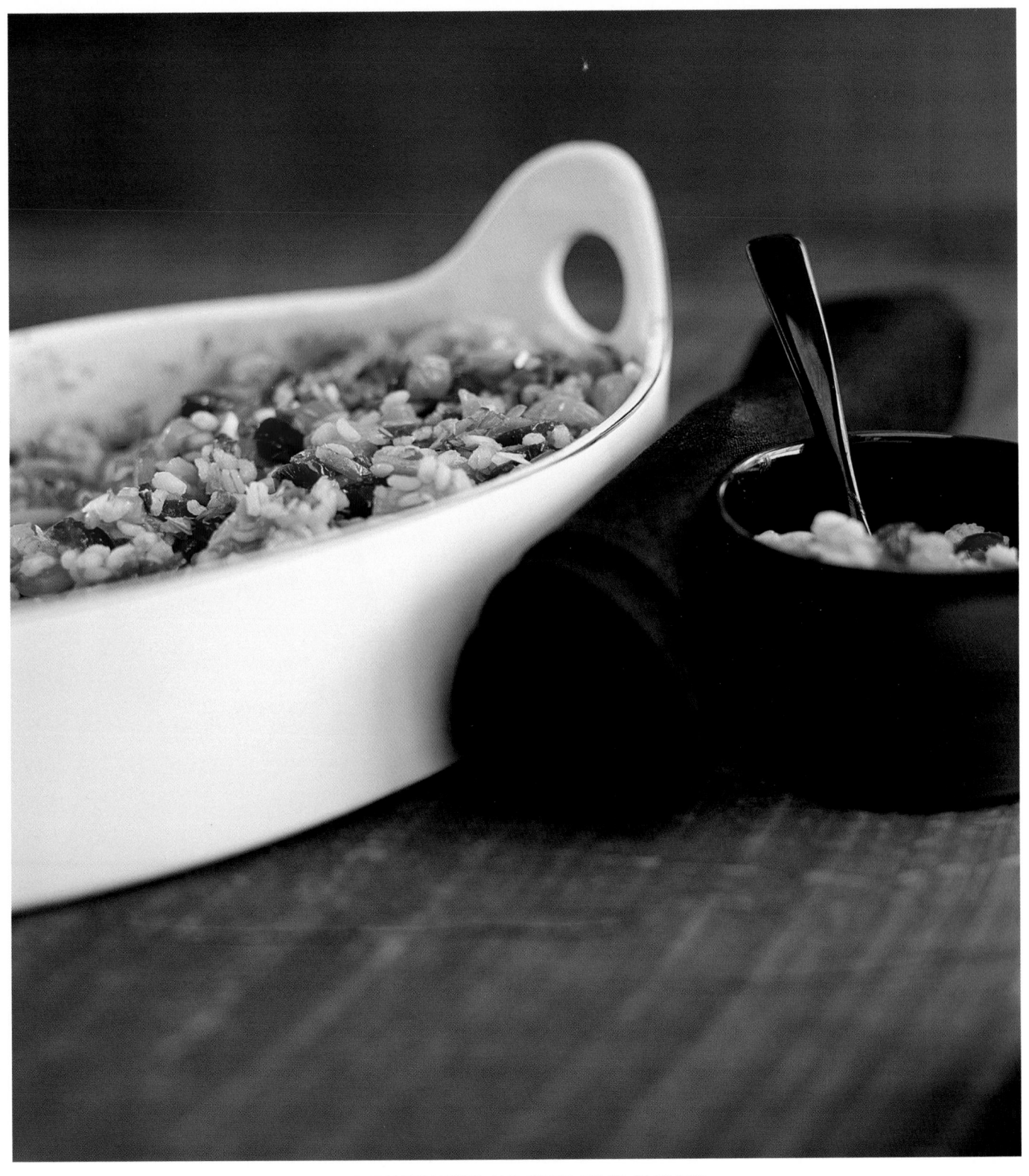

BARLEY WITH NUTS AND DRIED FRUIT, PAGE 332
OPPOSITE PAGE: MACARONI AND PARMESAN CHEESE, PAGE 323

POOR MAN'S LOBSTER (BUTTER-BAKED COD), PAGE 353
OPPOSITE PAGE: PROVENÇAL TOMATO CASSESROLE, PAGE 439

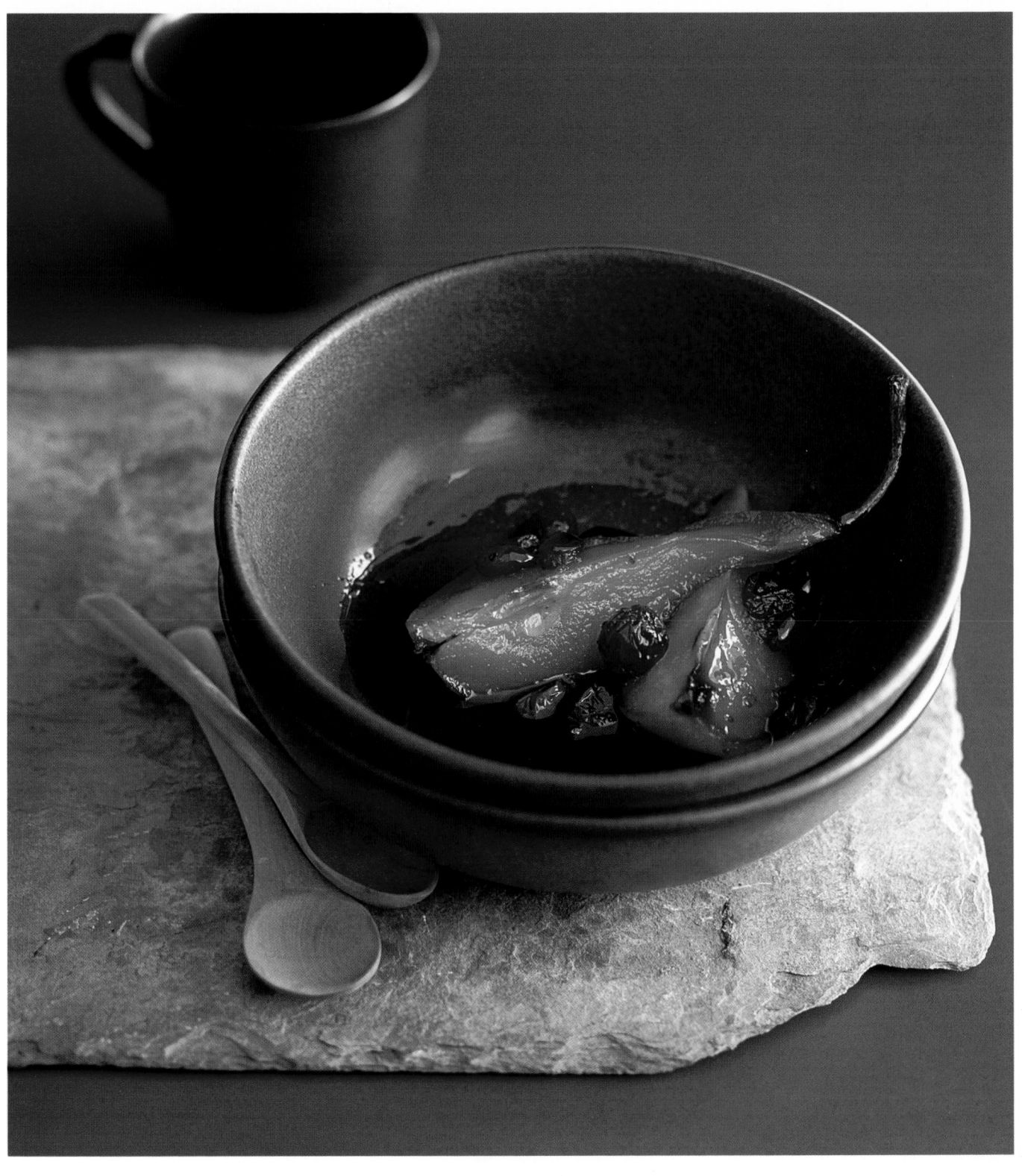

CRANBERRY PEARS, PAGE 587
OPPOSITE PAGE: CHOUCROUTE GARNI, PAGE 502

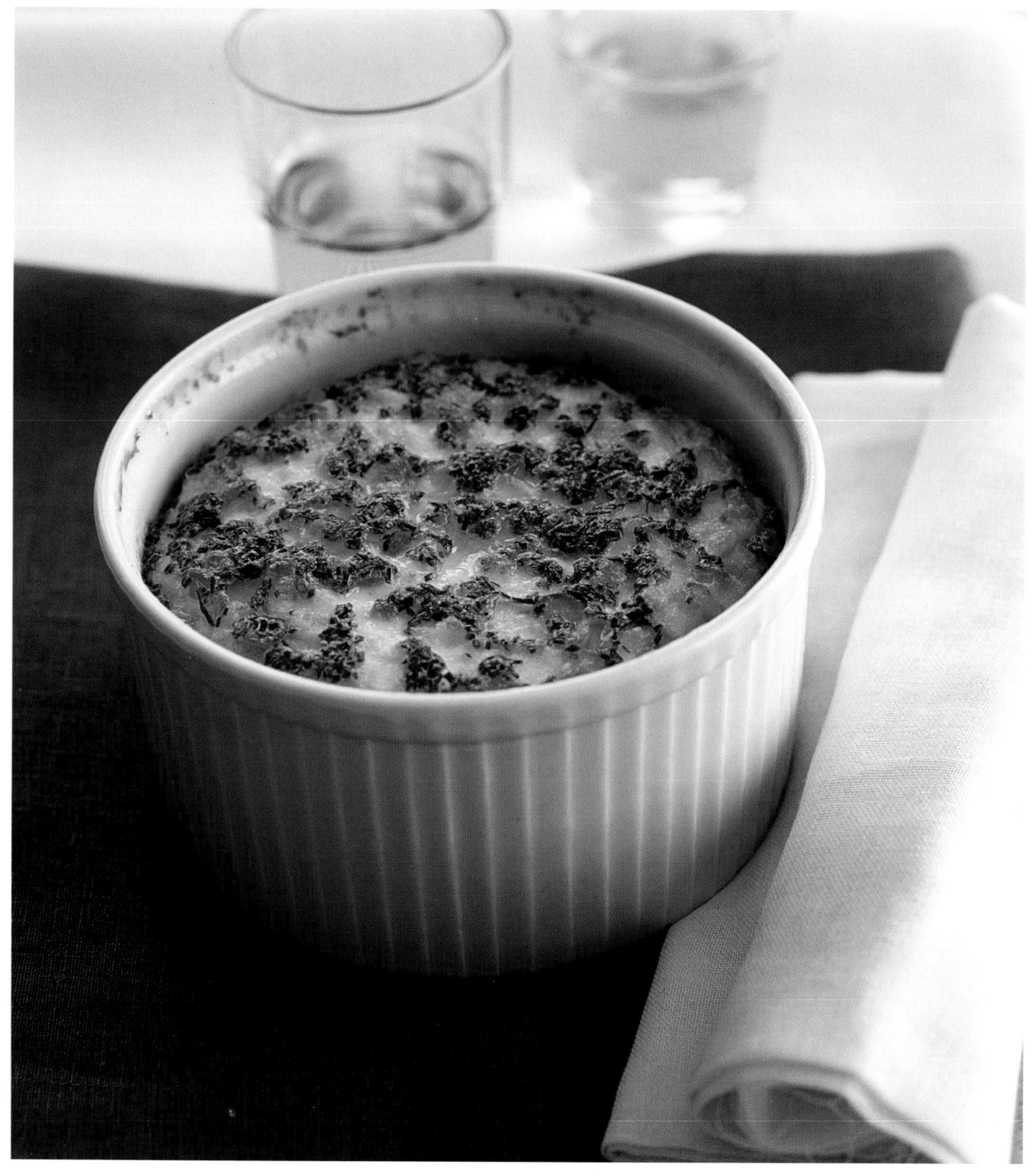

CORN AND CHIVE PUDDING

CORN AND CHIVE PUDDING

The corn bakes in a custard and almost persuades you it is a dessert. This soothing comfort food makes a fine companion for roasted or rotisserie chicken.

SERVES 8

4 tablespoons butter, melted and cooled, plus extra for the dish

1 package (1 pound) frozen corn kernels, thawed

¼ cup sugar

1½ teaspoons salt

2 cups milk

4 large eggs

3 tablespoons all-purpose flour

¼ cup chopped fresh chives, plus 3 tablespoons chopped chives for garnish

Pinch of ground nutmeg

1. Preheat the oven to 350°F. Butter a shallow 1½-quart casserole.

2. Put half of the corn into a blender and pulse until coarsely chopped. Transfer the chopped corn to a medium bowl and add the remaining corn kernels, the sugar, and salt, stirring until well mixed.

3. In another medium bowl whisk together the milk, eggs, the 4 tablespoons of butter, the flour, and the ¼ cup chives and stir into the corn until mixed. Pour the pudding into the buttered dish and sprinkle with nutmeg.

4. Bake until the center is just set, about 45 minutes. Garnish the pudding with the 3 tablespoons chives. Serve hot.

FRESH CORN PUDDING

More of a soufflé than a pudding, this is an excellent dish for Sunday brunch. Add fresh berries, garden greens, and fresh-baked muffins for a simple but elegant menu. You can make this with frozen corn, but do try it with fresh corn!

SERVES 4

3 large ears fresh corn, husked, or 1¼ cups frozen corn kernels, thawed

3 large eggs, separated

2 tablespoons butter

2 tablespoons cornstarch

1 cup milk

2 teaspoons sugar

½ teaspoon salt

1. Preheat the oven to 400°F. Coat a 1-quart soufflé dish with cooking spray.

2. With a sharp knife, slice the corn kernels off the cob. In a large bowl, beat the egg yolks and add the corn.

3. In a small saucepan, melt the butter over medium heat and stir in the cornstarch. Gradually whisk in the milk and bring to a boil. Lower the heat and simmer, stirring, until the sauce is smooth and thickened. Stir in the sugar and salt. Gradually stir the hot sauce into the corn mixture.

4. In a large bowl, whip the egg whites until stiff. Fold into the corn mixture. Turn the mixture into the soufflé dish. (At this point you can cover the dish and refrigerate for up to 2 hours. Add 5 minutes to the baking time.)

5. Bake for 25 to 30 minutes, or until the pudding is browned on top but still jiggles a little when tapped on the side. Serve hot.

CARROT CASSEROLE WITH CHEDDAR AND HORSERADISH

The great flavor of this vegetable casserole belies how simple it is to put together. Serve it with a braised brisket in the winter, and alongside a glazed roasted turkey breast in the fall.

6 SERVINGS

6 medium carrots, peeled

½ cup mayonnaise

1 tablespoon grated fresh horseradish

½ cup shredded Cheddar cheese

1 teaspoon minced fresh chives for garnish

1. Preheat the oven to 350°F. Coat a shallow 2-quart casserole with cooking spray.

2. Cut the carrots diagonally into ½-inch-thick slices. Cook in boiling salted water to cover until crisp-tender, about 10 minutes. Drain and transfer to the casserole.

3. Mix the mayonnaise and horseradish together in a small bowl and spread over the carrots. Sprinkle with the cheese. (At this point you can cover and refrigerate overnight. Add 5 to 10 minutes to the baking time.)

4. Bake for 25 to 30 minutes, until bubbly. Sprinkle with the minced chives.

CHILE-CHEDDAR POTATO CASSEROLE

Green chiles add just a bit of a bite here, which is mellowed by the creamy sauce. Serve this with a pot roast with Mexican flavors, such as hot peppers, cumin, and cilantro.

SERVES 6 TO 8

2½ pounds thin-skinned potatoes, peeled and cubed

3 cups Béchamel Sauce (page 21)

2 cups shredded Cheddar cheese

1 can (4 ounces) diced green chiles with their juice

2 teaspoons salt

2 cloves garlic, minced

½ cup fine dry breadcrumbs

3 tablespoons melted butter

1. Preheat the oven to 350°F.

2. In a medium saucepan, cook the potatoes in boiling salted water to cover until tender, about 20 minutes. Transfer to a 2-quart casserole.

3. In a large bowl, mix the Béchamel Sauce, cheese, chiles, salt, and garlic and pour over the potatoes. Mix the breadcrumbs with the melted butter and sprinkle over the potatoes.

4. Bake for 25 minutes, or until the crumbs are browned and the casserole is bubbly.

CORN, BACON, AND CHEDDAR SOUFFLÉ

The soufflé rule applies here: Have your guests seated at the table before you take the soufflé out of the oven for the most spectacular presentation.

¼ cup grated Parmesan cheese

6 slices bacon

1 package (10 ounces) frozen corn kernels, thawed

4 tablespoons butter

¼ cup all-purpose flour

¼ teaspoon salt

⅛ teaspoon pepper

1 cup milk

1 cup shredded Cheddar cheese

6 large eggs, separated

1. Preheat the oven to 350°F. Coat a 2-quart soufflé dish with cooking spray and sprinkle with the Parmesan cheese to coat evenly. Cut a sheet of aluminum foil long enough to wrap around the soufflé dish. Fold the foil in half lengthwise and coat with cooking spray. Wrap it around the soufflé dish so that it extends above the rim of the dish by 2 inches. Fold the ends of the foil together to fasten.

2. Cook the bacon in a medium skillet until crisp. Drain well on paper towels, and crumble.

3. Cook the corn according to package directions and drain.

4. Melt the butter in a medium saucepan over medium heat and blend in the flour, salt, and pepper. Gradually whisk in the milk and continue whisking until the mixture is smooth. Heat to boiling, whisking constantly, lower the heat, and simmer until thickened, 3 to 5 minutes. Remove from the heat and stir in the cheese and cooked corn. In a small bowl, beat the egg yolks and add a small amount of the hot mixture to the yolks to temper them. Whisk the egg yolk mixture into the sauce and set aside.

5. Beat the egg whites until stiff and fold into the cheese mixture until almost totally blended in. It is okay to have bits of egg white unblended. Transfer to the soufflé dish.

6. Bake for 35 to 40 minutes, or until puffy and golden. Serve immediately.

CREAMY POTATOES AND MUSHROOMS WITH SAGE

The combination of fresh sage leaves, mushrooms, cream, and potatoes is irresistible! Serve with a crusty bread to sop up any extra juices.

SERVES 6

6 medium thin-skinned potatoes

2 large onions

2 tablespoons chopped fresh sage

½ pound mushrooms, sliced

1 to 1½ cups heavy cream

2 tablespoons fine dry breadcrumbs

1 tablespoon butter, melted

1. Preheat the oven to 425°F. Coat a shallow 2-quart casserole with cooking spray.

2. Peel and rinse the potatoes. Cut the potatoes into ¼-inch-thick slices and cut the slices into ¼-inch strips. Peel the onions and trim off the ends. Cut the onions in half lengthwise. With the cut side down, cut the onions lengthwise into ¼-inch slices.

3. Spread out the onions, sage, and mushrooms in the prepared dish. Cover with the potato strips. Add just enough cream to cover the potatoes. Mix together the breadcrumbs and melted butter, then sprinkle over the potato layer.

4. Bake for 45 to 50 minutes, until the potatoes are tender and the top is browned.

CRUSTY ROASTED CARROT CASSEROLE

You wouldn't think that carrots covered with a thin batter could roast until very tender, but they do. And this preparation renders them sweet and flavorful, as well.

1 tablespoon cold butter, cut up, plus extra for the dish

6 medium carrots, peeled

¼ cup milk

1 egg, beaten

1 teaspoon salt

½ cup all-purpose flour

1. Preheat the oven to 350°F. Butter a shallow 2-quart casserole.

2. Quarter the carrots lengthwise. Beat the milk and egg in a shallow bowl. In another shallow bowl, combine the salt and flour. Dip the carrots first into the milk mixture, then into the flour mixture.

3. Arrange the carrots in the casserole dish in a single layer. Dot with the 1 tablespoon butter and bake until the carrots are tender, about 45 minutes.

EGGPLANT WITH GARLIC, BASIL, AND TOMATOES

This is a perfect buffet dish. Fill out the meal with simple-to-make Wild Rice Buffet Casserole (page 348), and add Rosemary and Parmesan Casserole bread (page 82) to the menu.

SERVES 6

1 clove garlic, crushed

¼ cup olive oil

4 tablespoons butter

1 large eggplant (about 1½ to 1¾ pounds), peeled and cubed

1 cup minced onion

3 large tomatoes, diced, or 1 can (14½ ounces) diced tomatoes with their juice

½ teaspoon dried basil

1½ teaspoons salt

¼ teaspoon pepper

½ cup shredded Swiss or Cheddar cheese

1. Preheat the oven to 375°F. Rub a 2-quart casserole with the garlic.

2. In a large skillet, heat the olive oil with 2 tablespoons of the butter over medium-high heat. Sauté the eggplant for 10 minutes until browned, then transfer to the casserole.

3. Melt the remaining 2 tablespoons butter in the skillet, add the onion, and sauté for 3 to 5 minutes, until the onion is softened. Stir in the tomatoes, the basil, salt, and pepper.

4. Pour the tomato mixture over the eggplant in the casserole. Sprinkle with the cheese. (At this point you can cover and refrigerate the casserole for a few hours. Add another 5 to 10 minutes to the baking time.)

5. Bake for 30 minutes, or until bubbly and browned.

CHEESY EGGPLANT AND TOMATO BAKE

This is an easy and appetizing way to serve eggplant. The combination of eggplant, tomatoes, and two types of cheese makes it a perfect companion for grilled fish or lamb chops.

SERVES 8

2 medium eggplants (about 3 pounds total)

Salt

½ cup olive oil, or more as needed

2 green bell peppers, seeded and cut into rings

2 medium onions, chopped

4 large cloves garlic, minced

1 teaspoon dried rosemary

1 teaspoon dried oregano

1 teaspoon dried basil

1 can (28 ounces) Italian-style tomatoes with their juice

Pepper

1 cup shredded Monterey Jack cheese

½ cup grated Parmesan cheese

1. Preheat the oven to 350°F. Coat a 9-by-13-inch baking dish with cooking spray.

2. Cut the eggplants into ½-inch-thick slices and spread out in a single layer on 2 thicknesses of paper towels. Sprinkle lightly with salt on both sides and let stand for 20 minutes. Rinse off the salt and pat the eggplant dry.

3. Heat 2 tablespoons of the olive oil in a large nonstick skillet over medium heat. Add the peppers, onions, and garlic and sauté until softened, about 10 minutes. Add the rosemary, oregano, basil, and tomatoes with their juice and bring to a boil. Reduce the heat and simmer until the mixture is reduced to 2½ cups. Season with salt and pepper to taste, transfer to a bowl, and set aside.

4. Heat the remaining 6 tablespoons olive oil in the skillet over medium-high heat. Working in batches, cook the eggplant until golden, adding more oil as necessary, about 5 minutes per side. Drain the eggplant slices on paper towels as they are done.

5. Layer half of the eggplant in the baking dish and top with half of the tomato sauce. Sprinkle lightly with salt and pepper and cover with the remaining eggplant. Spoon the remaining tomato sauce on top and sprinkle lightly with salt and pepper. Top with the Monterey Jack and Parmesan cheeses.

6. Bake, uncovered, until the eggplant is tender, about 40 minutes. Let stand for 15 minutes before serving.

FETA-TOPPED GREEN TOMATOES

If you're a fan of fried green tomatoes, you may decide that you like this simple casserole even more. Feta adds a bit of saltiness to counter the slightly acidic tomatoes.

SERVES 4

4 medium green tomatoes

Juice of ½ lemon

1½ teaspoons dried oregano

1 cup crumbled feta cheese

2 tablespoons olive oil

Pepper

1. Preheat the oven to 425°F.

2. Remove the cores from each tomato and cut into ½-inch-thick slices. Arrange in a shallow 1-quart casserole dish, overlapping the slices slightly,

3. Squeeze the lemon over the tomato slices. Sprinkle with the oregano and feta cheese, and drizzle with the olive oil.

(At this point you can cover and refrigerate for up to 1 day. Add 5 to 10 minutes to the baking time.)

4. Bake for 10 to 15 minutes, until the tomatoes are hot and the cheese is beginning to brown. Grind fresh pepper over the top and serve hot.

FRENCH POTATO GRATIN

An old-fashioned French classic, this is rich and creamy! It is still a perfect accompaniment for roasts, steaks, or chops.

SERVES 6

3 large baking potatoes, peeled

1 clove garlic

1 tablespoon butter

1 teaspoon salt

½ teaspoon pepper

⅛ teaspoon ground nutmeg

½ cup shredded Swiss or Jarlsberg cheese

1½ cups half-and-half or heavy cream

1. Preheat the oven to 350°F. Slice the potatoes thinly and rinse with cold water to prevent browning. Crush the garlic and work it into the butter. Spread over the bottom and sides of a shallow 1½-quart casserole or gratin dish.

2. Arrange the potato slices neatly in overlapping rows in the buttered casserole. Sprinkle with the salt, pepper, nutmeg, and half the cheese.

3. In a small saucepan, heat the half-and-half to boiling. Pour over the potato mixture in the casserole and sprinkle with the remaining cheese.

4. Bake, uncovered, for 45 minutes to 1 hour, or until the potatoes are browned and very tender.

FRESH VEGETABLES BAKED WITH ROSEMARY AND GRUYÈRE CHEESE

Serve these simply roasted vegetables with crusty bread. The dish has few seasonings, allowing the flavor of the vegetables to shine. If possible, when choosing the vegetables, select ones that have about the same diameter. It will make alternating them in the casserole dish easier and more visually appealing.

MAKES 6 SERVINGS

4 tablespoons olive oil, divided

2 medium baking potatoes, peeled and thinly sliced

2 small Japanese eggplants, thinly sliced on the diagonal

1 small zucchini, thinly sliced on the diagonal

4 Roma (plum) tomatoes, thinly sliced

½ teaspoon kosher salt

½ teaspoon pepper

2 tablespoons fresh rosemary leaves

1 head garlic, cloves separated, peeled, and bruised

⅓ cup shredded Gruyère cheese

1. Preheat the oven to 400°F. Brush 1 tablespoon of the olive oil on the bottom and sides of a shallow 2- to 3-quart casserole.

2. Arrange the vegetables in rows in the dish. Sprinkle with the salt, pepper, and rosemary.

Scatter the garlic cloves over all and drizzle with the remaining 3 tablespoons olive oil.

3. Bake for 25 to 30 minutes, or until the vegetables are tender. Remove from the oven and sprinkle with the cheese.

GREEN BEAN, MUSHROOM, AND ONION CASSEROLE

Perfect for the holiday table, this updated recipe is a big improvement over the mushy mass of canned green beans and mushroom soup that it replaces. I like to leave the green beans whole. If you make the casserole ahead, refrigerate it without the crumb topping, and add that just before you bake the casserole.

SERVES 6

1 pound green beans, trimmed

2½ tablespoons butter

½ pound baby portobello mushrooms, sliced

3 cloves garlic, minced

2 tablespoons all-purpose flour

¾ cup homemade (page 25) or prepared chicken broth

1 tablespoon dry sherry

½ cup heavy cream

Salt

Pepper

1 slice whole-grain bread

1. Preheat the oven to 425°F. Coat a shallow 2-quart casserole with cooking spray.

2. Cook the green beans in boiling salted water for 6 minutes, or just until crisp-tender and bright green. Drain and plunge into a bowl of ice water to stop the cooking. Drain well and transfer to the casserole.

3. Melt 1½ tablespoons of the butter in a skillet over medium-high heat and add the mushrooms and garlic. Cook for 6 minutes, or until the mushrooms are softened and somewhat juicy. Stir in the flour and cook for a minute. Add the chicken broth, sherry, and cream. Bring to a boil, stirring, lower the heat, and cook, continuing to stir, for

10 to 15 minutes, until the sauce thickens. Taste and add salt and pepper. Pour the sauce over the green beans. (At this point you can cover and refrigerate the casserole for up to 1 day. Then proceed with the recipe, adding 5 to 10 minutes to the baking time.)

4. For the topping, break the bread into pieces and, in a food processor fitted with the steel blade, process until crumbly. Add the remaining 1 tablespoon butter and pulse until blended with the crumbs.

5. Sprinkle the crumbs over the sauce. Bake for 15 minutes, uncovered, until the crumbs are lightly browned and the casserole is bubbly.

GREEN TOMATO CASSEROLE

A variation on the always-popular fried green tomatoes,
this casserole is simpler and just as delicious.

SERVES 6 TO 8

8 large green tomatoes, sliced

1½ teaspoons salt

½ teaspoon pepper

2 tablespoons chopped fresh chives

1 teaspoon chopped mixed fresh herbs, such as basil, oregano, and thyme, or ½ teaspoon dried herbes de Provence

¾ cup fine dry breadcrumbs or panko (see Note)

4 to 5 tablespoons cold butter, cut into small pieces

¼ cup grated Parmesan cheese

1. Preheat the oven to 350°F. Coat a shallow 3-quart casserole with cooking spray.

2. Arrange the tomatoes in layers, sprinkling each one with salt, pepper, chives, mixed herbs, breadcrumbs, and a few pieces of butter.

3. Top with the Parmesan cheese and bake for 45 to 55 minutes, until bubbly and browned.

NOTE: Panko are Japanese breadcrumbs. They are coarser than regular breadcrumbs and create a crunchier crust. Panko can be purchased in Asian markets, or in the Asian sections of large supermarkets.

GREEN ONION CASSEROLE

Eight cups of green onions looks like a lot, but don't worry.
They cook down to about a quarter of their original volume, giving
you 4 standard servings of this savory casserole.

───────────── SERVES 4 ─────────────

3 tablespoons unsalted butter

8 bunches green onions, roots trimmed, and cut crosswise into 1-inch pieces (about 8 cups, including most of the green parts)

2 cloves garlic, minced

¼ cup heavy cream

½ cup grated Parmesan cheese, divided

1 tablespoon olive oil

2 cups fresh breadcrumbs (see Note)

Salt

Pepper

1. Preheat the oven to 350°F. Coat a shallow 1½-quart casserole with cooking spray.

2. Heat the butter in a deep, heavy pot and add the green onions and garlic. Cook, stirring, over medium-high heat for 10 to 14 minutes, or until softened. Stir in the cream and ¼ cup of the Parmesan cheese. Transfer to the casserole dish.

3. In a skillet, heat the oil over medium-high heat until hot but not smoking and sauté the breadcrumbs, stirring, until golden brown, about 3 minutes. Transfer the breadcrumbs to a bowl and cool. Add the remaining ¼ cup Parmesan and season with salt and pepper. Sprinkle the casserole with the bread crumb mixture. (At this point you can cover the casserole and refrigerate for up to 1 day. Bring the casserole to room temperature before proceeding.)

4. Bake the casserole, uncovered, until hot, 15 to 20 minutes.

○ ○ ○ ○ ○

NOTE: To make fresh breadcrumbs, tear 1 or 2 slices of fresh bread into pieces and put in a food processor with the steel blade in place. Process with on/off pulses until the bread is broken down into crumbs.

MAKE-AHEAD MASHED POTATO CASSEROLE

I got this recipe from my sister Lil, who was in turn introduced to it by the Lindgren family in Minneapolis. The Lindgrens have a fun tradition for their holiday party, which is a potluck. Each year, they build their menu around a different letter of the alphabet. The same dishes may reappear, but they are cleverly retitled. One year, they had to bring something that started with "H," and so this casserole was called "Holiday Potato Casserole." Another year, the letter was "M," and the casserole was renamed "Make-Ahead Mashed Potato Casserole."

SERVES 10

10 tablespoons butter, divided, plus extra for the dish

10 medium thin-skinned potatoes, peeled and cubed

1 teaspoon salt

¼ teaspoon pepper

½ cup milk, scalded

1 package (8 ounces) cream cheese

½ cup fresh breadcrumbs (see Note)

1. Preheat the oven to 375°F. Butter a 3-quart casserole.

2. Cook the potatoes in boiling salted water to cover until fork-tender, about 15 minutes and drain.

3. With a hand-held mixer, whip the potatoes with 1 stick of the butter. Add the salt, pepper, hot milk, and cream cheese and beat until the mixture is light and fluffy.

4. Transfer the potatoes to the prepared casserole and sprinkle the breadcrumbs on top. Cut the remaining 2 tablespoons of butter into small pieces and dot the casserole with the butter. (At this point you can cover and refrigerate for up to 1 day, or wrap well and freeze for up to 1 month. Thaw if frozen, and bring to room temperature before baking.)

5. Bake for 30 to 35 minutes until the casserole is heated through and the top is browned.

———

Variation: Add 1 tablespoon chopped sautéed onion and 1 tablespoon fresh chives to the potato mixture. Omit the breadcrumbs and sprinkle the top with paprika or shredded Cheddar cheese before baking.

ooooo

NOTE: To make fresh breadcrumbs, tear 1 or 2 slices of fresh bread into pieces and put in a food processor with the steel blade in place. Process with on/off pulses until the bread is broken down into crumbs.

MAPLE BAKED BEANS

Baked beans is one of those classic dishes that ignites controversy. Of course, Boston baked beans immediately come to mind. Beans slowly baked with molasses has been a favorite Boston dish since colonial days. Therefore, molasses is often considered the *only* way to sweeten the beans. Other ingredients that might go into a bean pot can produce a lively discussion—for example, peppers, onions, garlic, or tomatoes. Our friend Charlie Matsch, who has spent many summers in New England, is known for his baked beans, and he brings them to holiday potluck parties. He insists that you should not follow a recipe and can vary the ingredients according to what is on hand. I like that approach. That's why this recipe is sweetened with maple syrup—I always have real, locally produced maple syrup on hand.

— SERVES 6 —

1 pound navy or pea beans, cooked until tender (see page 30)

⅓ cup vegetable oil

1 cup chopped onions

1 green bell pepper, seeded and chopped

1 stalk celery, chopped

2 to 3 cloves garlic, minced

½ cup pure maple syrup

½ cup canned tomato puree or crushed tomatoes

2 tablespoons blackstrap molasses

2 tablespoons cider vinegar

1 tablespoon Dijon mustard

1½ teaspoons salt

¼ teaspoon pepper

1 bay leaf

¼ cup chopped fresh parsley

1. Drain the beans and reserve the liquid. Cook the beans as directed.

2. While the beans cook, heat the oil in a large nonstick skillet over medium-high heat. Add the onions, bell pepper, and celery and sauté for 5 minutes, until tender, adding the garlic at the end. Remove from the heat and set aside.

3. Preheat the oven to 325°F.

4. In a large bowl, whisk together 1 cup of the reserved cooking water, the maple syrup, tomato puree, molasses, vinegar, mustard, salt, pepper, bay leaf, and parsley. Add the beans and sautéed vegetables and mix well. Pour everything into a 2-quart casserole and cover tightly. Bake for 2½ to 3½ hours. Check periodically to make sure the beans have enough liquid to not dry out, adding more of the reserved cooking water, if necessary. The beans are done when they are tender and juicy and the liquid has been absorbed.

MASHED CARROT CASSEROLE

This beautiful, deep golden casserole is a favorite in the winter, when root vegetables are choices.

2 pounds carrots, peeled and chopped

¼ cup chopped onion

2 tablespoons chopped green bell pepper

½ cup milk

2 tablespoons sugar

1 cup cracker crumbs, divided

6 tablespoons butter, melted

½ teaspoon salt

¼ teaspoon pepper

1. Preheat the oven to 350°F. Coat a shallow 1½-quart casserole with cooking spray.

2. Put the carrots in a medium saucepan and cover with water. Place over high heat and bring to a boil. Reduce the heat and simmer for 20 to 25 minutes, or until the carrots are tender. Drain, transfer to a food processor, and process until pureed.

3. In a large bowl, mix the pureed carrots, onion, bell pepper, milk, sugar, ½ cup of the cracker crumbs, 3 tablespoons of the butter, salt, and pepper. Transfer the mixture to the casserole dish. Top with the remaining ½ cup cracker crumbs and drizzle with the remaining 3 tablespoons melted butter.

4. Bake for 25 minutes, or until heated through and brown on top.

MASHED POTATO, RUTABAGA, AND PARSNIP CASSEROLE WITH CARAMELIZED ONIONS

Here's a family favorite that dates way back to my Finnish roots. It's absolutely essential on the Christmas table! I have modernized the recipe by adding garlic and herbs.

SERVES 8

¾ cup (1½ sticks) butter at room temperature, plus extra for the dish

7 cups low-sodium chicken broth

3 pounds russet potatoes, peeled and cut into 1½-inch pieces

1½ pounds rutabagas, peeled and cut into ½-inch pieces

1¼ pounds parsnips, peeled and cut into 1½-inch pieces

8 cloves garlic

1 bay leaf

Salt

Pepper

1 teaspoon dried thyme

3 large onions, thinly sliced

1. Preheat the oven to 375°F. Butter a 9-by-13-inch glass baking dish.

2. Combine the chicken broth, potatoes, rutabagas, parsnips, garlic, and bay leaf in a 4-quart soup pot, and bring the broth to a boil. Reduce the heat, cover partially, and simmer until the vegetables are very tender, about 30 minutes. Drain well. Remove the bay leaf.

3. Transfer the vegetables to a large bowl and add ½ cup of the butter. Using an electric mixer, beat the vegetables until mashed but still chunky. Season with salt, pepper, and thyme and transfer the vegetables to the buttered baking dish.

4. Melt the remaining ¼ cup butter in a large, heavy nonstick skillet over medium-high heat. Add the sliced onions and sauté until beginning to brown, about 5 minutes. Reduce the heat to medium-low and cook until the onions are tender and golden brown, about 15 minutes. Season the onions with salt and pepper and spread evenly over the mashed vegetables. (At this point the casserole can be covered and refrigerated for up to 1 day. Add 10 minutes to the baking time.)

5. Bake, uncovered, until heated through and the top begins to crisp, about 25 minutes.

MINNESOTA POTATO HOT DISH

"Oh casserole! Oh hot dish! Oh covered-dish meal!" wrote my friend Ann Burckhardt in her delightful book *Hot Dish Heaven*. Ann and I both agree that casseroles, hot dishes, and covered-dish meals are comfort food. This recipe is one that I've had kicking around my kitchen for a long time. Over the years, I've added garlic and chopped spinach or sometimes asparagus, when in season. Almost any kind of potato is fine, but I lean toward a russet, the potato grown in the Red River Valley of Minnesota and North Dakota. I like to save the water from cooking potatoes to make Finnish rye bread.

SERVES 6

6 medium potatoes, peeled and diced

2 teaspoons butter

2 cloves garlic, minced or pressed in a garlic press

1½ teaspoons salt

1 cup buttermilk

1 package (10 ounces) frozen chopped spinach, cooked according to package directions and well drained, or 1 bag (9 or 10 ounces) fresh spinach, blanched in boiling water and drained

1 cup shredded Cheddar cheese, divided

Dash of paprika

1. Preheat the oven to 350°F. Coat a 2-quart casserole with cooking spray.

2. Cook the potatoes in boiling salted water to cover until tender, about 15 minutes and drain. Transfer to a large bowl.

3. Meanwhile, as the potatoes cook, melt the butter in a small pan over medium heat and sauté the garlic until softened, about 5 minutes. Stir into the potatoes, and add the salt and buttermilk. Using a potato masher, mash the potatoes until almost smooth.

Add the spinach and ¾ cup of the cheese to the mashed potatoes and transfer to the prepared dish.

4. Sprinkle the potatoes and spinach with the remaining ¼ cup cheese and then with a dash of paprika. (At this point you can cover and refrigerate for up to 1 day. Add 10 minutes to the baking time.)

5. Bake, uncovered, for 15 to 20 minutes, until heated through.

MUSHROOM AND ONION CASSEROLE

Asiago cheese is a semi-firm Italian cheese with a rich, nutty flavor, which complements the mushrooms, onions, and peppers in this dish. If you cannot find Asiago in your market, you can substitute grated Parmesan cheese.

SERVES 4

1 tablespoon butter, divided

2 medium sweet onions, chopped

1 green bell pepper, seeded and chopped

¼ pound mushrooms, sliced

3 large eggs, lightly beaten

1 cup fine dry breadcrumbs

1 teaspoon dried basil

1½ cups shredded or grated Asiago cheese

1. Preheat the oven to 350°F. Coat a shallow 1½-quart casserole with about 1 teaspoon of the butter.

2. In a nonstick skillet over medium-high heat, melt the remaining butter and add the onions, pepper, and mushrooms. Sauté, turning and stirring the vegetables, for 5 to 8 minutes, until all of the vegetables are cooked.

3. Remove from the heat and add the eggs, breadcrumbs, and basil. Transfer to the casserole and top with the cheese.

4. Bake for 35 to 40 minutes, until the casserole is set.

MUSHROOM AND GREEN BEAN CASSEROLE

Most mushroom and green bean casseroles are made with canned soup. In this recipe the soup is replaced with a freshly made cream sauce, which we think is a big improvement.

SERVES 6

3 tablespoons butter

½ cup diced onions

½ cup sliced mushrooms

2 cups green beans, cut into 2-inch lengths

1½ cups light sour cream

2 tablespoons all-purpose flour

1 teaspoon seasoned salt

1 cup grated Cheddar cheese

1. Preheat the oven to 350°F. Coat a 1½- to 2-quart casserole with cooking spray.

2. Melt the butter in a skillet over medium-high heat. Add the onions and mushrooms and sauté for 4 to 5 minutes, until soft but not browned.

3. Cook the green beans in boiling salted water to cover for 10 minutes, or until crisp-tender. Drain and transfer to the casserole dish. Add the onions and mushrooms.

4. Stir the sour cream, flour, and seasoned salt together in a small bowl and pour over the beans. (At this point you can cover and refrigerate the casserole for up to 1 day. Add 10 minutes to the baking time or bake until heated through.)

5. Bake, uncovered, for 20 minutes. Top the casserole with the Cheddar and bake for 10 minutes longer, or until the casserole is hot and the cheese is melted.

SCALLOPED MUSHROOMS AND POTATOES

Mushrooms add moisture and a lot of flavor to these scalloped potatoes. When wild mushrooms are in season (it's a short one in Minnesota!), I add chanterelles, morels, and whatever else we can forage to replace the usual white button mushrooms from the market. When we have fresh sage growing in our herb garden, I add some to the casserole. The rest of the year, I use the dried leaves that I've harvested in the fall.

SERVES 6

6 medium potatoes, peeled and thinly sliced

½ pound mushrooms, sliced

2 tablespoons all-purpose flour

1 tablespoon chopped fresh sage, or 1 teaspoon dried sage, crumbled

1 teaspoon salt

½ teaspoon pepper

2 cups milk

⅓ cup shredded Swiss cheese

1. Preheat the oven to 350°F. Coat a shallow 2½-quart casserole with cooking spray.

2. Spread a layer of half the potatoes in the casserole and top with a layer of half the mushrooms. Sprinkle with half the flour, half the sage, half the salt and half the pepper. Top with remaining potatoes and remaining mushrooms. Sprinkle with remaining flour, sage, salt and pepper.

3. Pour the milk over all, cover, and bake for 45 minutes. Uncover and bake for 15 minutes longer. Sprinkle with the Swiss cheese and bake for 15 minutes more, until the potatoes are tender and the top is lightly browned.

PARMESAN SCALLOPED POTATOES

Potato peels contain important minerals and fiber. So, if you wish, you can scrub the potatoes well, and slice and cook them with the peels on. Either russets or thin-skinned red or white potatoes work well.

SERVES 4

4 large potatoes, thinly sliced

1 medium onion, thinly sliced

2 tablespoons all-purpose flour

2 tablespoons grated Parmesan cheese

Salt

Pepper

2 tablespoons butter

1¾ cups hot milk

1. Preheat the oven to 375°F. Coat a 1½-quart casserole with cooking spray.

2. Layer half of the potatoes in the casserole and cover with all of the onion. Sprinkle with 1 tablespoon of the flour, all of the Parmesan cheese, and some salt and pepper. Dot with 1 tablespoon of the butter. Cover with the remaining potatoes and dot with the remaining tablespoon butter.

3. Pour enough hot milk over to almost cover the potatoes. Cover and bake for 45 minutes. Uncover and bake for 15 minutes longer, or until the potatoes are tender and the top is golden.

PARSNIP AND POTATO CASSEROLE

The sweet taste of parsnips and the smooth texture of potatoes blend here to make a perfect side dish for roasted or baked chicken, beef, or pork.

SERVES 6

2 parsnips, shredded (about 3 cups)

2 large potatoes, peeled and shredded (about 3 cups)

2 green onions, minced (white and green parts)

1 teaspoon kosher salt

2 cups half-and-half

½ cup grated Parmesan cheese

1. Preheat the oven to 375°F. Butter a shallow 1½-quart casserole.

2. In a large bowl, mix the parsnips, potatoes, green onions, and salt. Transfer to the casserole and pat down with a spoon until smooth. Pour the half-and-half over all.

3. Bake for 1 hour, covered. Uncover and spread the Parmesan cheese over the top. Bake for an additional 15 minutes until bubbly and browned around the edges.

POLENTA AND ROASTED VEGETABLE CASSEROLE

Polenta creates a bottom crust for this casserole. The filling is a Mediterranean-inspired combination of roasted eggplant, bell peppers, onions, mushrooms, and plenty of garlic.

— MAKES 8 SERVINGS —

2 cups eggplant, cut into 2-inch cubes

1 yellow bell pepper, seeded and diced

4 medium zucchini, cut into 1½-inch lengths

1 sweet onion, quartered

8 mushrooms

6 cloves garlic, peeled

2 tablespoons olive oil

½ teaspoon salt

¼ teaspoon pepper

FOR THE POLENTA:

4 cups milk

1 cup hot water

1 teaspoon salt

¼ teaspoon pepper

1½ cups cornmeal

1 cup grated Parmesan cheese, divided

⅓ cup fresh basil leaves, chopped

¼ cup heavy cream

1. Preheat the oven to 400°F.

2. In a large bowl, mix the eggplant, bell pepper, zucchini, onion, mushrooms, garlic, oil, ½ teaspoon salt, and ¼ teaspoon pepper. Spread out in a single layer in a roasting pan.

3. Roast for 20 to 25 minutes, until the vegetables are tender, stirring halfway through the roasting time.

4. *To prepare the polenta:* In a large saucepan, combine the milk, water, salt, and pepper. Bring to a simmer over medium-high heat, whisk in the cornmeal, lower the heat, and simmer, stirring, until thick and smooth, about 3 minutes. If too thick, add a little more hot water. Stir in ½ cup of the Parmesan and the basil.

5. Spread out the polenta in a buttered 9-by-13-inch baking dish and arrange the roasted vegetables over the top evenly. (At this point you can cover and refrigerate the casserole for 4 or 5 hours before continuing with step 6. Add 5 to 10 minutes to the baking time.)

6. Drizzle the cream on top of the vegetables and sprinkle with the remaining ½ cup Parmesan cheese. Return to the oven and bake until the cheese is melted and the vegetables are hot, about 20 minutes. Let cool slightly before cutting.

PROVENÇAL TOMATO CASSEROLE

This casserole is best in summer, when the tomatoes ripen on the vine. But the herbs and the drizzle of balsamic vinegar perk up winter tomatoes, too, and we enjoy the casserole then, as well. If you like, assemble it ahead of time, and bake it at the last minute.

SERVES 6

6 medium tomatoes

1½ cups fresh breadcrumbs (see Note)

¼ cup minced green onions (white and green parts)

¼ cup minced fresh basil, or 2 tablespoons dried

2 tablespoons minced fresh parsley

2 teaspoons minced garlic

1 teaspoon chopped fresh thyme, or ½ teaspoon dried

1 teaspoon coarse kosher salt

2 tablespoons balsamic vinegar

½ cup shredded Gruyère cheese

2 to 3 tablespoons olive oil

1. Preheat the oven to 400°F. Coat a shallow 3-quart casserole with cooking spray.

2. Cut the tomatoes into 4 slices each and overlap the slices in the casserole to cover the bottom of the dish.

3. In a small bowl, mix the breadcrumbs, green onions, basil, parsley, garlic, thyme, and salt and sprinkle the mixture evenly over the tomatoes. Drizzle with the balsamic vinegar and sprinkle with the cheese. Drizzle with olive oil. (At this point the casserole can be covered and held at room temperature for up to 2 hours, or refrigerated overnight. If chilled, add 10 minutes to the baking time.)

4. Bake for 15 to 20 minutes, until the crumbs are crisp. Serve warm.

○ ○ ○ ○ ○

NOTE: To make fresh breadcrumbs, tear 1 or 2 slices of fresh bread into pieces and put in a food processor with the steel blade in place. Process with on/off pulses until the bread is broken down into crumbs.

RATATOUILLE

Many years ago, I started making this classic summertime dish in the oven rather than on the stove top because it was so much easier. The flavors meld and improve when prepared a day before serving.

SERVES 6

6 tablespoons olive oil, divided

2 small white onions, sliced

1 clove garlic, minced

1 medium eggplant (leave skin on), cut into 1-inch cubes

2 medium zucchini, cut into 1-inch slices

4 small fresh tomatoes, peeled and quartered, or 1 can (14½ ounces) diced tomatoes with their juice

1 teaspoon dried basil

Salt

Quartered mushrooms for garnish

Chopped fresh parsley for garnish

1. Preheat the oven to 400°F.

2. In a nonstick skillet, heat 3 tablespoons of the oil over medium-high heat. Add the onions and garlic and sauté until the onions are tender but not browned, about 5 minutes.

3. In a 3-quart casserole, mix the onion mixture, egg-plant, zucchini, and tomatoes. Sprinkle with the basil and drizzle with the remaining 3 tablespoons oil.

4. Bake, covered, for 2 hours, or until the eggplant is very soft, stirring twice during baking. Season with salt to taste. If the vegetables have too much liquid, pour off some into a skillet. Boil until reduced to a syrupy sauce, and pour over the vegetables in the casserole. (At this point you can cover and refrigerate for 1 day. Preheat the oven to 300°F and reheat the casserole before proceeding with step 5.)

5. Garnish with quartered tomatoes, mushrooms, and parsley. Serve hot or at room temperature.

ROASTED SWEET ONIONS WITH HERBS AND GRUYÈRE

It seems there is always one variety of sweet onion or another in the market. In addition to Vidalia onions, which are fairly common, there are Maui, Walla Walla, Oso Sweet, and Rio Sweet onions. They share in common their large size and mild flavor. Baked this way, any of these varieties would make a wonderful side dish.

———————————————— SERVES 8 ————————————————

4 large sweet onions (about 3½ pounds total), peeled and halved crosswise

2 teaspoons olive oil

1 teaspoon coarsely ground pepper

⅔ cup homemade (page 26) or prepared beef broth

2 teaspoons soy sauce

1 teaspoon rubbed dried sage

½ cup shredded Gruyère cheese

1. Preheat the oven to 400°F. Coat a 9-by-13-inch baking dish with cooking spray.

2. Arrange onions, cut sides up, in a single layer in the baking dish and brush the tops with the oil; sprinkle with pepper. Bake, uncovered, for 40 minutes.

3. Mix the broth and soy sauce and pour over the onions evenly. Bake for another hour, basting every 15 minutes. Sprinkle the sage and cheese evenly over the onions. Return to the oven for 5 minutes, or until the cheese melts.

RUTABAGA CASSEROLE WITH RYE CRUMB TOPPING

This classic Finnish dish is traditionally served on the Christmas table. The rye crumb topping is an old-fashioned preparation.

1 large rutabaga (about 2 pounds)

½ cup heavy cream

½ cup fine dry breadcrumbs

2 large eggs

¼ cup dark corn syrup

¼ teaspoon ground nutmeg

FOR THE RYE CRUMB TOPPING:

½ cup dark rye flour or rye meal

1 tablespoon butter

½ teaspoon salt

1. Preheat the oven to 350°F. Butter a shallow 2-quart casserole.

2. Peel the rutabaga and cut into 1-inch cubes. Cook in boiling salted water to cover for 30 minutes, or until soft. Meanwhile, mix the heavy cream and breadcrumbs in a large bowl.

3. When the rutabaga cubes are tender, drain and mash them. (You can puree them in the food processor if desired.) Add the mashed rutabaga to the cream and crumb mixture in the bowl. Blend in the eggs, corn syrup, and nutmeg.

4. *Make the rye crumb topping:* Spread out the rye flour in a large, heavy, dry skillet and place over medium heat. Stir until the flour is toasted and lightly browned, but not burned. Mix in the butter and salt and remove from the heat.

5. Sprinkle the crumb topping over the casserole and, with a spoon, make decorative indentations over the top. Bake for 45 minutes, or until browned and heated through.

SCALLOPED POTATOES WITH BELL PEPPERS AND CARROTS

The pepper and carrot add color and interest to what is otherwise a white, cheesy potato casserole. This is the sort of potato dish that transforms a simple roast chicken dinner into an appealing Sunday meal.

SERVES 4 TO 6

4 medium baking potatoes, peeled and thinly sliced

1 red bell pepper, seeded and sliced

1 carrot, peeled and shredded

1 medium onion, chopped

2 tablespoons butter

2 tablespoons all-purpose flour

2 cups milk

1 teaspoon salt

½ teaspoon pepper

½ cup shredded Swiss or Jarlsberg cheese

Chopped fresh parsley for garnish

1. Preheat the oven to 350°F. Coat a 2-quart casserole with cooking spray.

2. Arrange layers of the potato slices, bell pepper, carrot, and onion in the casserole. Dot with the butter and sprinkle with the flour. Pour the milk over the layers and sprinkle with the salt and pepper.

3. Cover and bake for 45 minutes. Uncover, sprinkle with the cheese, and continue baking for another 15 minutes, or until the potatoes are tender and the cheese is melted. Sprinkle with the parsley.

SHREDDED POTATO CASSEROLE

Bake this simple casserole alongside a roast or meat loaf for a homey and satisfying meal. While you've got the shredder out, peel and shred some carrots, too, and dress them with a few chopped green onions, chile oil, and the juice of a lime.

SERVES 6

2 large eggs, lightly beaten

1 cup milk

2 tablespoons all-purpose flour

1 teaspoon salt

6 large potatoes, peeled and shredded

2 tablespoons butter

Chopped fresh parsley or dill for garnish

1. Preheat the oven to 375°F. Coat a 1½-quart casserole with cooking spray.

2. In a large bowl, mix the eggs, milk, flour, salt, and potatoes. Pour the mixture into the prepared casserole dish, and dot the top with butter.

3. Bake for 45 to 50 minutes, until the potatoes are tender and the casserole is set. Serve hot, garnished with fresh herbs.

SPINACH AND ARTICHOKE CASSEROLE

Even children like this creamy spinach casserole, so it is perfect for a family holiday buffet. For a summer meal, poach boneless chicken breasts in dry white wine, season, and serve at room temperature on a bed of lettuce with a sour cream and herb dressing and this casserole.

———— SERVES 8 ————

2 packages (10 ounces) frozen chopped spinach

1 package (8 ounces) light cream cheese

½ cup (1 stick) plus 3 tablespoons butter

1 teaspoon fresh lemon juice

½ teaspoon salt

¼ teaspoon pepper

1 can (14 ounces) quartered artichoke hearts

⅓ cup fine dry breadcrumbs

1 cup halved cherry tomatoes for garnish

Sprigs of fresh herbs, such as rosemary or thyme, for garnish

1. Preheat the oven to 350°F. Coat a shallow 2-quart casserole with cooking spray.

2. Cook the spinach according to package directions, drain, and press out any excess moisture.

3. In a saucepan, heat the cream cheese and ½ cup of the butter, stirring until blended. Add the spinach, lemon juice, salt, and pepper and mix well.

4. Drain the artichoke hearts, rinse, and drain again. Arrange in the bottom of the baking pan in an even layer, and spread the spinach over the artichokes evenly.

5. Melt the remaining 3 tablespoons butter in a small saucepan and mix with the breadcrumbs. Sprinkle over the top of the casserole. (At this point you can cover and refrigerate for up to 1 day. Add 5 to 10 more minutes to the baking time.)

6. Bake for 20 to 30 minutes, until the crumbs are lightly browned and the casserole is heated through. Garnish with cherry tomatoes and sprigs of fresh herbs before serving.

SPINACH AND THREE-CHEESE GRATIN

Ricotta, Swiss, and Parmesan cheeses add creaminess and protein to this mixture of onions, spinach, and peppers. This makes a wonderful main dish for a light lunch or supper.

SERVES 8

1½ pounds baby spinach leaves

¼ cup water

3 red bell peppers, stemmed, seeded, and cut into 4 large pieces each

3 tablespoons olive oil

1 large sweet onion, thinly sliced

1 large shallot, chopped

3 cloves garlic, minced

1 cup heavy cream

4 large eggs

1 cup part-skim ricotta cheese

½ cup shredded Swiss cheese

¼ cup grated Parmesan cheese

1½ teaspoons salt

½ teaspoon freshly ground pepper

¼ teaspoon grated nutmeg

1. Preheat the broiler. Line a large rimmed baking sheet with aluminum foil and coat with cooking spray. Coat a shallow 3-quart casserole or a 9-by-13-inch baking dish with cooking spray and set aside.

2. In a large, deep nonstick skillet over medium-high heat, steam the spinach in the water in about 4 batches until wilted, about 2 minutes per batch. Squeeze the cooked spinach dry.

3. Toss the red peppers in a bowl with 1 tablespoon of the olive oil. Place the peppers in a single layer on the foil-covered baking sheet with the skin sides up. Broil until the peppers have dark brown spots on them, 7 to 10 minutes.

4. Remove the peppers from the broiler and wrap some of the foil around them to make a packet. Let cool for 10 minutes. Peel and cut the peppers into ¼-inch-wide strips.

5. Turn off the broiler and pre-heat the oven to 350°F.

6. Heat the remaining 2 table-spoons oil in the large nonstick skillet over medium heat and add the onion, shallot, and garlic. Cook until soft, about 5 minutes, and remove from the heat.

7. In a large bowl, whisk the cream and eggs together. Mix in all of the cheeses, the salt, pepper and nutmeg. Add the spinach, the onion mixture, and two-thirds of the roasted peppers, reserving the remain-der for the top. (At this point you can cover and refrigerate the casserole for up to 1 day. Add about 10 minutes to the baking time.)

8. Transfer the spinach mixture to the prepared baking dish and bake until a knife inserted in the center comes out clean, about 50 to 55 minutes. Arrange the remaining roasted pepper strips over the top and serve.

FRESH SPINACH CASSEROLE

Fresh baby spinach leaves come washed and bagged, and are handy to use. This is a simple and delicious side dish for any grilled or roasted meat, fish, or poultry.

SERVES 6

2 bags (about 9 ounces each) fresh spinach leaves

6 ounces light cream cheese, softened (see Note)

¼ cup skim milk

1 teaspoon fresh lemon juice

½ teaspoon grated lemon zest

Salt

Pepper

1. Preheat the oven to 350°F. Coat a shallow 1-quart casserole with cooking spray.

2. Put the spinach in a large colander and pour boiling water over it until wilted. Squeeze the spinach to remove excess moisture and chop coarsely. Transfer to a large bowl.

3. Mix in the cream cheese, milk, lemon juice, and lemon zest. Season with salt and pepper to taste and spoon into the casserole. Bake for 25 to 30 minutes, or until bubbly and the cheese is melted.

○ ○ ○ ○ ○

NOTE: To soften cream cheese, remove from the foil wrapper and place on a microwave-safe dish. Microwave for 10 seconds at high power.

SUMMER SQUASH WITH BASIL AND PARMESAN

Depending on what you have on hand (or in the garden), you can make this casserole with all zucchini or all yellow summer squash or a combination. Sometimes we like to brown sausages on the grill and serve them with this casserole.

SERVES 6

2 tablespoons plus 1 teaspoon olive oil, divided

3 medium zucchini, diced (3 cups)

3 medium yellow summer squash, diced (3 cups)

1 large sweet onion, sliced

2 tablespoons chopped fresh basil

1 teaspoon salt

⅓ cup grated Parmesan cheese

2 tablespoons pine nuts

1. Preheat the oven to 350°F. Coat a 2-quart casserole with cooking spray.

2. In a large nonstick skillet, heat 1 teaspoon of the oil and add the zucchini and yellow squash. Cook over medium-low heat for about 15 to 20 minutes, until the vegetables are soft. Transfer to a colander and drain off the liquid. Transfer to a large bowl.

3. Heat the remaining 2 tablespoons oil in the skillet and add the onion. Sauté for 5 minutes, until soft. Remove from the pan and add to the squash. Stir in the basil, salt, and cheese. Spread out the mixture in the casserole and sprinkle with pine nuts. (At this point, you can cover and refrigerate overnight. Add 5 or 10 minutes to the baking time.)

4. Bake for 25 to 30 minutes, until bubbly.

SWEET POTATO PUDDING

Shredded sweet potatoes are the basis for this perfect casserole for a holiday meal. This is especially good with a roasted turkey.

4 tablespoon butter, melted, plus extra for the dish

2 large eggs, beaten

1 cup firmly packed light or dark brown sugar

1 cup milk

½ teaspoon grated lemon zest

2 teaspoons fresh lemon juice

½ teaspoon ground cinnamon

¼ teaspoon ground nutmeg

2 cups shredded raw sweet potatoes (see Note)

1. Preheat the oven to 350°F. Butter a 1½-quart casserole.

2. In a large bowl, combine the eggs and brown sugar and stir until well mixed. Add the milk, the 4 tablespoons butter, the lemon zest, lemon juice, cinnamon, and nutmeg and mix well. Add the potatoes and blend well.

3. Transfer the mixture to the casserole dish and bake for 30 minutes. Remove from the oven and stir. Return to the oven and bake for 30 minutes longer.

○ ○ ○ ○ ○

NOTE: To keep the sweet potatoes from discoloring, rinse them in cold water and drain as soon as they are shredded. They will then keep, covered and refrigerated, for up to 1 day without discoloring.

TOMATO AND POTATO GRATIN

When tomatoes are in season during the summer, I always use fresh ones in this casserole. In the winter I use canned tomatoes because they have more flavor than the hothouse tomatoes at the market.

SERVES 4

3 tablespoons olive oil

2 onions, thinly sliced crosswise

1 cup diced and drained fresh or canned tomatoes

¾ teaspoon salt, divided

¼ teaspoon dried rosemary, crushed, divided

¼ teaspoon dried thyme, divided

¼ teaspoon pepper, divided

¼ cup grated Parmesan cheese

1½ pounds baking potatoes, peeled and cut into ⅛-inch-thick slices

1. Preheat the oven to 450°F. Coat a 2-quart shallow casserole dish with cooking spray.

2. In a large nonstick skillet, heat 2 tablespoons of the oil over medium-low heat. Add the onions and cook, stirring occasionally, until translucent, about 5 minutes. Remove from the heat and stir in the tomatoes. Add ¼ teaspoon of the salt, ⅛ teaspoon of the rosemary, ⅛ teaspoon of the thyme, and ⅛ teaspoon of the pepper.

3. In a small dish, mix in the remaining ½ teaspoon salt and the remaining ⅛ teaspoon rosemary, ⅛ teaspoon thyme, and ⅛ teaspoon pepper with the Parmesan cheese.

4. Spread out half the tomato and onion mixture in the casserole dish and layer half the potatoes on top. Sprinkle with half the Parmesan mixture. Repeat the layers with the remaining tomatoes and onions, potatoes, and Parmesan mixture. Cover with foil and bake for 30 to 40 minutes, just until the potatoes are tender.

WALNUT AND BROCCOLI CASSEROLE

Walnuts and broccoli have a natural affinity for one another. Here walnuts add a nice bit of texture as well as flavor to the casserole.

SERVES 6

2 packages (10 ounces each) frozen broccoli spears, cooked according to package directions and drained

½ teaspoon salt

¼ teaspoon pepper

1 cup Basic White Sauce (page 18), or 1 can (10¾ ounces) cream of chicken or cream of mushroom soup

⅔ cup hot water

4 tablespoons butter, melted

2 cups herb-flavored stuffing mix

⅔ cup chopped walnuts

1. Preheat the oven to 400°F. Coat a shallow 2-quart casserole with cooking spray. Arrange the cooked broccoli in the dish in a single layer. Sprinkle with the salt and pepper.

2. Prepare the white sauce and pour over the broccoli (or if you're short of time, use the soup).

3. Mix the water and melted butter. Put the stuffing mix in a large bowl and pour the butter and water over the stuffing. Stir until evenly moistened. Spread the stuffing over the top of the broccoli and sauce and sprinkle with the walnuts. Bake for 20 minutes, or until bubbly.

POTATO, MUSHROOM, AND ARTICHOKE CASSEROLE

Serve this hearty side dish with grilled or roasted pork or lamb. If you slice the potatoes in advance, hold them in cold water to cover to prevent discoloration, but drain well before you add them to the casserole.

SERVES 8

2 pounds Yukon Gold potatoes, thinly sliced, rinsed, and drained

1 can (14 ounces) quartered artichoke hearts, drained

4 large portobello mushroom caps, thinly sliced

6 ounces fresh goat cheese

3 cloves garlic, minced

1 teaspoon salt

½ teaspoon pepper

3 tablespoons grated Parmesan cheese

3 tablespoons olive oil

½ cup dry white wine

1. Preheat the oven to 425°F. Coat a 9-by-13-inch baking dish with cooking spray.

2. Arrange half of the potatoes in the baking dish, covering the bottom completely. Top with half of the artichoke hearts, and then half of the mushrooms. Coarsely crumble half of the goat cheese over the vegetables. Sprinkle with half of the garlic, ½ teaspoon salt, ¼ teaspoon pepper, and then 1 tablespoon Parmesan. Drizzle with 1 tablespoon oil. Cover with the remaining mushrooms, then artichokes, goat cheese, garlic, ½ teaspoon salt, and ¼ teaspoon pepper. Sprinkle with 1 tablespoon of the remaining Parmesan, and 1 tablespoon of the remaining oil. Top with the remaining potatoes. Pour the wine over all and drizzle with the remaining 1 tablespoon oil.

3. Cover the dish with foil and bake for 40 minutes. Reduce the oven temperature to 400°F. Sprinkle the top of the casserole with the remaining 1 tablespoon Parmesan. Bake, uncovered, until the potatoes are tender and the top is brown, about 25 minutes more.

Chapter 13
VEGETARIAN CASSEROLES

—○○○○○—

This chapter is devoted to meatless main dishes, which are heartier than the vegetable casseroles in the preceding chapter. Many are loaded with rice and beans in addition to vegetables. A crisp green salad and bread are usually all you will need to round out the meal.

AUTUMN VEGETABLE CASSEROLE STEW

A savory blend of green and root vegetables gives this classic Armenian casserole a juicy sweetness. It's great served either hot or at room temperature. Just add a crusty bread to make a light and satisfying lunch or supper. You will spend some time cutting and chopping, but then it goes together so easily!

— SERVES 8 —

1 can (14½ ounces) diced tomatoes with basil and garlic, with their juice

¼ cup olive oil

½ cup tomato ketchup

1½ teaspoons salt

1½ teaspoons sugar

1½ teaspoons dried basil

¼ teaspoon pepper

½ pound green beans, trimmed and cut into 1½-inch lengths

2 large thin-skinned potatoes, peeled and cut into 1-inch pieces

3 medium carrots, peeled and cut on the diagonal into ¾-inch pieces

2 large onions, cut into 1-inch chunks

2 stalks celery, cut into ½-inch pieces

2 large red or yellow bell peppers, seeded and cut into 1-inch squares

1 medium eggplant, cut into 1-inch cubes

3 small zucchini, cut into 1½-inch chunks

Yogurt for serving

1. Preheat the oven to 350°F.

2. In a medium bowl, mix the tomatoes with their juice, olive oil, ketchup, salt, sugar, basil, and pepper.

3. In a 6-quart casserole, combine the beans, potatoes, carrots, onions, celery, bell peppers, and eggplant. Pour the tomato mixture over the vegetables.

4. Cover and bake for 1½ hours, basting the vegetables with their juices every 30 minutes.

5. Mix the zucchini into the casserole and bake, uncovered, for an additional 25 minutes, or until the potatoes are tender.

6. Serve hot or at room temperature, topped with yogurt.

WINTER VEGETABLE COBBLER

Most people associate a cobbler with dessert, but vegetables bathed in sauce and crowned with a cobbler topping are delicious. This one is a classic.

SERVES 6

2 cups sliced carrots

1 cup sliced parsnips

2 cups baby red potatoes, scrubbed and quartered

1 large sweet onion, cut into 1-inch dice

½ cup chopped fresh parsley

1 cup homemade (page 27) or prepared vegetable broth

1 tablespoon cornstarch

1 teaspoon salt

Pepper

½ cup (1 stick) cold butter, cut into pieces

FOR THE COBBLER TOPPING:

2 cups all-purpose flour

4 teaspoons baking powder

½ teaspoon salt

½ cup (1 stick) cold butter, cut into pieces

¾ cup milk

1. Preheat the oven to 325°F.

2. Combine the carrots, parsnips, potatoes, and onion in a large saucepan. Bring to a boil and cook for 20 to 25 minutes until the vegetables are tender. Drain and mix with the parsley in a 9-by-13-inch baking dish.

3. In a small bowl, mix the vegetable broth and cornstarch and pour over the vegetables in the casserole; mix well. Sprinkle with the 1 teaspoon salt and pepper to taste. Dot the vegetables with the butter.

4. *Prepare the cobbler topping:* In a large bowl, combine the flour, baking powder, and ½ teaspoon salt. Add the butter and cut in with a pastry blender until the mixture resembles coarse crumbs. Alternatively, combine the dry ingredients in a food processor with the steel blade in place, add the butter, and pulse. Transfer the mixture to a large bowl if you used a food processor. Slowly stir in the milk with a fork. Gather the dough into a mass and knead 5 or 6 times to form a ball. Roll out on a lightly floured work surface so it is the size of the top of the baking dish. The dough will be about ⅓ inch thick.

5. Place the dough on top of the vegetables, but do not crimp the edges. (It's okay if the topping shrinks away from the edges of the casserole while baking.) Bake for 45 to 55 minutes, or until the crust is browned and the filling is bubbly.

BAKED ANCHO MEXICAN BEANS

This quick and easy casserole is made with canned beans. It's perfect to take to a potluck or to serve alongside cheese enchiladas.

SERVES 6

1 can (about 15 ounces) pinto beans, rinsed and drained

1 can (about 15 ounces) kidney beans, rinsed and drained

1 teaspoon salt (optional)

1 large onion, chopped

1 large clove garlic, chopped

3 tablespoons chopped canned green chiles

½ teaspoon dry mustard

1 teaspoon ancho chile powder

1 tablespoon molasses

2 tablespoons cider vinegar

½ cup tomato puree

1. Preheat the oven to 300°F. Coat a 1½-quart casserole with cooking spray.

2. Combine all of the ingredients in the casserole, cover, and bake for 30 minutes. Uncover and bake for 20 minutes longer, or until the casserole is bubbly.

BAKED PENNE WITH FOUR CHEESES

This is a simple meatless casserole. If you see a really busy week coming up on your calendar, make this in advance and freeze it.

SERVES 4

2 cups milk

1 teaspoon dried basil

½ teaspoon red pepper flakes

1¼ cups shredded provolone cheese

1¼ cups shredded mozzarella cheese

1¼ cups shredded Swiss cheese

6 tablespoons grated Parmesan cheese, divided

Salt

Pepper

2 large egg yolks, beaten

½ pound penne or another tube-shaped pasta, freshly cooked and drained

1. Preheat the oven to 375°F. Butter a 2-quart casserole.

2. In a large saucepan, heat the milk, basil, and red pepper to a simmer. Toss the provolone, mozzarella, Swiss, and 4 tablespoons of the Parmesan cheese together in a medium bowl. Add to the milk, a handful at a time, stirring after each addition. Continue stirring until the cheese is melted.

3. Season with salt and pepper and mix in the pasta. Turn into the casserole and sprinkle with the remaining 2 tablespoons Parmesan cheese.

4. Bake for 20 minutes, or until heated through. (At this point you can cool completely, cover, and refrigerate for up to 1 day. Or wrap well and freeze for up to 2 weeks. If refrigerated, reheat for an additional 10 minutes. If frozen, thaw overnight in the refrigerator and reheat for 35 to 40 minutes.)

BLACK BEAN AND RED PEPPER CASSEROLE

This hearty casserole is a great main-dish choice for a buffet.
You can assemble it in advance and bake it later—at your house
or at a friend's potluck.

SERVES 8 TO 10

1 small onion, chopped

2 cloves garlic, minced

1 large red bell pepper, seeded
and chopped

1 tablespoon olive oil

1 can (14½ ounces) diced tomatoes
with their juice

1 cup tomato salsa (mild, medium,
or hot)

1 teaspoon ground cumin

1 can (15 ounces) black beans,
rinsed and drained

1 can (7 ounces) corn kernels,
rinsed and drained

6 corn tortillas (8 inches)

1 cup shredded Monterey Jack
cheese, divided

2 cups shredded Pepper Jack
cheese, divided

1. Preheat the oven to 350°F.
Coat a 9-by-13-inch baking
dish with cooking spray.

2. In a large nonstick skillet
over medium heat, sauté the
onion, garlic, and bell pepper in
the oil, stirring, for 3 minutes.
Add the tomatoes with their
juice, salsa, cumin, beans, and
corn and bring to a simmer.
Continue simmering for 5 minutes, until the liquid is reduced
by half.

3. Spread a thin layer of the
bean mixture in the bottom
of the casserole. Top with a
layer of overlapping tortillas,
and sprinkle with half of the
Monterey Jack and half of the
Pepper Jack. Spread a thicker
layer of the bean mixture. Cut

the remaining tortillas into
1-inch strips and scatter them
on top. Spread with the remaining bean mixture. Coat a sheet
of aluminum foil with cooking
spray and cover the casserole.
(At this point you can cover and
refrigerate the casserole for up
to 1 day. Add 10 minutes to the
baking time.)

4. Bake the casserole, covered,
for 25 minutes. Remove the foil
and sprinkle with the remaining Pepper Jack and Monterey
Jack. Bake for about 15 minutes, until the cheese is melted
and bubbly. If you like, place
the casserole under the boiler
for a few minutes to brown the
cheese. Let stand for 10 minutes before serving.

BROWN RICE AND SPINACH CASSEROLE

This makes a hearty vegetarian casserole with a grainy, chewy texture. Add a platter of assorted melon spears sprinkled with black pepper and hot cornbread muffins for a colorful and healthy lunch or supper.

SERVES 6

3 tablespoons butter, plus extra for the dish

2 cups water

½ teaspoon salt

1 cup long-grain brown rice

1 cup chopped onion

2 cloves garlic, minced

1½ pounds regular or baby spinach, trimmed (if regular) and chopped

4 large eggs, beaten

1 cup milk

1½ cups shredded sharp Cheddar cheese

¼ cup chopped fresh parsley

1½ teaspoons salt

½ teaspoon pepper

¼ teaspoon cayenne pepper

¼ cup sunflower seeds

Paprika for sprinkling

1. Preheat the oven to 350°F. Butter a shallow 2-quart casserole.

2. In a medium saucepan, bring the water and salt to a boil and stir in the rice. Return to a boil, cover, and reduce the heat to low. Simmer the rice for 35 to 40 minutes, or until the rice is tender and the liquid is absorbed.

3. In a large skillet, melt the 3 tablespoons butter over medium heat and add the onion and garlic. Sauté for about 5 minutes, or until tender. Add the spinach, a few handfuls at a time, to the onion mixture and cook over medium heat until the spinach is wilted, 3 to 5 minutes.

4. In a large bowl, thoroughly combine the cooked rice, onion and spinach mixture, eggs, milk, cheese, parsley, salt, pepper, and cayenne. Transfer to the casserole and sprinkle with the sunflower seeds and paprika. Bake, uncovered, for 35 minutes, or until the casserole is set.

CARROT AND WILD RICE CUSTARD

Wild rice adds a chewiness and wholesome flavor to this recipe. Like many casseroles, this can be assembled a day ahead, and baked along with other food. The oven temperature is flexible, too. If you have something else (like a cake or dessert) baking at 350°F, just add this to the oven and check it for doneness at 45 minutes. Or, if you're baking biscuits at 400 or 425°F, bake this right along with them and check for doneness in 25 to 30 minutes. Add a plate of arugula, dressed with a bit of olive oil and vinegar, and serve a good red wine.

MAKES 6 SERVINGS

3 tablespoons butter, plus extra for the dish

1 cup cooked wild rice or brown rice

1 cup milk

5 large carrots, peeled and finely shredded

1 teaspoon salt

1 tablespoon dark brown sugar

2 large eggs

½ cup fine dry breadcrumbs

1. Preheat the oven to 375°F. Butter a shallow 1½-quart casserole.

2. In a large bowl, mix the rice, milk, carrots, salt, sugar, and eggs. Transfer the mixture to the casserole.

3. In a small skillet, melt the 3 tablespoons butter and mix in the breadcrumbs until the crumbs are completely coated. Sprinkle over the top of the casserole. Bake for 40 to 45 minutes, or until set and the top is lightly browned.

CAULIFLOWER MAC AND CHEESE CASSEROLE

We have grandchildren who are fussy eaters. But they love this casserole because I told them that cauliflower is nature's pasta. After all, it's white.

SERVES 6

1 large head cauliflower (about 2 pounds), cut into small florets

1 cup heavy cream

1 package (8 ounces) cream cheese, cut into small pieces

1½ teaspoons Dijon mustard

1½ cups shredded sharp Cheddar cheese, divided

½ teaspoon kosher salt

¼ teaspoon pepper

⅛ teaspoon garlic powder

1. Preheat the oven to 375°F. Coat a 2½-quart casserole with cooking spray.

2. Cook the cauliflower florets in boiling salted water until crisp-tender, about 5 minutes. Drain well and pat between several layers of paper towels to dry. Transfer the cauliflower to the baking dish and set aside.

3. Bring the cream to a simmer in a small saucepan, and whisk in the cream cheese and mustard until smooth. Stir in 1 cup of the cheese, the salt, pepper, and garlic powder, and whisk just until the cheese melts, about 1 to 2 minutes. Remove from the heat, pour over the cauliflower, and stir to combine. Top with the remaining ½ cup cheese and bake until browned and bubbly hot, about 15 minutes. Serve.

CHICKPEA CASSEROLE

Chickpeas are also called "garbanzo beans" and are used extensively in Mediterranean cooking. If you wish, you can cook dried chickpeas for this dish (see page 30).

SERVES 8

2 cans (15 ounces each) chickpeas (garbanzo beans) with their liquid, or 3 cups freshly cooked chickpeas

1 can (14 ounces) unsweetened coconut milk

½ cup water

¼ cup brown basmati rice

2 tablespoons olive oil

1 cup chopped onion

2 cloves garlic, minced

1 tablespoon curry powder

1 teaspoon dry mustard

1 teaspoon ground cumin

1 teaspoon ground coriander

¼ teaspoon ground ginger

¼ teaspoon ground allspice

1 teaspoon kosher salt

1 large potato, peeled and diced

1 tart apple, such as Granny Smith, peeled and diced

½ cup minced fresh parsley

1. Preheat the oven to 350°F. Lightly oil a 2½-quart casserole.

2. Mix the chickpeas, coconut milk, water, and rice in the casserole. Set aside.

3. In a medium nonstick skillet, heat the olive oil over medium heat and add the onion and garlic. Add the curry powder, mustard, cumin, coriander, ginger, allspice, and salt and sauté for 3 to 5 minutes, until the onion and garlic are softened and the spices are aromatic.

4. Transfer the onion mixture to the casserole and add the potato, apple, and parsley. Stir to blend well.

5. Bake for 1 hour, or until the potato and apple are tender.

CORNBREAD-TOPPED BLACK BEAN CASSEROLE

The mildly sweet cornbread that tops this pleasantly spiced mixture of beans and veggies makes a low-fat and satisfying meal.

SERVES 6

1 tablespoon canola oil

1 large onion, chopped

1 large clove garlic, minced

1 green bell pepper, seeded and diced

1 stalk celery, finely chopped

1 can (15 ounces) black beans, rinsed and drained

1 can (10 ounces) diced tomatoes and green chiles with their juice

2 teaspoons ground cumin

½ cup packed minced fresh cilantro

FOR THE CORNBREAD TOPPING:

1 cup yellow cornmeal

⅓ cup all-purpose flour

2 tablespoons sugar

1 teaspoon baking powder

½ teaspoon baking soda

¼ teaspoon salt

1 cup buttermilk

1 tablespoon canola oil

Sour cream for serving (optional)

Tomato salsa for serving (optional)

1. Preheat the oven to 400°F. Coat a shallow 3-quart casserole with cooking spray.

2. Heat the oil in a large non-stick skillet over medium heat, and add the onion and garlic. Saute for 2 to 3 minutes, until aromatic. Add the bell pepper and celery and sauté for another 5 minutes, stirring often. Add the beans, tomatoes and chiles with their juice, and cumin and simmer for another 5 minutes. Stir in the cilantro and spread out the mixture in the casserole dish.

3. *To make the cornbread topping:* In a large bowl, stir together the cornmeal, flour, sugar, baking powder, baking soda, and salt. Add the buttermilk and oil and stir just until the mixture is moistened. Pour over the beans and tomatoes.

4. Bake, uncovered, for 30 to 35 minutes, or until a toothpick inserted in the center of the topping comes out clean. To serve, cut into squares or wedges. Top with sour cream and salsa, if desired.

EASTER EGG HOT DISH

In order not to waste all those great hard-cooked Easter eggs, serve this with asparagus on the side for supper or lunch. For safety, though, make sure the eggs haven't been at room temperature for more than 2 hours.

SERVES 6

2 tablespoons butter

1½ cups sliced celery

1 cup chopped green bell peppers

1 medium onion, thinly sliced

1½ tablespoons flour

1 teaspoon salt

1 can (14½ ounces) diced tomatoes with their juice

¼ teaspoon Tabasco sauce

2 large eggs (uncooked)

2 cups cooked rice

6 hard-cooked eggs, peeled and chopped

½ cup shredded Cheddar cheese

1. Preheat the oven to 350°F. Coat a 2-quart casserole with cooking spray.

2. In a large nonstick skillet, melt the butter over medium heat and add the celery, bell peppers, and onion. Sauté for about 5 minutes, until the vegetables are tender. Add the flour and salt and stir until blended. Stir in the tomatoes with their juice and the Tabasco and heat to boiling. Lower the heat and simmer for 10 minutes, or until thickened. Remove from the heat and stir in the uncooked eggs.

3. Spread the cooked rice over the bottom of the casserole and top with the chopped eggs. Spread the vegetable mixture over the top.

4. Bake, uncovered, for 25 to 30 minutes, until thoroughly heated. Top with the cheese during the last 5 minutes of baking.

GREEK SPINACH AND FETA CASSEROLE

The nutty flavor of basmati rice combined with raisins, spinach, and feta makes this an outstanding vegetarian main dish. What's more, it is great reheated.

2 tablespoons olive oil

3 cups sliced onions

4 large cloves garlic, minced

2½ cups water

1 cup white or brown basmati rice

1 teaspoon salt

¼ teaspoon pepper

½ cup dark or golden raisins

½ cup slivered almonds

1 tablespoon dried dill

2 packages (10 ounces) chopped frozen spinach, thawed

1 can (14½ ounces) diced tomatoes with their juice

1½ tablespoons fresh lemon juice

2 cups crumbled feta cheese

1 medium tomato, sliced, for garnish

1. Preheat the oven to 350°F. Coat a 9-by-13-inch casserole with cooking spray.

2. In a large nonstick skillet, heat the oil over medium heat. Add the onions and garlic and sauté for 3 to 5 minutes, or until the onions are translucent. Transfer to a bowl and set aside.

3. In a medium saucepan, heat the water to boiling and add the rice, ½ teaspoon of the salt, ⅛ teaspoon of the pepper, the raisins, almonds, and dried dill. Lower the heat, cover, and simmer for 15 to 20 minutes, or until the rice has absorbed the water. Stir in half of the onion and garlic mixture and set aside.

4. In the skillet, over high heat, combine the spinach, diced tomatoes with their juice, lemon juice, and the remaining ½ teaspoon salt and ⅛ teaspoon pepper. Stir for 3 to 5 minutes, until heated thoroughly. Remove from the heat and add the cheese. Stir the remaining half of the onion and garlic mixture into the spinach mixture.

5. Spread out the rice, onion, and garlic mixture in the bottom of the casserole in an even layer. Top with the spinach mixture and arrange the fresh tomatoes over the top. Bake for 15 minutes, or until the casserole is bubbly and heated through.

HERBED ZUCCHINI AND TOMATOES

This French Provençal–style casserole is very different from its typical cheese- or egg-bound American counterpart. It combines garden-fresh vegetables, which are seasoned liberally with herbs and garlic and slow-baked in a shallow earthenware or enameled cast-iron gratin dish to concentrate their natural flavors. This is rustic, simple, and low-cal, but very tasty. It makes a delightful main dish, served with a good loaf of bread for mopping up the savory pan juices. For a side dish, try cooked white beans in a vinaigrette dressing.

MAKES 8 SERVINGS

3 tablespoons olive oil, divided

1 medium onion, thinly sliced

5 cloves garlic, finely chopped

6 medium zucchini (about 2½ pounds total), cut into ½-inch pieces

4 medium ripe, juicy tomatoes (about 1¼ pounds total), diced

¼ cup finely chopped fresh oregano

Salt

Pepper

1. Preheat the oven to 350°F.

2. Heat 1 tablespoon of the oil in a nonstick skillet over medium-high heat. Add the onion and garlic and sauté until pale gold and tender, about 5 minutes. Cool briefly.

3. In a large bowl, toss the onion mixture, zucchini, tomatoes, and oregano in large bowl. Sprinkle with salt and pepper to taste. Arrange the vegetable mixture in a shallow 2-quart casserole. Drizzle with the remaining 2 tablespoons oil.

4. Bake for 45 minutes, or until the vegetables are tender and golden brown on top. Tilt the dish several times during baking to collect the pan juices, and baste the vegetables with them.

ITALIAN STUFFED PEPPERS WITH MUSHROOMS AND RICOTTA

This makes a wonderful low-carb, meatless entrée. Or you can serve it as a side dish with pasta or a bean casserole.

SERVES 4 GENEROUSLY

4 large yellow, orange, red, or green bell peppers, or a combination

4 tablespoons olive oil, divided

1 pound mushrooms, chopped

1 teaspoon kosher salt

½ teaspoon pepper

2 tablespoons chopped fresh basil, or 2 teaspoons dried

1 tablespoon chopped fresh oregano, or 1 teaspoon dried

½ pound regular or part-skim ricotta cheese

2 teaspoons Dijon mustard

¾ cup grated Pecorino Romano, Parmesan, or Asiago cheese

1. Position a rack at the top of the oven and preheat to 500 or 550°F, depending on the capacity of your oven. If you have a convection option, choose that. Cover a rimless baking sheet with aluminum foil, and coat a shallow 9-by-13-inch baking dish with cooking spray.

2. Stem the bell peppers, remove the seeds, and cut in half lengthwise. Brush with about 1 tablespoon of the olive oil and place on the foil-covered baking sheet, cut side down. Roast the peppers until their skins are blistered and blackened in spots, about 10 minutes. Remove from the oven and wrap in the foil lining the cookie sheet. Let stand for 10 to 15 minutes until cooled. Peel away the loose skins from the peppers and rinse to remove any stray seeds. Pat dry and set aside.

3. Reduce the oven temperature to 350°F.

4. While the bell peppers are roasting, in a large nonstick skillet, cook the mushrooms in the remaining 3 tablespoons oil until soft and tender. Season with the salt, pepper, and herbs. In a medium bowl, mix the ricotta with the Dijon mustard and stir in the mushrooms.

5. Spoon an equal amount of the ricotta mixture into each pepper half.

6. Place the pepper halves (with the filling sides up) close together in the baking dish and sprinkle with the grated cheese. Bake for 20 to 25 minutes, or until heated through.

MEXICAN VEGETARIAN CASSEROLE

The corn, beans, and rice make a perfect protein here. All you need to add to this menu is a green salad.

1 can (15 ounces) corn kernels, drained

1 can (15 ounce) black beans, rinsed and drained

1 cup sour cream

1 cup tomato salsa (medium or hot)

2 cups shredded Colby and Monterey Jack cheese combined (see Note)

1 can (10 ounces) diced tomatoes and green chiles with their juice

2 cups cooked rice

¼ teaspoon pepper

1 green onion, chopped (white and green parts)

½ cup sliced black olives

2 cups shredded Monterey Jack cheese

1. Preheat the oven to 350°F. Coat a shallow 2½-quart casserole with cooking spray.

2. In a large bowl, stir together the corn, beans, sour cream, salsa, combined Colby and Jack cheeses, diced tomatoes with their juice, rice, pepper, and green onion. Spoon into the casserole evenly and sprinkle with the olives and Monterey Jack cheese.

3. Bake for 30 to 35 minutes, or until bubbly.

○ ○ ○ ○ ○

NOTE: You can buy packaged shredded Colby and Jack cheese, which is usually labeled "Co-Jack." An 8-ounce package equals 2 cups.

MOUSSAKA WITH LOTS OF VEGETABLES

Classic moussaka, a popular dish in the Middle East, usually contains beef or lamb. In this vegetarian version, the vegetables are layered and covered with a white sauce enriched with eggs and cheese.

SERVES 12

2 eggplants (about ¾ pound each), peeled, halved lengthwise, and cut into ½-inch-thick slices

1½ pounds zucchini, trimmed and cut into ¼-inch-thick rounds

1 pound red-skinned potatoes, scrubbed and cut into ¼-inch-thick rounds

1 tablespoon olive oil, plus extra for coating vegetables

Salt

Pepper

2 cups chopped sweet onions

3 cloves garlic, minced

2 teaspoons dried oregano

2 cans (14½ ounces each) diced tomatoes with herbs, with their juice

½ cup fine dry breadcrumbs, divided

2 large eggs, beaten

¼ teaspoon ground cinnamon

3 cups Basic White Sauce (page 18)

4 large tomatoes, cut into ¼-inch-thick rounds

1 package (9 ounces) frozen artichoke hearts, cooked according to package directions

2 tablespoons Parmesan cheese

1. Preheat the oven to 425°F. Cover two large baking sheets with aluminum foil and coat with cooking spray.

2. Arrange the eggplant slices and half the zucchini on one baking sheet, overlapping slightly. Arrange the remaining zucchini and the potatoes on the second baking sheet, overlapping again. Brush generously with olive oil or, if you prefer, coat with cooking spray. Sprinkle with salt and pepper.

3. Bake for about 25 minutes, or until the vegetables are tender and beginning to brown. Remove from the oven and cool. Reduce the oven temperature to 375°F.

4. Place a large nonstick skillet over medium heat and add the 1 tablespoon olive oil. Add the onions and garlic and sauté until the onions are tender, about 7 minutes. Stir in the oregano and add the tomatoes with their juice. Simmer until the mixture thickens slightly, about 15 minutes. Season with salt and pepper and remove from the heat. Mix in ¼ cup of the breadcrumbs, the eggs, cinnamon, and white sauce.

5. Coat a 9-by-13-inch baking dish with cooking spray. Sprinkle the bottom of the dish with the remaining ¼ cup breadcrumbs. Arrange the potatoes in the dish. Top with half of the sliced fresh tomatoes and the artichoke hearts. Cover with the eggplant slices and then the zucchini, and the remaining tomatoes, overlapping all of the slices slightly. Pour the white sauce mixture over all evenly and sprinkle with the Parmesan cheese.

6. Bake until golden, about 55 minutes. Let stand for 15 minutes before serving.

QUICK MEATLESS SPINACH AND PESTO LASAGNA

The no-boil lasagna noodles and prepared pasta and pesto sauces make this a super-quick casserole to put together. This goes well with marinated vegetables on the side and a loaf of garlic bread.

SERVES 8

3 cups ricotta cheese or small-curd cottage cheese

1 cup grated Parmesan cheese

1 large egg

1 teaspoon salt

½ teaspoon pepper

2 packages (10 ounces each) frozen chopped spinach, thawed and drained

1 cup prepared pesto

4 cups prepared chunky pasta sauce with herbs

1 package (9 ounces) no-boil lasagna noodles (12 noodles)

2 cups shredded fontina or mozzarella cheese

1. Preheat the oven to 350°F. Coat a 9-by-13-inch baking dish with cooking spray.

2. In a large bowl, mix the ricotta cheese, Parmesan cheese, egg, salt, and pepper.

3. In a medium bowl, mix the spinach and pesto.

4. Spread 1 cup of the pasta sauce over the bottom of the baking dish. Arrange 3 noodles over the sauce. Top with a third of the cheese mixture, then a third of the spinach mixture. Repeat the layers 2 more times. Top with the remaining 3 noodles and then 1 cup sauce. (At this point you can cover and refrigerate for up to 1 day. Add 10 to 15 minutes to the baking time.)

5. Bake, covered, for 35 minutes. Uncover and sprinkle with the fontina or mozzarella cheese. Return to the oven for 15 minutes, uncovered. Let stand for 10 minutes before serving.

SPICED BROWN RICE AND VEGETABLES

Rice combined with beans makes a perfect protein for this vegetarian main dish. Don't be put off by the length of the ingredients list, which contains a lot of spices.

SERVES 6

1½ cups long-grain brown or basmati rice

3 tablespoons vegetable oil, divided

Pinch of saffron threads

Pinch of ground turmeric

1 teaspoon salt

2¾ cups hot water, divided

1 large onion, chopped

2 teaspoons grated fresh ginger

1½ teaspoons ground cumin

1½ teaspoons ground coriander

½ teaspoon ground cinnamon

⅛ teaspoon cayenne pepper

1 small sweet potato or yam, peeled, cut into ½-inch dice, and rinsed in cold water

2 cups cauliflower florets

1 medium yellow, orange, or red bell pepper, seeded and diced

1 medium tomato, diced

½ cup peas

⅓ cup raisins

¾ cup chickpeas (garbanzo beans), canned or freshly cooked (see page 30), drained

Chopped cashews for garnish

Plain yogurt for serving

1. In a medium saucepan, sauté the rice in 1 tablespoon of the oil over medium-high heat, until each kernel is coated. Add the saffron, turmeric, salt, and 2¼ cups of the water. Bring to a boil, cover, and reduce the heat to low. Simmer for 30 minutes, or until the liquid is absorbed.

2. Preheat the oven to 350°F. Butter a 2½-quart casserole.

3. While the rice cooks, in a non-stick skillet, sauté the onion in the remaining 2 tablespoons oil over medium heat for 5 minutes, or until transparent. Add the ginger, cumin, coriander, cinnamon, cayenne pepper, the remaining ½ cup water, the sweet potato cubes, and the cauliflower and bring to a boil, lower the heat, and simmer, covered, for about 5 minutes, or until the vegetables are barely tender, adding more water if necessary. Stir in the bell pepper, tomato, peas, raisins, and chickpeas.

4. Spread half of the rice in the bottom of the casserole. Cover with the vegetables and top with the remaining rice.

5. Cover and bake for 30 minutes, or until bubbly. Garnish with the chopped cashews and serve with yogurt.

SPINACH AND RICOTTA CASSEROLE

Simple and tasty, this savory custard makes a satisfying main dish. Serve with a crisp salad and freshly baked whole-wheat baking-powder biscuits on the side.

SERVES 4

4 large eggs

1 teaspoon salt

½ teaspoon pepper

1 package (10 ounces) frozen chopped spinach, thawed and squeezed dry

2 cups ricotta cheese

1 bunch green onions, chopped (including most of the green tops)

1 cup shredded sharp Cheddar cheese

3 tablespoons chopped fresh dill, or 1 tablespoon dried

1. Preheat the oven to 350°F. Butter an 8-inch square glass baking dish.

2. In a large bowl, beat the eggs, salt, and pepper until blended. Mix in the spinach, add the remaining ingredients, and stir until well blended.

3. Spread out the mixture in the baking dish. Bake, uncovered, for 45 minutes, or until the center is firm.

VEGETABLE LASAGNA

This lasagna is loaded with vegetables and totally satisfying. Even die-hard carnivores will enjoy it. Serve with a salad of mixed leafy greens and shaved Asiago cheese.

SERVES 6

9 lasagna noodles

1 teaspoon vegetable oil

1 bag (1 pound) fresh baby spinach leaves

2 tablespoons water

1 tablespoon olive oil

½ cup chopped onion

1 cup shredded carrots

2 cups sliced mushrooms

1 can (15 ounces) tomato sauce

1 can (4½ ounces) chopped black olives, drained

½ teaspoon dried basil

½ teaspoon dried rosemary, crushed

¼ teaspoon dried sage

¼ teaspoon dried oregano

2 cups ricotta cheese

1 pound Monterey Jack cheese, sliced

½ cup grated Parmesan cheese, plus extra for serving

1. Cook the lasagna noodles according to package directions and drain. To prevent sticking, lay the cooked noodles in a shallow dish with cold water to cover; add the vegetable oil.

2. Put the spinach in a large saucepan with the water, cover, and place over high heat. After about 1 minute, when the water gives off steam, reduce the heat to low and cook for 3 minutes. Drain the spinach and set aside.

3. In a large skillet, heat the olive oil. Add the onion, carrots, and mushrooms. Sauté for 10 minutes, or until the onion is tender and the liquid has evaporated. Add the tomato sauce, olives, and herbs. Cook for 20 minutes, or until all the vegetables are tender.

4. Preheat the oven to 375°F. Coat a 9-by-13-inch baking dish with cooking spray.

5. Spread a third of the sauce in the bottom of the baking dish. Drain the noodles and arrange 3 noodles lengthwise over the sauce. Top with a third of the ricotta and then with a third of the spinach. Pour a third of the remaining sauce over and sprinkle with a third of the Monterey Jack cheese. Repeat the layers once, this time placing the noodles crosswise in the baking dish. Repeat the layers a third time, placing the noodles lengthwise in the dish. Sprinkle with the ½ cup Parmesan cheese.

6. Bake, uncovered, for 40 minutes, or until the lasagna is bubbly and the top is golden. Let stand for 10 minutes and serve with additional Parmesan cheese.

BAKED VEGETABLE STEW WITH CUMIN AND GINGER

Serve this curry-like stew over steamed rice or couscous. Add a green salad, a good loaf of bread, and a bottle of red wine to turn this into a special meal.

SERVES 6

2 tablespoons olive oil

2 cups sliced onions

1 cup sliced carrots

1 stalk celery, sliced

1 cinnamon stick

½ teaspoon ground cumin

½ teaspoon ground ginger

½ teaspoon ground turmeric

1 large pinch saffron threads

2 cups diced peeled russet potatoes

1½ cups low-sodium vegetable broth

2 tablespoons raisins

1 can (15 ounces) chickpeas (garbanzo beans), rinsed and drained

1 medium zucchini, halved lengthwise and cut crosswise into ½-inch pieces

1 medium tomato, seeded and diced

1. Preheat the oven to 350°F. In a large, heavy Dutch oven, heat the oil over medium-low heat. Add the onions, carrots, celery, cinnamon stick, cumin, ginger, turmeric, and saffron threads and sauté until the spices become aromatic, 5 to 10 minutes.

2. Add the potatoes, broth, raisins, chickpeas, zucchini, and tomato. Cover and bake for 30 minutes, or until bubbly.

CREOLE VEGGIE JAMBALAYA

True jambalaya includes sausages, shrimp, and chicken. This rich vegetarian version is made with beans and rice to provide a complete and delicious protein.

SERVES 6

1 tablespoon vegetable oil

1 large onion, chopped

1 green bell pepper, seeded and chopped

½ cup chopped celery

3 cloves garlic, minced

2 cups water

1 can (14½ ounces) diced tomatoes with their juice

1 can (8 ounces) tomato sauce

1½ teaspoons dried thyme

1 teaspoon dried basil

1 teaspoon dried oregano

¼ teaspoon red pepper flakes

1 cup brown rice

1 can (15 ounces) butter beans, rinsed and drained

1 can (15 ounces) small red beans, rinsed and drained

1. Preheat the oven to 350°F.

2. In a large nonstick skillet, heat the oil and add the onion, bell pepper, celery, and garlic. Sauté over medium-high heat until the vegetables are tender, 3 to 4 minutes. Add the water, tomatoes with their juice, tomato sauce, thyme, basil, oregano, pepper flakes, and rice. Transfer to a 2½-quart casserole and stir.

3. Cover and bake for 30 to 35 minutes, or until the rice has absorbed the liquid. Stir in the butter beans and red beans and return to the oven, covered, for another 15 minutes, or until heated through.

YAM AND CHICKPEA CURRY

Orange-fleshed yams are often mislabeled as "sweet potatoes," but actually they come from entirely different plant species. True yams have a higher sugar and moisture content, and for that reason they seem to have a lot more flavor. When combined with chickpeas (garbanzo beans), yams make a hearty main dish that carries the flavors of exotic spices wonderfully. Serve this with couscous and steamed broccolini to make a colorful and nutritionally balanced meal.

SERVES 6

2 medium red onions, coarsely chopped

1 clove garlic, minced

1 small hot pepper, such as jalapeño, seeded and minced

1 piece fresh ginger, 2½ to 3 inches long, peeled and cut into chunks

3 tablespoons canola oil

½ teaspoon red pepper flakes

½ teaspoon ground ginger

1 teaspoon ground coriander

1 teaspoon ground cumin

1½ teaspoons ground turmeric

3 cardamom pods, crushed

1 teaspoon salt

3 medium orange-fleshed yams or sweet potatoes (2 pounds total), peeled and cut into 1-inch cubes

1 can (14 ounces) unsweetened coconut milk

1 can (14 ounces) vegetable broth

4 cups cooked chickpeas (garbanzo beans), canned or freshly cooked (see page 30), drained

2 tablespoons chopped fresh cilantro

Couscous for serving

Steamed broccolini for serving

1. Preheat the oven to 350°F. Coat a deep 2½-quart casserole with cooking spray.

2. Combine the onions, garlic, hot pepper, and ginger in a food processor with the steel blade in place. Pulse until all ingredients are finely chopped.

3. Pour the oil into a large sauté pan over medium-low heat. Add the chopped onion mixture and sauté until softened, about 5 minutes. Add the red pepper flakes, ginger, coriander, cumin, turmeric, cardamom pods, and salt, and stir to blend well. Add the yams and stir in the coconut milk, broth, and chickpeas. Transfer to the casserole.

4. Cover and bake for 45 minutes, or until the yams are soft. Top with the cilantro and serve over couscous with steamed broccolini on the side.

ZITI WITH RICOTTA AND SPINACH

Double this recipe and freeze half of it. On a busy evening, you'll have dinner ready from the freezer. Pop it into the microwave or a slow oven until it is heated through.

SERVES 8

1½ pounds baby spinach leaves

½ cup water

1 pound ricotta cheese

3 large eggs, beaten

⅔ cup grated Parmesan cheese

⅓ cup chopped fresh parsley

Salt

Pepper

3 cups tomato sauce or bottled spaghetti sauce

1 pound ziti or penne pasta, cooked according to package directions and drained

1. Preheat the oven to 375°F. Put the spinach in a deep pot or wok. Add the water and bring to a boil. Cook, stirring, until the spinach wilts and heats through. Drain the spinach and press out the excess moisture.

2. In a large bowl, combine the spinach with the ricotta, eggs, Parmesan, parsley, salt and pepper to taste, and 2½ cups of the tomato sauce. Stir until blended and add the cooked pasta.

3. Spread the remaining ½ cup tomato sauce on the bottom of a 3-quart casserole and cover with the pasta mixture. Bake for about 20 minutes, or until heated through.

ZUCCHINI PARMESAN WITH TOMATO SAUCE

Zucchini replaces the eggplant in this classic dish. It is put together in much the same way as lasagna, but the zucchini (or, in most recipes, the eggplant) is layered with the tomato sauce instead of noodles. Parboiling the zucchini removes most of the juices, which otherwise would render the casserole rather soupy.

SERVES 6

1 tablespoon olive oil

1 medium onion, chopped

1 clove garlic, minced

2 tablespoons chopped fresh basil, or 2 teaspoons dried basil

1 tablespoon chopped fresh oregano, or 1 teaspoon dried oregano

1 teaspoon fennel seeds

½ cup dry white wine

2 cans (14½ ounces each) diced tomatoes with herbs, with their juice

6 large zucchini (about ½ pound each), cut lengthwise into 5 slices each

½ cup grated Parmesan cheese

Salt

Pepper

1. Preheat the oven to 350°F.

2. Heat the oil in a large non-stick skillet. Add the onion and garlic and sauté for 2 to 3 minutes, until the onion is softened. Add the basil, oregano, and fennel seeds and sauté for 1 minute. Add the wine and bring to a boil. Reduce the heat, add the tomatoes with their juice, and simmer until the sauce is reduced to about 3 cups.

3. In a sauté pan or skillet, bring about 1 inch of water to a boil. Add the zucchini slices and cook for 2 minutes to parboil. Drain and blot dry on paper towels.

4. Spread about 1 cup of the sauce over the bottom of a 9-by-13-inch baking dish. Top with half the zucchini slices, overlapping slightly. Sprinkle with 2 tablespoons Parmesan and salt and pepper. Top with 1 cup sauce, and repeat the layers, ending with 2 table-spoons Parmesan. (At this point the casserole can be covered and refrigerated over-night. Add about 5 minutes to the oven time.)

5. Bake, uncovered, for 30 minutes, or until the casserole is bubbly.

WISCONSIN MAC AND THREE-CHEESE CASSEROLE

Here a down-home casserole is updated with the adult taste of beer and flavorful cheeses. Check your cheese counter for aged Gouda from Wisconsin, which can almost be categorized as a hard cheese and adds a wonderful nutty flavor.

SERVES 8

1 pound macaroni

4 tablespoons butter

⅓ cup all-purpose flour

1 teaspoon salt

¼ teaspoon cayenne pepper

1½ cups milk

½ cup dark beer

1 can (12 ounces) evaporated milk

1 cup shredded sharp Cheddar cheese

1 cup shredded aged Gouda cheese

1 cup shredded Swiss cheese

¾ pound cooked smoked ham, cut into matchsticks

1½ cups diced Roma (plum) tomatoes with their juice

½ teaspoon paprika

1. Preheat the oven to 350°F. Coat a 3-quart casserole with cooking spray.

2. Cook the macaroni in boiling salted water according to package directions, until tender, but still firm to the bite. Drain and set aside.

3. Melt the butter in a large saucepan over low heat. Mix in the flour, salt, and cayenne pepper. Increase the heat to medium-high and whisk in the milk, beer, and evaporated milk. Bring to a boil and whisk until thickened. Remove from the heat and stir in the cheeses.

4. In a large bowl, combine the cooked macaroni, ham, cheese sauce, and tomatoes with their juice, stirring until well mixed. Transfer to the prepared casserole. (At this point the casserole can be covered and refrigerated for up to 1 day. Add 10 minutes to the baking time.)

5. Bake for 25 minutes, or until heated through, and sprinkle with the paprika.

TWO-CHEESE AND TOMATO CASSEROLE

Cheese, tomato, and chiles have a natural affinity for one another. This makes a great meatless main dish. Serve a green salad and crusty bread on the side.

SERVES 8

4 large eggs, separated

2/3 cup undiluted evaporated milk

1 tablespoon all-purpose flour

1 teaspoon salt

1/2 teaspoon pepper

2 cups shredded Monterey Jack cheese

2 cups shredded Cheddar cheese

2 cans (4 ounces each) diced green chiles, or 2 poblano chiles, roasted, peeled, and diced

1 can (14 1/2 ounces) stewed tomatoes with their juice, or 2 vine-ripened tomatoes, peeled and diced

1. Preheat the oven to 325°F. Butter a deep 3-quart casserole or soufflé dish.

2. Beat the egg yolks in a large bowl with the milk and add the flour, salt, and pepper.

3. Beat the egg whites in a medium bowl until stiff and fold into the egg yolk mixture.

4. In the buttered casserole, mix the cheeses, green chiles, and tomatoes with their juice. Pour the egg mixture over and stir with a fork until just mixed.

5. Bake for 30 to 35 minutes, until set and lightly browned.

BAKED CHEESE FONDUE

Cheese fondue is a classic dish from Switzerland, but it has become such a favorite of ours that we tend to think of it as an American dish. Nutty-flavored Jarlsberg, the cheese of Norway, melts beautifully, as do Gruyère or aged Emmentaler. You do need to use a cheese that is aged more than 3 months, or instead of melted cheese you will have a solid mass of curd surrounded by liquid.

SERVES 8 TO 10

1 clove garlic, cut in half

1 cup dry white wine

1 tablespoon fresh lemon juice

4 cups shredded Jarlsberg, Gruyère, or aged Emmentaler cheese

3 tablespoons all-purpose flour

3 tablespoons kirsch

Pinch of ground nutmeg, or more to taste

2 loaves crusty French bread, cut into 2-inch cubes

1. Preheat the oven to 325°F. Rub a deep 2-quart crockery casserole with the garlic, and leave the garlic in the dish. Add the wine and lemon juice.

2. In a medium bowl, toss the cheese with the flour and stir into the wine mixture. (At this point you can cover the casserole and leave at room temperature for up to 2 hours.)

3. Bake the casserole for 30 to 40 minutes, or until the cheese is melted, stirring once or twice during baking. Stir in the kirsch and nutmeg until smooth.

4. Keep warm over a fondue burner or candle warmer. Have long wooden skewers or fondue forks handy, and serve with French bread cubes for dipping.

CHEDDAR CHEESE SOUFFLÉ

The beauty of cheese soufflé is that one usually has all of the ingredients on hand. You can also substitute almost any kind of cheese for the Cheddar or Swiss.

3 tablespoons butter, plus extra for the dish

2 tablespoons grated Parmesan cheese

3 tablespoons all-purpose flour

1 cup milk

Dash of cayenne pepper

¼ teaspoon dry mustard

1 teaspoon salt

1 cup shredded sharp Cheddar or Swiss cheese

9 eggs, separated, at room temperature

1. Preheat the oven to 400°F. Butter a 2-quart soufflé dish and dust with the grated Parmesan cheese. Cut a sheet of aluminum foil long enough to wrap around the soufflé dish. Fold the foil in half lengthwise and butter one side. Wrap around the soufflé dish, buttered side facing in, so that it extends above the rim of the dish by 2 inches. Fold the ends of the foil together to fasten.

2. In a saucepan, melt the 3 tablespooons butter over medium heat and stir in the flour until blended. Gradually whisk in the milk and add the cayenne, mustard, and salt. Bring to a boil, reduce the heat, and simmer for 3 to 5 minutes, stirring, until thickened. Add the shredded cheese and continue stirring until the cheese is melted. Remove from the heat.

3. In a medium bowl, stir the egg yolks until broken. Whisk in a little of the hot sauce to temper the eggs, then add the eggs to the sauce in the pan, stirring until well blended. In a medium bowl, beat the egg whites with an electric mixer until they hold short, distinct, but soft peaks. Fold about half the whites thoroughly into the sauce, and then gently fold in the remaining whites.

4. Pour into the prepared soufflé dish and bake for 25 to 30 minutes, until puffed and golden. Serve right away.

CHILE AND CHEESE QUICHE

Cheese and eggs are the main source of protein in this quiche with Southwestern flavors. In the spring, when fresh asparagus is at its best, serve it, steamed, on the side. Stewed rhubarb with ginger makes a light and tasty dessert.

SERVES 6 TO 8

1 recipe Flaky Pastry (page 32), refrigerated for 30 minutes

1 cup shredded Cheddar cheese

1 cup shredded Monterey Jack cheese

3 large eggs

1 teaspoon salt

½ teaspoon chili powder

1½ cups half-and-half

1 can (4 ounces) chopped green chiles

½ cup sliced ripe black olives

2 tablespoons finely chopped green onion (white and green parts)

Guacamole for serving

Sour cream for serving

1. Preheat the oven to 350°F. Roll out the chilled pastry into a 12-inch circle and transfer to a 9-inch pie pan. Flute the edges.

2. Mix the cheeses together and spread over the bottom of the pastry. In a medium bowl, mix the eggs, salt, chili powder, half-and-half, chiles, olives, and green onion. Pour the mixture over the cheeses in the pie pan.

3. Bake for 45 minutes, or until a knife inserted in the center of the filling comes out clean. Serve each piece with a dollop of guacamole and sour cream.

CHILES RELLENOS

For lunch, brunch, or supper, this seems to please kids as well as adults. Fresh fruit, such as sliced melon, and a basket of corn muffins complete the menu.

½ pound Monterey Jack cheese

6 poblano or Anaheim chiles, roasted and peeled (see page 35)

8 large eggs, separated

⅓ cup all-purpose flour

¾ teaspoon salt

1. Preheat the oven to 400°F. Butter an 8- or 9-inch square baking dish.

2. Cut the cheese into strips ½ inch thick and 3 inches long. Remove the stem and seeds from the chiles and discard. Cut each chile lengthwise into 3 strips. Wrap a chile strip around each piece of cheese and set aside.

3. In a large bowl, beat the egg whites with an electric mixer until soft peaks form, and set aside. Without washing the beaters, beat the yolks in a small bowl until creamy, and beat in the flour and salt. Fold the egg whites into the yolk mixture.

4. Spread half of the egg mixture in the bottom of the casserole. Top with the chile-wrapped cheese. Cover with the remaining egg mixture.

5. Bake, uncovered, for 15 to 20 minutes, or until puffy and golden.

QUICK CHILES RELLENOS

All the flavors of classic chiles rellenos are here, but this version is a lot easier and quicker to put together. Canned diced green chiles replace the roasted poblanos.

SERVES 4

5 large eggs, separated

2 cups shredded Monterey Jack cheese

1 cup cottage cheese

2 tablespoons canned diced green chiles

¼ cup all-purpose flour

½ teaspoon baking powder

1. Preheat the oven to 350°F. Butter a 2-quart shallow casserole or quiche dish.

2. In a large bowl, combine the egg yolks, Monterey Jack cheese, cottage cheese, green chiles, flour, and baking powder. Beat the egg whites until stiff and fold into the egg yolk mixture. Pour into the casserole dish.

3. Bake for 20 to 25 minutes, until puffy. Remove from the oven, cut into quarters, and serve hot.

ROASTED RACLETTE WITH GRUYÈRE CHEESE AND ROASTED POTATOES

Raclette is both the name of a cheese that's made in Switzerland and the name of the dish it inspired. The dish is made by placing the cheese near intense heat, which traditionally is an open fire, and scraping off the melting cheese. (*Racler* is a French word that means "to scrape.") In this casserole version, we melt the cheese in the oven. I suggest using Gruyère or Swiss, which are more readily available than raclette cheese.

SERVES 4

FOR THE PICKLE:

2 medium red onions, sliced

1 teaspoon sugar

6 tablespoons red wine vinegar

1 teaspoon salt

Generous pinch of dried dill

FOR THE ROASTED POTATOES:

1 pound Yukon Gold potatoes, scrubbed and cut into 1-inch dice

10 cloves garlic, peeled

1 teaspoon olive oil

½ teaspoon kosher salt

½ teaspoon coarsely ground pepper

¾ pound sliced Gruyère or Swiss cheese

Sliced salami, sausages, or country-style ham for serving

1. *To make the pickle:* Spread out the onions in a shallow dish, pour boiling water over them to cover, and leave to soak until cooled, about 30 minutes. Mix the sugar, vinegar, salt, and dill in a small saucepan. Heat, stirring, until the sugar dissolves. Drain the onions, pour the vinegar mixture over, cover, and let stand for at least 1 hour. (You can do this as much as 1 day in advance and refrigerate.)

2. Preheat the oven to 450°F.

3. *To make the roasted potatoes:* In a large bowl, toss the potatoes and garlic cloves with the olive oil, salt, and pepper. Spread out the potatoes in a single layer in a shallow roasting pan. Roast for 10 to 15 minutes, until the potatoes are tender.

4. Lay the cheese slices over the potatoes, then return to the oven until the cheese melts, about 5 minutes. Serve hot with salami, sausages, or ham slices.

TRADITIONAL WELSH RAREBIT

Welsh rarebit is often served as a main course or at high tea in Britain. Tomatoes are the classic accompaniment. I think it makes a perfect brunch or supper dish. When it is topped with a poached egg, it's called a "golden buck."

SERVES 4

2 cups shredded sharp Cheddar cheese

2 tablespoons all-purpose flour

½ cup beer or milk

4 thick slices rustic, homemade-style bread

Paprika or cayenne pepper for sprinkling

Fresh basil leaves for garnish

Tomato wedges for garnish

1. Preheat the oven to 350°F.

2. Toss the cheese with the flour in a 1-quart casserole. Stir in the beer or milk.

3. Cover and bake for 25 to 30 minutes, until the cheese is melted. Stir until smooth.

4. Meanwhile toast the bread. Spoon the melted cheese over the bread and sprinkle with paprika or cayenne pepper. Top with basil leaves and tomato wedges.

Chapter 14
CASSEROLES FOR CROWDS

— ◦ ◦ ◦ ◦ ◦ —

What is a crowd? For one person, that might mean a dozen people, and for another, two dozen is more like it. In this chapter, we cover the range between 12 and 24. Most home kitchens don't have casserole dishes, ovens, and refrigerators large enough to handle extra-large quantities, so these quantities are easier to manage.

If you are planning a large gathering, such as a family reunion, you might consider making a casserole in this chapter several times. It is easier to repeat a recipe than to multiply it by, say, three, and then try to figure out what to bake it in. However, you may need to use all the casserole dishes in your pantry, or borrow a bunch from neighbors and friends.

Here's a plan of action to help you with a large party:

1. Select casseroles that can be easily prepared in advance. This chapter offers many ideas.

2. Read through the recipe ahead of time and note everything that must be purchased or borrowed.

3. If many of the recipes you choose include similar ingredients, say lots of chopped onions or garlic, consider chopping enough for all of the recipes. You can do that a day in advance, which will make the assembly a lot easier.

4. Consider food safety. When you are preparing large quantities of food, the chances for food spoilage are multiplied. Be extra careful when handling meat, fish, and dairy products. Keep hot things hot and cold things cold. Remember that the types of bacteria that can contaminate food and make people sick grow in food at temperatures between 45 and 140°F.

BAKED POTATO CASSEROLE

Assemble this casserole ahead of time if you wish, but bake it just before serving. It's absolutely a perfect one to tote to a potluck, as well. I have even frozen it 2 weeks before our holiday family buffet, and nobody knew the difference. Most potato casseroles frozen in advance have a telltale flavor and texture that give the secret away, but not this one.

SERVES 12

8 large baking potatoes, peeled and cut into 1-inch dice

4 cups shredded Cheddar cheese (about 1 pound)

2 cups sour cream

6 slices bacon, cut into ½-inch pieces

2 bunches chopped green onions (white and green parts)

1. Preheat the oven to 325°F. Butter a 9-by-13-inch baking dish.

2. Cook the potatoes in boiling salted water for about 20 minutes, until tender. Drain, spread out in the baking dish, and top with the cheese and sour cream.

3. In a medium nonstick skillet, cook the bacon until crisp over medium-high heat. Drain the bacon on paper towels, and pour off all but 1 tablespoon of the fat. Add the green onions to the skillet and sauté for 2 to 3 minutes, until soft. Sprinkle the bacon and green onions over the casserole. (At this point, you can cover and refrigerate the dish for up to 1 day. Or you can wrap it well and freeze it; see the Note below. Thaw overnight in the refrigerator.)

4. Bake for 30 minutes, or until bubbly.

○ ○ ○ ○ ○

NOTE: To freeze, place a piece of waxed paper down on top of the potato mixture, then wrap in a double layer of foil, so it's airtight.

SPAGHETTI AND BEEF CASSEROLE

Think of this casserole when there are kids in the crowd.
Simple accompaniments will go over well, like raw vegetable sticks
and toasted French bread slices. Assemble the casserole in advance,
if you like, and refrigerate.

SERVES 10 TO 12

2 pounds ground beef

½ cup diced onion

½ cup diced green bell pepper

2 cloves garlic, chopped

1 can (14½ ounces) diced tomatoes with their juice

1 can (8 ounces) tomato sauce

1 cup water

¼ cup chopped fresh parsley

1½ teaspoons Italian seasoning

2 teaspoons salt

1½ teaspoons sugar

2 small bay leaves

½ pound angel hair pasta or spaghetti

1½ cups shredded Cheddar cheese

1½ cups shredded mozzarella or Monterey Jack cheese

1. Preheat the oven to 350°F.

2. Crumble the beef into a large skillet. Add the onion, bell pepper, and garlic. Cook, stirring, over medium-high heat for 5 to 10 minutes, until the meat is no longer pink. Drain the fat. Add the tomatoes with their juice, tomato sauce, water, parsley, seasoning, salt, sugar, and bay leaves. Bring to a boil and remove from the heat.

3. Cook the pasta according to package directions. Cover the bottom of a 9-by-13-inch baking dish with a third of the meat sauce. Add half of the pasta in an even layer, and sprinkle with ½ cup of each cheese. Cover with another third of the meat sauce and the remaining pasta. Top with the remaining sauce and ½ cup of each cheese.

4. Bake for 30 minutes. Top the casserole with the remaining ½ cup Cheddar and ½ cup mozzarella cheese. Return it to the oven, and continue to bake until the cheese is melted and bubbly, about 5 more minutes. Cut into squares before serving.

BLACK BEAN TORTILLA CASSEROLE

Here's a great party dish that lends itself to a fiesta theme. I like a fresh orange and jicama salad with this, dressed simply with oil, vinegar, and a pinch of chili powder.

SERVES 12

2 tablespoons vegetable oil or cooking spray

2 cups coarsely chopped onion

2 cloves garlic, minced

1 large red bell pepper, seeded and chopped

1 large green bell pepper, seeded and chopped

½ cup tomato salsa (mild, medium, or hot)

1½ teaspoons ground cumin

2 cans (15 ounces each) black beans, rinsed and drained

1 can (14½ ounces) diced tomatoes with their juice

12 corn tortillas

2 cups shredded reduced-fat Monterey Jack cheese, divided

TOPPINGS:

Shredded iceberg lettuce

Chopped fresh tomato

Diced avocado

Sour cream

Tomato salsa (mild, medium, or hot)

1. Preheat the oven to 350°F.

2. Coat a large skillet with the vegetable oil or cooking spray. Place over medium heat, add the onion and garlic, and sauté for 4 minutes, or until tender. Add the red and green bell peppers and sauté for 3 minutes, or until the vegetables are tender. Add the salsa, cumin, black beans, and diced tomatoes with their juice. Cook for 5 minutes, stirring occasionally. Remove from the heat.

3. Coat a 9-by-13-inch baking dish with cooking spray. Spoon 1½ cups of the bean mixture into the baking dish. Arrange 6 tortillas in a single layer over the bean mixture. Top with 1 cup of the cheese. Spoon the remaining bean mixture over the cheese. Arrange the remaining 6 tortillas over the bean mixture.

4. Coat a sheet of aluminum foil with cooking spray. Cover the casserole and bake for 30 minutes. Uncover and top with the remaining cup of cheese. Bake, uncovered, for another 5 to 7 minutes, or until the cheese melts. Let stand for 5 minutes and cut into squares to serve. Set out the toppings so people can help themselves.

BLUEBERRY BRUNCH FOR A CROWD

When our whole family is together, this is the perfect solution for a no-stress breakfast. It's best to use fresh blueberries for this seasonal dish; frozen berries will discolor the casserole. In a commercial oven, you can bake this in a 12-by-20-inch pan with 2-inch sides. I have found, however, that in a home oven, it is best to divide the recipe between two 9-by-13-inch baking dishes so that the center of the food gets cooked evenly.

○——————————— SERVES 24 ———————————○

36 slices thick-cut crusty white bread, cut into 1-inch cubes

2 packages (8 ounces each) cream cheese, cubed

4 cups blueberries

2 tablespoons grated orange zest

36 large eggs

4 cups milk

1 cup pure maple syrup

FOR THE BLUEBERRY SAUCE:

3 cups sugar

2/3 cup cornstarch

3 cups water

3 cups blueberries

1 tablespoon fresh lemon juice

3 tablespoons butter

1. Butter 2 shallow 9-by-13-inch baking dishes.

2. Scatter half the bread cubes in the bottom of the pans. Scatter the cream cheese and blueberries on top evenly and sprinkle with the orange zest. Top with the remaining bread cubes.

3. Mix the eggs, milk, and maple syrup in 1 or 2 large bowls and pour evenly over the ingredients in pans. Cover with aluminum foil coated with cooking spray and refrigerate overnight.

4. Preheat the oven to 350°F.

5. Bake, covered, for 40 minutes. Uncover and bake an additional

20 to 30 minutes, or until puffed, browned, and set.

6. *While the casseroles bake, make the sauce:* Blend the sugar and cornstarch in a large saucepan. Add the water and cook over medium-high heat, stirring occasionally, until the mixture boils, thickens, and becomes clear, about 8 minutes. Stir in the blueberries and simmer until the berries burst. Remove from the heat and stir in the lemon juice and butter.

7. To serve, cut each pan into 12 squares. Serve warm with warm blueberry sauce spooned over each serving.

BRAZILIAN FEIJOADA

Brazil's national dish is loaded with black beans and a variety of meats. It's a great party dish, and is not difficult to make. It does require hours of unattended long, slow cooking, so you need to plan your time accordingly. Feijoada is served with toasted manioc, which is ground cassava root, the same substance that comprises tapioca. Feijoada is sometimes served with stewed kale or other greens or garnished with sliced oranges.

SERVES 12 TO 15

1 pound dried black beans

1 teaspoon salt

½ teaspoon pepper

8 cloves garlic, coarsely chopped

¾ pound salt pork, rind trimmed off, and diced

1 ham shank (about 1½ pounds)

1 corned beef brisket (3 to 3½ pounds) with the spice packet, if desired

1 can (28 ounces) whole or stewed tomatoes with their juice

1 large sweet onion, chopped

4 cups water, plus extra as needed

1 pound spicy sausage, such as linguiça or Spanish chorizo

Sautéed Greens (facing page) for serving

FOR THE BUTTERED MANIOC:

1 tablespoon butter

1 cup manioc flour or uncooked farina

½ cup chopped fresh parsley

½ cup light or dark raisins

½ cup sliced stuffed green olives

Hot cooked rice for serving

1. Put the beans in a 3- to 4-quart casserole. Add water to cover (by about 4 inches) and soak overnight. Drain the beans.

2. Preheat the oven to 325°F.

3. Add the salt, pepper, garlic, salt pork, ham shank, beef brisket, tomatoes with their juice, onion, and the 4 cups water to the beans.

4. Cover tightly and bake for 4 hours. Check occasionally, adding more water to keep the mixture moist, if necessary.

5. Uncover and stir in the sausage. Reduce the oven temperature to 300°F. Bake, uncovered, for 30 minutes to 1 hour longer, or until the liquid is thickened.

6. Slice the sausage and beef. Remove the meat from the ham hock and cut it up. Stir the beans and arrange the meats on top. Make the Sautéed Greens and transfer to a serving dish. Keep warm while you make the buttered manioc.

7. *To make the buttered manioc:* In a medium skillet, melt the butter over medium-low heat and add the manioc flour or farina. Stir so the grains stay loose and dry and turn golden. Stir in the parsley, raisins, and olives.

8. *To serve:* Sprinkle some of the buttered manioc over the dish and put the rest in a serving bowl so people can help themselves. Spoon rice around the edges of the feijoada dish. Or put the rice in a serving bowl and spoon the feijoada over individual servings. Offer the Sautéed Greens on the side.

SAUTÉED GREENS
SERVES 12 TO 15

Feijoada is traditionally served with *couve à mineira,* or sautéed greens. This dish can be prepared with broccoli rabe or green cabbage, but the most popular choice is kale.

2 pounds kale

3 tablespoons olive oil

1 medium onion, minced

2 cloves garlic, minced

1. Wash the kale and bunch it together in 2 or 3 bunches. Take each bunch, roll it up tightly, and cut crosswise into thin strips. Wash the strips and drain thoroughly.

2. Heat the oil in a large heavy skillet over medium heat, then cook the onion and garlic, stirring, until lightly browned. Add the kale strips and cook, stirring, for another 5 minutes so until the greens are soft, but still retain their bright green color. Serve hot.

SOUR CREAM AND BROCCOLI CASSEROLE

We all know that broccoli is healthy, but how do you make it more interesting? Why, with some sour cream, Cheddar cheese, and sweet onion. Be sure the broccoli is fresh. If it smells strong, it will taste even stronger after cooking. I am always careful to check expiration dates on bags of fresh broccoli.

SERVES 12

2 tablespoons butter, melted, plus extra for the dish

1 bag (20 ounces) fresh broccoli florets

1 cup light sour cream

1 cup shredded Cheddar cheese

¼ cup minced sweet onion

1 teaspoon salt

½ cup seasoned fine dry breadcrumbs

1. Preheat the oven to 350°F. Butter a shallow 3-quart casserole.

2. Cook the broccoli in salted boiling water to cover for 3 minutes, then drain. In a large bowl, mix the broccoli with the sour cream, cheese, sweet onion, and salt. Transfer to the casserole dish. (At this point you can cover and refrigerate the casserole for up to 1 day.)

3. Mix the breadcrumbs with the 2 tablespoons butter and sprinkle over the top of the casserole evenly. Bake for 15 to 20 minutes, or until the breadcrumbs are browned and the casserole is heated through.

CAULIFLOWER AND BROCCOLI CASSEROLE

Think of cauliflower and broccoli as siblings in the cabbage family. A characteristic they share is that they should not be overcooked. Cheese and a bit of ham transform them into a convenient main dish.

SERVES 12

1½ pounds cauliflower florets

1½ pounds broccoli florets

½ cup (1 stick) butter, divided

3 tablespoons all-purpose flour

3 cups milk, heated

1½ cups shredded Cheddar cheese

1 cup grated Parmesan cheese

½ teaspoon salt

3 cups chopped cooked ham

3 cups fresh breadcrumbs (see Note)

1. Preheat the oven to 350°F. Cook the cauliflower and broccoli in boiling salted water to cover, just until crisp-tender. Drain and set aside.

2. Melt 4 tablespoons of the butter in a medium saucepan over medium heat. Add the flour and stir until blended. Gradually whisk in the milk and bring to a boil, stirring constantly. Lower the heat and simmer, for 3 to 5 minutes, stirring constantly until thickened. Add the cheeses and salt and stir over low heat until the cheese melts.

3. Transfer the cooked vegetables to an ungreased 3-quart casserole and scatter the ham on top. Pour the sauce over all.

4. Melt the remaining 4 tablespoons butter in a small skillet and stir in the breadcrumbs. Make a border of buttered crumbs around the edges of the casserole. Bake, uncovered, for 20 to 30 minutes, or until the breadcrumbs are lightly browned.

○ ○ ○ ○ ○

NOTE: To make fresh breadcrumbs, tear 1 or 2 slices of fresh bread into pieces and put in a food processor with the steel blade in place. Process with on/off pulses until the bread is broken down into crumbs.

CHICKEN AND MUSHROOM CASSEROLE

Here's a tasty candidate for a family reunion buffet or to tote to a potluck. Depending on availability and the adventurousness of your guests, try substituting wild mushrooms for common white button mushrooms. For a more complex flavor, add a little truffle oil to the sauce.

SERVES 12

3 chickens (3 pounds each), cut into 8 serving pieces per chicken

2 tablespoons salt

2 teaspoons pepper

2 teaspoons paprika

½ cup (1 stick) butter

2 pounds mushrooms, sliced

½ cup all-purpose flour

2 cups homemade (page 25) or prepared chicken broth

¾ cup dry sherry

1 tablespoon dried rosemary, crushed

1. Preheat the oven to 350°F. Wash the chicken pieces and pat dry. Sprinkle with salt, pepper, and paprika.

2. In a 5-quart Dutch oven, melt 4 tablespoons of the butter over medium-high heat. Add the chicken pieces, a few at a time, and brown on both sides, removing them to a dish as they are done.

3. When all of the chicken pieces are browned, add the remaining butter and the mushrooms to the Dutch oven and sauté until browned. Sprinkle flour over the mushrooms and add the chicken broth, sherry, and rosemary, stirring until blended. Bring to a boil, lower the heat, and simmer until thickened.

4. Return the chicken to the pot. Spoon the sauce over the chicken and bake, covered, for 1 hour, or until the chicken is cooked through.

CHICKEN BREASTS WITH CARAMELIZED ONIONS

Although this is a relatively simple casserole, the caramelized onions, paprika, mushrooms, wine, and roasted bell peppers add up to a richly flavored chicken dish. To complete the menu, add a vegetable casserole, a salad, and crusty artisanal bread.

SERVES 24

24 boneless, skinless chicken breast halves (4 to 6 ounces each)

½ cup all-purpose flour

1 teaspoon salt

1 teaspoon Hungarian paprika

1 cup (2 sticks) butter

2 pounds mushrooms, sliced

1 recipe Caramelized Onions (page 31)

1½ cups green onions, chopped (white and green parts)

¾ cup dry white wine

1½ cups homemade (page 25) or prepared chicken broth

6 red bell peppers, roasted and quartered (see page 35)

24 fresh basil leaves

24 slices mozzarella cheese

1. Preheat the oven to 450°F.

2. Wash the chicken pieces and pat dry. Combine the flour, salt, and paprika in a shallow dish and coat the chicken with the mixture evenly. Arrange in two 9-by-13-inch baking dishes or one 12-by-20-inch baking pan. Set aside the remaining seasoned flour.

3. Melt ½ cup of the butter in a small skillet and drizzle the chicken breasts with the butter. Bake in the oven, uncovered, for 15 minutes, or until the chicken breasts are browned. Reduce the oven temperature to 350°F.

4. While the chicken breasts brown, melt the remaining ½ cup butter in a large skillet over high heat and add the mushrooms, caramelized onions, and green onions. Cook until the mushrooms

are softened, about 3 minutes. Sprinkle the reserved seasoned flour over the mushrooms and stir until the mushrooms are evenly coated. Whisk in the wine and broth and bring to a boil. Reduce the heat and simmer for 2 minutes until thickened.

5. Pour the mushroom and onion mixture over the browned chicken breasts and top with the roasted pepper pieces. (At this point you can cover and refrigerate for up to 2 hours. Then proceed with the final baking.)

6. Return the chicken to the oven and bake, uncovered, for 15 to 20 minutes, or until the chicken breasts are cooked through. Top with the basil leaves and cheese and return to the oven for 5 minutes, or until the cheese is melted. Serve hot.

CHOUCROUTE GARNI

Translated literally from the French, *choucroute garni* means "garnished cabbage"! The success of this dish depends on the quality of the sauerkraut, so use a good one, preferably the kind that comes fresh in a bag and not the canned variety—unless, of course, you make your own!

MAKES 12 GENEROUS SERVINGS

2 pounds fresh sauerkraut

2 large Golden Delicious apples, peeled, cored, and sliced

4 slices bacon, diced

6 black peppercorns

6 juniper berries

1 cup dark beer

12 smoked pork chops, or 2 pounds smoked ham, cut into ½-inch-thick slices

12 garlic-flavored smoked sausage links (about 3 pounds), such as kielbasa

¼ cup chopped fresh parsley for garnish

1. Preheat the oven to 300°F.

2. In a heavy 5-quart casserole, layer the sauerkraut, apples, and bacon. Sprinkle with the peppercorns and juniper berries and pour the beer over all. Cover tightly and bake for 2½ hours. Arrange the pork chops or ham on top. Cover and bake for another 30 minutes.

3. Cut the sausages diagonally into 3-inch-thick slices. Tuck the sausage slices into the sauerkraut mixture in the casserole. Cover and bake for another 30 minutes, or until the sausages are heated through.

4. To serve, spoon the sauerkraut onto a rimmed platter and arrange the meat and sausages over the sauerkraut. Garnish with chopped fresh parsley.

DUDE RANCH PORK AND BEANS

A couple of years ago, I was privileged to visit a half dozen dude ranches in Colorado. I even learned to ride a horse! The ranches ranged from very rustic to very posh. But the one thing they had in common was the pork and beans on their buffet menus. Maybe it was because beans have an important place in early American culinary history and live on as the mainstay in the diets of the cowboys. And they really wanted to turn me into a cowgirl! Go ahead and visit the dude ranches in Grand County, Colorado, where you're likely to be served a dish of beans like this one.

SERVES 10

4 strips bacon, cut into ½-inch pieces

3 tablespoons canola oil

2 pounds lean pork loin, cut into 1-inch cubes

2 cups chopped onions

3 large cloves garlic, minced

3 tablespoons chili powder

1 teaspoon ground cumin

¼ teaspoon cayenne pepper

1 teaspoon salt, or more to taste

1 teaspoon Worcestershire sauce

2 cans (14½ ounces each) diced tomatoes with their juice

½ cup water

3 cans (15 ounces each) pinto beans, rinsed and drained

Cornbread squares for serving

1. Preheat the oven to 350°F.

2. In a heavy Dutch oven, brown the bacon over medium-high heat. Drain the bacon on paper towels and pour off the bacon fat from the pot.

3. Add the oil to the pan and stir in the pork cubes. Brown the meat, stirring occasionally, over medium-high heat. Add the onions, garlic, chili powder, cumin, cayenne pepper, and salt. Cook over high heat, stirring, for 5 minutes. Stir in the Worcestershire sauce, tomatoes with their juice, and water.

4. Cover and bake for 1 hour. Stir in the beans and add more water, if they seem dry. Bake for 30 minutes longer, or until the pork is very tender. Add the bacon. Taste and add more salt, if desired.

5. Serve with squares of cornbread.

EGGPLANT AND SPINACH TIAN

Tian is a French word that describes both a shallow earthenware casserole and the food it contains. The most common tian is a dish of gratinéed vegetables (topped with breadcrumbs or cheese). This one makes a pretty spectacular presentation.

SERVES 10 TO 12

3 firm large eggplants (about 3½ pounds total), cut crosswise into ¼-inch-thick rounds

2 to 3 tablespoons kosher salt

½ cup olive oil, divided, plus extra for the baking sheet

1 large onion, halved lengthwise and thinly sliced crosswise

6 cups packed spinach leaves

Salt

Pepper

1 cup packed fresh basil leaves

2 garlic cloves, minced

6 medium vine-ripened tomatoes, cut into ¼-inch-thick slices

½ cup grated Parmesan cheese

1. Line a baking sheet with paper towels and arrange the eggplant in a single layer on top. Sprinkle with 1½ teaspoons of the kosher salt. Turn over and spread the other side with another 1½ teaspoons of kosher salt. Cover with a layer of paper towels and top with another layer of eggplant, sprinkling with kosher salt in the same way. Continue in this way until you've salted all the eggplant slices. Let stand for 20 minutes, or until the paper towels have absorbed the liquid from the eggplant.

2. Preheat the broiler.

3. Oil a baking sheet with 1 tablespoon of the olive oil and top with one layer of eggplant. Broil 3 inches from the heat until pale gold, about 3 minutes. Turn the eggplant over and broil until pale gold and tender, about another 2 minutes. Transfer the cooked eggplant to a platter and broil the remaining eggplant slices the same way.

4. In a large nonstick skillet, heat 1 tablespoon of the oil

over medium heat. Add the onion and cook, stirring, until soft and pale gold; transfer to a bowl. Add the spinach to the skillet and increase the heat to medium-high. Toss and turn the spinach until wilted. Season with salt and pepper and stir into the onion.

5. In a blender, puree the basil, garlic, and 6 tablespoons of the oil until smooth. Season the basil mixture with salt and pepper an transfer to a bowl.

6. Preheat the oven to 450°F. Brush an earthenware casserole or soufflé dish, about 10 inches in diameter, with oil. Line the bottom and sides of the casserole with a layer of eggplant. Brush with some of the basil mixture and top with a layer of the spinach mixture. Add a layer of tomato slices, and brush with more basil mixture. Repeat the layers with the remaining eggplant, basil mixture, spinach, and tomatoes, ending with the tomatoes.

7. Bake for 20 minutes. Cool in the dish on a rack for 1 hour. Invert the tian onto a serving dish with shallow sides (some liquid will drain from the tian). Sprinkle with the Parmesan cheese and cut into wedges to serve.

FINNISH CABBAGE ROLLS (KAALIKÄÄRYLEET)

This recipe has many virtues: it can be made ahead, served to a crowd, and anything left over tastes even better the next day! To soften the cabbage leaves, you can blanch them, as described in step 1. Or you can freeze the cabbage whole, then thaw it just before you plan to use it. When thawed, the leaves separate beautifully and are flexible enough to encase the filling.

SERVES 24

24 large green cabbage leaves, separated, and coarse ribs removed

1½ cups pearl barley or rice

1¼ cups water

4 tablespoons butter, melted, plus extra for the dish(es)

3 teaspoons salt

¾ teaspoon white pepper

1½ pounds lean ground beef

1½ pounds lean ground pork

1½ pounds onions, diced

1½ cups diced red bell peppers

2 tablespoons chopped garlic

1 cup dark corn syrup

About 4 cups boiling water

1. If you choose not to freeze the cabbage (see headnote), blanch the cabbage leaves in boiling salted water to cover until they become soft and bright green; remove from the water and pat dry with paper towels.

2. Peel off as many large leaves as possible from the cabbage head and set aside for filling. The center will be a tight ball of leaves too small to fill. Shred this part of the cabbage and set aside.

3. Combine the barley or rice and water in a heavy saucepan and bring to a boil over medium-high heat; cover and simmer until most of the water is absorbed. Remove from the heat and cover; let stand for 10 minutes.

4. Preheat the oven to 350°F. Butter a 12-by-20-inch baking pan with 2-inch sides, a 7½-quart casserole, or two 9-by-13-inch baking dishes.

5. Spread the shredded cabbage in a single layer on the bottom of the dish(es). Sprinkle with half the salt and pepper and drizzle all the melted butter over the cabbage evenly.

6. In a large bowl, mix the cooked barley or rice, ground beef, ground pork, onion, bell pepper, garlic, and the remaining salt and pepper.

7. Place an egg-sized ball of the meat mixture onto the stem end of a softened cabbage leaf. Wrap the leaf around the meat, tuck in the sides, and roll up. Place, seam side down, on top of the shredded cabbage. Fill and roll up the remaining cabbage leaves and place on the shredded cabbage.

8. Brush the rolls with the corn syrup. Coat a sheet of aluminum foil with cooking spray. Cover the casserole and bake for 30 minutes. Uncover, pour the boiling water over, and bake for another hour, or until the filling is cooked through.

GARDEN-STYLE LASAGNA

For this you will need a lasagna pan with straight sides, at least 14 inches long. Lasagna pans vary in size, but they are all at least 3 inches deep. If you use a standard 9-by-13-inch baking pan with sloping sides, you will find that you can't fit all the noodles and filling in it. If that's all you have, reduce the number of noodles to 9, or make a second, smaller lasagna in a smaller dish.

SERVES 12

2 cups chopped onions

4 cloves garlic, minced

2 teaspoons olive oil, divided

2 cups chopped zucchini

2 cups chopped yellow squash

2 cups thinly sliced carrots

2 cups chopped broccoli

2 teaspoons salt, divided

5 tablespoons butter

5 tablespoons flour

3½ cups milk, heated

1 cup grated Parmesan cheese, divided

10 fresh basil leaves, chopped

¼ teaspoon pepper

⅛ teaspoon ground nutmeg

1 package (10 ounces) frozen chopped spinach, thawed and drained

1½ cups regular or part-skim ricotta cheese

2 cups shredded part-skim mozzarella cheese, divided

1 package (9 ounces) no-boil lasagna noodles (12 noodles), divided

1. Preheat the oven to 375°F. Coat a 9-by-15-inch or 10-by-15-inch lasagna pan with 3-inch sides with cooking spray.

2. Place a large Dutch oven over medium-high heat. Coat the pan with cooking spray. Add the onions to the pan and sauté 4 minutes, or until lightly browned. Add the garlic and sauté for 1 minute. Spoon the onion mixture into a large bowl.

3. Heat 1 teaspoon of the oil in the Dutch oven over medium-high heat. Add the zucchini and yellow squash and sauté for 4 minutes, or until tender and just beginning to brown. Add to the onion mixture.

4. Heat the remaining 1 teaspoon oil in the pan over medium-high heat. Add the sliced carrots and sauté for

4 minutes, or until tender. Add the chopped broccoli and sauté for 4 minutes, or until crisp-tender. Add to the onion mixture. Sprinkle the vegetables with 1 teaspoon of the salt and toss well to combine.

5. Melt the butter in a medium saucepan and whisk in the flour. Over medium-high heat, gradually add the milk, stirring with a whisk until blended. Bring to a boil and simmer for 2 minutes, or until thick, stirring constantly. Remove from the heat. Add ½ cup of the Parmesan, the remaining 1 teaspoon salt, the basil, pepper, and nutmeg. Stir until smooth and then stir in the spinach.

6. In a large bowl, combine the ricotta and 1½ cups of the mozzarella and stir well.

7. Spread ½ cup spinach mixture in bottom of the lasagna pan.

8. Arrange 4 noodles over the spinach mixture in the dish. Top with half of the cottage cheese mixture, half of the vegetable mixture, and about 1 cup of the spinach mixture. Repeat the layers, ending with the noodles. Spread the remaining spinach mixture over the noodles. Sprinkle with the remaining ½ cup Parmesan and the remaining ½ cup mozzarella.

9. Coat a sheet of aluminum foil with cooking spray. Cover the casserole and bake for 20 minutes. Uncover and bake for an additional 20 minutes, or until the cheese is bubbly and beginning to brown. Let stand for 10 minutes before serving.

EASY CORN AND ORZO CASSEROLE

This could hardly be a simpler dish. The orzo thickens the mixture so that it can be easily cut into serving pieces. If you prefer, substitute 1 cup of a small shell pasta for the orzo.

SERVES 12

2 tablespoons butter at room temperature

1 cup orzo

1 cup shredded mild Cheddar cheese

2 cans (16 ounces each) corn kernels, drained

2 cans (16 ounces each) cream-style corn

1 can (4 ounces) chopped green chiles

1. Preheat the oven to 350°F.

2. Spread the butter in a 9-by-13-inch baking dish.

3. Combine all of the remaining ingredients in the casserole.

4. Cover and bake for 30 minutes. Stir, and bake, uncovered, for another 25 to 30 minutes. Cut into 3-inch squares to serve.

HAM AND BROCCOLI STRATA

A strata is usually a filled sandwich made juicy with eggs and milk. Here, the bread is torn into pieces and layered with vegetables, cheese, and meat. But look in your refrigerator for some good substitutes—cooked vegetables or another kind of cheese, for example.

SERVES 12

12 slices thick-cut crusty white or whole-wheat bread

12 slices sharp Cheddar cheese, ¼ inch thick

1 package (10 ounces) frozen chopped broccoli, thawed

1 package (10 ounces) frozen chopped spinach, cooked and drained

½ cup chopped roasted red bell peppers

2 cups chopped cooked ham

3 cups half-and-half or milk

12 large eggs

2 tablespoons finely chopped green onion (white and green parts)

1 teaspoon dry mustard

1. Coat a 9-by-13-inch baking pan with cooking spray. With a cookie cutter, cut designs out of each bread slice. Tear the remaining bread into pieces and place in the bottom of the baking pan.

2. Top the bread with an even layer of cheese, and in layers add the broccoli, spinach, red bell peppers, and ham. Top with the bread cut-outs.

3. Beat the half-and-half and eggs together in a large bowl and stir in the onion and mustard. Pour the mixture evenly over the layers in the baking pan. Cover with plastic wrap and refrigerate for 8 hours or overnight.

4. Preheat the oven to 350°F.

5. Uncover the casserole and bake for 1 to 1¼ hours, or until set and golden brown. If the strata is browning too quickly, loosely cover with aluminum foil. Let stand for 15 minutes before serving.

BREAKFAST HAM AND CHEESE STRATA

This is an old breakfast favorite for a crowd. In fact, I put this together at home, chilled it, and packed it in the ice chest before taking our family to a rustic lodge in northern Minnesota. It was so nice to have the first breakfast all ready to pop into the oven the next morning. To round out the menu, serve a platter of fresh fruit, a selection of juices, and coffee or hot chocolate.

SERVES 12

12 slices day-old French bread, cubed

2 cups shredded Cheddar cheese

3 cups diced cooked ham

24 large eggs, beaten

4 cups milk

2 teaspoons dry mustard

1 teaspoon salt

2 teaspoons pepper

1. Butter a 9-by-13-inch baking dish or a 3-quart casserole.

2. Arrange half the bread cubes evenly in the bottom of the casserole.

3. Distribute the cheese and ham evenly over the bread cubes. Top with the remaining bread.

4. In a large bowl, beat the eggs with the milk, mustard, salt, and pepper. Pour over the bread cubes in the pan, cover, and refrigerate for at least 12 hours.

5. Preheat the oven to 350°F.

6. Bake for 1 hour, or until the casserole is set. Cut into squares and serve hot.

Variations

Crab and Havarti Strata: Substitute 3 cups cooked crabmeat for the ham and 2 cups diced havarti cheese for the Cheddar cheese.

Veggie Strata: Replace the ham with 3 cups blanched and well-drained chopped broccoli.

Shrimp and Artichoke Strata: Omit the ham and add 2 cups diced cooked shrimp and 2 cups diced cooked artichoke hearts.

HOLIDAY CORN CASSEROLE

This is Christmassy enough to serve as a vegetable on a holiday buffet, or at a potluck for a large group.

SERVES 12

¾ cup (1½ sticks) divided, plus 2 tablespoons butter, plus extra for the dish

1 cup chopped green onions (white and green parts)

1 cup chopped celery

1 green pepper, seeded and chopped

1 red bell pepper, seeded and chopped

2 cans (15 ounces each) yellow corn kernels, drained

2 cans (11 ounces each) white corn kernels, drained

2 cans (15 ounces each) yellow cream-style corn

⅔ cup evaporated milk

1½ cups shredded Swiss cheese

1½ cups shredded Cheddar cheese

3 large eggs, lightly beaten

1 teaspoon salt

1 teaspoon cracked pepper

2 cups snack crackers, crushed, such as Ritz

1. Preheat the oven to 350°F. Butter a 9-by-13-inch baking dish.

2. In a large skillet, melt the 2 tablespoons butter and add the green onions, celery, and bell peppers. Sauté for about 5 minutes, or until the vegetables are crisp-tender.

3. Meanwhile, in a small skillet, melt the remaining ¾ cup butter. In a large bowl, combine all three types of corn, the milk, cheeses, eggs, salt, pepper, and ½ cup of the melted butter. Add the sautéed vegetables and transfer to the prepared baking dish. (At this point you can cover and refrigerate for up to 1 day. Add 10 to 15 minutes to the baking time.)

4. Sprinkle with the cracker crumbs and drizzle with the remaining ¼ cup melted butter. Bake for 30 minutes, or until the crumbs are browned and crisp.

HOLIDAY MORNING EGG CASSEROLE

Here's a breakfast casserole that will serve a lot of people. It's great for brunch entertaining or if you have a house full of relatives! To make the casserole extra special, use shiitake mushrooms or wild mushrooms, such as morels.

SERVES 10 TO 12

2 tablespoons butter, plus extra for the dish (optional)

8 slices bacon, cut into little strips

½ pound dried chipped beef, shredded

½ pound mushrooms, sliced

½ cup all-purpose flour

4 cups milk, heated

FOR THE EGG LAYER:

4 tablespoons butter

20 large eggs, beaten

¾ teaspoon salt

1 cup undiluted evaporated milk

1. Preheat the oven to 275°F. Butter a 9-by-13-inch baking dish or coat with cooking spray.

2. In a skillet, cook the bacon over medium-high heat until crisp. Drain the bacon on paper towels, and pour off all but 2 tablespoons of the drippings. Over medium heat, add the beef, mushrooms, and 2 tablespoons butter to the pan. Sprinkle with the flour and mix until blended. Whisk in the milk slowly, bring to a boil, and continue whisking until the mixture is smooth and thickens. Add the bacon and set aside.

3. *To make the egg layer:* Add the 4 tablespoons butter to the pan and melt over medium heat. Beat the eggs, salt, and milk together in a large bowl. Add to the pan and cook, stirring, until softly scrambled. Remove from the heat.

4. Spread out half of the bacon and beef mixture in the bottom of the baking dish. Spoon the eggs over in an even layer. Top with the remaining meat mixture. Coat a sheet of aluminum foil with nonstick spray. Cover the casserole with the foil and bake for 1 hour. Serve immediately or cool completely and freeze (see Note).

○ ○ ○ ○ ○

NOTE: To freeze, wrap well and place in the freezer for up to 2 weeks. Thaw in the refrigerator. To reheat, place in a 275 degree F. oven until heated through, about 25 to 30 minutes.

KARELIAN HOT POT (KARJALAN PAISTI)

Karjalan Paisti is a Finnish stew made with three meats—beef (or veal), pork, and lamb. It is so simple and delicious that I use it as my "default meal" when I am entertaining a crowd and don't have a lot of time for preparation. I just pack all of the ingredients, except for the mashed potatoes, into a heavy casserole and let it bake in the oven for many hours at a low temperature. For make-ahead ease, consider the Mashed Potato and Cream Cheese Casserole for a Crowd (page 520) instead of the freshly cooked mashed potatoes.

SERVES 12 TO 16

2 pounds beef stew meat, cut into 1½ inch-inch cubes

1 pound lamb stew meat, cut into 1½ inch-inch cubes

1 pound boneless pork, cut into 1½-inch cubes

5 large onions, thinly sliced

1 teaspoon whole allspice berries

2 teaspoons salt

Hot buttered or mashed potatoes for serving

1. Preheat the oven to 275°F. In a deep, heavy casserole with a tight-fitting lid, preferably cast iron, layer the beef, lamb, and pork with the onions, allspice, and salt.

2. Press a piece of parchment or waxed paper right over the meat in the casserole, tucking the ends of the paper tightly around the edges. Cover and bake for at least 5 hours, or until the meat is very tender.

3. Remove the cover and paper, stir, and serve over hot buttered or mashed potatoes.

LAMB CURRY

This is a great party dish. Serve the curry surrounded by as many of the *sambals,* or toppings, as you like, and have guests make their selections. You don't need to add much more than a green salad and crusty bread for a very satisfying meal.

MAKES 10 TO 12 SERVINGS

4 pounds boneless lamb shoulder, cut into 1-inch cubes

5 tablespoons vegetable oil

1 cup coarsely chopped onion

5 large cloves garlic, chopped

2 cups homemade (page 25) or prepared chicken broth

⅔ cup mango chutney

3 tablespoons curry powder

¼ cup coriander seeds

¼ teaspoon ground mace

¼ teaspoon ground cloves

¼ teaspoon ground cinnamon

1 teaspoon salt

Pinch of cayenne pepper

2 tablespoons cornstarch

2 tablespoons cold water

Cooked rice for serving

SAMBALS (TOPPINGS):

1 cup golden raisins

1 cup toasted coconut

1 cup mango chutney

1 cup finely chopped peanuts

1 cup finely chopped red onion

1 cup finely chopped green onion tops

1 cup finely chopped cucumber

1 cup finely chopped tomato

1 medium green bell pepper, seeded and cut into 1-inch strips

1 cup bite-size banana chunks, sprinkled with lemon juice to prevent browning

1 cup bite-size apple chunks, sprinkled with lemon juice to prevent browning

1 cup drained pineapple tidbits or finely chopped fresh pineapple

1 cup drained mandarin orange segments

1 cup finely chopped hard-cooked egg

Crumbled crispy cooked bacon

1. Preheat the oven to 300°F. Pat the lamb cubes dry.

2. Heat 3 tablespoons of the oil over medium heat. Add the lamb cubes and brown, a few pieces at a time, and transfer to a 3-quart heavy Dutch oven.

3. When all the meat is browned, reduce the heat to low and add the remaining 2 tablespoons oil and the onion and sauté for 5 minutes. Add the garlic and sauté for 3 minutes longer. Remove from the heat and stir in the chicken broth, chutney, curry powder, coriander seeds, mace, cloves, cinnamon, salt, and cayenne. Pour over the lamb in the Dutch oven.

4. Cover and bake for 2 hours, or until the lamb is very tender. Mix the cornstarch and water and stir into the pan juices, and heat until thickened.

5. Prepare at least 8 of the *sambals* while the lamb cooks. Serve over cooked rice and offer the *sambals* in small dishes on the side for guests to add as they wish.

LASAGNA ROLLS

Instead of layering the lasagna noodles with the other ingredients, they are stuffed with a filling, rolled up, and then placed in the baking dish so that the rolls are standing on end. I like to cook the White Sauce and Herbed Tomato Sauce the day before to avoid last-minute cooking. This is a party dish for a lot of people. Add a salad of romaine lettuce, sliced onions, and black olives and a bottle of red wine to the menu.

SERVES 20 TO 24

½ cup (1 stick) butter

2 large onions, chopped

2 cloves garlic, minced

1¼ pounds extra-lean ground beef

1 pound ground turkey breast

2 cups ricotta or cream-style cottage cheese

1 cup grated Parmesan cheese

4 large egg yolks

1½ teaspoons salt

¼ teaspoon ground nutmeg

½ cup chopped fresh parsley

White Sauce (facing page)

Herbed Tomato Sauce (facing page)

2 packages (1 pound each) lasagna noodles

2 tablespoons olive oil

3 pounds mozzarella or Monterey Jack Cheese, sliced

1. Preheat the oven to 375°F.

2. In a large skillet, melt the butter over medium-high heat and add the onions and garlic. Sauté for 10 minutes, or until the onions are very tender. Add the ground meats and continue cooking, stirring often, until crumbly and no longer pink. Drain off the fat. Put the meat mixture in a large bowl and cool. Add the ricotta, Parmesan cheese, egg yolks, salt, nutmeg, and parsley and mix well.

3. Prepare the White Sauce and Herbed Tomato Sauce. Spoon half of each sauce into the bottom of two 9-by-13-inch pans.

4. Cook the lasagna according to package directions until al dente, or firm to the bite, and drain. Add the olive oil to the water and then drain the noodles. Lay them out flat on a work surface, side by side.

5. Spoon an equal amount of filling over two-thirds of each noodle. Roll up each noodle, starting from the filled end. Stand the rolls close together in the sauced baking pans. Spoon the remaining Herbed Tomato Sauce and White Sauce over the rolls, and top with the mozzarella cheese. Bake, uncovered, for about 45 minutes, or until heated through and the cheese is melted.

WHITE SAUCE

MAKES 5 CUPS

4 tablespoons butter

⅓ cup all-purpose flour

2 cups hot milk

3 cups hot homemade (page 25) or prepared chicken broth

In a medium saucepan, melt the butter over medium heat and stir in the flour until smooth. Gradually whisk in the hot milk and chicken broth. Bring to a boil, reduce heat to low and cook at a simmer, whisking constantly, until thickened and smooth. Cool and refrigerate if not using right away.

HERBED TOMATO SAUCE

MAKES 5 CUPS

3 tablespoons butter

¼ cup chopped green onion (white and green parts)

2 cans (15 ounces each) tomato sauce

1 cup homemade (page 25) or prepared chicken broth

1 teaspoon dried basil

½ teaspoon salt

In a large skillet, melt the butter. Add the green onion and sauté for 2 to 3 minutes, until soft. Add the tomato sauce, chicken broth, basil, and salt. Simmer, uncovered, for 30 minutes or until reduced and slightly thickened. Cool and refrigerate if not using right away.

MASHED POTATO AND CREAM CHEESE CASSEROLE FOR A CROWD

These mashed potatoes are light and fluffy, even after a couple of weeks in the freezer. Be sure to use brown-skinned russet potatoes.

SERVES 12 TO 16

¾ cup (1½ sticks) butter, divided, plus extra for the dish

5 pounds russet potatoes

1 cup half-and-half

¼ cup whole milk

1 package (8 ounces) cream cheese, cut up

2 teaspoons salt

Paprika for sprinkling

1. Preheat the oven to 350°F. Butter a 9-by-13-inch baking dish.

2. Peel the potatoes and cut into halves; cook in boiling salted water to cover until fork-tender. Drain and press through a potato ricer into a large bowl. Add ½ cup of the butter, the half-and-half, milk, cream cheese and salt. Mash together with a potato masher until smooth.

3. Spread the mashed potato mixture into the dish evenly. Dot with the remaining ¼ cup butter and drizzle the milk on top. Sprinkle with paprika.

4. Bake for 30 minutes. Serve immediately or cool completely and then freeze, well wrapped. Thaw in the refrigerator and heat through at 350°F just before serving.

MEXICAN CORNBREAD-CRUSTED PIE

I first made this pie when we lived in California decades ago. This spicy chili, baked under a thin cornbread crust, became a family favorite. Now I bring it to potlucks or make several to serve a crowd.

SERVES 10

FOR THE FILLING:

1½ pounds lean ground beef

1 medium onion, chopped

1 green bell pepper, seeded and chopped

2 cloves garlic, minced

2 teaspoons chili powder

1½ teaspoons ground cumin

1 teaspoon ground coriander

¼ teaspoon cayenne pepper

½ teaspoon salt

1 tablespoon all-purpose flour

2 cups frozen corn kernels

2 cans (14½ ounces each) chili-style diced tomatoes with their juice

FOR THE CORNBREAD TOPPING:

1 cup yellow cornmeal

½ cup all-purpose flour

1½ tablespoons sugar

2 teaspoons baking powder

¼ teaspoon salt

1 large egg

1 cup milk

¼ cup vegetable or canola oil

1. Preheat the oven to 400°F. Oil a 9-by-13-inch baking dish.

2. *To make the filling:* In a large nonstick skillet over medium-high heat, brown the beef, breaking it up with a wooden spoon. Drain the meat, keeping 3 tablespoons of the fat in the pan, and transfer the meat to the casserole dish.

3. Return the pan to medium-high heat and sauté the onion and bell pepper for 7 to 8 minutes. Add the garlic, chili powder, cumin, coriander, cayenne pepper, ½ teaspoon salt, and 1 tablespoon flour and stir until aromatic. Stir in the corn and the tomatoes with their juice. Cover the pan and bring the mixture to a gentle boil, stirring occasionally. Remove from the heat.

4. *To make the cornbread topping:* In a large bowl, stir the cornmeal, ½ cup flour, sugar, baking powder, and ¼ teaspoon salt together. Whisk the egg, milk, and oil together in a medium bowl and add to the dry ingredients, mixing until well blended. Pour the batter over the filling in the baking dish and spread it evenly with a spoon.

5. Bake for 20 to 25 minutes, or until the topping is lightly browned and a wooden skewer or toothpick inserted into the center comes out clean.

MINNESOTA CHICKEN HOT DISH

We've just got to include at least one Minnesota hot dish. A "hot dish" is strictly a Minnesota term for a casserole. We bring hot dishes to potlucks and family reunions, and we like to have them around for weekday nights when the family is going here and there. This makes enough to fill a 12-by-20-inch baking pan with 2-inch sides.

SERVES 24

10 cups diced cooked chicken

10 cups chopped celery

2 bunches green onions, sliced (white and green parts)

2 cans (4 ounces each) chopped green chiles

1 can (6 ounces) pitted ripe olives, drained and sliced

2 cups slivered almonds

1 teaspoon pepper

5 cups shredded Cheddar cheese, divided

2 cups regular or light mayonnaise

2 cups sour cream

5 cups crushed potato chips

1. Preheat the oven to 350°F. Butter two 9-by-13-inch baking dishes or one large full-sized steam-table pan, about 12 by 20 inches with 2-inch sides.

2. In a large bowl, combine the chicken, celery, green onions, green chiles, olives, almonds, pepper, and 2 cups of the cheese. In a small bowl, combine the mayonnaise and sour cream. Fold the sour cream mixture into the chicken mixture and spread out in the baking dishes or pan.

3. Sprinkle the casserole with the potato chips and the remaining cheese. (At this point you can cover and refrigerate the casserole overnight. Add 15 to 20 minutes to the baking time.)

4. Bake, uncovered, for 35 to 40 minutes, or until heated through.

MUSHROOM AND PINE NUT MEAT LOAF

Consider this as a main dish for a picnic. We toted this casserole along on a tasting trip through the Napa Valley, years ago. It is still one of our favorite meat loaves. Slice the loaf and keep it chilled. Serve with a hearty bread, pickles, vegetable relishes, fresh fruit, and a mellow cheese. Barbera, Zinfandel, Bordeaux, or Burgundy wines go well with this.

SERVES 16

1 medium onion, finely chopped

3 tablespoons butter

¼ pound mushrooms, finely chopped

¼ cup Cognac or another brandy

3 large eggs

½ cup homemade (page 26) or prepared beef broth

1 cup fresh or fine dry breadcrumbs

2 cloves garlic

½ teaspoon dried thyme

½ teaspoons ground allspice

½ teaspoon salt

1½ pounds lean ground beef

1 pound ground pork

½ pound cooked ham, diced ½ inch thick

⅔ cup pine nuts, divided

Whole-grain bread for serving

Mustard for serving

1. Preheat the oven to 325°F. Oil or butter a 2-quart loaf-shaped casserole or terrine.

2. In a large skillet, sauté the onion in 2 tablespoons of the butter for about 2 minutes over medium heat until translucent. Add the mushrooms, cognac, and remaining 1 tablespoon butter and sauté until the mushrooms are coated with butter, about 1 minute. Set aside.

3. In the container of a blender or the work bowl of a food processor, combine the eggs, broth, breadcrumbs, garlic, thyme, allspice, and salt and process until smooth. Transfer to a large bowl and add the ground beef, ground pork, and ham. Add the onions and mushrooms and ⅓ cup of the nuts and blend well.

4. Transfer the mixture to the prepared casserole and top with the remaining ⅓ cup pine nuts. Bake, uncovered, for 1½ hours, or until cooked through and the top of the loaf is browned.

5. Remove from the oven and cool completely. Then cover with waxed paper, and top with about a 1-pound weight (a wrapped pound of butter works well). Place in the refrigerator for at least 8 hours, until completely chilled and firm.

6. To serve, remove any congealed fat from the sides of the loaf. Slice ½ inch thick and serve on sliced whole-grain bread with a good mustard.

ONION GRATIN

This is a perfect buffet dish. Serve it alongside roast beef, and add a steamed vegetable in a vinaigrette dressing and a freshly baked loaf of bread.

SERVES 10

4 pounds sweet onions, such as Vidalia or Maui, sliced

7 tablespoons butter

5 hard-cooked eggs, chopped

2 cups Béchamel Sauce (page 21)

1 teaspoon dried tarragon

1 cup fine dry breadcrumbs

1. Preheat the oven to 375°F. Coat a shallow 3-quart casserole with cooking spray.

2. In a large skillet, cook the onions in 4 tablespoons of the butter over medium-high heat for 10 minutes. Reduce the heat to medium and cook for another 30 minutes, or until soft, stirring frequently. Transfer to the casserole and top with the hard-cooked eggs.

3. Make the Béchamel Sauce and add the tarragon. Pour over the onions in the casserole.

4. Melt the remaining 3 tablespoons butter in a small skillet and stir in the breadcrumbs. Sprinkle evenly over the casserole. Bake for 25 to 30 minutes, or until the breadcrumbs are browned and the casserole is bubbly around the edges.

POTATOES AND GREEN ONION GRATIN

Many casseroles are based on cubed cooked potatoes, and this one is a classic. The cheese topping is what makes it a gratin. Other gratins are topped with breadcrumbs.

SERVES 12

½ cup (1 stick) butter

¼ cup green onions, sliced (white and green parts)

½ cup chopped green bell pepper

½ cup chopped red bell pepper

1 teaspoon salt

¼ teaspoon pepper

1 tablespoon chopped fresh parsley

1 teaspoon paprika

6 tablespoons all-purpose flour

4 cups milk, heated

6 cups cubed cooked potatoes

2 cups shredded sharp Cheddar cheese, divided

1. Preheat the oven to 350°F. Coat a 9-by-13-inch baking dish with cooking spray.

2. In a large heavy skillet, melt the butter over medium heat. Add the green onions and green and red bell peppers and sauté for 1 minute. Add the salt, pepper, parsley, paprika, and flour and stir until blended. Gradually stir in the milk, heat to a simmer, and cook, stirring, until thickened. Add the cooked potatoes and 1 cup of the cheese and stir to blend.

3. Pour the sauce over the vegetables in the baking dish and sprinkle with the remaining 1 cup cheese. (At this point you can cover and refrigerate for up to 1 day. Add 10 to 15 minutes to the baking time.)

4. Bake, uncovered, for 30 to 35 minutes, or until bubbly.

POTATO AND ZUCCHINI CASSEROLE

When I was growing up on a farm in northern Minnesota, we did not know about zucchini, but today it's in just about every vegetable garden around. If you have one producing plant, you probably have too much zucchini. Although the first tiny fruits of the plant are relished by all, soon I need to do things like hide it between potatoes in a cream cheese sauce, as in this casserole.

SERVES 12

3 tablespoons butter, melted

2 packages (8 ounces each) cream cheese, softened (see Note)

½ cup milk

12 large eggs, lightly beaten

3 cups chopped peeled and cooked potatoes

¼ cup sliced green onions (white and green parts)

1 teaspoon salt

1 large or 2 medium zucchini, quartered lengthwise and cut into ¼-inch-thick slices (2 cups)

1 teaspoon dried basil, crushed

2 cups chopped tomatoes

1. Preheat the oven to 350°F.

2. Spread out the butter in the bottom of a 9-by-13-inch baking dish.

3. Mix 1 package of the cream cheese with the milk in a medium bowl until well blended. Mix in the eggs, and add the potatoes, green onions, and salt. Pour the mixture into the baking dish, and bake for 25 minutes.

4. Cut the second package of cream cheese into cubes and sprinkle over the top of the potatoes. Combine the zucchini, basil, and tomatoes and pour over the potatoes. Bake for 10 minutes longer, or until the potatoes and zucchini are tender.

○ ○ ○ ○ ○

NOTE: To soften cream cheese, remove from the foil wrapper and place on a microwave-safe dish. Microwave for 10 seconds at high power.

POTATOES AND MUSHROOMS IN PHYLLO CRUST

Phyllo (also spelled "filo") is a tissue-thin pastry that is used in various Greek and Middle Eastern preparations. In this savory one, the phyllo encases a creamy combination of potatoes, mushrooms, and fresh sage leaves. It makes a pretty buffet presentation.

SERVES 12

6 medium thin-skinned red or yellow potatoes

2 large onions, cut in half lengthwise and cut into ¼-inch strips

½ cup (1 stick) butter, cut into 8 tablespoons, divided

½ pound mushrooms, sliced

2 tablespoons chopped fresh sage

20 sheets phyllo dough

2 cups sour cream

1 large egg, beaten

2 tablespoons light cream

1. Preheat the oven to 350°F. Coat a 9-by-13-inch shallow baking dish with cooking spray.

2. Cook the potatoes in boiling salted water to cover for 10 to 15 minutes, or until tender; drain well and cool.

3. Meanwhile, in a large non-stick skillet, cook the onions in 1 tablespoon of the butter over medium-high heat until tender. Remove the onions to a bowl and set aside.

4. Melt another tablespoon butter in the skillet and add the mushrooms and sage. Sauté for 3 to 4 minutes over medium-high heat until the mushrooms are softened.

5. Pull the skins off the potatoes and cut the potatoes into ½-inch-thick slices.

6. Melt the remaining 6 tablespoons butter in a small saucepan. Unroll the phyllo dough and cover with a damp kitchen towel to prevent it from drying out. Place 1 sheet in the baking dish and brush with butter. Top with 2 more sheets of phyllo and brush with butter. Top with half of the sour cream, potatoes, onions, and mushroom mixture. Cover with 3 sheets of phyllo, and brush each sheet with butter. Layer the remaining sour cream, potatoes, onions, and mushroom mixture on top of the phyllo. Top with remaining 14 phyllo sheets, brushing between each with melted butter.

7. Mix the beaten egg and light cream and brush over the top of the casserole. Bake, uncovered, for 20 to 25 minutes, or until heated through and bubbly. Let stand for 5 minutes before cutting into squares.

SHRIMP AND CHICKEN PAELLA

It was on a a family-owned saffron farm in La Mancha, the land of Don Quixote in Spain, where I observed the most amazing preparation of paella. The pan measured 4 feet across and was set over an open fire. As the cooks stirred and fried chicken, sausage, and shrimp along with a myriad of other ingredients, we enjoyed roasted red bell peppers on crusty white bread with a glass of Spanish Tempranillo. The idea was to recognize the importance of the saffron in the paella. After watching the family painstakingly pull the stigmas from a mountain of saffron crocuses and learning that it takes 50,000 flowers to produce a pound of this, the world's most expensive spice, I felt a little guilty consuming this absolutely delicious dish.

SERVES 12 TO 16

1 cup extra-virgin olive oil

5 teaspoons dried oregano

5 teaspoons dried basil

4 cloves garlic, minced

2 teaspoons salt

1 teaspoon pepper

4 pounds boneless, skinless chicken breast halves, quartered

12 chicken legs

24 large shrimp, peeled, with tails left on, and deveined

2 pounds Spanish chorizo or pepperoni sausage, skinned and cut into 1-inch pieces

2 large onions, chopped

1 large green bell pepper, seeded and chopped

2 cups Arborio rice

3 cups hot homemade (page 25) or prepared chicken broth

4 large tomatoes, peeled, seeded, and chopped

Large pinch of saffron threads, crushed

2 cups fresh or frozen peas

¾ pound sea scallops, quartered

2 roasted red bell peppers, freshly roasted (see page 35) or from a jar, cut into matchsticks, for garnish

¼ cup chopped fresh cilantro for garnish

1. In a small bowl, combine the oil, oregano, basil, garlic, salt, and pepper.

2. Put the chicken breast pieces, chicken legs, and shrimp in a large bowl and pour the oil mixture over them. Cover and refrigerate for at least 4 hours and up to 1 day.

3. Preheat the oven to 350°F.

4. Remove the chicken from the marinade and put into a heavy 6-quart casserole or paella pan. (Leave the shrimp in the marinade, refrigerated.) Add the sausages, onions, bell pepper, rice, chicken broth, tomatoes, and saffron to the pot with the chicken.

5. Cover and bake for 25 minutes, or until the chicken and rice are tender and all the liquid has been absorbed. Add the shrimp, peas, and scallops. Bake, uncovered, for 15 to 20 minutes, or until the shrimp turn pink. Garnish with strips of bell pepper and the chopped cilantro.

SMOKED SALMON AND DILL CASSEROLE

You can assemble this casserole the night before baking, if you wish. The flavors will develop and blend during the chilling time. However, if you're in a rush, you can bake the dish right away.

SERVES 12

3 tablespoons butter at room temperature

12 slices day-old French bread, cubed

1 package (8 ounces) cream cheese, cubed

½ pound smoked salmon, flaked

12 large eggs

4 cups milk

1 teaspoon salt

½ teaspoon coarsely ground pepper

¼ cup coarsely chopped fresh dill, plus extra for garnish (optional)

1. Grease a 3-quart casserole with the butter. Arrange half of the bread in the dish. Distribute the cream cheese on top of the bread, then arrange the salmon evenly over the cheese. Top with the remaining bread cubes.

2. Mix the eggs, milk, salt, pepper, and dill in a large bowl and pour over the bread layer. If possible, cover and refrigerate for at least 12 hours and up to 1 day.

3. Preheat the oven to 350°F.

4. Uncover the casserole and bake for 45 minutes to 1 hour, or until set. Cut into squares to serve. Garnish with additional chopped dill, if desired, before serving.

ROGAN JOSH

The secret to Indian cooking is to brown the spices and onion slowly to bring out and develop their flavors. Serve this curry-like dish with cooked rice and peas.

SERVES 12

2 tablespoons vegetable oil

3 medium onions, finely chopped

1 piece fresh ginger, 2 inches long, finely chopped

3 pounds lean lamb stew meat, cut into 1-inch cubes

1 teaspoon ground ginger

1 teaspoon salt

2 cloves garlic, minced

½ teaspoon ground turmeric

½ teaspoon red pepper flakes

1 teaspoon garam masala (see Note)

½ teaspoon coriander, crushed

1 cup plain yogurt

1 can (14½ ounces) diced tomatoes with their juice

1. Preheat the oven to 325°F. Coat a 3- to 4-quart heavy-lidded casserole with cooking spray.

2. Heat the oil in a heavy skillet over medium heat. Add the onions and fresh ginger and cook slowly until browned, about 10 minutes. Push to the sides of the pan. Add the lamb, ground ginger, salt, garlic, turmeric, red pepper flakes, garam masala, and coriander and stir for 2 minutes. Stir in the yogurt and canned tomatoes with their juice. Transfer to the casserole, cover tightly, and bake for 3 hours, or until the lamb is very tender and aromatic.

NOTE: Garam masala is a blend of dry-roasted ground spices from northern India, and it adds a warm flavor to the dish. There are many different variations of garam masala, which often include black pepper, cinnamon, cloves, coriander, cumin, cardamom, dried chiles, fennel, mace, and nutmeg. You can buy premixed garam masala, which you will find with other spices or with Indian foods in a well-stocked market.

THANKSGIVING IN A CASSEROLE

The inspiration for this dish came from a small Lebanese food stand in Covent Garden, in London. I bought a slice of an attractive terrine, and made a sort of blueprint of it in my notebook. Then, at home in my own kitchen, I re-created its layers with the elements of our Thanksgiving dinner. Thus was born "Thanksgiving in a Casserole."

SERVES 10 AS A MAIN DISH,
OR 20 AS AN APPETIZER OR FIRST COURSE

1 recipe Flaky Pastry (page 32)

2 tablespoons whole-grain mustard

FOR THE TURKEY PÂTÉ:

1 clove garlic, peeled

1 pound ground turkey

1 large egg

1 teaspoon salt

½ teaspoon pepper

¼ teaspoon allspice

¼ teaspoon ground nutmeg

2 tablespoons brandy

FOR THE TURKEY LAYER:

1 ½ pounds fully cooked smoked turkey breast, thinly sliced

2 tablespoons whole-grain mustard

2 tablespoons brandy

FOR THE STUFFING:

4 tablespoons butter

1 small onion, minced

1 teaspoon dried thyme

½ cup homemade (page 25) or prepared chicken broth

2 tablespoons chopped fresh parsley

1 large egg

8 slices whole-wheat bread, cubed

FOR THE CRANBERRY LAYER:

1 package (12 ounces) fresh cranberries

1 cup water

1 cup sugar

1. Preheat the oven to 300°F. Prepare the pastry and roll out to a 12-inch circle. Transfer to a 10-inch springform pan, gently pressing the dough against the bottom and 2 inches up the sides of the pan. Crimp the edges and brush the bottom with mustard.

2. *To make the turkey pâté:* Combine all the ingredients in a food processor with the steel blade in place and process until smooth. Spread over the mustard-lined pastry in an even layer.

3. *To make the turkey layer:*
Top the pâté evenly with half of the turkey slices. Brush with 1 tablespoon mustard and sprinkle with 1 tablespoon brandy.

4. *To make the stuffing layer:*
Melt the butter in a skillet and add the onion; sauté for 5 to 10 minutes over medium heat until the onion is soft. Add the remaining stuffing ingredients and blend well. Pack the stuffing on top of the turkey layer in the pan. Top with the remaining turkey slices, 1 tablespoon mustard, and 1 tablespoon brandy.

5. Cut a piece of parchment paper or waxed paper and press on top of the turkey layer. Insert a meat thermometer into the center of the pie so that the tip is in the pâté. Bake for 2 hours, or until the thermometer registers 165°F. Cool the casserole.

6. *To make the cranberry layer:*
Combine the cranberries, water, and sugar in a saucepan. Heat to boiling and cook for 10 minutes at a gentle boil or until thick. Cool completely. Spread the cranberry mixture over

the top of the cooled casserole. Cover with aluminum foil and chill for about 4 hours. When ready to serve, uncover the casserole and remove the sides of the pan. Serve cold or at room temperature, cut into wedges.

TURKEY-NOODLE CASSEROLE FOR A CROWD

Perfect for a casual family gathering, this is soul food in a casserole. A green salad and fresh-baked bread or rolls round out the meal. Dessert? Ice cream sundaes!

SERVES 24

4 packages (8 ounces each) wide egg noodles

12 slices bacon, cut into ½-inch dice

5 pounds ground turkey breast

4 pounds mushrooms, sliced

4 large onions, chopped

1½ tablespoons salt

2 teaspoons pepper

1½ tablespoons dried thyme

2 cups dry white wine

4 cups homemade (page 25) or prepared chicken broth

1½ cups heavy cream

1 teaspoon ground nutmeg

8 cups shredded Gruyère cheese (about 2 pounds)

4 cups fine dry breadcrumbs

½ cup chopped fresh parsley for garnish

1. Preheat the oven to 350°F. Coat a 6- to 8-quart casserole with cooking spray.

2. Cook the noodles in boiling salted water until tender but still firm to the bite. Drain and set aside.

3. In a large sauté pan, cook the bacon until crisp and remove with a slotted spoon to drain on paper towels, leaving the drippings in the pan.

4. Brown the ground turkey in the pan in batches, stirring it to break it up, until crumbly. Remove to a dish as the turkey is cooked. Add the mushrooms and onions to the pan and cook until tender, 10 to 15 minutes. Return the turkey to the pan, season with the salt, pepper, and thyme, and cook the mixture for 5 minutes.

5. Pour the wine, broth, and cream into the pan, and bring to a boil, stirring to scrape up the browned bits from the bottom of the pan. Boil until reduced by about half and thickened. Add the nutmeg.

6. Combine the noodles with the turkey and sauce, and turn into the casserole dish. Top with the crumbled bacon, the cheese, and breadcrumbs. Bake until heated through, about 35 to 40 minutes. Garnish with the parsley and serve.

VEGETABLE FRITTATA

The Italians make an omelet by mixing eggs with other ingredients, and rather than folding the fillings inside, they finish the partially cooked dish in the oven. When you make a large frittata, big enough to serve a crowd, it needs to be baked. While it bakes, serve strawberry mimosas, and then add a fresh fruit salad and Cinnamon Bubble Bread (page 71) to the menu.

SERVES 24

6 pounds eggplant, cut into ½-inch-thick rounds

7 pounds potatoes, cut into ¼-inch-thick rounds

6 tablespoons oil

2½ tablespoons minced garlic

2½ pounds onions, chopped

¼ cup dried basil, or ¾ cup chopped fresh basil

6 pounds zucchini, cut into ¼-inch-thick rounds

6 cups diced fresh tomatoes, or 3 cans (15 ounces each) diced tomatoes with their juice

16 large eggs, beaten

4 cups shredded mozzarella cheese

2 cups grated Parmesan cheese

2 cups fine dry breadcrumbs

½ cup (1 stick) butter, melted

1. Preheat the oven to 400°F. Lightly oil two 9-by-13-inch baking dishes with 1 tablespoon oil in each.

2. Arrange the eggplant slices in the pans; cover tightly with aluminum foil, and bake until tender, about 45 minutes. Remove the eggplant from the pans and set aside. Lower the oven temperature to 350°F.

3. Boil the potatoes in boiling salted water to cover until just tender, and then drain.

4. Meanwhile, heat the remaining 4 tablespoons oil in a large skillet. Add the garlic and onions and cook until the onions are translucent. Add the dried basil (if using fresh basil, add it later). Stir in the zucchini and sauté until barely tender.

5. Combine the tomatoes with the fresh basil (if using).

6. Layer the ingredients in each pan in the following order: half of the potato slices, half of the eggplant, half of the zucchini mixture, half of the tomatoes, half of the eggs, 2 cups of the mozzarella cheese, and 1 cup of the Parmesan cheese. Mix the breadcrumbs with the melted butter and sprinkle evenly over the top of each casserole.

7. Cover and bake for 30 minutes. Uncover and continue baking for 15 minutes longer, or until the top is lightly browned. To serve, cut into 12 servings per pan.

Chapter 15
CASSEROLES FOR TWO

How many of us begin our cooking lives by preparing meals for two? But families tend to grow, and soon we are cooking for three, four, or five. Then, we end up cooking for two again (if we're so lucky). Often, it is really hard to return to preparing smaller amounts, and people either end up with lots of leftovers, or resort to eating out often.

The casseroles in this chapter are designed to help with those starting-up and winding-down processes, offering some interesting flavors and relatively simple preparations.

BAKED EGGS WITH ARTICHOKES AND PARMESAN

For an intimate brunch for two, this is perfect. Add a compote of bananas, pineapple, and fresh berries in season.

SERVES 2

2 teaspoons chopped fresh basil

1 teaspoon chopped fresh thyme

1 teaspoon chopped fresh oregano

8 canned artichoke heart quarters, or 8 frozen artichoke heart quarters, cooked according to package directions

Two 1-inch squares Brie cheese

2 large eggs

Salt

Pepper

2 tablespoons grated Parmesan cheese

1. Preheat the oven to 400°F. Coat the bottom and sides of two ¾-cup soufflé dishes or custard cups with cooking spray.

2. Sprinkle each cup with half of the herbs. Drain the artichokes and place 4 in each dish. Top each dish with 1 square Brie cheese.

3. Crack 1 egg into each dish, being careful not to break the yolk. Sprinkle with salt, pepper, and the cheese.

4. Bake until the eggs are softly set but still jiggly and the cheese is melted, 12 minutes. Serve immediately.

BAKED PASTA PUTTANESCA FOR TWO

This is a pasta with a spicy blend of ingredients. The name is actually derived from the Italian word *puttana*, which means "whore." According to Sharon Tyler Herbst, the author of *The Food Lover's Companion,* one explanation for the name is that the intense fragrance of the sauce was like an invitation to the men who visited such ladies of the night. This version of the popular pasta dish can be made ahead and finished off in the oven just before you plan to serve it.

SERVES 2

¼ pound linguine or vermicelli

2 tablespoons olive oil

3 cloves garlic, coarsely chopped

3 anchovy fillets, chopped

1 can (14½ ounces) stewed tomatoes with their juice

Salt

Pepper

½ cup pitted kalamata olives, coarsely chopped

2 tablespoons capers

Red pepper flakes

½ cup grated Parmesan cheese

Chopped fresh herbs such as parsley, oregano, marjoram, or basil for garnish

1. Preheat the oven to 350°F. Butter a shallow 1½-quart casserole.

2. Bring a pot of salted water to a boil and add the pasta. Cook according to package directions. Drain and transfer the pasta to the casserole dish.

3. In a large skillet, heat the olive oil over medium heat and add the garlic and anchovies. Cook, stirring occasionally, until the garlic is pale gold. Crush the tomatoes with a fork, add to the skillet with their juice, and season with salt and pepper to taste. Raise the heat to medium-high and cook, stirring occasionally, until the juices cook down and the mixture is saucy, about 10 minutes. Stir in the olives, capers, and red pepper flakes to taste. Pour the mixture over the pasta in the casserole. (At this point you can cover and refrigerate for up to 1 day. Add 5 to 10 minutes to the baking time.)

4. Sprinkle the casserole with the Parmesan and bake for 15 minutes, or until heated through. Sprinkle with the fresh chopped herbs.

BROCCOLI AND CHICKEN CASSEROLE FOR TWO

Layers of noodles, broccoli, and cooked chicken compose this casserole. For variety, you can use ham, shrimp, or another shellfish in place of the chicken.

SERVES 2

1½ tablespoons butter

2 cups sliced mushrooms

¼ cup finely diced onions

1 bunch broccoli, cut into florets

¼ pound egg noodles

¼ teaspoon salt

Dash of pepper

1 cup cubed cooked chicken

1 cup sour cream

1 cup grated Parmesan cheese, divided

1. Preheat the oven to 350°F.

2. Melt the butter in a small nonstick skillet. Brush a shallow 1½-quart casserole with some of the butter. Add the mushrooms and onions to the skillet and cook over low heat for 4 to 5 minutes, until the onions are soft.

3. Meanwhile, heat a pot of salted water to boiling, drop in the broccoli florets, and simmer for 3 to 4 minutes, or until the broccoli turns bright green. Remove the broccoli with a slotted spoon and set aside. Add the noodles to the boiling water and cook according to package directions until the noodles are al dente, or firm to the bite.

4. Transfer half of the cooked noodles to the buttered casserole dish, and top with the mushrooms and broccoli. Sprinkle with salt and pepper.

5. Mix the remaining noodles with the chicken, sour cream, and ½ cup of the Parmesan. Spread over the broccoli and mushrooms. (At this point you can cover and refrigerate the casserole for up 1 day and add 5 to 10 minutes to the final baking time.)

6. Bake for 25 to 30 minutes, or until heated through. Sprinkle with the remaining ½ cup Parmesan and return to the oven for 2 to 3 minutes, until the cheese melts.

CHEESE SOUFFLÉ FOR TWO

This elegant dish is perfect for lunch or supper. Add a salad of baby greens with red and yellow tomatoes, tossed with a lemon vinaigrette, and a crusty bread to round out the meal.

MAKES 2 SERVINGS

1½ tablespoons butter, plus extra for the dish and the foil

1 tablespoon grated Parmesan cheese

1½ tablespoons all-purpose flour

½ cup milk

Dash of cayenne pepper

⅛ teaspoon dry mustard

½ teaspoon salt

½ cup shredded sharp Cheddar or Swiss cheese

4 large eggs, separated, at room temperature

1. Preheat the oven to 400°F. Butter a 1-quart soufflé dish and dust with the grated Parmesan cheese. Cut a sheet of aluminum foil long enough to wrap around the soufflé dish. Fold the foil in half lengthwise and butter one side. Wrap around the soufflé dish, buttered side facing in, so that it extends above the rim of the dish by 2 inches. Fold the ends of the foil together to fasten.

2. In a medium saucepan, melt the 1½ tablespoons butter and stir in the flour. Gradually whisk in the milk and add the cayenne, mustard, and salt. Bring to a boil and cook at a gentle boil over medium heat, stirring constantly, until thickened. Add the cheese and continue stirring until the cheese is melted. Remove from the heat.

3. In a small bowl, stir the egg yolks until broken. Whisk in a little of the hot sauce to temper the yolks, then add to the saucepan, stirring until well blended.

4. In a medium bowl, beat the egg whites until they hold short, distinct, but soft peaks. Fold about half the whites thoroughly into the sauce, then fold in the remaining whites. Pour into the prepared soufflé dish.

5. Bake for 25 to 30 minutes, or until puffed and golden. Serve right away.

CHICKEN AND BROWN RICE FOR TWO

This one is perfect for the day after a hectic afternoon. Buy a rotisserie chicken from the supermarket for dinner on your busy day, and save the extra meat for this casserole. Round out the menu with a roasted mixed vegetable salad, which you can cook while this casserole bakes.

— SERVES 2 —

4 tablespoons butter, divided

1½ tablespoons all-purpose flour

1 cup homemade (page 25) or prepared chicken broth

2 tablespoons milk

1 tablespoon dry sherry

1 cup diced cooked chicken or turkey

Salt

Pepper

1 cup cooked brown rice

1 cup frozen peas

2 tablespoons grated Parmesan cheese

1 tablespoon seasoned fine dry breadcrumbs

1. Preheat the oven to 400°F. Coat a shallow 1½-quart casserole with cooking spray.

2. Melt 3 tablespoons of the butter in a saucepan over medium heat. Blend in the flour and cook for 1 minute without browning. Gradually whisk in the chicken broth, milk, and sherry, bring to a boil, and cook, stirring constantly, until thickened and smooth. Blend in the chicken and salt and pepper to taste, and remove from the heat.

3. Spread out the rice in the casserole and top with the peas. Spread the chicken mixture over the top. Dot with the remaining 1 tablespoon butter. Sprinkle with the Parmesan cheese and breadcrumbs.

4. Bake, uncovered, for 20 minutes, or until bubbly.

CHICKEN BREASTS COOKED WITH MORELS

Morels are among the most aromatic of the wild mushrooms. They are distinctive looking, too; their crinkly tops resemble the structure of brains. Morels can be found in the woods under dead or dying elms, sometimes under old pine trees, and in old apple orchards. Although they may be moving northward, typically they grow at the same latitude as southern Wisconsin. A much easier (but expensive) way to find morels is to buy them on the Internet or at a greengrocer. Dried morels can be reconstituted by simply soaking them in hot water for up to 30 minutes. Or, as in this recipe, they can be crushed and added to liquid ingredients during cooking.

SERVES 2

2 bone-in chicken breast halves

1 tablespoon all-purpose flour

½ teaspoon salt, plus extra for seasoning flour

Pepper

1½ tablespoons canola oil

1 small onion, chopped

3 cups homemade (page 25) or prepared chicken broth

1 bay leaf

1 sprig fresh parsley

1 teaspoon dried marjoram

1 teaspoon dried thyme

4 cloves garlic, minced

4 whole dried morels, crushed

Hot cooked rice for serving

1. Preheat the oven to 350°F. Wash the chicken, and pat dry. Mix the flour and salt and pepper to taste in a shallow bowl and coat the chicken.

2. Heat the oil in a heavy 3-quart Dutch oven. Add the onion and cook over medium heat for 5 minutes, or until translucent but not browned. Add the chicken and brown on both sides. Add the broth, bay leaf, parsley, marjoram, thyme, garlic, dried morels, and ½ teaspoon salt.

3. Cover and bake for 45 minutes, or until the chicken is tender. Remove and discard the bay leaf and parsley sprig. Serve over hot cooked rice.

CREAMY BAKED CHICKEN WITH MUSHROOMS AND GREEN OLIVES

This is an attractive dish. Sometimes I like to add a package of artichoke hearts along with the mushrooms. Serve the casserole with a side of buttered green noodles.

— MAKES 2 SERVINGS —

2 chicken legs and thighs, split (4 pieces)

½ teaspoon salt

¼ teaspoon pepper

Dash of paprika

1 tablespoon butter

1 teaspoon all-purpose flour

1 teaspoon Dijon mustard

¼ cup dry white wine

¼ cup homemade (page 25) or prepared chicken broth

¼ cup heavy cream

1 cup sliced mushrooms

¼ cup sliced stuffed green olives

2 tablespoons minced fresh parsley

1 teaspoon herbes de Provence (see Note)

¼ cup chopped salted sunflower seeds

1. Preheat the oven to 375°F. Wash the chicken and pat dry with paper towels. Sprinkle with the salt, pepper, and paprika.

2. In a large heavy skillet, melt the butter. Add the chicken and brown thoroughly on both sides. Transfer to a 1-quart casserole.

3. Stir the flour and mustard into the drippings in the skillet. Whisk in the wine, broth, and cream and bring to a boil, whisking constantly. Continue cooking at a gentle boil for about 3 minutes, or until the sauce is thickened. Stir in the mushrooms, olives, parsley, and dried herbs. Pour the sauce over the chicken in the casserole.

4. Cover and bake for 30 minutes, or until the chicken is tender. Sprinkle with the sunflower seeds and bake, uncovered, for 5 minutes longer.

NOTE: Herbes de Provence is an assortment of dried herbs that are commonly used in southern France. The mixture usually contains basil, fennel seed, lavender, marjoram, rosemary, sage, summer savory, and thyme.

ORZO CHICKEN

This casserole comes together in just a few minutes—and you can even assemble it ahead of time. Add a salad of Belgian endive, radicchio, and a leaf lettuce with a vinaigrette dressing and a generous sprinkling of fresh herbs and pine nuts.

SERVES 2

2 tablespoons all-purpose flour

1 teaspoon salt

½ teaspoon pepper

2 boneless, skinless chicken breast halves

¾ cup plain or multigrain orzo

1 cup hot homemade (page 25) or prepared chicken broth

½ cup finely chopped sweet onion

1 fresh tomato, diced

½ cup heavy cream

½ cup sour cream

½ cup shredded mozzarella cheese

1. Preheat the oven to 400°F. Coat a shallow 1½-quart casserole with cooking spray. Combine the flour, salt, and pepper in a shallow bowl and coat the chicken breast halves.

2. Spread out the orzo in the bottom of the casserole dish and pour the hot chicken broth over it. Top with the onion, tomato, and seasoned chicken breasts.

3. Mix the heavy cream and sour cream together and spoon over the chicken. Bake, uncovered, for 30 minutes, or until the chicken is cooked through. Sprinkle with the cheese and let stand for 5 minutes, until the cheese is melted.

EGG CASSEROLE FOR TWO

This is basically a breakfast bread pudding. It's perfect for a leisurely late breakfast or brunch. I've sometimes put this together as a quick supper after a busy day. The recipe lends itself to endless variations; see the suggestions below.

───────── SERVES 2 ─────────

3 large eggs

3 tablespoons milk

2 slices thick-cut white or whole-wheat bread, cut into 1-inch cubes

2 teaspoons fresh chopped basil

1 green onion, chopped (white and green parts)

⅓ cup shredded Cheddar cheese

⅓ cup chopped ham or crisp fried bacon

1. Preheat the oven to 350°F. Coat a shallow 3 or 4-cup casserole with cooking spray.

2. In a medium bowl, whisk the eggs and milk together. Add the bread, basil, green onion, cheese, and ham. Mix until all the bread is moistened.

3. Pour into the casserole and bake for 20 to 25 minutes, or until the egg mixture is set.

Variations

Crab and Egg Casserole: Add one 6-ounce package or can of crabmeat to the mixture along with the eggs and milk.

Herbed Egg Casserole: Add a couple of handfuls of chopped fresh herbs, such as basil, parsley, and fresh sage. Substitute ¼ cup grated Parmesan cheese for the Cheddar cheese.

FETA AND MUSHROOM CHICKEN BREASTS

Here's a dinner for two that you can prepare in about 30 minutes. While the chicken bakes, toss a salad and open up a nice chilled white wine.

SERVES 2

1 tablespoon butter

2 boneless, skinless chicken breast halves

½ teaspoon salt

¼ teaspoon pepper

Dash of paprika

1 teaspoon all-purpose flour

¼ cup heavy cream

1 teaspoon Dijon mustard

1 cup sliced mushrooms

6 tablespoons halved pitted kalamata olives

¼ cup crumbled feta cheese

2 tablespoons minced fresh parsley for garnish

1. Preheat the oven to 400°F. Put the butter in a shallow 1-quart casserole and put the casserole in the oven as it preheats. Watch carefully so the butter does not burn.

2. Remove the casserole from the oven and roll the chicken breasts in the melted butter. Arrange them in the casserole and sprinkle on both sides with the salt, pepper, paprika, and flour.

3. Whisk the cream and mustard together.

4. Spread the sliced mushrooms and ¼ cup of the olives on top of the chicken and pour the cream mixture over all.

5. Bake 20 to 25 minutes, or until the chicken is cooked through. Sprinkle with the remaining 2 tablespoons olives and the feta and return to the oven for 5 minutes until heated through. Sprinkle with the parsley and serve hot.

SPINACH AND JACK CHEESE CASSEROLE FOR TWO

Packaged fresh spinach is a great time-saver. It is already washed of all sand and grit. What looks like a large volume, however, cooks way down! When you shop for the spinach, you will find it in variously sized bags. The lightest one is usually 5 ounces.

SERVES 2

1 bag (5 ounces) fresh baby spinach

½ cup shredded Monterey Jack or Swiss cheese

1 small onion, minced

½ teaspoon salt

¼ teaspoon pepper

2 large eggs

1 tablespoon seasoned fine dry breadcrumbs

1. Preheat the oven to 350°F. Butter a shallow 3- to 4-cup casserole.

2. Chop the spinach and transfer to a large bowl. Mix in the cheese, onion, salt, pepper, and eggs. Press the mixture into the casserole.

3. Sprinkle with the breadcrumbs and bake for 45 minutes, or until the top is golden and the casserole is set.

HERBED ORECCHIETTE WITH SORREL AND ASIAGO

We have perennial sorrel in our herb garden. The leaves, which resemble spinach, have a lemony flavor. And like spinach, sorrel cooks down to next to nothing. Don't let its small volume fool you, though—it does pack a punch of flavor!

SERVES 2

2 tablespoons butter

¼ cup chopped green onions (white and green parts)

½ cup chopped fresh sorrel leaves

1 cup orecchiette (ear-shaped pasta)

1 cup low-sodium chicken broth, heated to boiling

1 tablespoon chopped fresh basil

¼ cup grated Asiago cheese

Salt

Pepper

1. Preheat the oven to 300°F. Smear a 1-quart casserole with 1 tablespoon of the butter.

2. Melt the remaining 1 tablespoon butter in a heavy, medium saucepan and add the green onions and sorrel leaves. Sauté for 2 minutes. Mix in the pasta and transfer the mixture to the buttered casserole. Pour the boiling broth over all and mix well.

3. Cover and bake for 15 minutes, or until the pasta has absorbed the broth. Uncover and sprinkle with the basil and Asiago cheese. Bake for 5 minutes longer, until the cheese is melted. Season with salt and pepper to taste.

TURKEY DRUMSTICK AND WILD RICE CASSEROLE

Slip this into a low oven, and let it cook throughout the day. The turkey drumsticks will bake to delicious tenderness. No time to assemble the dish in the morning? Get everything ready the night before.

SERVES 2

2 slices bacon

2 turkey drumsticks

½ cup chopped celery

⅓ cup chopped carrot

¼ cup chopped onion

1 can (14½ ounces) chicken broth

⅛ teaspoon dried marjoram

⅛ teaspoon pepper

½ cup wild rice, rinsed and drained

½ cup sour cream

1. Preheat the oven to 275°F.

2. Place a heavy, flameproof 2½-quart casserole over medium heat. Add the bacon and cook until crisp. Remove from the heat.

3. Add the turkey, celery, carrot, onion, chicken broth, marjoram, pepper, and wild rice. (At this point the casserole can be covered and refrigerated overnight.)

4. Place the casserole in the oven, tightly covered, and bake for 7 to 8 hours, or until the rice is tender and the liquid has been absorbed. Stir in the sour cream and serve.

HUNGARIAN GOULASH FOR TWO

When cooking a small amount of meat, as in this goulash, it is important to keep it from baking dry. See the Note below for instructions on sealing the casserole.

SERVES 2

1 tablespoon butter

2 tablespoons sweet Hungarian paprika

¾ pound lean beef stew meat, cut into 1-inch cubes

1 large onion, finely chopped

1 clove garlic, minced

½ teaspoon caraway seeds

½ teaspoon dried marjoram

Pepper

1 small bay leaf

½ pound lean smoked ham, cubed

½ cup dry red wine

Salt

½ cup sour cream

Chopped fresh parsley for garnish

Hot buttered noodles for serving

1. Preheat the oven to 325°F.

2. While the oven preheats, put the butter and paprika in a heavy 1-quart casserole and put it in the oven, uncovered, until the paprika is aromatic.

3. Add the stew meat, onion, garlic, caraway seeds, marjoram, pepper to taste, the bay leaf, ham, and wine. Cover and bake for 2½ hours, or until the meat is very tender. Taste and add salt and pepper if needed.

4. Just before serving, stir in the sour cream. Garnish each serving with chopped parsley and serve over hot buttered noodles.

○ ○ ○ ○ ○

NOTE: If the cover of the casserole is loose-fitting, seal the casserole with aluminum foil, then place the cover on top.

CASSEROLE PRIMAVERA

I like to assemble this casserole ahead of time, either hours ahead or the evening before a busy day. Vary the vegetables according to what's in season and what you have in your fridge. This would be fine all by itself, but it's also tasty with a good old grilled hamburger!

SERVES 2

½ teaspoon cumin seeds

¾ cup finely chopped sweet onions

1 small clove garlic, minced

½ cup finely diced carrot

1 small jalapeño pepper, seeded and finely chopped

1 cup chopped fresh tomato, or 1 cup canned diced tomatoes with their juice

⅓ cup fresh or frozen corn kernels

¾ cup diced zucchini

½ cup penne pasta, cooked according to package directions and drained

1 cup canned red kidney beans, drained and rinsed

¼ cup reduced-fat shredded sharp Cheddar cheese

1. Preheat the oven to 350°F. Coat a shallow 1½-quart casserole with cooking spray.

2. Place a large nonstick skillet over low heat and add the cumin seeds. Cook and stir until they become aromatic. Add the onions and garlic and cook until the onion is soft and translucent, 10 to 15 minutes. Stir occasionally and add a little water or stock, if necessary, to prevent scorching. Add the carrot, jalapeño, and tomato and simmer, uncovered, for 15 minutes. Add the corn and zucchini and simmer until the zucchini is tender, about 5 more minutes. Stir in the cooked pasta and drained beans and mix well.

3. Transfer the mixture to the casserole and top with the cheese. (At this point you can cover and refrigerate the casserole for 1 day. If you do this, remove from the refrigerator when you begin preheating the oven and add 5 minutes to baking time.)

4. Bake the casserole for about 10 minutes, or until the cheese is melted.

PORK CHOPS AND APPLES

Pork chops are the most popular cut from the pork loin, which runs from the pig's hip to its shoulder. Serve with a baked potato and a crisp slaw.

SERVES 2

1 tablespoon butter

1 small onion, sliced

1 clove garlic, minced

¾ pound boneless loin pork chops (about 2), cut into 1-inch cubes

2 teaspoons all-purpose flour

⅔ cup apple cider

3 tablespoons homemade (page 26) or prepared beef broth

½ teaspoon dried sage

Salt

Pepper

1 apple peeled, cored, and sliced

2 tablespoons light cream

Chopped fresh parsley for garnish

1. Preheat the oven to 350°F.

2. Melt the butter in a heavy skillet over medium-high heat. Add the onion and garlic and sauté until soft. Add the pork and brown quickly on all sides over high heat. Transfer the pork to a shallow 2-quart casserole, preferably an oven-to-table dish.

3. Lower the heat to medium, add the flour to the skillet, and cook for 1 minute. Gradually whisk in the cider and broth and simmer, stirring, until the sauce is thickened. Add the sage and season with salt and pepper to taste.

4. Arrange the pork in the casserole and top with the apple. Pour the sauce over both.

5. Cover and bake for about 30 minutes, or until the meat is cooked through and the apples are soft. Stir in the cream and sprinkle with parsley.

PORK CHOP AND POTATO BAKE

To my mind, meat that still has the bone in always has more flavor. Here's a simple casserole that you can put together while the oven preheats.

2 bone-in pork chops

2 medium baking potatoes, scrubbed, cut into lengthwise quarters

1 tablespoon olive oil

2 tablespoons fine dry breadcrumbs

2 cloves garlic, minced

1 teaspoon balsamic vinegar

½ teaspoon kosher salt

½ teaspoon pepper

1 medium tomato, diced

1 teaspoon dried sage, crushed

1. Preheat the oven to 400°F. Line a rimmed baking pan with aluminum foil or parchment paper and coat with cooking spray.

2. Brush the pork chops and potatoes with the olive oil and sprinkle with the breadcrumbs.

Place in the baking pan and sprinkle with the garlic, balsamic vinegar, salt, and pepper.

3. Bake for 30 minutes. Add the tomato and sage and return to the oven for 5 minutes longer.

POTATO-CRUSTED SALMON FILLET

Alaska salmon is our favorite. I like to bake it slowly to retain maximum moisture, then top it with mashed potatoes, and finish it off under the broiler.

SERVES 2

¾ pound salmon fillet

½ small onion, finely chopped

¼ teaspoon dried thyme

¼ cup dry white wine or apple cider

Salt

Pepper

4 to 5 tablespoons milk

1 tablespoon butter

2 tablespoons all-purpose flour

FOR THE TOPPING:

2 potatoes, peeled and chopped

Salt

Pepper

2 tablespoons butter

¼ cup heavy cream

1. Preheat the oven to 300°F.

2. Place the salmon in a shallow buttered casserole dish. Top with the onion, thyme, and wine. Sprinkle with salt and pepper. Cover and bake for 20 minutes, or until the salmon flakes when probed with a fork.

3. Strain the cooking liquid into a measuring cup. Add enough milk to equal ¾ cup. Melt the butter in a saucepan over medium-high heat and stir in the flour. Cook, stirring for 1 minute. Gradually whisk in the ¾ cup liquid. Bring to a boil and cook, stirring, until the sauce thickens. Season with salt and pepper to taste.

4. *To make the topping:* Cook the potatoes in boiling salted water to cover until fork-tender. Drain, mash, and add salt and pepper to taste. Whisk in the butter and cream. Preheat the broiler.

5. Spread the potatoes over the fish and score a pattern on top with a fork. Place under the broiler and brown for 2 to 3 minutes.

CHICKEN BREASTS WITH SWISS CHEESE

Making this dish is a snap. While the oven preheats, assemble the chicken breasts in a shallow casserole. Then, while the chicken bakes, toss a salad and warm up some crusty bread. You'll have an elegant meal in less than an hour.

SERVES 2

2 boneless, skinless chicken breast halves (about 1 pound)

½ teaspoon kosher salt

¼ teaspoon pepper

¼ teaspoon paprika

1 teaspoon cornstarch

2 tablespoons dry sherry

⅓ cup half-and-half

½ cup shredded Swiss cheese

Chopped fresh parsley for garnish

1. Preheat the oven to 350°F. Coat a shallow 2-quart casserole with cooking spray.

2. Rinse the chicken breasts and pat dry. Sprinkle with the salt, pepper, and paprika.

3. Combine the cornstarch, sherry, and half-and-half in a small bowl and pour over the chicken breasts evenly. Bake, uncovered, for 20 minutes. Spoon the pan sauces over the chicken to baste. Bake for 10 minutes longer. Sprinkle with the cheese and return to the oven just long enough to melt it, about 5 minutes longer. Sprinkle with the parsley.

SALMON SOUFFLÉ

To complete a meal, serve this salmon with roasted potatoes and a salad of blanched asparagus, dressed with a bit of soy sauce and sesame oil.

1 tablespoon grated Parmesan cheese

½ cup canned flaked salmon

1½ tablespoons butter, plus extra for the foil

1½ tablespoons all-purpose flour

½ cup milk, heated

Dash of cayenne pepper

¼ teaspoon dried dill

⅛ teaspoon dry mustard

½ teaspoon salt

½ cup shredded sharp Cheddar or Swiss cheese

4 large eggs, separated, at room temperature

1. Preheat the oven to 400°F. Coat a 1-quart soufflé dish with cooking spray and dust with the grated Parmesan. Cut a sheet of aluminum foil long enough to wrap around the soufflé dish. Fold the foil in half lengthwise and butter one side. Wrap around the soufflé dish, buttered side facing in, so that it extends above the rim of the dish by 2 inches. Fold the ends of the foil together to fasten.

2. Melt the 1½ tablespoons butter in a saucepan and blend in the flour. Gradually whisk in the milk, cayenne, dill, mustard, and salt. Bring to a boil and cook over medium heat, stirring constantly, until thickened. Add the cheese and continue stirring until the cheese is melted. Remove from the heat.

3. In a small bowl, stir the egg yolks until broken. Whisk in a little of the hot sauce to temper the yolks, and then pour into the saucepan, stirring until well blended.

4. In a medium bowl, beat the egg whites until they hold short, distinct, but soft peaks. Fold about half the whites thoroughly into the sauce, then fold in the remaining whites.

5. Pour into the prepared soufflé dish and bake for 25 to 30 minutes, until puffed and golden. Serve right away.

TUNA CASSEROLE FOR TWO

Celery and green bell pepper add crunch to this beloved classic.
And it is so easy and quick to prepare.

SERVES 2

2 quarts water

1 teaspoon salt

¾ cup elbow macaroni or shell pasta

1 can (6 ounces) solid tuna, drained

½ cup sour cream

⅛ teaspoon oregano

¼ cup sliced ripe olives

1 cup sliced mushrooms

½ cup chopped green bell pepper

¼ cup chopped celery

½ cup shredded Cheddar cheese

1. Preheat the oven to 350°F. Butter a shallow 1½-quart casserole.

2. Bring the water to a boil. Add the salt to the water, and then the macaroni, and cook for 8 to 10 minutes, or until tender but still firm to the bite. Drain and transfer to a large bowl. Add the tuna, sour cream, oregano, olives, mushrooms, green pepper, and celery. Mix well and transfer to the casserole.

3. Bake for 20 to 25 minutes, until bubbly. Remove from the oven and sprinkle with the cheese. Let stand 5 minutes until the cheese melts.

TUNA MELT SANDWICH FOR TWO

Assembled ahead and baked in a casserole, this can easily be multiplied to serve more than 2 people. Serve with potato chips and pickles.

SERVES 2

2 slices whole-wheat bread

2 teaspoons butter

1 can (6 ounces) water-packed tuna, drained

½ cup chopped celery

1 tablespoon finely chopped red onion

½ cup light mayonnaise

1 teaspoon fresh lime juice

¼ teaspoon dried dill

½ cup shredded Gruyère, Fontina, or Swiss cheese

2 slices tomato

1. Preheat the oven to 400°F. Coat the bottom of a shallow casserole, about 6 by 9 inches with cooking spray.

2. Spread each slice of bread with 1 teaspoon butter and place in the casserole.

3. Mix the tuna, celery, onion, mayonnaise, lime juice, and dill. Mound half of the tuna mixture on each slice of bread. Top each with ¼ cup of the shredded cheese.

4. Bake for 15 minutes, or until heated through and the cheese is melted. Top with the tomato and serve right away.

STEAK SMOTHERED WITH ONIONS AND MUSHROOMS

Cooking for two can often result in bits of leftovers, but not this dish. It is easily consumed in one sitting.

SERVES 2

2 tablespoons all-purpose flour

Salt

Pepper

2 sirloin steaks (about 4 ounces each)

2 tablespoons butter

2 medium onions, thinly sliced

3 cloves garlic, pressed in a garlic press

2 cups half-and-half or milk, heated

¼ cup sherry

½ pound mushrooms, sliced

1. Preheat the oven to 325°F. Coat a shallow 2-quart casserole with cooking spray.

2. Mix the flour with salt and pepper and dust the steaks with it. Reserve the extra flour.

3. Melt 1 tablespoon of the butter in a nonstick skillet. Add the steaks and brown quickly over medium-high heat, turning once. Place in the casserole dish.

4. Add the remaining 1 tablespoon butter to the skillet. Add the onions and garlic and stir over medium-high heat until aromatic, 3 to 4 minutes. Sprinkle with the reserved seasoned flour (about 1 tablespoon) and stir until blended. Gradually whisk in the half-and-half, bring to a boil, and cook until thickened. Add the sherry and cook for another 2 to 3 minutes.

5. Spread mushrooms over the steak in the casserole and pour the sauce over evenly. Cover and bake for 45 minutes. Uncover and bake for an additional 15 minutes, or until bubbly.

Chapter 16
CASSEROLES FOR KIDS

Cooking for kids can present multiple challenges when you are strapped for time and energy. And to complicate matters, kids don't care much for foods that are mixed up. But it is important to teach them good eating habits. Whenever possible, I incorporate whole-grain pasta and vegetables into casseroles.

BAKED NOODLES CASSEROLE

Consider this a template of a casserole for kids. It can be varied endlessly, depending on what the kids like and what is in your refrigerator.

2 tablespoons plus 2 teaspoons butter at room temperature

¼ pound whole-wheat noodles

2 large eggs

3 cups low-fat milk, heated

½ teaspoon salt

1. Preheat the oven to 325°F. Coat a 2-quart casserole with the 2 teaspoons butter.

2. Cook the noodles in boiling salted water according to package directions. Drain and toss with the remaining 2 tablespoons butter. Transfer to the casserole dish.

3. In a medium bowl, beat the eggs and mix in the milk and salt. Pour over the noodles in the casserole dish. Bake for 30 minutes, or until set.

———

Variations: Sprinkle with Parmesan cheese before baking, or add 1 cup shredded Cheddar cheese to the noodles before adding the egg and milk mixture. You may also add Italian seasonings such as basil and oregano to the milk-and-egg mixture.

HOT DOG AND BEAN CASSEROLE WITH BROWN RICE

Hot dogs are a favorite food with many kids, and it's no wonder; they are so easy to cook in a pinch. Here, the hot dogs are sliced and covered with a simple homemade barbecue sauce.

SERVES 6 TO 8

1 large can (28 ounces) baked beans

1 package (about 10) hot dogs, cut into ¼-inch-thick rounds

½ medium onion, diced

1 tablespoon mustard

1 tablespoon ketchup

1 tablespoon brown sugar

Cooked brown rice for serving

1. Preheat the oven to 325°F.

2. Pour the beans into a 2-quart casserole and add the hot dog rounds. Add the diced onion, and stir in the mustard, ketchup, and brown sugar.

3. Bake for 20 to 25 minutes, until bubbly and hot. Spoon over the cooked brown rice.

BEAN BURRITO CASSEROLE

If the kids like Mexican food, try this. If you don't have diced tomatoes with green chiles (I prefer the Rotel brand), you can substitute mild, medium, or hot tomato salsa. Offer an ice cream sundae for dessert.

SERVES 6

3 tablespoons olive oil

1 medium onion, finely chopped

4 cloves garlic, minced

2 cans (15 ounces each) red kidney beans, rinsed and drained

1 can (10 ounces) diced tomatos and green chiles, with their juice

2 teaspoons ground cumin or chili powder

Salt

Pepper

¼ cup chopped fresh cilantro (optional)

12 flour tortillas (8 inches), preferably whole-wheat

1½ cups shredded Monterey Jack cheese

Guacamole for serving

Tomato salsa for serving

1. Preheat the oven to 350°F. Coat a 9-by-13-inch baking dish with cooking spray.

2. Heat the oil in a large heavy skillet. Add the onion and garlic and cook over medium-low heat until the onion is softened, about 5 minutes. Add the beans, and mash about half of them with the back of a wooden spoon. Add the diced tomatoes and chiles with their juice and the cumin.

Season with salt and black pepper to taste. Simmer the mixture, stirring, for 5 minutes, or until thickened slightly, and stir in the cilantro, if desired.

3. To soften the tortillas, place them between sheets of dampened paper towels and microwave for 30 seconds to 1 minute.

4. Spread about 3 tablespoons of the bean mixture down the center of each softened tortilla. Roll up, enclosing the filling, but leaving the ends open.

5. Arrange the filled tortillas, seam side down, in a single layer in the baking dish. Sprinkle with the cheese and cover with aluminum foil. (At this point, you can cover and refrigerate the casserole for up to 1 day. Add 5 to 10 minutes to the baking time.)

6. Bake for 10 minutes, or until the cheese is melted and the burritos are heated through. Serve hot with guacamole and salsa.

BEEF NACHO CASSEROLE

Nachos are an all-time favorite, quick to make and even more nutritious if you use ripe, fresh tomatoes instead of the salsa, and you can whip it up in less than an hour. Layers of seasoned ground beef, corn, tortilla chips, and cheese are baked until warm and rich with melted cheese. Juicy slices of watermelon would be a perfect summertime dessert.

SERVES 6

1 pound lean ground beef

1½ cups chunky tomato salsa or chopped fresh tomatoes

1 can (10 ounces) corn kernels, drained

¾ cup low-fat sour cream

1 teaspoon chili powder

2 cups crushed low-salt tortilla chips

2 cups shredded mild Cheddar, colby, or Monterey Jack cheese

1. Preheat the oven to 350°F.

2. In a large skillet over medium-high heat, cook the beef, breaking it up, until it is browned and crumbled. Drain the grease. Remove from the heat, and stir in the salsa, corn, sour cream, and chili powder.

3. In a 2-quart casserole, layer half of the ground beef mixture, half of the tortilla chips, and half of the cheese. Repeat the layers, ending with the cheese. Cover with greased aluminum foil.

4. Bake for 20 minutes, until the cheese is melted and the dish is heated through.

BROCCOLI CASSEROLE WITH BUTTERFLIES

Our grandchildren love broccoli. That's a good thing. Their favorite is usually just plain buttered broccoli, but for variety, we serve this creamy broccoli with buttered bow tie pasta. The pasta is called *farfalle* in Italian, which actually means "butterflies," not "bow ties."

— SERVES 4 TO 6 —

1 package (10 ounces) frozen broccoli spears, or 1 bunch fresh broccoli cut into spears

1 cup light or regular sour cream

1 cup shredded Cheddar cheese

4 cups farfalle (bow tie pasta), preferably whole-wheat

2 tablespoons butter or olive oil

1. Preheat the oven to 350°F.

2. Cook the broccoli according to package directions and drain. Or, if using fresh broccoli, cook in boiling salted water to cover for 5 to 6 minutes, until crisp-tender. Drain and transfer to a 9-inch square baking dish or shallow 2-quart casserole.

3. Spread the sour cream evenly over the broccoli and sprinkle with the cheese.

4. Bake for 10 to 15 minutes, until the cheese is melted.

5. Meanwhile, cook the pasta according to package directions in boiling salted water. Drain and mix with the butter or olive oil. Serve the broccoli with the pasta.

EGG CASSEROLE FOR KIDS

This casserole contains mushroom, and while some kids adore them, others don't. As my mother used to tell me, "You have to learn to like them!" You can, of course, just leave them out. Leave out the mushrooms *and* the ham and you still have a delicious and nutritious breakfast or brunch dish.

SERVES 6

2 cups seasoned whole-wheat or regular croutons

1 cup shredded Cheddar cheese

½ pound mushrooms, sliced

1 cup diced cooked ham (optional)

6 large eggs

2 cups milk

½ teaspoon salt

⅛ ground pepper

½ teaspoon prepared mustard

1. Preheat the oven to 325°F. Butter a 9-by-13-inch baking pan.

2. Spread out the croutons over the bottom of the pan. Top with the cheese, mushrooms, and ham, if using.

3. In a medium bowl, mix the eggs, milk, salt, pepper, and mustard. Pour over the layers in the pan. Bake for about 1 hour, until the eggs are set.

KIDS' FONDUE

We taste-tested this dish with a group of five-to-thirteen-year-olds. They all ate it enthusiastically, except for one little niece, who would not even try it. The others thought it tasted like pizza. Alas, you can't win 'em all!

SERVES 6

1 large can (28 ounces) crushed Italian-style tomatoes with their juice

1 teaspoon dried oregano

1 teaspoon salt

¼ teaspoon pepper

3 cups shredded Cheddar cheese

Baguette cubes for serving

Celery sticks for serving

Sliced green bell pepper for serving

1. Preheat the oven to 350°F.

2. Put the tomatoes with their juice in a 1-quart casserole. Mix in the oregano, salt, and pepper.

3. Bake for 1 hour, or until the tomatoes are bubbly hot.

4. Add the cheese gradually, stirring to combine after each addition. Keep warm until ready to serve.

5. Center the casserole on a platter and surround with the baguette cubes, celery sticks, and green pepper (or whatever vegetables your kids prefer). Provide forks or skewers.

MAC AND CHEESE TO BEAT THE BOX

I've always been suspicious of macaroni and cheese from a box, which is actually a product of WWII, having been invented for feeding the troops. This recipe is mac and cheese in a hurry. Sometimes when the grandkids arrive (which can be in the middle of the afternoon or long after the dinner hour), they're hungry. It must be a conditioned response. When I serve this to them, it's comforting to know that they're eating good-quality whole foods, instead of powdered dark yellow cheese. I keep a package of shredded sharp Cheddar in the freezer, and I seem to always have cream cheese and good Parmesan on hand. Elbow macaroni is not one of our staples, but any other small pasta seems to be okay with the kids.

SERVES 4

2 cups whole-wheat or regular elbow macaroni (or, in a pinch, penne, farfalle, or cavatelli)

1 cup shredded Cheddar cheese (mild, medium, or sharp)

1 package (8 ounces) cream cheese or Neufchâtel cheese, cubed

1 cup undiluted evaporated milk

½ cup fine dry breadcrumbs

2 tablespoons butter, melted

½ cup grated Parmesan cheese

1. Preheat the oven to 400°F.

2. Cook the macaroni in boiling salted water according to package directions. Drain, but do not rinse.

3. Combine the macaroni with the Cheddar and cream cheese in a shallow 1-quart casserole. Stir until the cream cheese melts into the hot macaroni.

Stir in the milk and scrape down the sides of the dish.

4. In a small bowl, mix the breadcrumbs with the melted butter and grated Parmesan cheese. Sprinkle evenly over the macaroni and cheese. Bake for 30 to 35 minutes, or until the breadcrumbs are browned.

PIZZA CASSEROLE FOR KIDS

This is a simple and straightforward combination of ingredients that is kid-friendly. If there are leftovers, you'll be so glad you have something for their midnight snacks. Even though this looks similar to many hamburger casseroles, it has the distinct flavors of pizza. You can even top it all off with thinly sliced pepperoni—if that's how the kids "ordered" it.

SERVES 6 TO 8

1 package (8 ounces) elbow macaroni, preferably whole-wheat

1 pound ground beef

1 teaspoon dried oregano

½ teaspoon dried basil

½ teaspoon salt

1 medium onion, finely chopped

1 green bell pepper, seeded and finely chopped (optional)

1 can (15 ounces) tomato sauce

2 cups shredded part-skim mozzarella cheese

2 cups shredded low-fat Cheddar cheese

½ cup grated Parmesan cheese

¼ to ½ pound sliced pepperoni (optional)

1. Preheat the oven to 325°F. Lightly oil a 9-by-13-inch baking dish.

2. Cook the macaroni in boiling salted water according to package directions and drain.

3. In a large skillet over medium-high heat, brown the beef, breaking it up with a wooden spoon. Add the oregano, basil, salt, onion, and green pepper (if using).

4. Spread out the cooked macaroni in the baking dish and top with the meat in an even layer. Drizzle with the tomato sauce and sprinkle the top with the mozzarella and Cheddar cheeses. Bake for 25 to 30 minutes, until the cheese is melted and the casserole is bubbly. Top with the Parmesan and the pepperoni (if desired).

OUTSIDE-IN PIZZA SQUARES

This is really a very cheesy meat pie with a pizza-flavored filling. For the filling, you can choose the same ingredients as your favorite pizza toppings. In place of the Italian sausage, you could use ground beef, but in that case, be sure to season the filling more liberally.

SERVES 8

1 pound bulk Italian pork sausage (mild or medium)

½ teaspoon fennel seeds (optional)

1 can (8 ounces) tomato sauce

1 teaspoon Italian seasoning

4 recipes Flaky Pastry (page 32), combined into 2 large balls and refrigerated for 30 minutes

2 cups shredded mozzarella cheese

1 tablespoon sesame seeds

1. Preheat the oven to 350°F.

2. In a medium skillet, cook the sausage, stirring, over medium heat for about 10 minutes, until thoroughly cooked. Drain any excess fat. Stir in the fennel seeds (if using), tomato sauce, and Italian seasoning.

3. Roll out one ball of the pastry into a rectangle about 10 by 14 inches. Transfer to a 9-by-13-inch baking dish. The pastry should cover the bottom and come ½ inch up the sides of the dish.

4. Spread out the sausage mixture over the pastry and sprinkle with the cheese.

5. Roll out the remaining ball of pastry so it's a little bit smaller, about 9 by 12 inches, and lay it over the top of the filling. Crimp the edges and cut a few slits in the top to let steam escape. Sprinkle with the sesame seeds and bake for 30 to 35 minutes, or until the dough is golden brown. Cut into squares to serve.

ROTINI CASSEROLE

If your kids object to anything spicy, you can omit the chili powder. But you never know. We have a granddaughter who declared one day, "I like spicy!" For busy days, you can assemble this ahead of time, refrigerate it, and then pop it in the oven when you get home.

SERVES 4 TO 6

1 pound extra-lean ground beef

1 medium onion, chopped

1 tablespoon chili powder

1 teaspoon salt

1 can (14 ounces) stewed tomatoes with their juice

1 cup water

1½ cups rotini (spiral pasta)

1. Preheat the oven to 350°F.

2. Brown the beef in a large ovenproof skillet with a lid or in a Dutch oven, breaking it up with a wooden spoon. Add the onion, chili powder, and salt, and cook over medium-high heat for 5 to 10 minutes, until the beef is no longer pink. Stir in the tomatoes with their juice, water, and rotini. (At this point you can cover and refrigerate overnight. Add 10 minutes to the baking time.)

3. Cover and bake for 30 to 35 minutes, or until the pasta is cooked.

Chapter 17
DESSERT CASSEROLES

○ ○ ○ ○ ○

Desserts have been part of our culinary heritage since the beginning of American colonial history. Fruits have played a major role, especially when baked in a casserole. Early cooks delighted their families with hearth-warming stewed fruits, crisps, cobblers, betties, buckles, pies, and cakes. And let's not forget grunts, slumps, and roly polies! This chapter goes beyond American classics, however. In addition to cobblers and crisps, and puddings and custards, you will also find a Peruvian flan (page 602), a French clafouti (page 595), and a Jamaican pudding (page 594).

CRISP APPLE STREUSEL

The German word *streusel* means "to sprinkle" or "strew." Here, the streusel forms a crunchy topping for baked apples. This popular dessert is also known as "apple crisp."

SERVES 8

FOR THE STREUSEL TOPPING:

⅔ cup all-purpose flour

⅓ cup light or dark packed brown sugar

⅓ cup butter, plus extra for the dish

FOR THE FRUIT FILLING:

8 cups sliced apples (about 3 pounds)

¾ cup granulated sugar

2 tablespoons all-purpose flour

1 teaspoon ground cinnamon

½ teaspoon ground nutmeg

Whipped cream for serving

1. Preheat the oven to 350°F. Butter a shallow 1½-quart casserole.

2. *To make the topping:* In a large bowl, mix the flour and brown sugar. With a pastry blender, cut the ⅓ cup butter into the flour until the mixture resembles coarse crumbs. Set aside.

3. *To make the fruit filling:* Put the sliced apples in a large bowl and toss with the granulated sugar, flour, cinnamon, and nutmeg. Spread in an even layer in the buttered casserole.

4. Sprinkle the topping over the apples, patting it down evenly. Bake, uncovered, for 45 minutes to 1 hour, or until the apples are tender and juices bubble around the edge and the topping is browned. Serve warm or at room temperature with whipped cream.

BAKED FRUIT COMPOTE WITH STAR ANISE

Baked mixed dried fruit is a wintertime favorite, and star anise gives it a pleasant licorice flavor and aroma. Star anise is a small, dark brown seed pod shaped like an eight-pointed star.

—— SERVES 6 ——

1 package (12 ounces) mixed dried fruit

1 cup golden raisins

⅓ cup sugar

3 cups white wine, white grape juice, or water

Zest and juice of 1 lemon

Zest and juice of 1 orange

1 stick cinnamon, 3 inches long

3 whole star anise pods

Whipped cream or sour cream for serving

1. Preheat the oven to 300°F.

2. Combine the mixed fruit, raisins, sugar, and wine or water in a 2-quart casserole.

3. Place the zest on the fruit mixture. Add the cinnamon stick and star anise pods. Pour the juice over the fruit.

4. Bake, covered, for 1¼ hours. Remove and discard the zest, cinnamon stick, and star anise pods. Serve warm with whipped cream or sour cream.

BAKED PIE PLANT (RHUBARB)

Rhubarb, also known as "pie plant," is the unsung hero of American cooks, an effortlessly grown vegetable (botanically speaking), which offers its thick, juicy stalks from early spring through June. Estelle Woods Wilcox's *New Buckeye Cookbook,* published in 1883, advises the reader to "bake the rhubarb in a deep bean pot with a cover, using a teacupful of sugar to each quart of pie plant to make a superior sauce." Covering the rhubarb while it bakes doubles the baking time, but preserves more of the aroma and flavor of the fruit. I personally like to add a chunk of peeled fresh ginger to the rhubarb. Serve over ice cream or topped with whipped cream.

SERVES 6 TO 8

4 cups rhubarb, cut into 1-inch slices

1 cup sugar

1 piece fresh ginger, 1 inch long

Ice cream or whipped cream for serving

1. Preheat the oven to 325°F.

2. Combine the rhubarb, sugar, and ginger in a 1½-quart casserole or a bean pot with a cover. Cover and bake for 1 hour, or until the rhubarb is stewed and soft. Serve with ice cream or whipped cream.

BLUEBERRY AND PEACH BREAD PUDDING

Fruits that are in season at the same time often have a natural affinity for one another. Such is the case with blueberries and peaches.

SERVES 8

½ cup (1 stick) butter, melted, plus extra for the dish

5 cups combined blueberries and diced peaches

2 tablespoons plus 1¼ cups sugar

1 tablespoon tapioca flour (see Note)

½ teaspoon ground cinnamon

1 tablespoon fresh lemon juice

5 slices day-old bread, crusts removed

2 tablespoons all-purpose flour

2 large eggs, beaten

1 teaspoon vanilla extract

¼ teaspoon salt

Whipped cream or ice cream for serving

1. Butter a 9-inch square glass baking dish generously. Spread the fruit evenly over the bottom of the dish. Mix the 2 tablespoons sugar, tapioca flour, and cinnamon and sprinkle evenly over the fruit. Drizzle with the lemon juice.

2. Arrange the bread over the top of the fruit, cutting it as needed to fit the pan.

3. Whisk the 1¼ cups sugar, flour, eggs, the ½ cup butter, vanilla, and salt together in a medium bowl and pour over the bread layer evenly. Let sit for 15 minutes.

4. Meanwhile, preheat the oven to 350°F.

5. Bake for 45 to 55 minutes, until the custard is set and golden and the fruit is bubbly around the edges. Serve with whipped cream or ice cream.

○ ○ ○ ○ ○

NOTE: Tapioca flour is available in the natural foods section of most supermarkets.

CHEESE AND APPLE COBBLER

This dessert is perfect for a chilly evening. Like all cobblers, it is topped with a biscuit-like pastry. There are two old-fashioned desserts with quirky names that are variations on the same theme—grunts and slumps. A grunt was made in colonial days with berries and dough, which were cooked in a Dutch oven hanging over an open fire. The name "grunt" presumably came from the sound the fruit made as it bubbled and grunted beneath the biscuit-like topping. Likewise, a slump was made by dropping a soft, biscuit-like dough onto bubbling fruit. The dessert had a tendency to slump on the plate, hence its name. Louisa Mae Alcott was especially fond of slumps made with apples.

SERVES 6

FOR THE COBBLER TOPPING:

1 cup all-purpose flour

2 tablespoons sugar

1½ teaspoons baking powder

¼ teaspoon salt

⅓ cup cold butter, plus extra for the dish

1 egg

¼ cup milk

FOR THE FRUIT LAYER:

1½ pounds cooking apples

⅓ cup sugar

2 tablespoons quick-cooking tapioca

½ teaspoon ground cinnamon

¼ teaspoon ground nutmeg

1¼ cups water

2 tablespoons butter

1 cup shredded sharp Cheddar cheese

FOR THE VANILLA SAUCE:

2 cups milk

1 tablespoon cornstarch

¼ cup sugar

2 teaspoons vanilla extract

1 teaspoon butter

1. Preheat the oven to 425°F. Butter a shallow 8- or 9-inch round or square baking dish.

2. *To make the cobbler topping:* In a medium bowl, mix the flour, sugar, baking powder, and salt. With a pastry blender, cut in the ⅓ cup butter until the mixture resembles coarse crumbs. Mix the egg and milk together and stir into the crumbly mixture to make a soft dough.

3. *To make the fruit layer:* Peel, core, and slice the apples. You should have about 4 cups. Put in a medium bowl. Add the sugar, mix well, and set aside. In a medium saucepan, combine the tapioca, cinnamon, nutmeg, water, and butter. Place over medium-high heat and cook, stirring, until the mixture boils. Add the apples and remove from the heat. Let stand for 5 minutes. Transfer to the baking dish and top with the cheese.

4. Drop rounded spoonfuls of cobbler topping onto the cheese layer. Bake, uncovered, for 20 to 25 minutes, or until the cobbler is lightly browned.

5. *To make the vanilla sauce:* While the cobbler bakes, in a medium saucepan, blend the milk, cornstarch, and sugar. Bring to a boil over medium-low heat, stirring constantly. Cook, stirring constantly, until slightly thickened. Stir in the vanilla and butter.

6. Serve the cobbler hot from the oven or cooled to room temperature. Spoon some of the vanilla sauce over each serving.

CINNAMON-CHOCOLATE NUT BREAD PUDDING

For the chocolate lover, this bread pudding is loaded! It makes a great finale for a potluck at your home.

— SERVES 10 TO 12 —

5½ cups dried white or whole-wheat bread cubes (see Note, facing page)

2 cups semisweet chocolate chips

1 cup coarsely chopped toasted pecans (see Note, facing page)

3 cups light cream or half-and-half, heated

¾ cup granulated sugar

3 eggs plus 3 egg yolks

⅛ teaspoon salt

1½ teaspoons ground cinnamon, divided

3 squares bittersweet baking chocolate (1 ounce each)

1 cup whipping cream

2 tablespoons powdered sugar

1. Preheat the oven to 350°F. Butter a 2-quart soufflé dish.

2. Mix the bread, chocolate chips, and pecans in a medium bowl and spread out in the buttered dish.

3. In a medium saucepan, heat the light cream to boiling over medium heat.

4. In a medium bowl, whisk together the granulated sugar, whole eggs, egg yolks, salt, and 1 teaspoon of the cinnamon. Slowly whisk 1 cup of the hot cream into the egg mixture to temper it. Whisk the egg mixture into the remaining cream in the saucepan. Cook for 1 to 2 minutes over medium-low heat until the sugar dissolves. Add the 3 squares bittersweet chocolate, stirring until melted. Pour over the bread mixture in the soufflé dish, stirring carefully until mixed.

5. Place the soufflé dish into a larger baking dish, so there is about 1 inch all around between the sides of the soufflé dish and the sides of the larger dish. Carefully pour hot water into the larger pan to reach halfway up the sides of the soufflé dish. Bake for 1 hour, or until set.

6. While the pudding bakes, beat the whipping cream in a medium bowl until soft peaks form. Add the powdered sugar and the remaining ½ teaspoon cinnamon.

7. To serve, spoon some whipped cream over each serving of warm bread pudding.

○ ○ ○ ○ ○

NOTES: To make dried bread cubes, remove the crusts from white or whole-wheat bread slices and cut the bread into cubes. Spread them out on a baking sheet and toast in a 350°F oven for 10 minutes, or until lightly browned and dry.

To toast pecans, spread them out on a baking sheet and place into a 350°F oven for 10 minutes, stirring occasionally, until aromatic and lightly browned.

CINNAMON-CHOCOLATE FONDUE

Baking is an easy and controlled way to melt chocolate for dessert fondue. If you wish, you can just omit the rum or liqueur.

1 bar (12 ounces) milk chocolate, or 1 package (12 ounces) semisweet chocolate chips

¾ cup heavy cream

¼ teaspoon ground cinnamon

3 tablespoons rum, Cointreau, or another fruit-flavored liqueur (optional)

FOR DIPPING:

Bananas, cut into 1-inch chunks

Pineapple chunks

Fresh strawberries, cherries, and/ or grapes

Pound cake or angel food cake, cut into cubes

1. Preheat the oven to 325°F.

2. Break the chocolate bar into pieces and combine in a deep 1-quart casserole with the cream and cinnamon.

3. Bake, uncovered, for 25 to 30 minutes, or until the chocolate is soft. Stir to blend. Stir in the rum or liqueur (if desired). Place over a candle warmer and surround with bowls of fresh fruit or cake cubes for dipping.

CRANBERRY PEARS

Although I've placed this recipe in the dessert chapter, it makes a fabulous side dish for a company breakfast or brunch. Baked in a slow oven, the pears and cranberries meld into a delicious combination.

—○—————————— SERVES 6 ——————————○—

6 large Bosc pears, peeled, seeded, and quartered

1 cup cranberries

1 cup packed light or dark brown sugar

1 cup water

Heavy cream, mascarpone, or crème fraîche for serving

1. Preheat the oven to 300°F. Butter a shallow 2½- to 3-quart casserole.

2. Arrange the pear quarters in a single layer in the dish and sprinkle the cranberries evenly over the pears. Sprinkle with the brown sugar and pour the water over all.

3. Cover and bake for 1 to 1½ hours, until the pears are cooked. Cool completely and refrigerate for at least 4 hours. Serve chilled with cream.

CRANBERRY PUDDING

This easily assembled pudding is pretty when baked in a fancy mold, but a loaf pan is the most convenient for serving. This recipe is adapted from one that I received from my hairdressers, Chuck and Bill, who make it every year for their Christmas party. You can use fresh, frozen, or dried cranberries. If your cranberries are frozen, don't bother to thaw them—just mix them right into the batter. Dried berries are often sweetened, and that is okay.

SERVES 6

1 large egg

½ cup light molasses

⅓ cup warm water

1⅓ cups all-purpose flour

1 teaspoon baking powder

½ teaspoon salt

½ teaspoon baking soda

2 cups fresh, frozen, or dried cranberries

FOR THE CARAMEL SAUCE:

2 tablespoons butter

1 cup heavy cream

1 cup sugar

1 teaspoon vanilla extract

1. Preheat the oven to 325°F. Butter a 1-quart fancy metal mold, or a 4½-by-8½-inch loaf pan.

2. In a large bowl, beat the egg, molasses, and water together. In a small bowl, mix the flour, baking powder, salt, and baking soda.

3. Put the cranberries in a bowl and add 2 tablespoons of the flour mixture to coat thoroughly. Stir the remaining flour mixture into the egg mixture, blending until smooth. Fold in the cranberries. Transfer the batter to the buttered pan. Coat a sheet of aluminum foil with cooking spray and cover the pan tightly.

4. Put the buttered pan into a larger pan. Carefully pour boiling water to a depth of 1 inch in the larger pan. Bake for 2 hours, or until a skewer inserted in the center comes out clean.

5. *While the pudding bakes, prepare the caramel sauce:* Combine the butter, cream, and sugar in a medium saucepan. Bring to a boil, stirring constantly, and continue boiling, while stirring constantly, for about 5 minutes, or until syrupy. Stir in the vanilla.

6. The pudding can be eaten hot from the oven or at room temperature. Spoon some of the warm sauce over each serving.

UPSIDE-DOWN APPLE COBBLER

A classic cobbler has a biscuit-like topping baked over fruit. Here, the fruit is baked on top of the batter, which bubbles up around the fruit as it bakes.

SERVES 6

¾ cup plus 2 tablespoons sugar

Pinch of cinnamon

½ cup (1 stick) butter, melted

1 cup all-purpose flour

1 teaspoon baking powder

1 teaspoon vanilla extract

¾ cup milk

2 cups sliced peeled apples

Heavy cream for serving

1. Preheat the oven to 400°F. Coat a shallow 1½-quart casserole with cooking spray. In a small dish or cup, mix 2 tablespoons of the sugar with the cinnamon and set aside.

2. In a medium bowl, mix the butter, flour, baking powder, the remaining ¾ cup of sugar, the vanilla, and milk to make a batter. Pour into the prepared casserole dish.

3. Arrange the apple slices over the top of the batter. Sprinkle with the cinnamon sugar.

4. Bake for 25 to 30 minutes, or until nicely browned. Serve warm and offer a pitcher of cream for people to pour over their cobbler.

GINGER BLUEBERRY CRISP

Blueberries and ginger have a natural affinity for each other, and they are a perfect pair in this fresh-tasting dessert.

SERVES 6

⅓ cup butter at room temperature, plus extra for the dish

½ cup plus 4 teaspoons all-purpose flour

1 tablespoon granulated sugar

1 tablespoon chopped candied ginger

3 cups blueberries

2 tablespoons fresh lemon juice

⅔ cup packed light or dark brown sugar

½ cup quick-cooking rolled oats

Whipped cream or ice cream for serving

1. Preheat the oven to 375°F. Butter a 6-cup shallow casserole.

2. In a large bowl, combine 4 teaspoons of the flour, the granulated sugar, and ginger. Add the blueberries, toss, and sprinkle with the lemon juice. Pour the berries into the casserole dish.

3. In a medium bowl, mix the brown sugar, the remaining ½ cup flour, the rolled oats, and the ⅓ cup butter to make a crumbly mixture. Sprinkle over the blueberries.

4. Bake, uncovered, for 30 minutes, or until the topping is golden and the edges are bubbly. Serve warm with whipped cream or ice cream.

GREEN TOMATO COBBLER

There is just a short window of time, at least where I live, when green tomatoes are on my countertop in abundance. They either gradually turn red or they rot. I love them fried or baked with a topping of feta cheese. Sometimes I make a green tomato salsa if I have the time and the tomatoes. One evening, I needed a quick and easy dessert for a party. This turned out to be just perfect. I assembled the whole thing and let it sit for about an hour before I baked it. It turned out great, and there were lots of compliments!

SERVES 6 TO 8

3 tablespoons butter, melted, plus extra for the dish

4 cups chopped green tomatoes

1 cup packed light or dark brown sugar

2 tablespoons quick-cooking tapioca

1 tablespoon all-purpose flour

1 tablespoon freshly squeezed lemon juice

1 teaspoon ground cinnamon

½ cup chopped raisins

½ teaspoon salt

¼ teaspoon ground cloves

¼ teaspoon ground nutmeg

½ cup blanched almonds

FOR THE TOPPING:
1½ cup all-purpose flour

¼ granulated cup sugar

3 teaspoon baking powder

½ cup (1 stick) butter, melted

½ cup light cream or half-and-half

Whipped cream for serving

1. Preheat the oven to 425°F. Butter a 2-quart casserole.

2. Put the tomatoes in a saucepan, cover with water, and bring to a boil over high heat. Remove from the heat and drain in a colander.

3. In a large bowl, combine the tomatoes, brown sugar, tapioca, flour, lemon juice, cinnamon, raisins, the 3 tablespoons butter, salt, cloves, and nutmeg. Mix well and transfer to the casserole dish. Sprinkle with the almonds.

4. *To make the topping:* In a medium bowl, stir together the topping ingredients to make a stiff, biscuit-like dough. Scoop out the dough to make small mounds on the tomato mixture.

5. Bake for 25 to 30 minutes, or until the tomato filling is bubbly and the topping is lightly browned. Serve warm or at room temperature with whipped cream.

HOLIDAY CASSEROLE COOKIES

Talk about stretching the idea of casseroles; this is really different!
You bake the dough in a casserole and then shape it into delicious balls—
perfect as an after-dinner holiday treat.

MAKES 3 DOZEN

2 large eggs

1 cup packed light brown sugar

2 tablespoons dark rum

1 cup sweetened shredded or flaked coconut

1 cup finely chopped walnuts or almonds

1 cup snipped pitted dates

Granulated sugar for coating the cookies

1. Preheat the oven to 350°F.

2. In a large bowl, using an electric mixer, beat the eggs, sugar, and rum until fluffy. Stir in the coconut, walnuts, and dates. Transfer to an ungreased 2-quart casserole.

3. Bake for 35 minutes. Remove from oven and, while hot, stir well with a wooden spoon. Cool and shape into 1-inch balls, and roll in granulated sugar.

HUCKLEBERRY OR BLUEBERRY BUCKLE

Last summer our son, Greg, gifted me with a bowlful of huckleberries from his country home in Missouri. So I made this dessert. This buckle has a cake-like texture with berries folded into the batter, and more berries spooned on top of it. Then the berries are covered with a crispy topping.

SERVES 4

4 tablespoons butter, plus extra for the dish

¾ cup sugar

1 large egg

1 teaspoon vanilla extract

1 cup all-purpose flour

1¼ teaspoons baking powder

¼ teaspoon salt

¼ cup milk

1½ cups fresh huckleberries or blueberries

FOR THE TOPPING:

¼ cup sugar

¼ cup all-purpose flour

½ teaspoon ground cinnamon

2 tablespoons butter, softened

1. Preheat the oven to 350°F. Butter a 1-quart oven-to-table casserole.

2. In a large bowl, cream the 4 tablespoons butter and the sugar together with an electric mixer until smooth. Beat in the egg and vanilla and continue beating until light. In a medium bowl, stir together the flour, baking powder, and salt. Add the dry ingredients to the creamed mixture, and stir in the milk. Beat until light and fluffy.

3. Stir half the berries into the batter and transfer the mixture to the prepared casserole. Top with the remaining berries.

4. *To make the topping:* In a small bowl, blend together all of the topping ingredients to make a crumbly mixture. Sprinkle evenly over the berries.

5. Bake for 30 to 35 minutes, until the topping is crisp and the center of the buckle is cooked through and a wooden skewer inserted into the topping comes out clean. Serve warm or at room temperature.

JAMAICAN SWEET POTATO PUDDING

We often confuse sweet potatoes and yams. Sweet potatoes are the pale, creamy tubers we often mistake for the deeper-hued yams. For this recipe, Jamaicans traditionally use some of each. If all you have is one or the other, either will be fine in this recipe. Coconut milk, spices, vanilla, and rum transform the sweet potatoes (and yams) into a silky, spicy pudding. It would be perfect for any special meal between Thanksgiving and New Years'. This makes a very substantial dessert. Just be careful not to overbake it, or it will behave like an overbaked custard and separate.

SERVES 8

2 tablespoons butter, plus extra for the dish

1½ pounds sweet potatoes, yams, or a combination, peeled and cut into ½-inch dice (about 4 cups)

1 can (14 ounces) unsweetened coconut milk

1 cup heavy cream

1 teaspoon ground cinnamon

1 teaspoon ground allspice

1 teaspoon ground nutmeg

½ teaspoon ground ginger

1½ teaspoons vanilla extract

½ teaspoon salt

1 cup packed light or dark brown sugar

¾ cup raisins

¾ cup all-purpose flour

2 tablespoons Jamaican rum

Whipped cream for serving

1. Preheat the oven to 325°F. Butter a shallow 2½-quart casserole.

2. Put the sweet potatoes and/or yams in a blender or a food processor with the steel blade in place with the coconut milk, cream, cinnamon, allspice, nutmeg, ginger, vanilla, and salt. Process until pureed.

3. Transfer to a large bowl and mix in the brown sugar, raisins, flour, and rum. Transfer to the prepared casserole dish and dot with the 2 tablespoons butter.

4. Bake for 1½ hours, or until set and a knife inserted near the center comes out clean. Serve warm, or cooled and chilled, with whipped cream.

MIXED FRUIT CLAFOUTI

In this French dessert, the fruit (usually cherries) is traditionally baked with a light batter on top and served warm. In this recipe, however, the fruit bakes on top of the batter.

SERVES 6

2 tablespoons butter

¼ cup all-purpose flour

¼ teaspoon salt

2 large eggs

2 tablespoons sour cream

⅓ cup apple cider or milk

1 tablespoon grated lemon zest

¼ cup sugar

2½ to 3 cups mixed fruit in any combination, including sliced pears, apples, bananas, and peaches; halved and pitted apricots and plums; strawberries, blueberries, raspberries, and pitted cherries

2 tablespoons dark rum or fruit-flavored liqueur

Whipping cream for serving

1. Preheat the oven to 375°F. Put the butter in a 1-quart soufflé dish and place into the oven as it preheats. When the butter is melted, spread it evenly over the dish.

2. In a medium bowl, mix the flour, salt, eggs, sour cream, apple cider or milk, and lemon zest. In another medium bowl, combine the sugar, fruit, and rum.

3. Pour the batter into the hot, buttered soufflé dish and top with the fruit mixture. Bake, uncovered, for 35 to 40 minutes, or until the batter is puffed and the top is lightly browned. Serve hot with whipped cream.

MOCHA FUDGE PUDDING

This has a cake-like top and a fudgy pudding layer on the bottom.
It's best served the day it is made, while the top is still moist.

SERVES 6

1¼ cups granulated sugar, divided

1 cup all-purpose flour

2 teaspoons baking powder

Dash of salt

7 tablespoons dark unsweetened cocoa powder, divided

4 tablespoons butter, melted

½ cup milk

1 teaspoon vanilla extract

½ cup packed light or dark brown sugar

1½ cups cold strong coffee

Powdered sugar for dusting

Whipped cream or ice cream for serving (optional)

1. Preheat the oven to 350°F. Coat an 8- or 9-inch square baking dish with cooking spray.

2. In a large bowl, combine ¾ cup of the granulated sugar, the flour, baking powder, salt, and 3 tablespoons of the cocoa.

3. In a small bowl, combine the butter, milk, and vanilla and add to the dry ingredients. Mix until just blended, and pour into the prepared baking dish.

4. Scatter over the top of the pudding, without first mixing, the brown sugar and the remaining ½ cup granulated sugar and 4 tablespoons cocoa. Pour the cold coffee over the pudding.

5. Bake for 40 minutes, or until puffy and the cake is cooked through and a wooden skewer inserted into the center of the cake comes out dry. Cool completely, but do not chill. Dust with powdered sugar, and serve with whipped cream or ice cream, if desired.

NORWEGIAN LEMON CUSTARD

When this bakes, it separates into two layers and becomes a sponge cake-topped custard, which is why it's sometimes called a "pudding cake." It's so easy to make and the ingredients are simple, but it's a perfectly refreshing dessert.

SERVES 6

2 tablespoons butter at room temperature, plus extra for the dish

1 cup sugar

3 large eggs, separated

¼ cup all-purpose flour

¼ teaspoon salt

⅓ cup fresh lemon juice

1 tablespoon grated lemon zest

1½ cups half-and-half or whole milk

1. Preheat the oven to 350°F. Butter a 1-quart casserole.

2. In a medium bowl, with an electric mixer, beat the 2 tablespoons butter, the sugar, and egg yolks until light. Add the flour, salt, lemon juice, and lemon zest. Mix in the half-and-half or milk. In a large bowl, beat the egg whites until soft peaks form. With a rubber spatula, fold the beaten whites into the egg yolk mixture.

3. Pour the batter into the casserole and place the casserole in a larger pan. Pour boiling water to a depth of 1 inch in the pan. Bake, uncovered, for 30 to 40 minutes, or until the top is lightly browned.

OLD-FASHIONED RICE PUDDING

According to Scandinavian tradition, a whole almond is placed into the center of this pudding on Christmas Eve, and the person who gets the almond will enjoy good luck all year. If there are young children in the family, the person with the almond gets to play Santa and distribute gifts from under the tree.

SERVES 6

1½ cups undiluted evaporated milk or light cream

2 large eggs

½ cup sugar

1 teaspoon vanilla extract

½ teaspoon ground cinnamon

Dash of salt

1¼ cups cooked medium-grain rice

⅓ cup raisins

Whipped cream or ice cream for serving

1. Preheat the oven to 350°F. Butter a 1-quart casserole.

2. Mix the milk, eggs, sugar, vanilla, cinnamon, salt, rice, and raisins in a large bowl. Pour the mixture into the prepared casserole.

3. Bake for 30 to 35 minutes, or until the center is set. Serve with whipped cream or ice cream.

PEACH BUCKLE

Culinarily speaking, a buckle is an old American term for a single-layer cake made with fruit. For this recipe, you'll need to peel some peaches. The traditional way to peel a peach is to dip it in boiling water (see the Note below). But today there are razor-sharp peelers that do a nice job, and you won't have to wash a pan.

SERVES 8

FOR THE CAKE LAYER:

4 tablespoons butter, plus extra for the dish

½ cup sugar

1 cup all-purpose flour

1 teaspoon baking powder

¼ teaspoon salt

½ cup milk

FOR THE FILLING:

8 fresh ripe peaches, peeled and sliced (see Note)

¾ cup sugar

½ cup boiling water

1 tablespoon butter

Whipped cream or vanilla ice cream for serving

1. Preheat the oven to 375°F. Butter the bottom of a 2-quart casserole.

2. *To make the cake layer:* In a large bowl, with an electric mixer, cream the 4 tablespoons butter and the sugar. In a separate small bowl, combine the flour, baking powder, and salt. Stir into the butter mixture with a wooden spoon, and then stir in the milk. The mixture will be thick and lumpy. Spread the batter into the prepared casserole dish.

3. *To make the filling:* In a large bowl, combine the peaches, sugar, and boiling water. Pour over the batter in the pan. Dot the top with the 1 tablespoon butter.

4. Bake for 45 to 50 minutes, until the batter that bubbles up through the filling is golden. Serve warm or at room temperature with whipped cream or ice cream.

∘∘∘∘∘

NOTE: To remove the peels from the peaches, heat a saucepan of water to boiling. Drop in the peaches, one at a time, for 15 seconds. With a slotted spoon, lift the peaches out. When cool enough to handle, slip the peels off.

PEACHES AND CREAM DESSERT CASSEROLE

This is a wonderful dessert to make when peaches are in season. For a low-fat version, use the evaporated skim milk instead of cream.

1½ cups old-fashioned rolled oats

¼ cup light or dark brown sugar

4 large peaches or nectarines, peeled (see Note on page 599) and diced

2 large eggs

2 teaspoons vanilla extract

1 cup cream or undiluted evaporated milk

1. Preheat the oven to 350°F. Butter an 8-inch square baking dish.

2. Combine the rolled oats and sugar in a small bowl and set aside. Distribute the peaches evenly in the prepared pan.

3. Mix the eggs, vanilla, and cream in a medium bowl, and pour over the peaches in the pan. Top with the rolled oat mixture.

4. Bake for 35 to 45 minutes, or until the oats are browned and the peaches bubble up around the edges of the pan. Serve hot or at room temperature.

PINEAPPLE RUM–BAKED STUFFED APPLES

Well, it doesn't have to be pineapple rum, but I think the flavors go together really well. We bought this rum on a trip to the Caribbean, and I wondered what to do with it, besides drink it. So, I just poured it over apples ready for baking, and the fruity aroma filled the kitchen!

— MAKES 2 SERVINGS —

2 tablespoons raisins

2 tablespoons chopped toasted pecans (see Note)

3 tablespoons firmly packed light brown sugar, divided

Pinch of apple pie spice mix

2 large Golden Delicious or pippin apples

1 tablespoon cold butter, cut into small pieces

½ cup pineapple rum, dark rum, or apple cider

Heavy cream for serving

1. Preheat the oven to 375°F. Combine the raisins, pecans, 1 tablespoon of the brown sugar, and the apple pie spice mix.

2. Core the apples and peel the top half of each one. Press the raisin and nut mixture into the centers of the apples and place in a shallow baking dish just large enough to accommodate them.

3. Dot the apples with the butter and sprinkle with the remaining 2 tablespoons brown sugar. Pour the pineapple rum over the apples.

4. Bake until the apples are tender, 45 to 50 minutes. Serve hot or warm, and offer the heavy cream in a pitcher to pour over.

○ ○ ○ ○ ○

NOTE: To toast pecans, spread them out on a baking sheet and place into a 350°F oven for 10 minutes, stirring occasionally, until aromatic and lightly browned.

PERUVIAN FLAN

I was first served this silken flan in Peru at a buffet luncheon. Although this might be stretching the definition of a casserole a bit, this is a really great recipe, and easy to make, too. A ring mold helps the flan to bake evenly, and it makes for a pretty presentation when you fill the center with berries.

SERVES 16

1 cup sugar

10 large eggs, lightly beaten

2 cans (14 ounces each) sweetened condensed milk

2 cans (12 ounces each) evaporated milk

1 teaspoon vanilla extract

Dash of cinnamon

Fresh berries, such as raspberries, strawberries, or blackberries, or edible flowers for garnish

1. Preheat the oven to 350°F. Coat an 11-cup metal ring mold with cooking spray.

2. Put the sugar in a dry heavy skillet and stir over medium heat until the sugar is melted and caramelized. Pour the caramelized sugar into the ring mold and turn it from side to side until the bottom and part of the sides are coated with the sugar. Set aside and allow the sugar to harden. (Set the mold in a pan of ice water, if necessary.)

3. In a large bowl, stir together the beaten eggs, sweetened condensed milk, evaporated milk, vanilla, and cinnamon until well blended.

4. Pour the egg mixture into the caramel-coated mold. Place in a larger pan and pour 2 inches of hot water into the larger pan. Bake for 1 hour, or until the custard is set.

5. Let cool. With a knife, loosen the edges and then invert the flan onto a serving platter or plate.

6. Decorate the flan with fresh berries or edible flowers.

○ ○ ○ ○ ○

NOTES: Sweetened condensed milk is a mixture of whole milk and sugar, heated until 60 percent of the water is evaporated and the milk becomes sticky, thick, and sweet. If you see a recipe that calls for "condensed milk," it almost certainly means sweetened condensed milk, not evaporated. If you do not have sweetened condensed milk on hand, to replace 1 cup you can do the following: Combine 1 cup plus 2 tablespoons nonfat dry milk powder, ½ cup warm water, and ¾ cup sugar in a saucepan. Heat until dissolved.

Evaporated milk is concentrated milk. It comes either whole or nonfat. The milk is sold with varying amounts of butterfat, ranging from whole evaporated milk to the equivalent of skim milk. To reconstitute, mix with an equal amount of water.

ALMOND PUMPKIN PUDDING

If you're not much for rolling out pie crusts, try this instead for your next holiday dinner. This pumpkin pudding has the rich flavor of pumpkin pie.

SERVES 8

2 tablespoons butter, plus extra for the dish

1 can (16 ounces) pureed pumpkin

2 large eggs, lightly beaten

1 cup packed light or dark brown sugar, divided

¼ cup slivered almonds, toasted (see Note), divided

2 tablespoons raisins

2 tablespoons all-purpose flour

1½ cups milk

1½ teaspoons pumpkin pie spice (see Note)

¼ teaspoon salt

¼ teaspoon vanilla extract

1. Preheat the oven to 350°F. Butter a 1½-quart soufflé dish or a deep 1½-quart casserole.

2. In a large bowl, thoroughly combine the pumpkin, eggs, ½ cup of the brown sugar, half of the almonds, and 1 tablespoon of the raisins; set aside.

3. In a medium, heavy saucepan, melt the 2 tablespoons butter over medium heat. Add the flour and stir until blended. Gradually whisk in the milk, bring to a boil, lower the heat, and simmer, whisking constantly, until thickened and smooth.

4. In a small bowl, mix the pumpkin spice, salt, and the remaining ½ cup brown sugar. Stir into the sauce and add the vanilla. Add half of the sauce to the pumpkin mixture, blend well, and pour into the buttered dish.

5. Pour the remaining sauce over the top and sprinkle with the remaining almonds and raisins. Bake, uncovered, for 60 minutes, or until set and a knife inserted near the center comes out clean. Serve warm or chilled.

ooooo

NOTES: To toast the almonds, spread them out on a baking sheet and place in a 350°F oven for 5 to 10 minutes, stirring occasionally, until aromatic and lightly browned.

Pumpkin pie spice is a mixture of cinnamon, nutmeg, ginger, and cloves. It is available in most markets. If you do not have the mixture, substitute 1 teaspoon cinnamon, ¼ teaspoon ground ginger, ⅛ teaspoon ground nutmeg, and ⅛ teaspoon ground cloves for the tablespoon pumpkin pie spice.

PUMPKIN-HAZELNUT CASSEROLE

It seems pumpkin tastes best in the fall, when the leaves are turning and we're looking forward to the holiday season. Hazelnuts (also known as "filberts") are a perfect complement to the spiced pumpkin.

SERVES 6

2 tablespoons butter, melted, plus extra for the dish

1 can (16 ounces) pureed pumpkin

1 cup firmly packed light brown sugar

1 teaspoon salt

1 teaspoon ground cinnamon

½ teaspoon ground nutmeg

¼ teaspoon ground cloves

2 cups half-and-half

3 large eggs

1 cup chopped hazelnuts

Whipped cream for serving

1. Preheat the oven to 350°F. Butter a 1½-quart casserole.

2. In a large bowl, stir the pumpkin puree and add the brown sugar, salt, and spices. Stir to blend well.

3. In another bowl, whisk the half-and-half and the eggs until frothy. Add to the pumpkin mixture, and pour into the casserole. Sprinkle the hazelnuts over the top and drizzle with the 2 tablespoons butter.

4. Bake for 50 to 55 minutes, or until a knife inserted near the center comes out clean. Cool and serve at room temperature, topped with whipped cream.

PUMPKIN PUDDING WITH TOASTED PECAN CRUST

Here is another delicious alternative for pumpkin pie lovers who are timid about rolling out pie crusts, and are reluctant to use the commercial variety. This ground pecan crust is pressed into the casserole dish and toasted in the oven.

SERVES 10

1 cup finely ground pecans (see Note)

1¼ cups firmly packed dark brown sugar

1 tablespoon cornstarch

½ teaspoon salt

1 tablespoon mixed pumpkin pie spice (see Note)

1 can (15 ounces) pureed pumpkin

3 large eggs

1 cup heavy cream

⅓ cup milk

1. Preheat the oven to 375°F. Butter a 2-quart shallow casserole generously.

2. Press the ground pecans evenly onto the bottom and up the sides of the dish. Place in the oven to toast for 15 minutes while preparing the pudding.

3. In a large bowl, whisk together the brown sugar, cornstarch, salt, pumpkin pie spice, pumpkin, eggs, cream, and milk until well blended.

4. Pour the filling into the nut-lined dish and bake until the center is set and a knife inserted near the center comes out clean, 45 to 50 minutes. Cool completely before serving.

NOTES: To grind the pecans, put them in a food processor with the steel blade in place and process until they have the texture of breadcrumbs. Be careful not to process too long, or you'll end up with pecan butter!

Pumpkin pie spice is a mixture of cinnamon, nutmeg, ginger, and cloves. It is available in most markets. If you do not have the mixture, substitute 1 teaspoon cinnamon, ¼ teaspoon ground ginger, ⅛ teaspoon ground nutmeg, and ⅛ teaspoon ground cloves for the tablespoon pumpkin pie spice.

RHUBARB COBBLER

A cobbler is a baked fruit dessert with a thick, biscuit-like topping, which is usually sprinkled with sugar. Rhubarb can vary in tartness, depending on the variety and where it is grown, so I give a range for the sugar in the filling recipe.

SERVES 6

2 cups diced fresh rhubarb

2/3 to 1 cup sugar

1 tablespoon all-purpose flour

1 teaspoon ground cinnamon

1/8 teaspoon salt

1 teaspoon grated orange zest

FOR THE TOPPING:

1 cup all-purpose flour

2 tablespoons sugar

1/4 teaspoon salt

2 teaspoons baking powder

1/4 cup shortening

1 large egg, beaten

3 tablespoons milk

1. Preheat the oven to 350°F.

2. Arrange the rhubarb in the bottom of a 9-inch pie pan. Mix the sugar, flour, cinnamon, salt, and orange zest in a small bowl and sprinkle over the rhubarb.

3. *To make the topping:* Mix the flour, sugar, salt, and baking powder together in a medium bowl. Cut in the shortening with a pastry blender until the mixture resembles coarse crumbs. Mix the egg and milk together, stir into the flour mixture, and continue stirring just until the dry ingredients are moistened.

4. With a tablespoon, drop the dough over the rhubarb mixture, and spread the mounds together with a spatula. Bake for 35 minutes, or until the topping is lightly browned and the filling is bubbly.

STRAWBERRY-RHUBARB CRISP

Rhubarb and strawberries are a natural combination because they are both in season at the same time. Rhubarb is actually a vegetable. It is often planted as a green "filler" around buildings in cool climates. The stalk is the only edible part of the plant. The giant, heart-shaped, wide-veined leaves contain oxalic acid, which is toxic—so don't eat them!

SERVES 6

FOR THE TOPPING:

½ cup all-purpose flour

⅓ cup old-fashioned rolled oats

½ cup light or dark brown sugar

½ cup chopped walnuts

½ teaspoon ground cinnamon

4 tablespoons butter, melted, plus extra for the dish

FOR THE FILLING:

3 cups diced or sliced rhubarb

1 pint fresh strawberries, hulled and sliced

½ cup granulated sugar

1 tablespoon cornstarch

1 tablespoon cold butter, cut into small pieces

Vanilla ice cream or whipped cream for serving

1. Preheat the oven to 350°F. Butter an 8-inch glass pie dish.

2. *To make the topping:* Mix the flour, rolled oats, brown sugar, walnuts, and cinnamon in a medium bowl. Stir in the 4 tablespoons melted butter to make a crumbly mixture. Spread half the topping in the prepared pie dish.

3. *To make the filling:* Gently mix the rhubarb and strawberries together and spread out in the dish.

4. In a small bowl, mix the granulated sugar and cornstarch. Sprinkle over the rhubarb and strawberries evenly. Cover with the remaining topping. Sprinkle the 1 tablespoon cold butter onto the topping.

5. Bake for 45 minutes to 1 hour, or until bubbly and the top is crisp. Serve warm with vanilla ice cream or whipped cream.

SLOW-BAKED PEACHES

These are so good and yet so simple! If you find Georgia peaches, grab them!

———— SERVES 4 ————

4 peaches

½ cup sugar

Heavy cream for serving

1. Preheat the oven to 300°F. Coat a casserole dish just large enough to accommodate the peaches with cooking spray.

2. Rinse the peaches and pat dry. Place (with skins on and pits intact) in the casserole in a single layer. Sprinkle the sugar over the peaches. Cover tightly and bake for 1½ hours, or until the peaches are soft and wrinkled.

3. Cool the peaches completely and refrigerate until cold. Serve with cream in a pitcher for people to pour over their serving.

TABLE OF EQUIVALENTS

○ ○ ○ ○ ○

The exact equivalents in the following tables have been rounded for convenience.

LIQUID/DRY MEASUREMENTS

U.S.	Metric
¼ teaspoon	1.25 milliliters
½ teaspoon	2.5 milliliters
1 teaspoon	5 milliliters
1 tablespoon (3 teaspoons)	15 milliliters
1 fluid ounce (2 tablespoons)	30 milliliters
¼ cup	60 milliliters
⅓ cup	80 milliliters
½ cup	120 milliliters
1 cup	240 milliliters
1 pint (2 cups)	480 milliliters
1 quart (4 cups, 32 ounces)	960 milliliters
1 gallon (4 quarts)	3.84 liters
1 ounce (by weight)	28 grams
1 pound	448 grams
2.2 pounds	1 kilogram

LENGTHS

U.S.	Metric
⅛ inch	3 millimeters
¼ inch	6 millimeters
½ inch	12 millimeters
1 inch	2.5 centimeters

OVEN TEMPERATURE

Fahrenheit	Celsius	Gas
250	120	½
275	140	1
300	150	2
325	160	3
350	180	4
375	190	5
400	200	6
425	220	7
450	230	8
475	240	9
500	260	10